Vegan Planet

Vegan Planet

Revised Edition

More Than 425 Irresistible Recipes
with **Fantastic Flavors** *from* **Home**
and **Around the World**

ROBIN ROBERTSON

The Harvard Common Press
Boston, Massachusetts

The Harvard Common Press
www.harvardcommonpress.com

Printed in the United States of America
Printed on acid-free paper

Library of Congress Cataloging-in-Publication Data
Robertson, Robin.
 Vegan planet : more than 425 irresistible recipes with fantastic flavors from home and
around the world / Robin Robertson. -- Revised edition.
   pages cm
  ISBN 978-1-55832-831-0 (pbk.)
1. Vegan cooking. 2. International cooking. I. Title.
 TX837.R6253 2014
 641.5'636--dc23
                        2013022919

Special bulk-order discounts are available on this and other Harvard Common Press
books. Companies and organizations may purchase books for premiums or resale, or may
arrange a custom edition, by contacting the Marketing Director at the address above.

Book design by Michelle Thompson | Fold & Gather Design
Cover and text illustrations by Susy Pilgrim Waters

10 9 8 7 6 5 4 3 2 1

Contents

Acknowledgments

I am indebted to many people who have helped to make this revised edition of *Vegan Planet* as good as it can be. First and foremost I want to thank the many readers and fans of the first edition for helping to make *Vegan Planet* a "classic."

Many thanks to my recipe testers who tested the new and revised recipes for this edition: Melissa Chapman, Zsu Dever, Lyndsay Orwig, Jonathan and Nancy Shanes, Lori Maffei, and Barbara Bryan. I appreciate your enthusiasm and your helpful feedback more than I can say.

I want to again express my very special appreciation to Neal Barnard, MD, of the Physicians Committee for Responsible Medicine (PCRM), for his compassionate spirit and vital work and for writing the foreword to this book. Thanks also to Jen Keller, RD, of PCRM, for her assistance with nutritional information.

My gratitude goes to my husband, Jon Robertson, for his unwavering support and encouragement. An extra-special thank-you goes to Jenna Patton for her valued assistance, and many thanks also to Dianne Wenz for her help.

Much appreciation goes to my agent, Stacey Glick of Dystel & Goderich Literary Management, and the team at The Harvard Common Press: Bruce Shaw, Dan Rosenberg, Adam Salomone, Emily Geaman, Virginia Downes, Pat Jalbert-Levine, Karen Wise, Vicki Rowland, and Michelle Thompson. Your hard work and enthusiasm for this new edition of *Vegan Planet* means the world to me.

Foreword

As you page through the recipes in this book—from appetizers to desserts—you'll find that not only are they mouthwateringly delicious, but these great-tasting foods can change your life.

In research studies at the Physicians Committee for Responsible Medicine in Washington, DC, we have put various diets to the test. Whether our goal is cutting cholesterol levels, taming diabetes or high blood pressure, or trimming waistlines, the clear winner is a low-fat, vegan diet. As savory as spaghetti marinara, split pea soup, or rice pilaf may be, they are also incredibly powerful for health. They contain no animal fat and no cholesterol—if they are properly made. And that means that they, along with other vegan foods, can tackle cholesterol problems like no other diet can, and weight loss kicks in effortlessly without the need to impose any artificial calorie limit—even when people do not change their exercise routines.

Young people who eat this way can stay trim and healthy and keep their arteries open throughout life. Older people whose unhealthy diets may have already brought on health problems—heart disease, for example—can use these foods to get a new lease on life. The research studies of Dr. Dean Ornish and his colleagues at the Preventive Medicine Research Institute showed that diets based on plant foods rather than animal products actually reversed existing heart disease in more than 80 percent of participants without medications or surgery. We have shown that this same sort of diet helps many people with type 2 diabetes to reduce their medications or even stop them completely. Other researchers have found much the same benefit for people with high blood pressure.

A vegan diet is as close to a perfect menu as you can have. Unfortunately, many people have made wrong turns. A switch from red meat to white meat, for example, does not do the job. If a person scrupulously limits meat intake to no more than six ounces per day, choosing only chicken and fish while trimming away visible fat, and chooses skim over whole milk and egg whites over whole eggs, the results are embarrassingly modest. Cholesterol levels fall by only about 5 percent. Body weight and blood pressure improve only modestly. Inside the arteries, blockages continue to worsen. All in all, there is little reward for all this effort. Americans now eat, believe it or not, 1 million chickens per hour, and collectively we are more out of shape than at any time in our nation's history.

A vegan diet puts health into high gear, cutting cholesterol by 20 to 25 percent, trimming body weight by a pound or more per week, and helping most people with diabetes or high blood pressure free themselves from their medications.

If you are tempted to put it to the test, I suggest that you take a week or two and try out as many of these delicious recipes as you can. Then, when you've found your favorites, block out a three-week period to eat low-fat, vegan foods exclusively. Don't dabble with it—do it all the way. As you get started, your body will begin to transform itself. In all likelihood, you'll start to lose weight, your cholesterol level will fall, your energy will improve, and you'll feel better than you've felt since you were a kid.

After three weeks, see how you feel. If you like the feeling of a trimmer, healthier body, you can stick with it—and you now have the tools you need to do it.

These foods give you a chance to be on as perfect a diet as humanly possible, and your body will be delighted that you made this choice. Robin has done a magnificent job in bringing this volume together, and I hope you enjoy *Vegan Planet* as much as I have.

— Neal D. Barnard, MD
President, Physicians Committee
for Responsible Medicine

Introduction

Vegan is the new vegetarian. What was once considered a fringe offshoot of vegetarianism is now a household word, with many celebrities embracing a vegan lifestyle. It also is easier to enjoy a vegan diet now than ever before. Vegan-friendly ingredients are becoming more visible in natural foods stores and many supermarkets, and creative vegan cookbooks are showing up on bookshelves everywhere. Although the vegetarian menu choices of many restaurants remain dairy-laden, vegan selections are becoming more widely available. At the same time, upscale vegan restaurants in metropolitan areas are thriving.

Those of us who enjoy a plant-based diet are often quizzed with questions such as these: *Do you live on salad? No meat or dairy at all? What do you eat? And, of course, Where do you get your protein?*

The more than 425 recipes in this revised edition of *Vegan Planet* are my answer to those questions.

Quite simply, a well-balanced vegan diet can provide all of the nutrition we need with astonishingly varied recipes. The truth is there is a world of choice in the vegan diet. In fact, I hesitate to use the word *diet* because it may imply austerity or deprivation, and a vegan diet is anything but that. In this book, fresh vegetables and fruits, whole grains, beans, and nuts are used to make infinitely varied, full-flavored dishes for breakfast, lunch, dinner, and everything in between.

Chapter 1 introduces the basics of a vegan diet, from its history and health benefits to an overview of ingredients, cooking tips, and basic recipes. From there, you will discover that by creatively using a variety of vegetables, beans, grains, and other healthful ingredients, you can make soups, stews, entrées, breads, and even desserts that are satisfying and delicious—good food that just happens to be meatless and dairy-free. From *Chilled Ginger-Peach Soup with Cashew Cream* and hearty *White Bean Cassoulet* to *Chocolate Layer Cake* and *Maple-Pecan French Toast,* the dishes you prepare will be noticed for their great taste rather than for "what's missing."

When you first begin to cook without animal products, it can be a liberating experience. You are free to explore the cuisines of other lands, using ingredients you never knew existed. Fragrant spices, colorful vegetables, and numerous beans, grains, and other ingredients await your pleasure. What will it be tonight? A Moroccan stew or a Thai stir-fry? How about a Tuscan soup or a French gratin? It can be an exciting experience to try a new cuisine each week, pick up new vegetables at the market that you have never cooked before, and learn how to prepare them. Soon you will find creative ways to incorporate more fresh vegetables into your meals, perhaps by making a lovely composed salad or whipping up a relish or chutney.

For those times when only good old-fashioned comfort food will do, you can explore new ways to make old favorites with healthier plant-based ingredients. Use tofu to make creamy sauces, lasagna, and even cheesecake. Sauté some seitan when you crave a "meaty" entrée. When you cook vegan, you can have it all—the flavors you enjoy, the nutrients you need, and, best of all, the freedom to move beyond the Standard American Diet (SAD).

The twenty chapters in this book range from appetizers, soups, and sauces to breads, beverages, and desserts. In between, there are a number of main-course chapters that are organized by ingredients such as grains, beans, and pasta. Others are grouped by cooking method, such as sautés and stir-fries, stews, and oven-baked dishes. Also included are chapters on sandwiches and pizza, and even one devoted to breakfast.

Within these chapters, you will find a wide range of recipes. First are the naturally vegan recipes that celebrate the natural goodness of vegetables, grains, beans, and other plant-based ingredients. Recipes such as *Ancient Grains on Wild Greens, Brandy-Glazed Winter Squash with Apple-Pecan Topping,* and *Marjoram-Scented Artichoke and Chickpea Stew* fall under that heading.

Other recipes drawn from the cuisines of the world include exciting, robust dishes such as *African Sweet Potato and Peanut Stew,* Thai *Drunken Noodles,* and *Cuban Black Bean Soup,* as well as recipes that feature some of the world's best vegetable-based protein sources, such as tofu, tempeh, and seitan.

Many of the recipes are what I call transformation recipes. They include dishes that traditionally contain meat or dairy but have been transformed into vegan versions by changing some of the ingredients. Examples include *Easy Vegan Hollandaise, Seitan Reubens,* and *Fresh Lime Cheesecake.*

In developing the recipes, it was important to me that they be accessible to everyone. The great majority of the ingredients called for in my recipes are available in most supermarkets and natural foods stores, and the remainder can be found in ethnic markets or online. I have made a point not to use heirloom produce or other esoteric ingredients that are available only to a small portion of the population. For those who do not live near a natural foods store or ethnic grocer, mail-order and online sources for ingredients are provided in the resource list beginning on page 517.

In *Vegan Planet,* you will traverse the globe with internationally inspired, straightforward recipes that show how varied, flavorful, and exciting vegan food can be. It is my hope that, with this book, you will discover new ways to enjoy the many natural ingredients available to us, and a whole new world of delicious vegan cuisine.

Vegan Basics

Although there have long been vegetarians who do not eat or use any animal products, the term *vegan* (pronounced VEE-gun) came into being in 1944 in London. The first official Vegan Society in America was established in 1948, and today the American Vegan Society is a thriving entity that publishes a quarterly magazine, *American Vegan* (formerly *Ahimsa*, a Sanskrit word meaning "harmlessness to all life").

In some editions of the *Oxford English Dictionary,* a vegan is defined as a "strict vegetarian." Other sources refer to a vegan diet as "pure vegetarian," since it consists solely of plant-based ingredients. The reasons for going vegan are usually based on health, ethics, environment, or religion.

Veganism is actually as old as recorded history if you consider Genesis 1:29, where God says, "Behold, I have given you every herb-bearing seed, which is upon the face of all the earth, and every tree, in which is the fruit of a tree-yielding seed; to you it shall be for meat." In the archaic English usage, *meat* merely meant "meal."

By the close of the 20th century, the steady increase of diet-related maladies such as high cholesterol, heart disease, and diabetes prompted many Americans to consider switching to a diet that emphasizes whole grains, vegetables, and fruits. In this way, the vegetarian diet established itself as an important fixture in mainstream America. Among the types of vegetarian diets now shared by millions are lacto-vegetarian, which includes dairy; lacto-ovo-vegetarian, which includes dairy and eggs; and vegan, which contains no eggs, dairy, or other animal products, including honey.

In terms of health, many people give up meat in order to avoid cholesterol and saturated fat. If they still rely on eggs and dairy products, however, they have not solved their cholesterol problem. A vegan diet is cholesterol-free and naturally low in saturated fat. Other health concerns include food allergies, such as lactose (milk sugar) intolerance or other dairy allergies; the hormones and antibiotics that are given to livestock; and the pesticides from animal feed that find their way into many meat and dairy products.

People who initially go vegan for their health often remain vegan for ethical reasons. Some vegetarians give up meat because they do not believe in killing animals for food and prefer to rely on eggs and dairy for their protein because "it doesn't kill

> "I am in favor of animal rights as well as human rights. That is the way of a whole human being."
>
> —ABRAHAM LINCOLN

the animal." What they often do not realize is that the factory-farming practices of the egg and dairy industries can be just as brutal as the meat industry. For that reason, ethically based vegans eliminate all animal-derived products—and their commitment does not end with diet. Many ethical vegans wear no leather, silk, fur, or wool and avoid products such as soaps and cosmetics that contain animal byproducts or are tested on animals. Vegans espouse compassion for all life, holding that animals should not be exploited for food, clothing, or any other reason.

Enjoying a Healthy Vegan Diet

To successfully adopt a vegan diet, common sense and an understanding of basic nutritional needs are important. For example, choosing a diet of French fries and diet cola may qualify as vegan, but that does not make it healthy. The key to a healthful vegan diet is eating a variety of fresh fruits and vegetables, whole grains, legumes, nuts, and seeds every day. This will ensure that you are getting adequate amounts of protein, calcium, fat, and iron.

Protein is made up of amino acids, and we need to obtain nine essential amino acids from the foods we eat. All nine of these essential amino acids are found in animal products such as meat, milk, and eggs. However, it is quite easy to get too much protein by eating a diet that includes these products, and too much protein can damage your bones and organs. Animal products also contain high amounts of cholesterol and saturated fat, which put us at

a higher risk for developing heart disease, cancer, hypertension (high blood pressure), and diabetes, among other ailments. For this reason, it is best to get protein from plant foods, since they are naturally cholesterol-free, low in fat, and high in fiber and complex carbohydrates.

Since most individual plant foods, such as whole grains, legumes, and vegetables, contain varying amounts of the essential amino acids, they are said to be *incomplete proteins*. An exception is the soybean, which contains an abundance of all nine essential amino acids and is, therefore, a *complete protein*.

It was once thought that certain foods, such as beans and grains, needed to be carefully combined at the same meal to make a complete protein. In recent years, we have learned that these and other wholesome plant-based ingredients can be eaten at any time during the day to have the same benefits. Of course, since grains and beans are frequently paired in scores of tasty dishes, it's often a simple matter to enjoy them at the same meal.

The dairy industry tells us that if we do not drink milk, we will not get enough calcium. However, calcium is found in abundance in tofu, nuts, vegetables such as broccoli and dark leafy greens, and sea vegetables. In addition to providing enough protein and calcium, a well-balanced vegan diet has ample sources of vitamins, minerals, and other nutrients.

Since iron is abundant in many plant foods, vegans are not at any particular risk for iron deficiency, as long as they include daily servings of iron-rich foods. Beans, dark green vegetables, dried fruits, nuts, and seeds, as well as blackstrap molasses and whole-grain or fortified breads and cereals, all contain high amounts of iron.

If you are wondering how you will get your vitamin D if you stop drinking milk, you should know that cow's milk does not naturally contain vitamin D; it's added later, just as it is in soy milk. Vitamin D, in fact, is not really a "vitamin" but a hormone that our bodies manufacture when our skin is exposed to as little as 15 minutes of sunlight.

Vitamin A is readily stored in the liver, and thus daily sources are not critical. In fact, since it is not excreted, overdoses can be toxic. Good sources of vitamin A are yellow and dark green vegetables and orange fruits, as well as fortified nondairy milk.

Vitamin B_{12} is found mostly in animal products, but it is also found in some fortified foods, as well as in our own mouths and intestines. We require only 2 micrograms of vitamin B_{12} per day, and our bodies store and recycle it, so a B_{12} deficiency is not a problem for most vegans. Still, if you are concerned about getting enough, you can take a vitamin B_{12} supplement.

Some dietitians maintain that omega-3 fatty acids are best when derived from fish and fish oils. Other researchers, however, have found that the omega-3 molecules from fish sources can be unstable and release free radicals as they decompose. A more stable form of omega-3s is found in vegetables, fruits, beans, and, most notably, flaxseeds. Additionally, the antioxidants present in certain vegetables and fruits help neutralize the free radicals.

Many respected medical doctors and other health professionals conclude that a vegan diet not only is safe but also can produce significant health benefits. (For more information on the health benefits of a vegan diet, read the Foreword by Dr. Neal Barnard on page ix.)

By learning to think of plant-based ingredients in new ways, you can help make your vegan meals more interesting and delicious. For example, whereas you may have once thought of nuts as simply an occasional snack food, you are now encouraged to consider them as a good protein source and versatile ingredient for sauces, spreads, salads, and entrées. In addition, many Asian, Indian, Italian, Mexican, and Middle Eastern dishes are vegan or easily adaptable

Getting Enough Iron?

A well-balanced vegan diet can provide ample iron for most people. Iron-rich vegan foods include blackstrap molasses, leafy greens, sea vegetables, beans, nuts, nutritional yeast, wheat germ, dried fruits, prune juice, and fortified cereals. If you decide to take an iron supplement, here are some tips.

- Look for a supplement that contains ferrous fumarate—it is easier on the stomach.

- Do not take iron supplements at the same time as calcium supplements, because the iron may inhibit calcium absorption.

- To increase the absorption of iron, take vitamin C or drink juice high in vitamin C when you take your iron supplement.

and use wonderful combinations of grains, beans, and vegetables. Ethnic cuisines and ingredients offer opportunities for tremendous variety in your meals. Cooking vegan has given me a broader appreciation for the natural flavors of foods and, at the same time, has inspired me to develop ways to use these ingredients to their full potential.

Whatever your reason for cooking vegan, it is almost certain to have far-reaching benefits for you, your fellow beings, and the entire planet. If you wish to learn more about a vegan lifestyle, see the resource list on page 517.

The Vegan Kitchen

A vast array of culinary resources can add flavor, texture, and nutrition to your meals. Whether it's fresh organic produce, or protein-rich beans, nuts, and soy foods, or exotic global seasonings, quality ingredients are the key to enjoying satisfying vegan meals.

A Firm Foundation

Cooking with a variety of whole grains, beans or legumes, and fresh vegetables and fruits can provide the firm foundation of a healthful vegan diet.

Considered staple foods throughout the world, grains can be an economical source of high-quality nutrition. Among the many grains to choose from are rice, millet, quinoa, barley, wheat, kamut, and others. Grains can be used in soups, stuffings, pilafs, puddings, and desserts, as well as to make breads and pasta. Each type of grain has its own nutritional value, unique flavor, and cooking characteristics. When combined with beans, vegetables, and seasonings, grains provide great taste and texture, in

addition to good nutrition. Grains are discussed in more detail in chapter 8.

Dried beans, also known as legumes, are widely used throughout the world as a major protein source. Beans are inexpensive, easy to prepare, low in fat, and an important part of a well-balanced vegan diet. Popular bean varieties include chickpeas (also known as garbanzo beans), black-eyed peas, lentils, split peas, black beans, pinto beans, kidney beans, lima beans, fava beans, and various white beans (such as Great Northern, navy, and cannellini). Once called "poor man's meat," beans are high in protein, fiber, carbohydrates, and B vitamins. They are becoming more popular on dinner tables throughout the United States, where they are used to make soups, stews, burgers, breads, spreads, and more. More information about beans can be found in chapter 10.

Whereas some vegetables are especially high in vitamin C, others are loaded with iron. For that reason, eating a wide variety of vegetables helps ensure optimum nutritional benefits. It also can add interest and variety to your meals. Many vegetables are delicious raw as well as steamed, stir-fried, baked, or boiled. In a plant-based diet, you are more apt to find vegetables featured as an integral part of a meal rather than as a side dish. However you prepare them, vegetables are best when grown without pesticides and eaten while at their peak of freshness.

Naturally sweet fruit is a refreshing, ready-to-eat snack or dessert that can be eaten raw with little or no preparation. In addition, many fruits, from the tiniest berry to the largest melon, can add appeal to appetizers, soups, entrées, salads, and sauces.

Always wash fruits and vegetables well before using to rinse off pesticides and bacteria. Potatoes and root vegetables should be well scrubbed, and any wilted or damaged areas should be removed from produce before using.

Egg and Dairy Alternatives

In childhood we learned to associate milk and other dairy products with nurturing and comfort, as well as good health. Much of this association is due to the advertising campaigns that taught us from an early age that dairy is good for us and that we need to drink milk to "build strong bones." Recent medical studies show that dairy products contribute to heart disease, many forms of cancer, psoriasis, respiratory ailments, allergies, sinus trouble, migraines, and other health problems. Once thought to aid in the prevention of osteoporosis, meat and dairy products in excessive amounts can actually contribute to osteoporosis. Medical researchers now report that excessive consumption of protein raises the acid level in the blood, which causes calcium to be lost. In fact, the protein in milk can actually inhibit the body's ability to absorb calcium from dairy products. Fortunately, calcium is found in abundance in plenty of nondairy foods, such as tofu, nuts, and many vegetables.

Humans are the only animals that drink the milk of another species and the only animals that drink milk after childhood. One might conclude that people who use dairy products often do so out of deeply ingrained habit and because they taste good.

Indeed, many American "comfort foods" are made with dairy products. For this reason, vegetarians who find it easy to give up meat may find it difficult to renounce dairy products, especially if they have come to rely on these products for protein. Fortunately, there are plant-based alternatives to dairy products that allow us to enjoy many of our favorite "creamy" dishes.

Eggs served sunny-side up and milk in a carton are easy ingredients to recognize. The trick is learning to detect them when they are hidden in baked goods and prepared foods. In addition to reading labels closely, the best defense against hidden dairy products may be to "bake your own," using some of the many available egg and dairy alternatives.

Nondairy milks made from soy, almonds, rice, oats, and coconut can be used to replace cow's milk in cooking. They are widely available in most supermarkets and natural foods stores. Several types can be found in the refrigerator case and must stay refrigerated even if unopened, but many brands are available in one-quart aseptic containers that may be stored unrefrigerated until opened. Plain unsweetened nondairy milk is best for savory dishes—my favorite is almond milk. Nondairy milks that contain sweeteners should be reserved for desserts or poured over cereal. You can now find coconut milk sold in a variety of ways: in refrigerated cartons next to the soy and almond milk, or the canned variety, which has a richer texture and distinctive flavor, making it

Did You Know?

Osteoporosis is less a disease of calcium deficiency than one of protein excess. Studies show that osteoporosis tends to occur in countries where calcium intake via dairy products is highest. Instead, it's better to get your calcium from plant sources such as figs, rice, fortified cereals, nuts, sesame seeds, molasses, dark greens, sea vegetables, and soy foods.

most suitable for Thai or Indian recipes or in certain desserts.

In addition to nondairy milks, you can buy dairy-free mayonnaise, sour cream, cream cheese, and a variety of cheeses made from nuts, soy, and rice. When buying such products, read the label to be sure the product does not contain casein or other dairy byproducts that are sometimes added to make the cheese melt better. Vegan cheese is usually labeled as such or has the words "contains no animal products" on the label.

Recipes for homemade vegan sour cream, mayonnaise, cream cheese, and a cheesy sauce can all be found in chapter 5.

Instead of butter, you can opt for high-quality expeller-pressed or cold-pressed oils, which are made without the use of harsh solvents and heat. I prefer extra-virgin olive oil for most salads and savory dishes and grapeseed oil as a good all-purpose neutral vegetable oil. When only a solid butter alternative will do, check out the refrigerator case of your natural foods store for a nonhydrogenated vegan buttery spread. Consider switching to nut butters for toast—they contain about the same amount of calories as butter but with no cholesterol and lots of protein and essential fatty acids.

There are several ways to replace eggs in recipes. Depending on the recipe and the function eggs serve in it, alternatives include ground flaxseeds blended with water, silken tofu, and egg replacement powder made from vegetable starch and leaveners (see page 457).

Meat Alternatives

Although it is possible to fulfill all our nutritional needs with a plant-based diet, many people hold firm to the habit of eating meat. Since most people do not eat their meat raw but prefer it cooked and sauced in a variety of ways, it seems apparent that the surrounding flavors play a role in their choices. Taste and tradition, it would seem, are an important part of why we eat what we do.

But the change to a vegan diet does not mean that you must give up familiar flavors, textures, and traditions. You can often enjoy many of the same dishes by simply swapping some ingredients. Soy foods such as tofu, tempeh, and textured vegetable protein (TVP), along with seitan (also called wheatmeat) and the many varieties of beans, are excellent protein choices that can be used to make soups, stews, and other dishes with many of the same flavors and chewy textures you enjoy.

Although a vegan menu does not have to include tofu, soy foods can add variety and nutritional benefits to a vegan diet and are worth considering. Evidence indicates that eating more soy protein can produce a number of health benefits, whether you are trying to lower your cholesterol, relieve the symptoms of menopause, or reduce the risks of heart disease, osteoporosis, and certain cancers. A recent medical study on soy protein's effect on menopause showed such remarkable results that tofu is now being referred to as "natural estrogen." In 1999, the FDA permitted soy food manufacturers to label their products as being associated with a reduced risk of coronary disease.

TOFU TALK

If you are among those who avoid tofu because you do not know what to do with it, I encourage you to try it. Think of it as an ingredient, like flour, rather than a ready-to-eat food, like bread. This will make it easier to understand that tofu needs to be combined with other ingredients to be at its best. You would not eat raw chicken without first cooking and seasoning it, and the same is true for tofu. It's like an empty canvas waiting for the creative cook to transform it into a masterpiece.

Regular tofu is also known as Chinese bean curd, and silken tofu is called Japanese-style tofu. Both are available in soft, firm, and extra-firm varieties. Firm and extra-firm regular tofu are generally used in stir-fries and other dishes that require a sturdy texture that retains its shape during cooking. Soft regular tofu can be used in recipes where a softer texture is desired. Silken tofu is more or less the same whether soft or firm; the softer kind just contains more water. Silken tofu is primarily used in recipes requiring a smooth, creamy texture, such as smoothies, sauces, and puddings. Both regular and silken tofu are available in low-fat versions. Regular tofu is also sold baked and marinated in a number of flavors, which you can use without further seasoning. For best results, regular and silken tofu should be treated as different products and not used interchangeably.

Storing Tofu

Regular tofu may be stored unopened in the refrigerator up to the expiration date on the package. Once tofu is opened, it is best to use it right away, although it can be submerged in fresh water in a covered container (to prevent it from absorbing surrounding flavors) and kept in the refrigerator for several days. Silken tofu is usually sold in aseptic

Did You Know?

Soy products are high in protein and a good source of calcium, B vitamins, phosphorus, and potassium. In addition, soy has been shown to help lower blood cholesterol in some people.

containers that can be kept unrefrigerated until opened. Once opened, however, it should be used within 3 days.

Draining, Blotting, and Pressing Tofu

Since tofu is generally packaged in water, it is essential to drain it before using it in recipes. To remove even more moisture, cut the tofu into slabs and place them on a cutting board or baking sheet lined with two or three layers of paper towels. Cover the tofu with more paper towels and blot to enable the tofu to better absorb flavors. To remove most of the moisture from regular tofu (you can't do this with silken tofu) and thereby achieve a firmer texture, place a baking sheet on top of the tofu after blotting. Weight down the sheet with canned goods or a heavy skillet and allow to sit for one hour, then use as desired.

Freezing and Thawing Tofu

Another way to change the texture of regular tofu is to freeze it. (Do not freeze silken tofu.) Once thawed, the tofu will be chewier and more porous, making it ideal for marinating and sautéing. It is also easily crumbled for use in chili and other recipes.

To freeze tofu, cut drained and pressed tofu into thin slices and wrap in plastic or place in an airtight container. When you are ready to use the tofu, defrost it, then squeeze it to remove any excess moisture. Once thawed, it should be used within 3 days. Since frozen tofu will keep for several months, this is a good way to store tofu that is near its expiration date.

BAKED TOFU

Baked marinated tofu is widely available in natural foods stores and supermarkets in a variety of flavors, including teriyaki, Italian, and Thai. It is ready to eat and can be served hot or cold, but it is also expensive. A more economical choice is to bake your own, using whatever seasonings you like—such as the simple soy-sesame marinade in the recipe that follows. To give it a teriyaki taste, add a teaspoon or two of pure maple syrup or agave nectar and a little grated fresh ginger to the marinade. For a Thai flavor, whisk in a little peanut butter and Asian chili paste or sriracha. If you want to go Italian, simply marinate the tofu in your favorite Italian salad dressing.

Baked tofu is extremely versatile and can be sliced, cubed, or cut into strips. It's great cold when added to salads, made into sandwiches, or eaten as a snack. Served hot, it can be added to pasta and grain dishes or served as an entrée.

Baked Marinated Tofu

Use this recipe for as a guideline to make baked tofu, changing up the marinade as desired or as described above. Different brands of tofu come in different package weights, usually from 12 to 16 ounces. Use whatever brand you like—in most cases the recipes using tofu will be fine with any of these amounts unless a specific cup amount is noted.

1 (12- to 16-ounce) package
extra-firm tofu, drained

⅓ cup low-sodium tamari

¼ cup water

2 tablespoons toasted sesame oil

2 tablespoons fresh lemon juice

1. Blot the tofu with paper towels to remove excess liquid, then cut it into ½-inch-thick slices. Place the tofu slices on a baking sheet lined with paper towels. Cover with more paper towels and place another baking sheet on top. Press more liquid out of the tofu by placing some canned goods on top of the top baking sheet. Let it sit for 20 minutes.

2. In a small bowl, combine the tamari, water, sesame oil, and lemon juice. Blend well.

3. Place the pressed tofu slices in a glass baking dish and pour the marinade on top. Cover and refrigerate for at least 3 hours or as long as overnight, turning the tofu once.

4. Preheat the oven to 375°F. Remove the tofu from the marinade and place on a lightly oiled baking sheet. Bake until the tofu is well browned and very firm, turning once about halfway through, 45 to 50 minutes total. Serve hot or allow to cool. Store leftovers in a tightly covered container in the refrigerator for up to 3 days.

Serves 4

Lemon-Ginger Tofu

This is another good basic recipe for baked tofu. This one doesn't require marinating, but gets its flavor from a sprightly lemon-ginger sauce.

1 (12- to 16-ounce) package
extra-firm tofu, drained

1 teaspoon toasted sesame oil

1 garlic clove, minced

2 teaspoons grated fresh ginger

½ cup fresh lemon juice

2 tablespoons natural sugar

2 tablespoons agave nectar

2 tablespoons low-sodium tamari

1 teaspoon Asian chili sauce

2 teaspoons cornstarch

½ cup vegetable broth or water

1. Cut the tofu into ½-inch-thick slices and arrange in a single layer in a large oiled baking pan. Set aside. Preheat the oven to 350°F.

2. Heat the sesame oil in a small saucepan over medium heat. Add the garlic and ginger and cook, stirring, for about 2 minutes. Add all of the remaining ingredients except the cornstarch and broth and heat until boiling. Mix the cornstarch with the vegetable broth until smooth and stir it into the sauce. Cook, stirring, until the mixture thickens slightly.

3. Pour the hot lemon-ginger sauce over the tofu and bake for 30 minutes. Flip the tofu in the pan and spoon any remaining sauce over the top. Drizzle with a little sesame oil or broth if the tofu is becoming too dry. Bake for 15 minutes longer. Serve hot or allow to cool. Store leftovers in a tightly covered container in the refrigerator for up to 3 days.

Serves 4

Organically Yours

Coming up with an enforceable standard for what can be called "organic produce" has been debated for a long time. In 2001, the USDA passed strict guidelines for labeling organic foods. These guidelines made it easier for consumers to understand what they were buying. Previously, organic labeling was mostly unregulated and varied largely based on geographic region.

The USDA organic seal for foods that are at least 95 percent organic will make it easier for you to make your selections. This label means that synthetic pesticides or fertilizers were not used in the growing of the produce and that the ingredients were not exposed to irradiation or biotechnology. Try to buy locally grown organic produce, not only for maximum nutrition and that "just picked" flavor but also for the peace of mind you get by buying from someone you trust.

TEMPEH: THE OTHER SOY MEAT

Tempeh is a versatile meat alternative made from fermented soybeans that are compressed into a cake. Like tofu, tempeh readily absorbs flavors and is especially suited to hearty stews, stir-fries, and sautés. It marinates well and turns a crisp, golden brown when fried. Indonesian in origin, tempeh is a good source of high-quality soy protein with a chewy, meat-like texture. Some varieties of tempeh contain only soy; others are blended with one or more grains, giving them a mellower flavor. I prefer the tempeh-grain blends because they lend themselves to a wider variety of preparations.

Purchasing and Storing Tempeh

Tempeh is available in the refrigerator or freezer case of natural foods stores and some supermarkets. Sold in slabs, it can be found in 8- or 12-ounce packages, depending on the brand. The slabs can be sliced lengthwise, cut into strips, cubed, or grated. Tempeh must be stored in the refrigerator, where it will keep unopened for several weeks (check the expiration date). Once opened, however, it should be tightly wrapped and used within 4 days. Tempeh also may be stored in the freezer for a month or so.

Steaming Tempeh

As a general rule, I recommend steaming tempeh before using it in recipes to mellow the flavor and increase digestibility. Tempeh should be steamed over simmering water for at least 15 minutes. Once it is steamed, tempeh can then be used as desired in recipes.

One of my favorite ways to use tempeh is transforming it into these tasty and versatile "bacon bits." You can use these tasty morsels as a topping for salads, soups, or grain or pasta dishes. They also make a great addition to tofu scrambles.

Nutrient-Rich Foods

Many vegans are concerned about getting enough of the nutrients often associated with animal products. As the following list shows, a plant-based diet can supply these nutrients as well.

- *Calcium:* tofu (made with calcium sulfate); soy nuts; fortified nondairy milk; collards and other dark leafy greens; sesame seeds and other nuts and seeds; beans; dried figs; blackstrap molasses

- *Iron:* sea vegetables; tofu; blackstrap molasses; nutritional yeast; wheat germ; dried fruits; beans; nuts; leafy greens; enriched breads, cereals, and grains

- *Protein:* beans; nuts; seeds; whole grains; soy foods such as tofu and tempeh

- *Vitamin B$_{12}$:* fortified cereals; fortified soy milk; nutritional yeast

Tempeh "Bacon Bits"

Thanks to the miracle of liquid smoke, you can make "bacon" out of just about anything, from tempeh to eggplant to coconut.

8 ounces steamed tempeh (page 10)

1 tablespoon olive oil

2 tablespoons low-sodium tamari

1 tablespoon agave nectar
or pure maple syrup

1 tablespoon water

½ teaspoon liquid smoke

½ teaspoon toasted sesame oil

¼ teaspoon smoked paprika

¼ teaspoon freshly ground black pepper

1. Finely chop or crumble the steamed tempeh to "bacon bit" size.

2. Heat the olive oil in a medium-size skillet over medium-high heat. Add the crumbled tempeh and cook, stirring occasionally, until browned all over. Stir in the remaining ingredients and cook, stirring to combine well and coat the tempeh. Continue to cook, stirring, until the liquid is absorbed and the tempeh is nicely browned, 8 to 10 minutes. Use immediately or set aside to cool, then cover and refrigerate for up to 3 days.

Makes about 2 cups

TEXTURED VEGETABLE PROTEIN (TVP)

With the huge influx of vegan products that include everything from meatless Buffalo wings to bratwurst, textured vegetable protein (TVP) is found more often as an ingredient in other products than on its own.

Back in the early 1970s, when I first attempted vegetarianism, TVP was one of the few meat substitutes I could find. Sold as dehydrated granules or chunks that doubled in size when reconstituted with a hot liquid, TVP was one of the most economical meat alternatives you could buy. Made from compressed soy flour, it often tasted "grainy" and flavorless, but its ability to take on the flavor of surrounding ingredients made it popular for use in vegetarian chili, spaghetti sauce, and other "ground beef" recipes. TVP is a registered trademark of the Archer Daniels Midland Company, but it has come to be used generically to describe all dehydrated textured soy or vegetable protein products.

Although you can still find grainy and flavorless textured soy protein at the supermarket, some new and improved varieties have a better texture and taste. Look for TVP in natural foods stores and well-stocked supermarkets, where it is often sold in bulk. To rehydrate, place the desired amount in a heatproof bowl and cover with boiling water.

You can also buy refrigerated or frozen vegan burger crumbles that are convenient to use and generally have a good flavor. They often contain both soy and wheat gluten.

A popular TVP-like product is Butler Soy Curls, which are made from textured non-GMO soybeans. They have a great texture and can be used in most recipes calling for seitan, tempeh, or extra-firm tofu.

THE MEAT OF WHEAT

Seitan is one of the few meat alternatives not made from soy. Also known as wheat-meat, seitan is made from the protein part of wheat, which is known as gluten when mixed with liquid and kneaded. Seitan is perhaps the most versatile meat alternative, owing to its meaty texture and chameleon-like qualities. It can be sliced thin and sautéed; diced or cut into strips for stir-fries, stews, and soups; shredded or ground to use as you would ground beef; or even turned into a roast. If you're looking for an ingredient to win over a meat eater, this is the one that could do the trick.

Vital wheat gluten is the main ingredient used to make seitan. Sometimes called wheat gluten flour, vital wheat gluten is wheat flour with the starch and bran removed. It is more than 75 percent protein. You can find it in well-stocked supermarkets, natural foods stores, or online.

Made with vital wheat gluten and water (along with various seasonings), seitan can be purchased ready-made in the refrigerated or freezer sections of most natural foods stores. Ready-made seitan is sometimes sold in a marinade that may not be compatible with your recipe. To remedy this, drain and rinse the seitan before using.

Because it can be expensive to buy and is easy to make at home, I recommend making your own seitan with the following recipe. To save time, I like to make a large amount at once and then portion and freeze the rest. In addition to being a good source of protein, vitamin C, and iron, seitan is also low in fat and calories: one 4-ounce serving contains only 70 calories and 1 gram of fat.

Did You Know?

Seitan is a cholesterol-free food that is high in protein and a good source of iron. This "wheat-meat" also is low in calories, carbohydrates, and fat.

Seitan from Scratch

It's easy to make your own homemade seitan (wheat-meat). It can be simmered in broth on top of the stove or inside a slow cooker. Directions are provided for both cooking methods.

1¾ cups vital wheat gluten

¼ cup chickpea flour

¼ cup nutritional yeast

1 teaspoon onion powder

½ teaspoon garlic powder

½ teaspoon salt

¼ teaspoon freshly ground black pepper

6 tablespoons low-sodium tamari

1 tablespoon olive oil

1¾ cups water

1 medium-size onion, quartered

1. In a large bowl, combine the vital wheat gluten, chickpea flour, nutritional yeast, onion powder, garlic powder, salt, and pepper. Stir in 3 tablespoons of the tamari, the olive oil, and the water, and continue stirring until well mixed. Knead for 2 to 3 minutes.

SLOW COOKER METHOD:

2. Pour about 2 quarts of water into a slow cooker. Divide the seitan dough into 4 to 6 pieces and add to the water along with the onion pieces and remaining 3 tablespoons tamari. Cover and cook for 4 to 6 hours on Low.

STOVETOP METHOD:

3. Pour about 2 quarts of water into a large pot. Divide the seitan dough into 4 to 6 pieces and add to the water along with the onion pieces and remaining 3 tablespoons tamari. Simmer, uncovered, for 1 hour, keeping the seitan submerged. Do not boil.

AFTER COOKING (EITHER METHOD):

4. Transfer the cooked seitan to a baking sheet to cool. Once cool, tightly wrap the portions of seitan in plastic wrap, putting the portions that you won't be using in a few days in the freezer and the rest in the refrigerator. Seitan will keep in the refrigerator for up to 5 days and in the freezer for several weeks. The cooking liquid may be strained and used as a broth in sauces, soups, and other recipes or frozen in a tightly covered container and used to make the next batch of seitan.

Makes about 2 pounds

All-Purpose Seitan Loaf

The addition of white beans makes this seitan loaf slightly lighter than an all-gluten seitan loaf. It's called "all-purpose" because you can use it in a variety of ways: slice it very thin for sandwiches, slice it a little thicker for sautés, grind it up for chili and tacos, cut it into strips for stir-fries, dice or chop it for stews and soups, or serve it whole as a roast.

1 cup cooked or canned white beans, rinsed and drained

1 garlic clove, crushed

1½ cups vital wheat gluten

1 cup vegetable broth

⅓ cup nutritional yeast

3 tablespoons low-sodium tamari

3 tablespoons instant tapioca

1 tablespoon olive oil

2 teaspoons onion powder

½ teaspoon ground dried sage

½ teaspoon ground dried thyme

½ teaspoon salt

1. Preheat the oven to 350°F. Spray a 12 x 14-inch sheet of aluminum foil with cooking spray.

2. Combine the beans and garlic in a food processor and process until pureed. Add the remaining ingredients and process until well combined. The texture should be like a soft dough.

3. Transfer the mixture to the prepared foil and shape it into an oval loaf, with the ends of the loaf within about 2 inches of the width of the foil. Wrap the foil around the loaf, closing up the ends.

4. Transfer the loaf to a 9 x 13-inch baking dish, seam side up. Pour about 1 inch of water into the pan and place in the oven. Bake until firm, about 1½ hours, turning once about halfway through. If serving right away, set aside to cool for several minutes before slicing with a serrated knife. For best results, allow the loaf to cool to room temperature, then cover and refrigerate until chilled. Once chilled, the seitan will be easier to slice. You can then cut and portion to use as desired.

Makes about 1½ pounds

Spicy Sausage Links

My recipe testers who tried these sausage links prefer them to commercial brands—and they're a lot less expensive, too. Preparing the mixture in the food processor and baking the sausages in the oven are both time-savers. Once baked, they're ready to brown up in a skillet to enjoy as is or in other recipes.

1¼ cups vital wheat gluten

⅓ cup nutritional yeast

¼ cup tapioca flour

2 teaspoons smoked paprika

1 teaspoon ground fennel seeds

½ teaspoon red pepper flakes

½ teaspoon garlic powder

½ teaspoon onion powder

¼ teaspoon cayenne

½ teaspoon salt

¼ teaspoon freshly ground black pepper

⅔ cup cooked or canned dark red kidney beans, rinsed, drained, blotted dry, and lightly mashed

2 tablespoons low-sodium tamari

1 tablespoon olive oil

1 tablespoon ketchup

½ teaspoon liquid smoke

½ cup water, as needed

1. Preheat the oven to 350°F. In a food processor, combine the vital wheat gluten, nutritional yeast, tapioca flour, paprika, ground fennel seeds, red pepper flakes, garlic powder, onion powder, cayenne, salt, and pepper. Pulse to mix. Add the mashed kidney beans, tamari, oil, ketchup, liquid smoke, and about ⅓ cup of the water and process until well mixed. If the mixture is too dry, add more water, a little at a time, until you have a workable (not wet) dough.

2. Turn the dough out onto a work surface and knead for about 3 minutes, then divide into 8 equal pieces. Roll and shape each piece into a link about 5 inches long. Wrap each link separately in aluminum foil, twisting the ends to seal.

3. Arrange the links in a single layer in a shallow baking dish, seam sides up. Pour enough water into the baking dish to come halfway up the sides of the links. Cover the baking dish tightly with foil and bake until firm, about 45 minutes. Remove the links from the pan, unwrap, and set aside to cool, then refrigerate for at least 1 hour to allow them to firm up before using. When ready to use, the sausage links may then be sautéed in a skillet in a little oil until browned.

Makes 8 links

As mentioned in the section on TVP, manufacturers have discovered ways to add spices and seasonings to tofu, tempeh, and seitan to create products that resemble foods normally made with animal products, such as burgers, hot dogs, bacon, pepperoni, Buffalo wings, and pastrami. The number of products and companies making them has skyrocketed in recent years. Many of the products are vegan, but some are not. It is important to read the labels, looking for ingredients such as egg whites, cheese, casein, and milk solids. (See page 26 for a list of hidden animal ingredients in foods.)

There are two main schools of thought on these products. One is that they are processed foods and not natural. For that reason, many vegans do not eat them because they are not whole foods and also because they resemble animal products.

The other perspective is that they are practical convenience foods for people with limited time to cook, finicky children, or reluctantly vegan spouses. They also are viewed as good transitional foods to have on hand when you are new to veganism and trying new recipes. A veggie burger slathered with barbecue sauce goes a long way when you are too tired to cook and want something quick and easy.

My own view is that fresh, unadulterated whole foods are best. Vegetables, fruits, grains, beans, and the basic meat alternatives (tofu, tempeh, seitan) offer an amazing variety of textures and flavors, and provide maximum nutrition. At the same time, I do enjoy grilling vegan hot dogs on the Fourth of July or biting into a BLT made with crisp, smoky vegan bacon. One way to enjoy vegan sausage, burgers, and other such foods without buying products that are either expensive or highly processed or both is to make your own. In this book, you will find recipes for homemade vegan sausage, burgers, burger crumbles, and other "meaty" ingredients.

Regarding prepared vegan meat alternative products, I think that it is a personal decision. If you find a brand of vegan burgers or sausage that you enjoy, then keeping some on hand for a quick meal when you don't have time to cook seems like a practical thing to do.

The same thing holds true for baked marinated tofu. While it is easy and economical to make your own, it's also quite convenient to buy the prepared version when time is short.

Oils

Since many vegan ingredients are naturally low in fat, a moderate use of cooking and salad oils can add some "good" fat to your diet. The best-quality oils are cold-pressed, or unrefined. I like to use extra-virgin olive oil for salads and most cooking, except for high-heat stir-fries, where you want an oil that has a higher smoking point and will not start breaking down before you get it to the right temperature. In addition to great flavor, olive oil provides many health benefits.

A good "all-purpose" oil is grapeseed oil. It has a fairly high smoke point, so it can be used for high-temperature cooking such as stir-frying or sautéing. Because of its light flavor, it also makes a good component in dressings and sauces.

Toasted or dark sesame oil adds an Asian flavor to salads and other recipes, but think of it as a seasoning rather than a cooking oil, because it is unstable at high temperatures. Add it at the last minute for flavor. Flaxseed oil is an excellent source of omega-3 fatty acids, which are so important for good health. Like toasted sesame oil, flaxseed oil is unstable at high temperatures and should not be used for cooking. Unlike toasted sesame oil, it is virtually flavorless, but you can use it on salads to boost your intake of omega-3s. All of these oils are highly perishable, so be sure to store them in the refrigerator.

Coconut oil is another choice you may want to consider. It can withstand high temperatures and is especially useful for frying. Studies show a very low incidence of heart disease among people who consume coconut oil on a regular basis. In addition, coconut oil aids calcium absorption and is rich in antimicrobial properties. Organic, unrefined food-grade coconut oil is available at natural foods stores and online.

In order to make this book more accessible to those who follow a no-oil diet, most of the recipes in this book now offer a no-oil option.

Nuts and Seeds

Nuts and seeds are staple foods in many cultures and important protein sources for vegans. Many nuts and seeds are available both in and out of the shell, whole, halved, sliced, chopped, raw, roasted, or made into nut butter. Nuts are popular in both sweet and savory dishes and are often enjoyed as a snack food. Due to their high oil content, nuts and seeds go rancid quickly once shelled and should be stored in an airtight container in the refrigerator, where they will keep for several months. Some nuts are sold shelled in cans, jars, and bags. Many are available in bulk at natural foods stores and many supermarkets.

Studies have shown that eating just two ounces of almonds, pecans, or other nuts each day as part of a high-fiber vegan diet can dramatically lower "bad" (low-density lipoprotein, or LDL) cholesterol.

NUT AND SEED BUTTERS

When nuts or seeds are ground into a paste, they are referred to as butters. Not long ago, the only nut butter found in most pantries was peanut butter, and a highly processed version at that. Over the past several years, however, a wide variety of natural nut butters have become widely available, including almond butter, cashew butter, hazelnut butter, macadamia butter, pistachio butter, tahini (sesame paste), and even soy nut butter.

Nut and seed butters are rich in protein, fiber, and essential fatty acids and can be used to replace

Fabulous Flaxseeds

The tiny flaxseed is a nutritional powerhouse that is especially prized for its high amounts of omega-3 and omega-6 essential fatty acids. High in protein, flaxseeds also contain good amounts of calcium, phosphorus, potassium, magnesium, and boron. Flaxseeds provide abundant soluble fiber, which is helpful in controlling blood-sugar levels and reducing cholesterol. Flaxseeds are also the richest known source of the anticarcinogens known as lignans and phytoestrogens.

Flaxseeds can be purchased in bulk at natural foods stores and well-stocked supermarkets. They should be ground in a blender or coffee grinder before using to provide maximum nutrient absorption and increase digestibility. Since they go rancid quickly, they should be stored in the refrigerator or freezer. They can be sprinkled on breakfast cereals, salads, or grain dishes or added to smoothies for an energy boost. Blended with water, ground flaxseeds can be used to replace eggs in baking (see page 457).

butter or margarine on bread or toast. At least half of the fat in nuts is monounsaturated, which can actually be good for blood cholesterol. Nut butters are a boon to vegans as a versatile source of protein and can be used to make sauces, to enrich soups and stews, and as a healthy fat replacement in baking. They are easier to digest than whole nuts and are easy to make at home using a blender. They should be stored in tightly covered jars in the refrigerator, where they will keep for about a month. Since nut butters become stiff when chilled, it is best to bring them to room temperature before using. In addition, the oil in nut butters will rise to the top of the jar, so you will need to stir the butter before using.

Natural nut butters do not contain the stabilizers and additives found in most national brands. They are made, quite simply, with nuts and perhaps a little salt. Nothing more.

Know Your Nuts and Seeds

Most of us know that nuts and seeds are important sources of protein, but did you also know that they are rich in vitamins, minerals, and other nutrients as well? In addition, although most nuts and seeds are high in fat, most of that is unsaturated fat—the "good" fat we all need. Here's a look at the nutrient content of some nuts and seeds.

- *Almonds:* High in calcium, potassium, magnesium, and zinc, almonds also contain folic acid, phosphorus, and iron and are about 18 percent protein.

- *Brazil nuts:* Rich in calcium, magnesium, thiamine, and potassium, Brazil nuts contain significant amounts of vitamin B6, zinc, and iron.

- *Cashews:* They contain high amounts of calcium, magnesium, iron, and zinc, as well as phosphorus and potassium.

- *Chestnuts:* They are a good source of calcium, potassium, B vitamins, magnesium, and iron.

- *Coconuts:* High in fiber, coconuts contain a good amount of calcium, potassium, iron, phosphorus, zinc, and magnesium.

- *Flaxseeds:* Especially high in protein and rich in essential fatty acids, flaxseeds also contain good amounts of calcium and phosphorus.

- *Hazelnuts:* Also known as filberts, they are high in fiber and a good source of calcium, iron, potassium, magnesium, and vitamins A, B, and E.

- *Macadamia nuts:* They are rich in magnesium, calcium, potassium, iron, thiamine, and niacin.

- *Peanuts:* Rich in protein (about 26 percent) peanuts are an excellent source of niacin and contain other B vitamins—thiamine and riboflavin—as well as potassium, magnesium, calcium, and iron.

- *Pecans:* High in fiber, pecans are a good source of calcium, iron, magnesium, and potassium. They also contain small amounts of vitamins A, B, C, and E.

- *Pine nuts:* A rich source of fiber, pine nuts contain iron, magnesium, potassium, and folic acid.

- *Pistachios:* Pistachios are a good source of calcium, magnesium, potassium, iron, folic acid, and vitamins B_6 and C.

- *Pumpkin seeds:* Extremely high in protein (29 percent), pumpkin seeds are rich in iron, calcium, phosphorus, and vitamins A and B.

- *Sesame seeds:* They are rich in iron, calcium, and vitamins A, B, and E.

- *Sunflower seeds:* Rich in omega-6 fatty acids, sunflower seeds are a good source of calcium, iron, and other nutrients.

- *Walnuts:* An excellent source of vitamin E, copper, and magnesium, walnuts also contain potassium, vitamin B_6, thiamine, and essential fatty acids.

Dried Fruits

Dried fruits have become increasingly popular in recent years, showing up in sweet and savory dishes from breads, muffins, and compotes to sauces, chutneys, stuffings, and stews. Choices range from dried cranberries and papaya spears to banana chips and apple rings. Raisins, dried dates, dried figs, and even dried apricots are important ingredients in many cuisines, and prunes are now called dried plums in an effort to update their image.

Because most of the water content has been removed from dried fruits, they have a higher concentration of sugar than fresh fruits, which results in more calories on a weight-for-weight basis. Still, dried fruits are a chewy, sweet snack with good nutritional content, despite the fact that some of the nutrients are lost during the drying process. To keep the nutritional losses to a minimum, store your dried fruits in airtight containers in a cool, dark place. Dried fruits can be reconstituted by soaking them in hot water for 30 minutes.

Although their vitamin C content is diminished, virtually all dried fruits are high in potassium, calcium, and fiber, and many actually have an increased mineral content when dried. In particular, raisins, dried pears, and dried figs are abundant in iron, phosphorus, and magnesium, while dried apples and dates contain a good amount of magnesium. Dried apricots, peaches, and plums (prunes) are high in vitamin A, iron, and magnesium, and dried papayas are abundant in vitamin A.

Miso

Miso is a salty fermented paste made from soybeans, often in combination with a grain such as rice or barley. It is versatile and can be used in soups and stews, casseroles, marinades, sauces, dressings, and dips. Available in different colors and degrees of saltiness, miso is high in protein and rich in enzymes.

Miso paste is generally aged from one month to three years and can be made using either traditional or commercial methods. The traditional method relies on natural ingredients and sea salt and allows the miso to age in large, wooden fermentation casks. The commercial method accelerates the fermentation process in plastic or stainless steel holding tanks.

The longer the soybeans are fermented, the darker and stronger in flavor the miso is. Miso paste can range in color and pungency from white to dark brown, with white being the weakest in flavor and dark brown the most pungent. White and yellow miso are well suited for soups, salad dressings, and sauces. Red and brown miso are strong and salty and are generally used for stews, soups, and braised foods. Often two or more kinds of miso are combined in a recipe. Some of the more common varieties are *hatcho miso,* made with soybeans and sea salt; *genmai miso,* made with soybeans and brown rice; and *mugi miso,* made with soybeans and barley.

Several varieties of miso paste are available in natural foods stores and Asian markets under different brand names. Miso paste may be refrigerated for up to a year in a tightly sealed container.

Salt

From the delicate, pricey *fleur de sel* to the coarse, economical kosher variety, salt is an important element in cooking. Just a pinch can sometimes make the difference between a well-seasoned dish and one that lacks flavor. The best salt for general use is sea salt, because it is naturally derived, has a good flavor, and contains minerals that are nutritionally beneficial. Steer clear of refined table salt. It is bitter, devoid of nutrition, and loaded with chemicals that are added to make it flow freely.

If you do not need to avoid salt for medical reasons, I encourage a judicious use of sea salt in your cooking to bring out and balance the natural flavors of foods. If you must eliminate salt from your diet, consider using an herbal salt substitute. You also may want to experiment with spices, herbs, and ingredients such as garlic, onions, lemon juice, and wine to add flavor to your dishes.

The more processed a food is, the higher its sodium content. Therefore, the more naturally you eat, with lots of fresh vegetables, fruits, and grains, the less sodium you will consume. For that reason, most people can use sea salt when they cook and not worry about getting too much sodium. It is important to add salt to your food *while it is cooking,* not afterward, so that the salt has a chance to dissolve into the dish, thus allowing your body to absorb the minerals in the salt. If you add salt at the table, the absorption process is bypassed, and the salt is simply flushed out of your system, which can overtax your kidneys.

Soy sauce is often used to replace salt, although many brands of soy sauce are full of sodium and additives and the flavor can be bitter and harsh. Read the label when buying soy sauce to avoid any undesirable ingredients. For the best flavor and nutritional value, use a traditionally brewed shoyu or tamari. Although these products do contain salt, they are naturally fermented and have a mellow flavor. Low-sodium tamari also is available. The downside of these soy sauces is the cost: the best-quality, cold-pressed organic tamari and shoyu can be very expensive.

Sea Vegetables

Not long ago, the only sea vegetable on the American horizon was nori, famed for its use in sushi.

These days, however, you can find several varieties of sea vegetables on supermarket shelves and seaweed salads on some restaurant menus.

Sea vegetables are sold in dehydrated form and will keep indefinitely when stored in airtight containers in a cool, dark place. With flavors ranging from delicate and mild to salty and spicy, sea vegetables contain high concentrations of protein, iron, calcium, and other nutrients. Because most sea vegetables are dried, they require soaking in water prior to use. Two exceptions are nori sheets and dulse, which can be eaten right from the package.

Know Your Sea Vegetables

Here is a list of the most common sea vegetables.

- *Agar:* Also called kanten, this is a tasteless natural gelatin alternative used to make gelatin-type desserts. Available in bars or flakes, it is extremely high in iodine.

- *Alaria:* Resembling wakame in appearance, taste, and nutrition, alaria is high in calcium, vitamin A, and B vitamins. It is good in stews, grain dishes, and miso soup.

- *Arame:* Similar to hijiki in appearance, arame is rich in calcium and iodine. It has a delicate flavor and can be used in soups or combined with tofu or land vegetables.

- *Dulse:* With its soft, chewy texture and a salty, spicy flavor, this is an appealing choice for those new to sea vegetables. Native to the North Atlantic coast, dulse is high in protein, iron, potassium, and vitamins B_6 and B_{12}. It cooks quickly when added to recipes but also is a nice snack right from the package or when lightly fried.

- *Hijiki:* The strongest-tasting sea vegetable, hijiki is often paired with onions and root vegetables or added to soups. Dehydrated, hijiki looks like black strings. When cooked, it expands to up to five times its dry volume. Hijiki is high in calcium and iron.

- *Kelp:* Ranging from light brown to dark green, kelp is similar to kombu and is used in much the same ways—in stews and soups or cooked with grains or beans. It contains a natural tenderizer that helps beans cook quickly and aids in digestion. Kelp is high in calcium, iron, potassium, magnesium, chromium, and iodine.

- *Kombu:* Sometimes called "natural MSG," kombu is used to brighten the flavors of soups and stews and to tenderize beans. It is usually sold as blackish-green dried strips.

- *Nori:* Though deep purple when fresh, nori turns dark green when toasted, which is how it is commonly sold. Known for its role in sushi making, nori is available in pretoasted, ready-to-use sheets and can be chopped or crumbled to use in soups and salads.

- *Wakame:* The traditional leafy addition to miso soup, wakame has a mild flavor that works well in salads or stir-fries with other vegetables or grains. It is high in calcium, B vitamins, and vitamin C.

The soaking time for sea vegetables varies, and some expand more than others when soaked. For correct preparation, follow the instructions on the package or in a particular recipe.

Many sea vegetables are best enjoyed in soups or salads or cooked with vegetables or grains. A few have other uses. For example, agar has natural jelling properties, making it useful as a vegan alternative to gelatin. Kombu or kelp can be added to the cooking water of dried beans to help them cook faster and make them easier to digest.

It is best to buy only certified organic sea vegetables. Although Asian markets carry less expensive products, they are not of the same high quality as certified organic brands. If you are worried about the extra expense, remember that sea vegetables expand dramatically when soaked, so only a small amount is needed.

Flours

When considering what kind of flour to use in baking, you have a "field of flours" from which to choose, each with its own flavor and textural characteristics. Here is a bouquet of the more common (and some uncommon) flours.

•AMARANTH FLOUR: Though difficult to find, it can be made at home by grinding the tiny amaranth grains. Because of its strong, distinctive flavor, it is best used in small quantities to add nutrients and flavor to your favorite bread recipes.

•BROWN RICE FLOUR: This is especially useful for people allergic to wheat. However, because rice contains no gluten, it is best to use rice flour in quick-bread recipes.

•BUCKWHEAT FLOUR: Just a small amount of this flour added to a bread recipe creates a hearty, dense loaf with a strong, distinctive flavor.

•CORNMEAL: Available in both white and yellow varieties, cornmeal is used to make breads, muffins, and other baked goods. Because many of the nutrients are removed during processing, cornmeal is often sold enriched with vitamins and minerals.

•WHEAT GLUTEN FLOUR: This high-protein flour is refined from wheat flour and rises better because it is low in starch.

•OAT FLOUR: Oat flour has a delicate, sweet flavor and can be used in cookies, quick breads, and muffins. Because it contains no gluten, it is often used by people with wheat allergies. You can make your own oat flour by grinding rolled oats to a powder in a blender.

•RYE FLOUR: To make rye bread, you should use at least 1 cup of wheat flour for every 3 cups of rye flour in order to activate the yeast. Rye is a popular bread flour in eastern Europe and Scandinavia.

•SOY FLOUR: Extremely rich in high-quality protein, soy flour also is an excellent source of iron, calcium, and B vitamins. Made from finely ground roasted soybeans, soy flour adds protein to baked goods, as well as a dense texture and nutty flavor. Because it has no gluten, you should use only a small amount of soy flour in combination with wheat flour for baking.

Toasting soy flour lightly will give it a nuttier flavor.

- **Triticale flour:** This hybrid of rye and wheat has a hearty flavor and extra protein. Boost the protein in your bread recipe by replacing half of the whole-wheat flour with triticale flour.

- **Unbleached all-purpose flour:** Refined wheat flour is less nutritious than whole-wheat flour. Combine unbleached all-purpose flour and whole-wheat flour in bread recipes to provide the nutrients of whole-wheat and the lighter texture and mellower flavor of all-purpose.

- **Whole-wheat flour:** For bread recipes, use whole-wheat bread flour, which is made from hard red spring wheat or red winter wheat and is high in gluten, which helps produce light, airy loaves. For pastries, muffins, and cookies, use whole-wheat pastry flour, which has less protein than regular whole-wheat.

Sweeteners

The use of white sugar in a vegan diet is a matter of personal preference. Many people need to avoid sugar for health reasons. Others do not use it because it is devoid of nutritional value. If you need another reason to avoid sugar, consider the fact that about one-quarter of the white table sugar in the United States is processed using charred animal bones. To many vegans, this is considered a minuscule point in the grand scheme of things, and they continue to use sugar.

Among the alternatives to sugar and honey are natural sweeteners such as pure maple syrup, agave nectar, barley malt, rice syrup, pureed fruit (such as raisins or dates), and natural fruit sweeteners available under a variety of brand names. In addition to

The Buzz About Honey

Although honey may be considered a natural sweetener by many, it is not considered a vegan ingredient. This is because many bees are killed, harmed, or otherwise exploited to procure honey from their hives.

During the harvesting of honey and other bee byproducts, bees are removed from their hives by harsh methods, such as shaking or smoking the hives or dousing them with gases or blasts of air. A number of bees are invariably killed in the process.

Although the exploitation of bees may be inconsequential to many people, especially when compared to the cruel and inhumane treatment of other animals raised for food, many vegans do not use honey as a matter of principle. Ethical vegans strive to eliminate from their lives any product that involves the exploitation or suffering of any creature.

A vast number of alternative sweeteners, candles, and personal care products that do not contain bee products are available.

providing nutritional benefits, natural sweeteners do not cause a sugar "rush," because they metabolize more slowly in the system.

The sweetness level of sugar alternatives can vary greatly, so it is best to experiment to find the ones you like best. Several alternatives can be substituted in equal measure for white table sugar. One of the most popular and widely available is naturally processed granulated sugar cane, sold as Sucanat or Florida Crystals.

Another option is date or palm sugar, which can be found in ethnic markets. Its deep, almost caramelized flavor is ideally suited to Southeast Asian recipes and can be fun to experiment with, although it does not dissolve as well as other sugars.

Among the natural liquid sweeteners that can be substituted in equal measure for honey are pure maple syrup, agave nectar, and coconut nectar. These work best when the liquid-to-solid ratio is important to the outcome of a recipe. Sweeteners such as barley malt and brown rice syrup are about half as sweet as honey, so you may need to experiment to achieve the desired results. Soaked and pureed dates and raisins, as well as molasses, are good natural sweeteners, but their dark color and distinctive flavors make them appropriate for only certain recipes.

When substituting a natural liquid sweetener for granulated sugar in recipes, you will need to reduce the amount of the other liquids in the recipe so that the finished product retains the intended texture. For each cup of liquid sweetener added, reduce the other liquids by a total of ¼ cup.

Stevia is another sweetener worth considering. Available in liquid or powder form, stevia is derived from dried stevia leaves, an herb native to Paraguay. It differs from other sweeteners in that it is highly concentrated. Just a drop or pinch of this natural sugar alternative can sweeten a cup of liquid. Stevia can be used for baking, as it is stable to 390°F, although determining the proper ratio can be hit or miss. If you use too much, it can leave a strong, overly sweet aftertaste.

Food Allergies

Many people today seek recipes that are gluten-free, soy-free, or low in fat. As I mentioned, the recipes in this book have been revised to offer options with no added oils. For example, in many cases, a choice is given to sauté ingredients in either water or a small amount of oil. In addition, the oils that are used have been significantly reduced.

As for people who are sensitive to gluten, soy, or nuts, I have done my best to provide alternatives to these ingredients wherever possible so that most of the recipes can be made accessible to as many people as possible, regardless of any dietary restrictions. Many of the recipes are also either gluten-free or soy-free, or both, and it's often quite simple to make a particular recipe either gluten-free or soy-free. For example, substitute gluten-free pasta for regular pasta or use coconut aminos instead of soy sauce.

Important: If you have a specific food sensitivity, be sure to read all labels carefully to be sure the products you are buying are free of those ingredients. For example, certain commercially available products, such as hoisin sauce, tamari, and vegetable broth (and soup base pastes and bouillon cubes) may contain gluten, although gluten-free versions are easily found in most markets.

Buying Breads

When buying breads, it is important to read the list of ingredients. Like many other prepared products, many commercially baked breads contain animal products or other ingredients you may not want to consume.

To get the most nutrition from bread, consider trying some of the delicious whole-grain sprouted breads available in natural foods stores and some supermarkets. Some brands contain only organic sprouted grains and beans, filtered water, fresh yeast, and sea salt.

Wheat-free and gluten-free breads are available for those with wheat allergies or gluten sensitivities. For those who cannot tolerate yeast, there are yeast-free breads available as well.

Hidden Animal Ingredients

Many animal-based ingredients lurk in seemingly vegetarian and vegan foods. Beyond the obvious anchovy-laced Worcestershire sauce and the "milk" contained in milk chocolate, animal products such as gelatin and lard can be found in commercial items such as marshmallows, cookies, crackers, chips, candies, pastries, and refried beans.

Vegetarians who eat cheese should know that most dairy cheese is made with pepsin, rennet, or lipase, coagulated enzymes from the stomach linings of slaughtered cows and pigs. An alternative to dairy cheese is soy cheese, which contains no animal byproducts. However, most soy cheeses are made with casein, which is obtained from cow's milk. A few brands of soy cheese are casein-free, but they do not melt well. They are usually labeled "vegan."

Vegans also should be aware that many products labeled as "vegetarian" may contain egg and dairy byproducts. In addition to avoiding products that contain butter, milk, eggs, and honey, vegans should be on the lookout for products with ingredients such as casein, albumin, whey, and lactose.

Fortunately, virtually every animal-based ingredient has a plant-based alternative. For example, there are vegan versions of Worcestershire sauce and chocolate chips, and gelatin-like desserts and puddings can be made with vegetable-based jelling ingredients such as the sea vegetables agar and carrageen.

The best defense against unwittingly buying foods with animal-derived ingredients is quite simple: read the labels. As a rule, the more processed a food item is, the more likely it is to contain animal products—often not listed in easily recognizable terms. To cut down on the chances of ingesting hidden animal ingredients, try to eat more fresh whole foods, such as vegetables, fruits, grains, and beans, and to make more foods, such as salad dressings, from scratch. Not only will this help you avoid hidden animal ingredients, but homemade dressings and other foods generally taste better and are more economical.

Avoiding Hidden Animal Ingredients

Here are some common hidden animal-based ingredients and the types of foods in which they are often found.

- *Albumin:* Used to thicken or bind baked goods, soups, cereals, puddings, and other products, albumin is a protein found in eggs, milk, and blood.

- *Carmine, cochineal, or carminic acid:* A common red food dye made from ground beetles, it is used to color juices, baked goods, candies, and other processed foods.

- *Casein:* This protein derived from animal milk is used in dairy products such as sour cream and cream cheese. It is also added to nondairy cheese to improve the texture.

- *Gelatin:* This thickener is made by boiling the bones, skin, and other parts of cows and other animals. It is found in gelatin desserts, marshmallows, candies, puddings, and other products.

- *Lactose:* Also called milk sugar, it is derived from cow's milk and is found in baked goods and processed foods.

- *Lard:* This fat taken from hogs is an ingredient in crackers, pie crusts, and baked goods, as well as refried beans and other fried or processed foods.

- *Suet:* This hard, white fat from cattle and sheep is sometimes found in margarine and baked goods.

- *Whey:* Derived from milk as it is processed into cheese, whey is found in commercial food products such as crackers and breads.

Stocking the Pantry

A well-stocked pantry is the first step toward making meatless and dairy-free cooking convenient, fun, and delicious. With a variety of ingredients at your fingertips, you can prepare interesting, healthful meals in a snap.

The following list of pantry items is especially important in a vegan kitchen. It includes staples such as canned and dried beans, grains, pasta, and tomato products. Also included are meal enhancers such as peanut butter, tahini, tamari, salsa, and chutney—indispensable ingredients for the creative cook.

In addition to the items listed here, you should, of course, keep on hand a supply of dried herbs, spices, sea salt, and other basic seasonings, as well as various flours, baking soda, baking powder, and extracts. Your vegan larder should include a number of perishable staples, such as onions, carrots, and celery, so that you always have the makings for a soup or stew; fresh lettuce and other salad ingredients; fresh vegetables and fruits; and fresh herbs.

Many of the ingredients integral to a vegan pantry are highly perishable. This applies not only to fresh fruits and vegetables but also to nuts, seeds, certain oils, and whole-grain flours, which can go rancid quickly. As an extra precaution against spoilage, I suggest storing such items in the refrigerator. Once packages are opened, other nonperishable items may require refrigeration.

Vegan Pantry List

Dried and canned beans: kidney beans, chickpeas, lentils, pintos, etc.

Grains: rice, quinoa, millet, barley, bulgur, rolled oats, couscous

Whole-grain flours, cornmeal, vital wheat gluten, etc.

Pasta and noodles: Italian pasta, rice sticks, soba, etc.

Soy foods: tofu, tempeh, miso paste, etc.

Nuts and seeds

Nondairy milk: soy, rice, oat, or almond

Unsweetened coconut milk (canned)

Canned tomato products (diced, whole, puree, paste)

Canned vegetables: artichoke hearts, roasted red peppers, hearts of palm, etc.

Condiments: soy sauce (tamari and shoyu are best), salsa, chutney, mustard, etc.

Dried fruits

Nutritional yeast

Thickeners: cornstarch, arrowroot, tapioca flour

Egg replacement powder (Ener-G Egg Replacer is a popular brand)

Sweeteners: pure maple syrup, agave nectar, raw sugar (brands include Sucanat or Florida Crystals), brown rice syrup, barley malt, palm sugar

Vegetable broth or soup base (aseptic containers, canned, paste, powder, or cube—preferably low sodium)

Dried mushrooms (porcinis, shiitakes, etc.)

Dried chiles

Sun-dried tomatoes (dehydrated or oil-packed)

Dried sea vegetables, including nori and agar

Oils: olive, flaxseed, sesame, grapeseed

Peanut butter, tahini, almond butter

Nondairy ice cream, mayonnaise, cheese, sour cream, yogurt

Bread products: whole-grain breads, tortillas, pita breads, bagels, etc.

Lemons and limes (for cooking)

Fresh ginger

Garlic

Olives (bulk)

Miscellaneous: vinegars, pickles, jellies, capers, Asian chili paste, hoisin sauce, wasabi powder, chipotle chiles in adobo, etc.

TWO

Love at First Bite

"I have no doubt that it is part of the destiny of the human race, in its gradual improvement, to leave off eating animals, as surely as the savage tribes have left off eating each other when they came into contact with the more civilized."

—HENRY DAVID THOREAU

Appetizers usually herald a special event, be it an intimate dinner for two, a family celebration, or a party. Whether you call them hors d'oeuvres, finger foods, or even amuse-bouches, these tasty bites don't have to be reserved for special occasions. Serving a first course prior to Tuesday night's casserole or setting out a plate of crostini before your usual Thursday night pasta dinner can lend a festive air to the rest of the meal. On nights when you're serving leftovers or a light supper, an appetizer can elevate the meal from dull to dramatic and add substance and nutrition at the same time. Your family will feel special for the extra effort, and that will make you feel good, too.

Appetizers are a great way to introduce new tastes and recipes to your family—in little bites. Plus, they're a good way to be sure your family is getting enough veggies. A finicky child (or spouse) who avoids certain vegetables on the dinner plate is almost certain to enjoy them served up as "fun food" in a fritter, alongside (or in) a dip, or wrapped in a savory pastry.

Planning an appetizer party without meat and dairy removes the guesswork from entertaining friends, since most people can enjoy the food whether they are vegetarians or meat eaters. This chapter contains a planet full of naturally vegan appetizers, including a spicy rendition of Middle Eastern hummus, *Stuffed Grape Leaves with Pine Nuts and Dill*, and *Minted Baba Ganoush*, as well as *Caponata Crostini*, *Black Olive Bruschetta*, and *Hot and Spicy Stuffed Mushrooms*. Asian bites include tempting *Vegetable Spring Rolls with Spicy Peanut Dipping Sauce*, *Scallion Pancakes with Sesame Seeds*, and *Portobello Satays*, as well as elegant *Sesame-Asparagus Sushi Rolls*. Other worldly wonders include *Baked Sweet Potato and Green Pea Samosas*, a French-inspired *Wild Mushroom Pâté*, and an all-American *Artichoke-Sunflower Spread*.

Walnut-Crusted Artichoke Hearts

This is a delicious way to combine these two complementary favorites into one amazing appetizer. Quartered artichoke hearts are coated with a walnut batter and pan-fried. Succulent and tender inside, with a crusty nutty outside and punctuated by bits of lemon zest, the result is heaven on a plate. This recipe works well with cooked frozen artichoke hearts, with canned artichoke hearts, or with marinated artichoke hearts from a jar. They are best served hot as an appetizer accompanied by lemon wedges.

½ cup toasted walnut pieces (page 203)

½ cup plain unsweetened nondairy milk

3 tablespoons all-purpose flour, chickpea flour, or fine cornmeal

2 tablespoons cornstarch

1 teaspoon very fine lemon zest (optional)

½ teaspoon salt

¼ teaspoon freshly ground black pepper

Neutral vegetable oil, for frying

1½ cups cooked frozen or canned artichoke hearts, well drained and quartered

Lemon wedges, to serve

1. In a food processor, process the walnuts until finely ground. Add the nondairy milk, flour, cornstarch, lemon zest (if using), salt, and pepper. Process until smooth and well blended (the batter will be thick). Transfer to a shallow bowl.

2. Heat a thin layer of oil in a large skillet over medium-high heat. Dip the artichoke hearts in the batter, turning to coat all over, then add them to the hot pan, working in batches if needed. Cook until nicely browned on both sides, turning once, about 4 minutes per side. Serve hot, with lemon wedges.

Serves 4

Did You Know?

Artichokes are believed to serve a number of medicinal purposes, including blood cleanser and diuretic. This vegetable, which is actually the flower bud of a plant, is also a good source of potassium and magnesium.

Nachos with Presto Queso

The healthy but flavorful take on *queso* sauce is made with protein-rich cannellini beans. In addition to being terrific for nachos, the sauce can also be used as a topping for cooked vegetables, grains, and even chili.

1½ cups cooked cannellini beans
or 1 (15-ounce) can beans, rinsed and drained

½ cup plain unsweetened nondairy milk

⅓ cup nutritional yeast

1 tablespoon fresh lemon juice

1 teaspoon smoked paprika

1 teaspoon chili powder

½ teaspoon salt

1 large bag tortilla chips

1 cup Fresh Tomato Salsa
(page 157) or purchased salsa

½ cup pickled jalapeño slices

Optional toppings: guacamole, sliced black olives, warmed vegan chili, warmed vegan refried beans, vegan sour cream, chopped red onion or scallions

1. In a food processor or high-speed blender, combine the beans, nondairy milk, nutritional yeast, lemon juice, paprika, chili powder, and salt. Blend until smooth. Transfer to a small saucepan and heat over medium-low heat until warm, stirring the *queso* so it doesn't burn. Taste and adjust the seasonings if needed.

2. To assemble, arrange the tortilla chips on a large platter and drizzle with the *queso*. Spoon on the salsa, and sprinkle with the pickled jalapenos and any of the optional toppings, if desired. Serve immediately.

Serves 4 to 6

Ginger-Scented Vegetable Pot Stickers

These vegetable dumplings are called pot stickers because—you guessed it—they tend to stick to the bottom of the pot. Look for wonton or dumpling wrappers in the produce section of well-stocked supermarkets and Asian grocery stores. They can be served with a small bowl of plain tamari or a dipping sauce such as Ginger-Lime Dipping Sauce (page 145).

1 cup minced napa cabbage

1 cup drained and crumbled extra-firm tofu

¼ cup finely shredded carrots

1 garlic clove, minced

2 teaspoons grated fresh ginger

1 teaspoon toasted sesame oil

½ teaspoon cornstarch

Salt and freshly ground black pepper

24 vegan wonton or dumpling wrappers, thawed if frozen

2 tablespoons neutral vegetable oil

1 tablespoon low-sodium tamari

1 cup water

1. In a food processor, combine the cabbage, tofu, carrots, garlic, ginger, sesame oil, cornstarch, and salt and pepper to taste. Pulse until well combined, but with some texture remaining.

2. Place 1 wonton wrapper on a work surface and spoon 1 tablespoon of the filling mixture on the lower third of the wrapper. Fold the wrapper over the filling to form a triangle (if using square wrappers) or a semicircle (if using round wrappers). Moisten the edges of the wrapper with water to seal. Repeat with the remaining wrappers and filling.

3. Heat 1 tablespoon of the oil in a large nonstick skillet over medium-high heat. Place half of the dumplings in the pan and cook until golden on the bottom, about 3 minutes. Do not crowd.

4. Stir in half of the tamari, then half of the water. Cover, reduce the heat to medium, and cook for 5 minutes. Uncover and continue cooking until the water evaporates, 2 to 3 minutes. Transfer the dumplings to a plate and tent with aluminum foil so they stay warm.

5. Repeat with the remaining dumplings, tamari, and water. Serve hot.

Makes 24

Stuffed Grape Leaves
with Pine Nuts and Dill

Piquant grape leaves wrap tightly around a tasty filling of basmati rice and pine nuts to make the classic Middle Eastern appetizer called *dolmas* or *dolmades*. Jars of grape leaves packed in brine are available in well-stocked supermarkets and specialty food stores.

1 (16-ounce) jar grape leaves

1 tablespoon olive oil or ¼ cup water

1 medium-size onion, minced

¾ cup basmati rice

¼ cup pine nuts, toasted (page 203)

3 tablespoons minced fresh dill

½ teaspoon ground cinnamon

Salt and freshly ground black pepper

1¼ cups vegetable broth

1 tablespoon fresh lemon juice

1. Remove the grape leaves from the jar and rinse under running water to remove the brine. Pat dry and trim off the stems. Set aside.

2. Heat the olive oil or water in a large skillet over medium heat. Add the onion, cover, and cook until softened, about 5 minutes. Stir in the rice, pine nuts, dill, cinnamon, and salt and pepper to taste, then pour in 1 cup of the broth. Cover and simmer, stirring occasionally, until all of the liquid has evaporated, 30 to 40 minutes. Transfer the filling to a bowl and allow to cool completely.

3. On a work surface, place one of the grape leaves shiny side down, with the stem end toward you. Place a tablespoon of the cooled filling near the stem end and fold in the sides of the leaf over the filling. Firmly roll up the leaf away from you. Repeat the process with the remaining leaves and filling. Transfer the *dolmas* to a large skillet.

4. Pour the remaining ¼ cup broth and the lemon juice over the *dolmas*, then add enough water to just barely cover them with liquid. Bring to a simmer over medium heat and cook, covered, until the grape leaves are tender, about 30 minutes. Remove from the heat, uncover, and allow to cool.

5. Using a slotted spoon, transfer the *dolmas* to a serving plate and serve. They will keep for up to 5 days in a tightly sealed container in the refrigerator but are best served at room temperature.

Makes 20 to 24

Thai Leaf-Wrapped Bites

This refreshing appetizer is a popular snack food in Thailand, where it is called *miang kam* and is often sold by street vendors. I've enjoyed it served elegantly at Arun's, an extraordinary Thai restaurant in Chicago, and have since begun making it at home. The key to the unique flavor is a small amount of several ingredients—sweet, sour, hot, and salty—which, when wrapped in a leaf and popped in the mouth, provide an experience not unlike a burst of fireworks. Since the wild leaves (often *shaploo*, wild pepper, or wild betel leaves) used to make *miang kam* can be difficult to find, I use leaf lettuce, torn into small pieces, but spinach or tender young kale leaves may be used instead.

5 or 6 large leaf lettuce leaves

SAUCE

½ cup unsweetened shredded coconut, toasted (page 453)

¼ cup unsalted dry-roasted peanuts

¼ cup palm sugar or other natural sugar

3 tablespoons low-sodium tamari

⅓ cup water

FILLING

2 or 3 Thai chiles, to your taste, seeded and cut into very thin rounds

1 lime, sliced and finely chopped, including peel

½ cup coarsely chopped unsalted dry-roasted peanuts

½ cup unsweetened shredded coconut, toasted (page 453)

¼ cup minced shallots

¼ cup grated fresh ginger

¼ cup chopped fresh cilantro

1. Carefully wash and dry the lettuce leaves and tear into 20 pieces total, about 4 inches square. Arrange on a serving platter and set aside.

2. To make the sauce, combine the ingredients in a small saucepan over medium heat and bring to a boil. Reduce the heat to low and simmer until thickened, about 5 minutes. Remove from the heat and allow to cool slightly. Transfer to a blender or food processor and process until smooth. Place in a small serving bowl and set the bowl on the platter with the leaves. Set aside.

3. For the filling, place each of the ingredients in a separate small bowl and arrange on a large platter or tray.

4. To eat, cup one of the lettuce leaves in your hand and place a small amount of each filling in the center of the leaf. Top with a bit of sauce, close up the leaf, and pop it in your mouth.

Serves 4

ALTERNATIVE SERVING IDEAS: Having your guests assemble their own *miang kam* can be fun, but you may prefer a more elegant presentation. Arrange 5 lettuce squares on each of 4 plates (square plates are perfect for this) and place a small amount of each filling and a small amount of sauce in the center of each leaf. Then the diners simply have to close up each leaf packet as they eat it.

When serving a crowd, you can go one step further and turn the appetizer into easy "pickup" food by closing up the leaf bundles and skewering them shut with a toothpick.

Party Planning

When I think of parties, I think of appetizers. Whether you're hosting an intimate dinner party or a lavish gathering of scores of your closest friends, appetizers help make the party special. When planning your menu, strive for variety in shape, color, and texture, but with a theme of some kind to tie it together.

My personal favorite is an international appetizer buffet—a festive mix of hot and cold, savory and sweet, and mostly fun finger foods. Include items that are special but not fussy—easy to make ahead with a quick reheat or other final touch. To reduce stress, plan no more than two hot appetizers that require last-minute attention, concentrating on dishes that do well cold or at room temperature. If a meal is to follow the appetizers, plan on three to five small hors d'oeuvres per person. If the appetizers are the main event, allow 10 to 12 per person.

Sesame-Asparagus Sushi Rolls

A sushi roll, called *nori maki*, can be filled with vegetables instead of fish. Tender, thin asparagus is used here, but other choices include strips of avocado, cucumber, carrot, and bell pepper. Nori seaweed sheets, as well as wasabi powder, pickled ginger, and short-grain rice (sometimes called sushi rice), are readily available in well-stocked supermarkets, natural foods stores, and Asian markets.

2 cups short-grain white rice

2¾ cups water

¼ cup rice vinegar

1 tablespoon natural sugar

1 teaspoon salt

6 nori sheets

2 tablespoons sesame seeds, toasted (page 171)

6 thin asparagus spears, trimmed and lightly steamed until crisp-tender

1 tablespoon wasabi paste

2 tablespoons pickled ginger

Low-sodium tamari

1. Rinse the rice under cold running water until the water runs clear, then drain in a colander for 1 hour.

2. Place the drained rice in a medium-size saucepan with a tight-fitting lid. Add the water, cover, and bring to a boil over medium-high heat. Boil for about 2 minutes, then reduce the heat to medium and simmer for 5 minutes. Reduce the heat to low and cook until all of the water has been absorbed, 12 to 15 minutes. Remove from the heat, remove the lid, and place a clean kitchen towel over the pot. Replace the lid and let stand for 10 minutes.

3. While the rice is cooking, heat the vinegar, sugar, and salt in a small saucepan over low heat, stirring until the sugar is dissolved. Remove from the heat and let cool to room temperature.

4. While the rice is still warm, place in a wide nonreactive container (such as a glass baking dish) and spread out evenly using a rice paddle or large wooden spoon. Bring the paddle through the rice in slicing motions to separate the grains. While doing this, slowly pour the vinegar mixture over the rice. Set aside to cool at room temperature while you prepare the rest of the ingredients.

5. Place one nori sheet on a bamboo sushi mat or cloth napkin. Spread ½ cup of the rice evenly over the nori, spreading it right to the side edges and to within ½ inch of the top and bottom edges. Sprinkle the rice evenly with the sesame seeds. Along the edge nearest you, place one asparagus spear on top of the rice. Beginning at that edge, roll up the mat or napkin, pressing firmly against the nori. Use your fingers to keep the edge of the sushi mat from rolling into the sushi. Continue rolling slowly up to the top edge. Wet the exposed edge of the nori with a little water to seal the roll. Gently squeeze the mat around the sushi roll and remove the mat.

6. Using a sharp knife, cut the sushi roll into 6 pieces. Stand the pieces on end and place on a large platter. Repeat with the remaining nori sheets, rice, sesame seeds, and asparagus.

7. Shape the wasabi paste into a small mound and place it on the sushi platter. Also place the pickled ginger in a mound on the platter. Serve with small dipping bowls of tamari. Sushi is best eaten shortly after it is made, since refrigeration can toughen the rice and cause the nori to go limp. If you must make it ahead, it should be no longer than 1 hour so that it can remain at room temperature. If you must make it further in advance, cover tightly and refrigerate until needed.

Makes 6 rolls or 36 pieces

Hot Like Wasabi

Wasabi isn't just for sushi anymore. Thanks to the popularity of fusion food, wasabi, among many other Asian ingredients, is being used in a number of Western dishes, with tasty results. The fiery green paste has found its way into marinades, salad dressings, sauces, spreads, and even mashed potatoes.

The wasabi plant is a semiaquatic member of the cabbage family. Its stem is ground into a powder that is in turn blended into a paste. A 10th-century Japanese medical encyclopedia documents wasabi as an antidote for food poisoning. In fact, it is traditionally served as a sushi condiment because of its ability to kill bacteria in food.

Prepared wasabi paste and powdered wasabi can be found at Asian markets and well-stocked supermarkets. Powdered wasabi is prepared in much the same way as dry mustard. Simply add water to form a paste, and this bright green condiment with the pungent, fiery flavor is ready to use. Just remember—a little goes a long way.

Vegetable Spring Rolls
with Spicy Peanut Dipping Sauce

Unlike deep-fried egg rolls, these fresh-tasting spring rolls are uncooked. Spring roll wrappers made of delicate rice paper are available in Asian markets. Vietnamese and Thai brands are common, and the shape can be round or square. The wrappers are brittle and quite fragile when you buy them, but they soften quickly in water just prior to use. Feel free to experiment by varying the filling ingredients according to personal preference.

1 cup shredded napa cabbage	½ cup fresh bean sprouts
¾ cup shredded carrots	½ cup chopped fresh cilantro or Thai basil
1 small red bell pepper, seeded and cut into thin strips	8 rice paper spring roll wrappers
	Spicy Peanut Dipping Sauce (page 145)

1. Before assembling your spring rolls, prepare all of the filling ingredients and have them at hand. Fill a shallow bowl with warm water, and place a sheet of plastic wrap on a flat work surface.

2. Carefully dip one wrapper into the water to soften. Remove from the water and place on the plastic wrap.

3. Arrange a small amount of each ingredient on the bottom third of the wrapper, not quite to the bottom edge. Bring the bottom edge over the filling and fold in the sides tightly. Roll up tightly, using the plastic wrap to help you roll. Place the roll seam side down on a serving platter. Repeat with the remaining wrappers and filling ingredients.

4. Serve the rolls with small bowls of the dipping sauce. These spring rolls are best eaten shortly after they are assembled, but they will keep for a few hours in the refrigerator if wrapped tightly in plastic wrap.

Serves 4

Spinach-Mushroom Phyllo Triangles

These bite-size versions of spanakopita are the hit of any party. The great taste of the spinach filling enveloped by the flaky phyllo pastry is a testimony to the vegan ingredients: olive oil and tofu stand in for the traditional butter and feta cheese. For a variation, use cooked kale or other greens instead of the spinach.

2 (10-ounce) packages frozen chopped spinach

1 tablespoon olive oil, plus more for brushing

1 medium-size onion, minced

2 cups chopped white mushrooms

3 garlic cloves, minced

1 (12- to 16-ounce) package soft silken tofu, drained

1 tablespoon fresh lemon juice

1 teaspoon salt

¼ teaspoon freshly ground black pepper

Pinch of freshly grated nutmeg

1 (16-ounce) package phyllo pastry, thawed overnight in the refrigerator

1. Cook the spinach according to the package directions. Drain well, then squeeze it inside a clean tea towel to remove any remaining moisture. Set aside.

2. Heat the oil in a large skillet over medium heat. Add the onion, cover, and cook until softened, about 5 minutes. Add the mushrooms and garlic and cook, uncovered, for 3 minutes. Add the spinach and cook until all of the liquid is absorbed, about 3 minutes.

3. Transfer the spinach mixture to a food processor. Add the tofu, lemon juice, salt, pepper, and nutmeg and process until smooth.

4. Preheat the oven to 375°F. Lightly oil a baking sheet. Unwrap the phyllo pastry and remove about half of the sheets. Rewrap the remaining phyllo and set it aside. Cut the phyllo sheets lengthwise into thirds. Take 1 strip and place it on a flat surface. Cover the remaining pastry with a damp towel. Lightly brush the phyllo strip with olive oil. Top with another strip and brush with a little more oil. Spoon a small spoonful of the filling in one corner of the pastry and fold over into a triangle. Continue folding the triangle as if you were folding a flag, until you end up with a small triangular packet. Place on the baking sheet and brush with oil. Repeat with the remaining ingredients until all of the filling is used.

5. Bake until golden brown, about 15 minutes. Serve warm or at room temperature.

Makes about 18

Baked Sweet Potato and Green Pea Samosas

These are actually twice-baked—if you count the fact that the sweet potato is baked before being turned into the fragrant samosa filling. Since these samosas are baked instead of fried, there's no need to feel guilty about filling your plate.

1 cup unbleached all-purpose flour

¼ cup water

1 tablespoon plus 2 teaspoons neutral vegetable oil, plus more for brushing

1 small onion, minced

1 large sweet potato, baked until tender, peeled, and diced

½ cup fresh or frozen peas

1 garlic clove, minced

2 teaspoons curry powder

½ teaspoon ground coriander

¼ teaspoon salt

1. In a medium-size bowl, combine the flour, water, and 2 teaspoons of the oil until well blended. Cover and let stand for 30 minutes.

2. Meanwhile, heat the remaining 1 tablespoon oil in a large skillet over medium heat. Add the onion, cover, and cook until softened, about 5 minutes. Add the remaining ingredients and cook, stirring occasionally, until the onion and garlic are soft and the flavors have developed, about 10 minutes. Mash the filling slightly to combine. Set aside to cool.

3. Preheat the oven to 375°F. Lightly oil a baking sheet and set aside. On a floured work surface, roll out the dough into a 16-inch square that is about ⅛ inch thick. Cut into sixteen 4-inch squares. Place a small amount of the filling in the center of each square. Dab a little water on the edges, and fold one corner over the filling to the opposite corner to make a triangle. Seal the edges. Place the samosas on the baking sheet and brush lightly with oil. Bake until golden brown, about 20 minutes. Serve hot.

Serves 4

Curried Cauliflower Pakoras

Much like the tempura of Japan or *fritto misto* of Italy, these classic batter-dipped fritters of India lend themselves to almost any vegetable. Try the cauliflower as suggested here, or use sliced zucchini, bell pepper, broccoli, or onion—or any combination. Serve with chutney.

1 small head cauliflower, trimmed and cored

½ cup unbleached all-purpose flour

½ cup chickpea flour

1 teaspoon salt

¾ teaspoon baking powder

½ teaspoon ground cumin

½ teaspoon ground coriander

1 cup water or club soda, as needed

Neutral vegetable oil, for frying

Chaat masala (optional; see Note)

Chutney, to serve

1. Preheat the oven to 275°F. Cut the cauliflower into slices about ¼ inch thick. You will end up with cross sections of the florets and some of them will fall apart—that's okay. Set aside.

2. In a large bowl, combine the flours, salt, baking powder, cumin, coriander, and enough water to make a smooth batter. Mix well.

3. Heat about 1 inch of oil in a large, deep skillet over medium-high heat. It's hot enough when a small piece of bread dropped in the oil turns golden brown in about 1 minute. Place the cauliflower slices and pieces in the batter to coat, letting any excess drip off, then place them in the hot oil. Do not crowd. Cook until golden brown on both sides, turning once, about 3 minutes per side. Transfer to paper towels to drain and sprinkle with *chaat masala,* if using. Place in a baking pan and keep warm in the oven until all of the slices are fried. Serve hot with your favorite chutney.

―――――――――――――――――― *Serves 4* ――――――――――――――――――

NOTE: *Chaat masala* is a spice blend used as a condiment to sprinkle on Indian appetizers such as pakoras. This seasoning usually contains powdered mango and dried pomegranate seed.

Did You Know?

Cauliflower is rich in vitamin C and potassium. Believed to be more than 2,500 years old, this member of the cabbage family also contains a fair amount of vitamin B_6 and copper.

Harissa-Spiced Hummus

Hummus is an ideal vegan food, at once creamy and flavorful, while also being loaded with calcium and protein. No wonder everyone loves it, whether it is served as a dip or used as a spread for sandwiches. To keep your hummus from becoming ho-hum, try this spiced-up variation made with fiery harissa, a North African chili sauce that contains garlic, cumin, and coriander. Canned harissa is available at ethnic markets for those who don't want to make it from scratch. For a more traditional hummus, omit the harissa.

1½ cups cooked chickpeas or 1 (15-ounce) can chickpeas, rinsed and drained

2 garlic cloves, crushed

¼ cup tahini

3 tablespoons fresh lemon juice

2 teaspoons harissa, homemade (page 144) or purchased, or to taste

½ teaspoon salt

1 tablespoon minced fresh parsley

1. Place the chickpeas and garlic in a food processor and process until smooth. Add the tahini, lemon juice, harissa, and salt. Process until smooth and well blended.

2. Transfer to a tightly covered container and refrigerate for at least 1 hour before serving to allow the flavors to develop. Serve chilled or at room temperature, sprinkled with the parsley. Store leftovers in a tightly covered container in the refrigerator for up to 3 days.

Makes about 2 cups

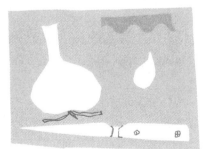

Minted Baba Ganoush

Baba ganoush is a delicious eggplant puree that can be used in much the same way as hummus. It is a must-have on any Middle Eastern *meze* platter (small dishes similar to Spanish *tapas*), where it is delicious accompanied by brine-cured black olives and warm pita wedges. Roasting the eggplant brings out its natural sweetness, which the mint complements nicely. Traditional baba ganoush usually contains a small amount of yogurt to enhance the creamy texture, but that is omitted here with good results.

1 large or 2 medium-size eggplants

3 large garlic cloves, slivered

⅓ cup tahini

Juice of 1 lemon

1 tablespoon olive oil

Salt

2 tablespoons minced fresh mint

1. Preheat the oven to 375°F. Using a sharp knife, make several deep cuts in the eggplant and place the garlic pieces inside. Place on a baking sheet and bake until soft, about 40 minutes. Allow to cool. Remove the eggplant skin and discard.

2. Transfer the eggplant flesh and garlic to a food processor or blender. Add the tahini, lemon juice, olive oil, and salt to taste and process until smooth.

3. Transfer to a serving bowl and sprinkle with the mint. Serve at room temperature. Store leftovers in the refrigerator in a tightly sealed container for up to 3 days.

Serves 4 to 6

Blushing Guacamole

Tomato salsa and a touch of chili powder add a rosy blush to this popular avocado dip. Guacamole is best made just before serving to keep it from turning brown.

2 medium-size ripe Hass avocados

1 tablespoon fresh lime juice

½ teaspoon chili powder

¼ teaspoon salt

1 ripe tomato, finely chopped

2 scallions, minced

2 tablespoons minced fresh cilantro

Tortilla chips, for serving

Halve and pit the avocados and scoop the flesh into a bowl. Add the lime juice, chili powder, and salt and mash well. Stir in the tomato, scallions, and cilantro. Mix well to combine. Taste and adjust the seasonings, if needed. Serve with tortilla chips.

Serves 4

Chili-Avocado Dip

A fun way to serve this dip is in what I call "chili parfaits." Instead of a large serving bowl, use individual dessert glasses and proceed with the recipe, dividing the ingredients evenly among the glasses. Each guest will have his or her own personal dip goblet.

2 medium-size ripe Hass avocados

1 tablespoon fresh lime juice

¼ teaspoon salt

⅛ teaspoon cayenne

2 cups of your favorite vegan chili (pages 290–301), heated

1 cup Fresh Tomato Salsa (page 157) or purchased salsa

½ cup vegan sour cream

1 (4-ounce) can diced mild green chiles, drained

½ cup sliced black olives

Tortilla chips

1. Halve and pit the avocados and scoop the flesh into a bowl. Add the lime juice, salt, and cayenne and mash until well combined.

2. In a serving bowl (preferably clear glass), spread half of the chili in a layer, followed by the salsa. Spread the avocado mixture over the salsa and top with the remaining chili. Spread the sour cream evenly over the chili, and scatter the green chiles and olives on top. Serve with tortilla chips.

Serves 6

Creamy Cashew Bean Dip

This recipe make a lot, but once you taste it you'll be glad there's some extra. It's great to serve to a crowd, or you can use the leftovers to top burritos, rice and beans, or chili.

¾ cup raw cashews, soaked for at least 3 hours or up to overnight

2 cups plain unsweetened nondairy milk

1 tablespoon olive oil or ¼ cup water

¼ cup minced onion

2 garlic cloves, minced

⅓ cup nutritional yeast

2 tablespoons fresh lemon juice

1 tablespoon white miso

½ teaspoon ground cumin

½ teaspoon salt

¼ teaspoon freshly ground black pepper

2 tablespoons cornstarch or arrowroot mixed with 3 tablespoons water

1 cup canned diced tomatoes with green chiles, well drained

1 cup cooked or canned pinto beans

Tortilla chips, to serve

1. Drain the cashews and place them in a food processor or high-speed blender. Add 1 cup of the nondairy milk and process until smooth. Set aside.

2. Heat the oil or water in a saucepan over medium heat. Add the onion and garlic and cook, stirring, until softened, about 4 minutes. Stir in the remaining 1 cup nondairy milk, reserved cashew mixture, nutritional yeast, lemon juice, and miso. Add the cumin, salt, and pepper. Stir in the cornstarch mixture and cook, stirring, until thickened and smooth, about 3 minutes. Stir in the tomatoes and beans and cook 1 minute longer to heat. Taste and adjust the seasonings, if needed. Transfer to a bowl and serve with tortilla chips.

===== *Makes about 3½ cups* =====

Artichoke-Sunflower Spread

This flavorful spread can be used on crackers, warm pita bread, or crostini. Or, thin it with a little nondairy milk to use as a dip for vegetables or crackers.

½ cup hulled raw sunflower seeds

1 (9-ounce) package frozen artichoke hearts, cooked according to package directions and drained, or one (14-ounce) can artichoke hearts, drained

2 garlic cloves, crushed

1 teaspoon minced fresh oregano or ¼ teaspoon dried oregano

½ teaspoon salt

Splash of Tabasco sauce

1. Soak the sunflower seeds in warm water to cover for 3 to 4 hours.

2. Drain the sunflower seeds, then transfer them to a food processor and process until smooth. Add the remaining ingredients and process until well blended.

3. Serve at once or transfer to a tightly covered bowl and refrigerate until ready to serve. This spread is best eaten the day it is made.

=========== *Makes about 1½ cups* ===========

Did You Know?

Garlic has been widely touted for its medicinal properties. In addition to perking up bland-tasting food, garlic has been credited with relieving ailments such as the common cold, bronchitis, hypertension, and high cholesterol. Garlic was even used for its antibiotic properties during World War I.

Wild Mushroom Pâté

Garnish this pâté with ground nuts and fresh herbs, and serve whole or sliced on a buffet table with an assortment of crackers and breads. If displaying whole, consider sautéing a few more mushrooms to garnish the top.

½ cup dried porcini mushrooms, soaked in very hot water to cover for 20 minutes

2 tablespoons olive oil or ¼ cup water

1 medium-size onion, minced

1 garlic clove, minced

2 cups chopped white mushrooms

1 cup chopped fresh shiitake mushroom caps

1 cup chopped cremini mushrooms

2 tablespoons dry white wine

1 teaspoon dried thyme

½ teaspoon salt

⅛ teaspoon cayenne

½ cup pecan pieces (or other nuts)

2 tablespoons chopped fresh parsley

2 tablespoons unbleached all-purpose flour

1. Preheat the oven to 350°F. Lightly oil a 6-cup loaf pan or pâté mold. Drain the porcinis and chop. Set aside.

2. Heat the oil or water in a large skillet over medium heat. Add the onion and garlic, cover, and cook until softened, about 5 minutes. Add all of the mushrooms, the wine, thyme, salt, and cayenne. Cook until all of the liquid evaporates, about 5 minutes. Remove from the heat and set aside.

3. Coarsely grind the pecans in a food processor. Add the parsley and flour and pulse to combine. Add the mushroom mixture and process until combined but not pureed, leaving some texture. Taste and adjust the seasonings, then spoon into the prepared pan. Bake until firm, about 45 minutes.

4. Let the pâté cool in the pan, then refrigerate until well chilled for easier slicing.

5. When ready to serve, remove the pâté from the pan and transfer to a plate. If necessary, run a knife along the edge of the pan to loosen the pâté. Serve at room temperature.

Serves 6 to 8

Portobello Satays

Traditional Indonesian satays are made with marinated meat or seafood threaded onto skewers and are usually served with a spicy peanut sauce. Here the flavor of the peanut sauce is built right into the marinade, although they're even better when also served with a side of Spicy Peanut Dipping Sauce (page 145). If you like, you may grill or broil these satays until lightly browned. If grilling or broiling, soak the bamboo skewers in water for 30 minutes before using to prevent them from burning.

4 large portobello mushroom caps, gills scraped out

1 large red or green bell pepper, seeded and cut into 2-inch squares

¼ cup water

3 tablespoons tamari

2 garlic cloves, chopped

2 tablespoons peanut butter

2 tablespoons fresh lime juice

1 tablespoon natural sugar

1 teaspoon grated fresh ginger

½ teaspoon ground cumin

½ teaspoon ground coriander

⅛ teaspoon cayenne

1. Cut the mushrooms crosswise into ¼-inch-thick slices and place in a shallow bowl or baking dish along with the bell pepper pieces.

2. In a food processor, combine the remaining ingredients and process until smooth. Spread the mixture over the mushrooms and peppers, turning to coat the vegetables with the marinade. Cover and set aside for 30 minutes.

3. Preheat the oven to 425°F. Lightly oil a baking sheet. Remove the mushrooms and peppers from the marinade, reserving the marinade. Thread the mushrooms and peppers onto bamboo skewers. Place on the baking sheet and bake until softened and lightly browned, 10 to 12 minutes, turning once and brushing with the reserved marinade. Serve hot.

Serves 4

Hot and Spicy Stuffed Mushrooms

The spiciness of the cherry peppers combines with the sweetness of the raisins for a balance of flavors that makes these mushrooms a favorite at our house. Jars of hot cherry peppers are available in well-stocked supermarkets and Italian specialty stores.

8 to 12 ounces white mushrooms	½ cup ground walnuts
1 tablespoon olive oil	½ cup raisins
1 garlic clove, minced	1 tablespoon minced fresh parsley
4 hot cherry peppers, seeded and minced	½ teaspoon natural sugar
1½ cups fresh bread crumbs	Salt and freshly ground black pepper

1. Preheat the oven to 400°F. Lightly oil a baking sheet. Remove the stems from the mushroom caps and set the caps aside. Chop the mushroom stems and set aside.

2. Heat the oil in a large skillet over medium heat. Add the mushroom caps and cook for 2 minutes to soften slightly. Remove from the pan with a slotted spoon and set aside.

3. Return the skillet to the heat. Add the garlic and cook until fragrant, about 30 seconds. Add the chopped mushroom stems, cherry peppers, bread crumbs, walnuts, raisins, parsley, sugar, and salt and pepper to taste. Cook for 2 to 3 minutes, mixing well. Add a little water, vegetable broth, or dry white wine, if needed, to get the stuffing to hold together.

4. Fill the mushroom caps evenly with the stuffing mixture and arrange on the baking sheet. Bake until the mushrooms are soft and the tops are lightly browned, about 10 minutes. Serve hot.

Serves 4 to 6

Caponata Crostini

Caponata is a piquant eggplant salad that hails from southern Italy. I think it makes an ideal topping for crostini. Make the caponata ahead of time so the flavors can mingle. Caponata is best served at room temperature.

CAPONATA

1 tablespoon olive oil or ¼ cup water

1 medium-size onion, finely chopped

1 medium-size eggplant, peeled and chopped

1 small red bell pepper, seeded and finely chopped

3 garlic cloves, minced

1 (14.5-ounce) can diced tomatoes, drained

Salt and freshly ground black pepper

2 tablespoons capers, drained and chopped

1 tablespoon red wine vinegar

1 tablespoon minced fresh parsley

2 teaspoons natural sugar

CROSTINI

8 to 12 (½-inch-thick) slices French bread

Olive oil, for brushing

1. To make the caponata: Heat the oil or water in a large skillet over medium heat. Add the onion, cover, and cook until softened, about 5 minutes. Remove the lid and stir in the eggplant. Cook, stirring occasionally, until the eggplant begins to soften, about 5 minutes. Add the bell pepper, garlic, tomatoes, and salt and pepper to taste. Cook until the vegetables soften but still hold some shape, about 15 minutes. Stir in the capers, vinegar, parsley, and sugar. Taste and adjust the seasonings.

2. Transfer to a bowl and allow to cool to room temperature. (You can make the caponata ahead up to this point, refrigerate, and bring back to room temperature before serving. It will keep, tightly covered, in the refrigerator for up to 4 days.)

3. To make the crostini: Preheat the oven to 400°F. Lightly brush both sides of the bread slices with olive oil and place on a baking sheet. Bake until lightly browned, 1 to 2 minutes. Remove from the oven, spread the caponata on the bread, and serve at once.

Serves 4

Black Olive Bruschetta

The topping for this bruschetta is a black olive tapenade. Although the name *tapenade* refers to the requisite capers (*tapeno* means capers in the Provençal dialect), the olives are really the star of the show. If you prefer a deeper flavor, use oil-cured black olives instead of the brine-cured kalamata olives. In any event, avoid using regular canned supermarket olives, because they lack the true olive flavor you want in a tapenade. In this recipe, the bread is run under the broiler, but it can be grilled or toasted instead.

2 teaspoons olive oil, plus more for brushing

2 garlic cloves, chopped

1½ cups pitted kalamata olives

3 tablespoons chopped fresh flat-leaf parsley

2 tablespoons capers, drained

½ teaspoon salt

8 (½-inch-thick) slices Italian or French bread

1. Preheat the broiler. Heat the oil in a small skillet over medium heat. Add the garlic and cook until soft and fragrant, about 1 minute. Transfer to a food processor. Add the olives, parsley, capers, and salt and pulse to blend, retaining some texture. Set aside. (The tapenade may be prepared ahead of time and refrigerated in a tightly sealed container. It will keep for up to 4 days. Bring it back to room temperature before using.)

2. Lightly brush both sides of the bread with olive oil and place on a baking sheet. Broil until golden brown on both sides.

3. Spread the tapenade on the prepared bread and serve at once.

Serves 8

Scallion Pancakes with Sesame Seeds

These golden brown pancakes make a delicious first course for an Asian meal or a wonderful addition to a dim sum buffet.

2 cups unbleached all-purpose flour

¾ teaspoon salt

1 cup boiling water, or more as needed

1 tablespoon toasted sesame oil

¾ cup minced scallions

2 tablespoons sesame seeds

1 tablespoon neutral vegetable oil

Ginger-Lime Dipping Sauce (page 145)

1. Place the flour and salt in a food processor. With the machine running, slowly add the water through the feed tube, adding a little more water, if necessary, until a dough ball forms. Remove from the food processor, cover with plastic wrap or a damp cloth, and let rest for 30 minutes.

2. Divide the dough into 2 pieces. Set one aside and cover. On a floured work surface, roll out the other piece of dough into a circle about ¼ inch thick. Brush on half of the sesame oil and press half of the scallions and half of the sesame seeds into the dough. Set aside and repeat with the remaining dough ball, sesame oil, scallions, and sesame seeds.

3. Heat half of the vegetable oil in a large nonstick skillet over medium heat. Place one of the pancakes in the pan and cook until golden brown on both sides, turning once, 5 to 7 minutes total. Repeat with the remaining oil and pancake.

4. Cut the pancakes into wedges and serve hot with the dipping sauce on the side.

=== *Makes 2 large pancakes* ===

Three-Onion Appetizer Pie

Onion lovers will enjoy this fresh take on the ever-popular onion dip, turned into an appetizer pie with a potato chip crust. Although it looks like a pie, it is essentially still a dip and should be served with raw vegetables or more chips.

1 (6-ounce) bag potato chips

¼ cup coarsely chopped red onion

1 large shallot, quartered

2 scallions, coarsely chopped

8 ounces vegan cream cheese, homemade (page 126) or purchased, at room temperature

¾ cup vegan sour cream

¼ cup minced fresh parsley

2 tablespoons vegan mayonnaise, homemade (page 125) or purchased

1 teaspoon Dijon mustard

½ teaspoon Tabasco sauce

½ teaspoon salt

Cherry tomatoes, cut in half, for garnish

Black olives, pitted and halved, for garnish

1. Lightly oil a 9-inch pie plate or tart pan or an 8-inch springform pan. Grind the chips in a food processor until they are fine crumbs. Reserve 2 tablespoons of the crumbs and press the remaining crumbs into the bottom of the prepared pan. Set aside.

2. Place the onion, shallot, and scallions in a food processor and process until minced. Add the cream cheese, sour cream, parsley, mayonnaise, mustard, Tabasco, and salt and process until well combined. Spread the onion mixture evenly over the crumb crust and smooth the top. Cover and refrigerate for at least 2 hours or overnight.

3. Just before serving, arrange a border of cherry tomato halves along the edge of the pie. Then arrange a ring of olive halves inside the tomatoes. Repeat with additional concentric rings of tomatoes and olives, if desired, leaving the center of the pie uncovered. Sprinkle the reserved chip crumbs in the center and serve.

Serves 8

Savory Pumpkin Bites with Green Chile Aioli

Pumpkin, walnuts, and sage combine to give these tasty bites a rich depth of flavor. But it's the accompanying green chile aioli that sends them over the top.

1 tablespoon olive oil or ¼ cup water

½ cup chopped onion

2 garlic cloves, minced

2 teaspoons chopped fresh sage

½ cup old-fashioned rolled oats

¾ cup finely ground walnuts

⅔ cup canned solid-pack or pure pumpkin puree

½ teaspoon baking powder

½ teaspoon salt

¼ teaspoon freshly ground black pepper

Green Chile Aioli (recipe follows)

1. Preheat the oven to 375°F. Coat a baking sheet with cooking spray and set aside. Heat the oil or water in a small skillet over medium heat. Add the onion, cover, and cook for 5 minutes to soften. Uncover, stir in the garlic and sage, and cook until the liquid is absorbed, about 1 minute longer. Set aside.

2. In a food processor, process the oats to a powder. Add the walnuts, pumpkin, baking powder, salt, and pepper. Add the reserved onion mixture and process until well combined. Shape the mixture into 1½-inch balls and transfer to the prepared baking sheet. Bake until firm and the bottoms are golden brown, about 15 minutes. Serve with the aioli.

Serves 4

GREEN CHILE AIOLI

This easy and flavorful aioli is fabulous with the pumpkin bites, but can also be slathered onto sandwiches or used as a dipping sauce for vegetables or baked tofu.

½ cup vegan mayonnaise, homemade (page 125) or purchased

2 garlic cloves, crushed

2 tablespoons fresh lemon or lime juice

2 tablespoons finely minced mild canned green chiles

1 teaspoon green Tabasco sauce

Salt and pepper to taste

Combine all of the ingredients in a small bowl and mix well. Taste and adjust the seasonings, if needed. Serve with the pumpkin bites.

Makes about ¾ cup

THREE

Soups that Satisfy

Soup is the common denominator of the world's cuisines. Since ancient times, when humankind first made fire and learned to boil water, pots of soup have been simmering everywhere on the planet. Throughout history, the wealthy and impoverished alike have shared in the pleasure of soup, where countless combinations of both humble and opulent ingredients have been ladled for sustenance.

Many warming soups are naturally vegan, such as those that feature beans and vegetables. Others can be made vegetarian by simply using a vegetable broth to replace a meat-based one. Where the real vegan magic comes into play is in transforming "cream" soups into dairy-free marvels. Creaminess is accomplished in several ways, through the use of either a dairy-free milk or pureed vegetables, beans, or nuts.

This chapter includes brothy vegetable soups, such as *Italian Wedding Soup, Sassy Vegetable Gumbo, Szechuan Hot and Sour Soup,* and *Miso Soup with Tofu and Baby Spinach;* hearty bean soups, such as *Tuscan White Bean Soup, Cuban Black Bean Soup,* and *Yellow Split Pea Soup with Green Pea Garnish;* and creamy soups, including velvety *Winter Vegetable Bisque, Potato-Watercress Soup with Sesame,* and *Orange and Chipotle–Kissed Butternut Squash Bisque.* For those hot summer nights, you can enjoy a selection of cold soups, including *Chilled Ginger-Peach Soup with Cashew Cream* and *Cool Cucumber Soup with Cilantro and Lime.*

Broth Options

The use of vegetable broth can add flavor and nutrition to many recipes. Making vegetable broth is not difficult, nor does it need to be time-consuming. It can be as easy as boiling water—all you have to do is add some vegetables and walk away. After about an hour of simmering, you can strain out the vegetables, and the resulting liquid is your broth.

An all-purpose vegetable broth made with little more than onions, carrots, celery, and water is a modest investment that will provide dividends to many of your meals. Begin by sweating the vegetables in a little oil to deepen the flavors. I usually roughly chop the vegetables, often keeping the skins, peels, stems, and leaves on for added taste. Just be sure that all the ingredients are well washed before adding them to the pot. Many of the recipes in this book call for broth or water. In these cases, water will work just fine in the recipe, but using broth will enrich the flavor. If you're trying to get as much flavor (and nutrition) as possible out of a recipe, opt for the broth.

Another variation is to roast the vegetables before adding them to the water. To do this, toss the vegetables with olive oil and spread in a baking pan. Roast in a preheated 425°F oven for about 45 minutes, turning frequently to brown. Transfer the vegetables to the stockpot, add the remaining ingredients, and proceed with the recipe. Roasting the vegetables intensifies the flavors and deepens the color of the final broth.

In addition to adding a little salt, I like to use a splash of tamari because it also adds its own flavor and a little color. The amount of salt you add is up to you, but less is better than more. Although salt does help bring out the flavors of the vegetables, adding too much salt will impair the flavors, especially if the broth is reduced further, which will intensify the saltiness. I usually begin with 1 teaspoon salt, then adjust the seasoning toward the end, after the flavors have had a chance to develop. At that time, I decide whether the broth will benefit from a bit more salt or perhaps another dash of tamari. More often than not, I leave it alone.

When there's no time to make homemade broth but you want a more complex flavor than you would achieve with water, you can buy commercial vegetable broth in cans or aseptic cartons or use vegetable bouillon cubes or powdered vegetable soup base as a quick and easy substitute. These products vary in saltiness, so experiment to find ones you like, and remember to adjust the seasonings in your recipes accordingly.

Sometimes when I don't have broth, I add a splash of tamari or a little dissolved miso paste to enrich the flavor of a recipe. More frequently, I will combine a spoonful of high-quality vegetable broth paste with water to make an instant broth. I like Better than Bouillon brand vegetarian bases as they have a good flavor and are vegan-certified.

The following broth recipes are examples of the subtle differences just a few ingredients can make. Basic Vegetable Broth is an all-purpose broth that can be used as a soup base or to make sauces, risottos, pilafs, or any recipe requiring broth. Mushroom Broth and Super-Rich Vegetable Broth can be used in the same ways as the basic recipe, but they impart more complex flavor notes.

Cooling the Heat with Chilled Soups

Combining the comforting goodness of hot soup with the invigorating coolness we crave in the summer, a chilled soup can be a welcome addition to a hot-weather meal. Since most chilled soups need to be refrigerated before eating, they are best made ahead, so plan to prepare them the night before or early in the day. Additionally, many chilled soups require no cooking, so you can be in and out of the kitchen quickly without heating it up.

Two of the best-known chilled soups, vichyssoise and gazpacho, couldn't be more different from each other. Vichyssoise, the cold leek and potato soup from France, with its delicate flavor and silky texture, is on the opposite end of the spectrum from the zesty Spanish gazpacho, a spicy tomato-based elixir brimming with refreshing chopped vegetables.

In addition to vegetables, fruits are often used to make chilled soups, with some so decadent they beg to be served as dessert and others sublime enough to be enjoyed as a dazzling first course. Making chilled soups can be as simple as pureeing your favorite fruits or vegetables in a blender or food processor with some fruit juice or vegetable stock, depending on the type of soup you are making. To add creaminess, finish the soup with a swirl of vegan yogurt or whisk in a small amount of nondairy milk. Garnish with a sliver of an appropriate fruit or vegetable, chopped nuts, or a fresh herb sprig.

Basic Vegetable Broth

Use this basic broth as a guideline, adding other vegetables or seasonings according to personal preference. It is best to stay away from boldly colored or strongly flavored vegetables, which will overpower the broth. Feel free to add vegetable trimmings, such as carrot peelings, parsley stems, and other discards.

1 tablespoon olive oil or ¼ cup water

1 large onion, coarsely chopped

2 celery ribs, chopped

2 medium-size carrots, coarsely chopped

8 cups water

2 garlic cloves, crushed

½ cup coarsely chopped fresh parsley

1 large bay leaf

1 tablespoon low-sodium tamari

½ teaspoon black peppercorns

Salt

1. Heat the oil or water in a large stockpot over medium heat. Add the onion, celery, and carrots. Cover, and cook until slightly softened, about 5 minutes. Add the water, garlic, parsley, bay leaf, tamari, peppercorns, and salt to taste. Bring to a boil, then reduce the heat to medium-low and simmer, uncovered, for 1 hour to reduce the liquid and bring out the flavors of the vegetables.

2. Strain through a fine-mesh sieve into a large bowl or pot, pressing against the solids with the back of a large spoon to release the liquid. The broth is now ready to use. If a stronger broth is desired, return the broth to a boil and reduce the volume by one-quarter. If stored tightly covered in the refrigerator, the broth will keep for up to 3 days. Alternatively, it can be portioned and frozen for up to 4 months.

Makes about 6 cups

Mushroom Broth

Mushroom broth adds exceptional depth of flavor to recipes. It is especially good in soups, sauces, risottos, and pilafs. I like to make this broth with mushrooms that are a bit past their prime for a richer taste. The addition of a few dried mushrooms lends a deep, woodsy flavor to the broth.

4 dried shiitake or porcini mushrooms, soaked in 1 cup very hot water for 20 minutes

1 tablespoon olive oil or ¼ cup water

1 large onion, quartered

1 celery rib, coarsely chopped

8 cups water

8 ounces white mushrooms, coarsely chopped

3 garlic cloves, crushed

½ cup coarsely chopped fresh parsley

2 bay leaves

1 tablespoon low-sodium tamari

½ teaspoon black peppercorns

Salt

1. Drain the shiitakes, reserving the soaking liquid. Strain the liquid and set aside.

2. Heat the oil or water in a stockpot over medium heat. Add the onion and celery, cover, and cook until softened, about 5 minutes. Add the water, all of the mushrooms, the mushroom soaking liquid, garlic, parsley, bay leaves, tamari, peppercorns, and salt to taste. Bring to a boil, then reduce the heat to low and simmer for 1 hour.

3. Strain through a fine-mesh sieve into a large bowl or pot, pressing against the solids with the back of a large spoon to release the liquid. Use at once or let cool and refrigerate, covered, for up to 3 days. Alternatively, you may portion the broth and freeze it for up to 3 months.

Makes about 6 cups

ASIAN-STYLE MUSHROOM BROTH: Omit the bay leaves and add a few slices of peeled fresh ginger, a piece of kombu sea vegetable, and a splash of sake, mirin, or dry sherry.

Super-Rich Vegetable Broth

This full-bodied broth tastes similar to chicken broth and can be used in any recipe to enrich the flavor. The use of potatoes and root vegetables gives the broth more body and a deeper character than vegetable broth. You may add other vegetables, such as leeks or mushrooms, but stay away from anything too assertive in color or flavor, such as beets or broccoli.

1 tablespoon olive oil or ¼ cup water

1 large onion, unpeeled and quartered

2 large Yukon Gold potatoes, unpeeled and quartered

2 medium-size carrots, coarsely chopped

1 medium-size parsnip, coarsely chopped

1 cup peeled and chopped celery root

8 cups water

3 garlic cloves, unpeeled and crushed

½ cup coarsely chopped fresh parsley

2 bay leaves

1 tablespoon low-sodium tamari

½ teaspoon black peppercorns

Salt

1. Heat the oil or water in a stockpot over medium heat. Add the onion, potatoes, carrots, parsnip, and celery root. Cover and cook until the vegetables are slightly softened, about 5 minutes. Add the water, garlic, parsley, bay leaves, tamari, peppercorns, and salt to taste. Bring to a boil, then reduce the heat to low and simmer, uncovered, for 1 hour.

2. Strain through a fine-mesh sieve into a large bowl or pot, pressing against the solids with the back of a large spoon to release the liquid. Use at once or let cool and refrigerate, covered, for up to 3 days. Alternatively, you may portion the broth and freeze it for up to 4 months.

=== *Makes about 6 cups* ===

NOTE: If celery root is unavailable, use regular celery instead.

Cool Cucumber Soup with Cilantro and Lime

"Cool as a cucumber" takes on new meaning with this light and luscious soup, made smooth and creamy with unsweetened coconut milk, which, along with the cilantro and lime juice, adds a hint of Southeast Asian flavor.

3 scallions, chopped

1 teaspoon salt

2 large cucumbers, peeled, seeded, and coarsely chopped

1 (14-ounce) can unsweetened coconut milk

1½ cups vegetable broth

2 tablespoons fresh lime juice

1 tablespoon minced fresh cilantro

8 thin cucumber slices, for garnish

Whole fresh cilantro leaves, for garnish

1. Place the scallions and salt in a food processor and process to form a paste. Add the cucumbers and process until smooth. Add the coconut milk, broth, lime juice, and minced cilantro and process until smooth. Taste and adjust the seasonings.

2. Transfer the soup to a container and refrigerate, covered, for a few hours to blend the flavors.

3. To serve, ladle the soup into bowls and garnish with the cucumber slices and whole cilantro leaves.

Serves 4

Chilled Ginger-Peach Soup
with Cashew Cream

A fresh fruit soup is a refreshing way to begin or end a meal during the summer. This is best made when peaches are ripe and plentiful. For a decadent flourish, make some extra cashew cream and swirl a spoonful into each portion of soup.

½ cup raw cashews, soaked for at least 3 hours or up to overnight

1 cup water, or more as needed

1½ pounds ripe peaches, peeled, pitted, and sliced

2 teaspoons grated fresh ginger

¼ cup frozen orange juice concentrate

1 tablespoon fresh lemon juice

Natural sugar, if needed

Fresh mint sprigs, for garnish

Chopped raw cashews, for garnish

1. Drain the cashews and place them in a blender with 1 cup water. Blend until smooth. Set aside.

2. Place the peach slices and ginger in a food processor and process until smooth. Add the cashew cream, orange juice concentrate, and lemon juice and blend well. Add a little more water if the soup is too thick. Taste and adjust the seasonings, adding a little sugar, if needed, for sweetness.

3. Pour into a container with a tight-fitting lid and refrigerate for several hours.

4. Serve chilled, garnished with the mint sprigs and chopped cashews.

Serves 4

Gazpacho Verde

This refreshing gazpacho is nontraditional in that it features mostly green vegetables, including green tomatoes, although it is garnished with chopped red tomatoes. If green tomatoes are unavailable, you can substitute tomatillos or an additional cucumber. Omit the jalapeño if you don't like the heat.

2 large green tomatoes, peeled, seeded, and chopped

2 medium-size cucumbers, peeled, seeded, and chopped

1 small green bell pepper, seeded and chopped

¼ cup chopped sweet onion

3 tablespoons minced scallions

2 tablespoons minced celery

2 tablespoons capers (optional), drained and chopped

2 tablespoons rice vinegar

1 jalapeño, seeded and minced

2 garlic cloves, minced

1 tablespoon olive oil

1 teaspoon salt

1 teaspoon green Tabasco sauce (optional)

3 cups vegetable broth

¼ cup minced fresh parsley

1 large ripe red tomato, seeded and chopped, for garnish

1. In a food processor, combine the green tomatoes, half of the cucumbers, half of the bell pepper, and the onion and process until smooth.

2. Transfer the vegetable puree to a large bowl and add the remaining cucumbers and remaining bell pepper. Stir in the scallions, celery, capers (if using), rice vinegar, jalapeño, garlic, olive oil, salt, and Tabasco (if using). Stir in the broth and 2 tablespoons of the parsley.

3. Cover and refrigerate for at least 2 hours. Taste and adjust the seasonings.

4. Serve chilled, garnished with the remaining 2 tablespoons parsley and the red tomato.

Serves 4 to 6

Szechuan Hot and Sour Soup

This version of the classic soup is as spicy and flavorful as the original but is made lighter with vegetable broth and pieces of tofu.

1 cup canned or fresh sliced bamboo shoots

1 tablespoon neutral vegetable oil
or ¼ cup water

2 garlic cloves, minced

2 teaspoons grated fresh ginger

8 ounces shiitake mushrooms,
stemmed and sliced

4 cups vegetable broth

2 tablespoons low-sodium tamari

2 tablespoons rice vinegar

1 teaspoon Asian chili paste or sriracha

½ teaspoon natural sugar

1 teaspoon cornstarch dissolved
in 1 tablespoon water

6 ounces extra-firm tofu, drained
and cut into ½-inch dice

4 scallions, chopped

1 tablespoon chopped fresh cilantro

1 teaspoon toasted sesame oil
or Chinese hot oil

Salt and freshly ground black pepper

1. If using canned bamboo shoots, drain and rinse, then cut into thin strips and set aside. If using fresh, soak in water to cover for 30 minutes. Cut into thin strips, cook in boiling water until tender, and set aside.

2. Heat the vegetable oil or water in a large pot. Add the garlic, ginger, and shiitake mushrooms. Cook until fragrant, about 30 seconds. Add the broth, tamari, vinegar, chili paste, and sugar. Bring to a boil over high heat, then reduce the heat to medium and simmer until the mushrooms are tender, about 5 minutes.

3. Stir in the cornstarch mixture and cook until heated through, about 5 minutes. Stir in the tofu, bamboo shoots, scallions, cilantro, sesame oil, and salt and pepper to taste. Serve hot.

Serves 4

Miso Soup with Tofu and Baby Spinach

Because of its many health benefits, miso soup is considered the "chicken soup" of a macrobiotic diet. Miso paste is made from aged soybeans that are often combined with other ingredients to make several varieties, from the salty, assertive barley miso to the slightly sweet, mellow white miso.

6 cups water

4 cups baby spinach leaves, cut into thin strips

2 cups thinly sliced white mushrooms

¼ cup minced scallions

1 tablespoon low-sodium tamari, or more to taste

⅓ cup mellow white miso paste

6 ounces extra-firm silken tofu, drained and cut into ¼-inch dice

1. Place the water in a large pot and bring to a boil over high heat. Add the spinach, mushrooms, scallions, and tamari. Reduce the heat to medium and simmer until the vegetables soften, 3 to 6 minutes. Reduce the heat to low.

2. Transfer ½ cup of the hot soup mixture to a small bowl and add the miso, blending well. Stir the mixture back into the soup, add the tofu, and simmer for 2 minutes, being careful not to boil. Taste and adjust the seasonings, if needed. Serve hot.

Serves 4

What Does Organic Mean?

Organic refers to farming practices that sustain soil health and fertility in a natural way without relying on synthetic fertilizers and that use natural methods to control pests, diseases, and weeds. Instead of chemicals, for example, weeds, insects, and other pests are managed with earth-friendly methods such as beneficial insects.

Produce labeled "100 percent organic" was grown by a farm certified organic by the USDA. Only certified operations may apply the USDA seal to their products.

Thai-Style Coconut Soup

I love the creamy elegance of Thai coconut soup. A favorite in many Thai restaurants, this soup is made with ingredients such as kaffir lime leaves, lemongrass, and galangal, which can be difficult for many people to find. I've devised a recipe that comes close to the original. Made substantial with tofu and mushrooms, it is seasoned with ingredients that are available in most supermarkets.

1 tablespoon neutral vegetable oil or ¼ cup water

3 shallots, minced

2 cups thinly sliced white mushrooms

3 cups vegetable broth

2 tablespoons low-sodium tamari

1 tablespoon grated fresh ginger

1 teaspoon Asian chili paste or sriracha

½ teaspoon natural sugar

1 (14-ounce) can unsweetened coconut milk

6 ounces extra-firm tofu, drained and cut into ¼-inch dice

Juice and grated zest of 1 lime

1 tablespoon chopped fresh cilantro, for garnish

1. Heat the oil or water in a large pot over medium heat. Add the shallots and cook, stirring, until tender, about 5 minutes. Add the mushrooms and cook, stirring, for 3 minutes. Stir in the broth, tamari, ginger, chili paste, and sugar and bring to a boil. Reduce the heat to low and simmer for 2 to 3 minutes, stirring to dissolve the sugar.

2. Stir in the coconut milk, tofu, lime juice, and zest, and simmer until the flavors have blended and the soup is hot, about 5 minutes. Taste and adjust the seasonings. Serve hot, garnished with the cilantro.

Serves 4

Smoke and Fire Pinto Bean Soup

This quick and easy soup is loaded with flavor and hearty enough to serve as a main dish with a salad on the side.

1 tablespoon olive oil or ¼ cup water

1 large onion, chopped

1 red bell pepper, seeded and chopped

3 garlic cloves, minced

1 (14.5-ounce) can diced fire-roasted tomatoes, undrained

1 or 2 chipotle chiles in adobo, minced

1 teaspoon ground cumin

1 teaspoon smoked paprika

½ teaspoon dried oregano

2 cups vegetable broth

3 cups cooked pinto beans or 2 (15-ounce) cans beans, rinsed and drained

Salt and freshly ground black pepper

1 cup fresh or frozen corn kernels

½ teaspoon liquid smoke

1. Heat the oil or water in a large pot over medium-high heat. Add the onion and cook, stirring, until softened, about 5 minutes. Stir in the bell pepper and garlic. Cook for 1 more minute, then stir in the tomatoes and juice, chipotle chiles, cumin, paprika, and oregano.

2. Add the broth and beans and bring to a boil. Reduce the heat to a simmer and season to taste with salt and pepper. Cook for 30 minutes. Stir in the corn kernels and liquid smoke and cook 10 minutes longer. Taste and adjust the seasonings, if needed. Serve hot.

Serves 4

Indian-Spiced Lentil Soup

Although lentils are enjoyed in various parts of the world, I think they are most flavorful prepared with Indian spices. Instead of the traditional dal, or lentil puree, the flavors here are combined in an aromatic soup, made colorful with the delicious, if inauthentic, addition of diced sweet potato.

1 tablespoon neutral vegetable oil or ¼ cup water

1 small onion, chopped

1 celery rib, chopped

1 small sweet potato, peeled and diced

1 garlic clove, minced

1 (14.5-ounce) can petite diced tomatoes, undrained

1 teaspoon grated fresh ginger

½ teaspoon ground cumin

½ teaspoon ground coriander

¼ teaspoon cayenne

1½ cups dried brown lentils, picked over and rinsed

6 cups vegetable broth or water

¼ cup minced fresh cilantro

Salt and freshly ground black pepper

1. Heat the oil or water in a large pot over medium heat. Add the onion, celery, sweet potato, and garlic. Cover and cook until softened, about 10 minutes. Add the tomatoes and their juice, and stir in the ginger, cumin, coriander, and cayenne. Add the lentils and broth and bring to boil. Reduce the heat to low, cover, and simmer, stirring occasionally, until the lentils are tender, about 30 minutes.

2. Add the cilantro, season to taste with salt and pepper, and cook for 10 minutes to blend the flavors. Serve hot.

Serves 4 to 6

Lentil Soup with Chard and Orzo

Although chard is often called "Swiss" chard after a Swiss botanist, it is actually a Mediterranean vegetable. Nutrient-rich chard and lentils combine for a healthful wintertime soup with a rich, complex flavor. A loaf of crusty bread is all that you need for a complete and satisfying meal.

1 tablespoon olive oil or ¼ cup water

1 large onion, chopped

1 large carrot, chopped

2 celery ribs, chopped

3 garlic cloves, minced

7 cups vegetable broth or water

1 cup dried brown lentils, picked over and rinsed

½ cup dry red wine

⅓ cup minced fresh parsley

2 tablespoons tomato paste

1 teaspoon minced fresh thyme or ½ teaspoon dried thyme

1 bay leaf

Salt and freshly ground black pepper

4 cups coarsely chopped Swiss chard (tough stems removed)

½ cup orzo

1. Heat the oil or water in a large pot over medium heat. Add the onion, carrot, celery, and garlic. Cover and cook until softened, about 5 minutes. Add the broth, lentils, wine, parsley, tomato paste, thyme, bay leaf, and salt and pepper to taste. Bring to a boil, then reduce the heat to medium-low and simmer, stirring occasionally, until the lentils are tender, about 30 minutes.

2. About 10 minutes before the end of the cooking time, remove the bay leaf and stir in the chard.

3. Meanwhile, cook the orzo in a pot of boiling salted water, stirring occasionally, until al dente, about 5 minutes. Drain. When ready to serve, stir the cooked orzo into the hot soup, then ladle immediately into bowls.

Serves 4 to 6

Yellow Split Pea Soup
with Green Pea Garnish

You can make this soup using green split peas, but the yellow ones have a milder flavor, and I like the color contrast when garnished with the vivid green peas.

1 tablespoon olive oil or ¼ cup water

1 large onion, chopped

1 large carrot, minced

1 large Yukon Gold potato, peeled and diced

6 cups vegetable broth or water

1¾ cups dried yellow split peas, picked over and rinsed

2 teaspoons minced fresh savory or marjoram or 1 teaspoon dried savory or marjoram

2 bay leaves

1 teaspoon salt

Cayenne

½ teaspoon liquid smoke

¾ cup fresh or frozen baby peas

1. Heat the oil or water in a large saucepan over medium heat. Add the onion, carrot, and potato. Cover and cook, stirring occasionally, until the vegetables are soft, about 10 minutes. Stir in the broth, split peas, savory, bay leaves, salt, and cayenne to taste. Bring to a boil, then reduce the heat to low, cover, and cook, stirring occasionally, until the vegetables are soft and the soup thickens, about 45 minutes. If the soup becomes too thick, add a little water. Remove and discard the bay leaves. Stir in the liquid smoke, then taste and adjust the seasonings, if needed.

2. Just before serving, heat the green peas in a small saucepan of boiling water. Drain and set aside. To serve, ladle the soup into bowls and garnish with the green peas.

Serves 4 to 6

Cuban Black Bean Soup

Black beans are popular in Cuban cooking, and this spicy soup is a terrific way to enjoy them. The cayenne is optional, since it adds another layer of heat beyond the chile. If you prefer a milder taste, you may omit the chile and cayenne with good results. This recipe calls for dried black beans, but if you're short on time, substitute two 15-ounce cans of black beans, rinsed and drained.

1½ cups dried black beans, picked over and rinsed

8 cups water

2 bay leaves

1 tablespoon olive oil or ¼ cup water

1 large red onion, chopped

1 medium-size carrot, chopped

1 small red bell pepper, seeded and minced

3 garlic cloves, minced

1 small, fresh hot chile, seeded and minced

1 (14.5-ounce) can petite diced tomatoes, undrained

6 cups vegetable broth or water

1 teaspoon dried oregano

1 teaspoon ground cumin

1 teaspoon salt

¼ teaspoon cayenne (optional)

¼ cup dark rum (optional)

2 tablespoons minced fresh cilantro, for garnish

1. Soak the beans in water to cover for several hours or overnight (or use the quick-soak method on page 251).

2. Drain the beans and transfer to a large pot. Add the 8 cups water and bay leaves and bring to a boil over medium heat. Reduce the heat to medium-low, cover, and simmer until the beans are soft, about 1½ hours. Stir occasionally, skimming off any foam that rises to the top. Drain the beans, discard the bay leaves, and set the beans aside.

3. Heat the olive oil or water in a large pot over medium heat. Add the onion, carrot, bell pepper, garlic, and chile. Cover and cook until softened, about 5 minutes. Add the tomatoes and their juice, then stir in the beans, broth, oregano, cumin, salt, and cayenne (if using). Simmer for 30 minutes.

4. Carefully transfer 2 cups of the soup to a blender or food processor. Process until smooth and return to the pot. Add a little water if the soup is too thick. Simmer for 15 minutes to blend the flavors. Taste and adjust the seasonings.

5. About 5 minutes before serving, stir in the rum (if using). Serve hot, garnished with the cilantro.

Serves 4 to 6

Chickpea and Tomato Soup

This flavorful, easy-to-make soup takes the chill off a cold winter night. For extra kick, use fire-roasted tomatoes with green chiles.

1 tablespoon olive oil or ¼ cup water

1 medium-size onion, chopped

4 garlic cloves, chopped

1 teaspoon dried basil

½ teaspoon dried oregano

½ teaspoon dried marjoram

¼ teaspoon cayenne (optional)

3 cups cooked chickpeas or 2 (15-ounce) cans chickpeas, rinsed and drained

3 cups vegetable broth

2 tablespoons low-sodium tamari

1 (14.5-ounce) can diced fire-roasted tomatoes, undrained

Salt and freshly ground black pepper

3 tablespoons chopped fresh parsley

1. Heat the oil or water in a large pot over medium heat. Add the onion and garlic and cook until softened, about 5 minutes. Stir in the basil, oregano, marjoram, and cayenne, if using. Add the chickpeas, broth, and tamari and bring to a boil. Reduce the heat to medium and simmer for about 15 minutes to blend the flavors.

2. Use an immersion blender to blend about half of the soup in the pot or transfer about half of the soup to a food processor to puree, then return to the pot. Stir in the tomatoes and juice, then season to taste with salt and pepper. Cook for a few minutes longer, until hot. Serve hot, sprinkled with parsley.

Serves 4 to 6

Tuscan White Bean Soup

Also known as *pasta e fagioli*, this classic bean soup has many variations. This version, made with cannellini beans and a touch of red pepper flakes, is thick with chewy pasta and makes a hearty and economical meal when served with a green salad.

8 ounces elbow macaroni or other small pasta

1 tablespoon olive oil or ¼ cup water

1 small onion, minced

1 large garlic clove, minced

1 (6-ounce) can tomato paste blended with 1 cup warm water

6 cups vegetable broth

1½ cups cooked cannellini or other white beans or 1 (15-ounce) can beans, rinsed and drained

¼ teaspoon red pepper flakes, or to taste

2 bay leaves

¼ teaspoon dried oregano

Salt and freshly ground black pepper

1. Cook the pasta in a pot of boiling salted water, stirring occasionally, until just al dente, 6 to 8 minutes. Drain and set aside.

2. Heat the oil or water in a large pot over medium heat. Add the onion, cover, and cook until softened, about 5 minutes. Add the garlic and cook for 1 minute. Reduce the heat to low and stir in the diluted tomato paste. Add the broth, beans, red pepper flakes, bay leaves, oregano, and salt and pepper to taste. Bring to a boil, reduce the heat to low, and simmer for 30 minutes.

3. Remove the bay leaves. Add the reserved pasta and cook for 10 minutes to blend the flavors. Serve hot.

Serves 4 to 6

Thyme-Scented Wild Mushroom Bisque

This creamy, elegant soup is a far cry from the canned mushroom soup we grew up with. Use white button mushrooms for all or part of the fresh mushrooms to cut down on the cost—the dried porcinis will impart a sufficient "wild" mushroom flavor.

1 tablespoon olive oil or ¼ cup water

1 large onion, chopped

1 celery rib, minced

3 garlic cloves, chopped

2 teaspoons minced fresh thyme
or 1 teaspoon dried thyme

1 teaspoon salt

¼ cup dry vermouth or white wine

8 ounces cremini mushrooms, thinly sliced

4 ounces oyster mushrooms, thinly sliced

2 portobello mushroom caps,
gills scraped out, chopped

1 cup dried porcini mushrooms,
soaked in very hot water to cover for
20 minutes, drained and sliced

6 cups vegetable broth,
mushroom broth, or water

¾ cup cooked or canned white beans

Fresh thyme sprigs, for garnish (optional)

1. Heat the oil or water in a large pot over medium heat. Add the onion and celery. Cover and cook until softened, about 10 minutes. Add the garlic, thyme, and salt and cook for 2 minutes. Stir in the vermouth, increase the heat to high, and cook for 1 to 2 minutes to reduce the liquid slightly. Add all of the fresh mushrooms, reduce the heat to medium, and cook for 5 minutes, stirring occasionally.

2. Slice the porcinis and add to the pot along with the broth. Reduce the heat to medium-low and simmer for 20 to 30 minutes. Taste and add more salt, if necessary.

3. Working in batches, carefully transfer the soup to a blender or food processor, add the beans, and process until smooth. Pour each batch of soup into a second pot and place over low heat to keep warm until ready to serve, being careful not to boil. Serve hot, garnished with the thyme sprigs, if desired.

Serves 6

Winter Vegetable Bisque

Made with those dependable vegetables that are often overlooked during summer's bounty, this velvety soup soothes on a cold winter night. A garnish of fresh chives adds a fresh taste and a bit of contrast.

1 tablespoon olive oil or ¼ cup water	1 garlic clove, minced
1 medium-size onion, chopped	¼ cup dry white wine
3 large parsnips, peeled and thinly sliced	5 cups vegetable broth
2 large carrots, thinly sliced	1½ teaspoons minced fresh thyme or 1 teaspoon dried thyme
1 medium-size Yukon Gold potato, peeled and diced	Salt and freshly ground black pepper
1 celery rib, thinly sliced	2 tablespoons snipped fresh chives, for garnish

1. Heat the oil or water in a large pot over medium heat. Add the onion, cover, and cook until softened, about 5 minutes. Add the parsnips, carrots, potato, and celery. Cover and cook until the vegetables are soft, about 10 minutes. Stir in the garlic, wine, and broth. Increase the heat to medium-high and bring to a boil, then reduce the heat to low. Add the thyme, season to taste with salt and pepper, and simmer for 30 minutes.

2. Working in batches, carefully transfer the mixture to a blender or food processor and process until smooth. Pour each batch of soup into a second pot and heat through. Taste and adjust the seasonings.

3. To serve, ladle into bowls and garnish with the chives.

Serves 4 to 6

Orange and Chipotle-Kissed Butternut Squash Bisque

The smoky chipotle chile and sweet hint of orange add layers of flavor to this creamy bisque. Chipotle chiles are smoke-dried jalapeños, also available canned in adobo sauce, and can be found in ethnic markets and well-stocked supermarkets.

1 tablespoon olive oil or ¼ cup water

1 medium-size onion, chopped

1 medium-size butternut squash, peeled, seeded, and thinly sliced

1 celery rib, chopped

Salt

5 cups vegetable broth

1 chipotle chile in adobo, chopped

2 tablespoons frozen orange juice concentrate

2 tablespoons roasted pumpkin seeds, for garnish (optional)

1. Heat the oil or water in a large pot over medium heat. Add the onion, cover, and cook until softened, about 5 minutes. Add the squash, celery, and salt to taste. Cook, stirring, until softened slightly, about 5 minutes. Add the broth, cover, and cook until the vegetables are soft, about 15 minutes.

2. In a blender or food processor, puree the chipotle. Working in batches, add the orange juice concentrate and squash mixture and process until smooth. Pour each batch of soup into a second pot and heat through. Taste, adjust the seasonings, and serve hot, garnished with the pumpkin seeds, if desired.

Serves 4 to 6

Roasted Corn Chowder

Roasting (or grilling) intensifies the naturally sweet flavor of the corn in this wholesome chowder. A garnish of fresh tomato and basil completes my favorite summer produce trilogy. Although you can make this chowder using frozen corn kernels instead of fresh, it will not be as flavorful.

3 cups corn kernels (frozen or fresh from 4 ears of corn)

1 tablespoon olive oil or ¼ cup water

1 large onion, chopped

1 celery rib, chopped

1 large Yukon Gold potato, peeled and diced

4 cups vegetable broth

1 cup plain unsweetened nondairy milk

Salt and freshly ground black pepper

1 large ripe tomato, peeled, seeded, and finely chopped, for garnish

2 tablespoons minced fresh basil, for garnish

1. Preheat the oven to 450°F. Spread the corn kernels on a baking sheet lined with parchment paper and roast until lightly browned, 15 to 20 minutes. Remove from the oven and set aside.

2. Heat the oil or water in a large pot over medium heat. Add the onion and celery, cover, and cook until softened, about 5 minutes. Add the potato and broth and bring to a boil. Reduce the heat to low, cover, and cook until the vegetables are tender, about 25 minutes. Uncover, add the roasted corn, and cook for 15 minutes.

3. Remove from the heat, ladle 2 cups of the soup into a food processor or blender, and process until smooth, then stir the puree back into the chowder. Alternatively, you can use an immersion blender to puree a portion of the chowder right in the pot.

4. Add the nondairy milk, and season to taste with salt and pepper. Ladle the soup into bowls and garnish with the tomato and basil.

Serves 4 to 6

New England-Style Chowder

This chowder gets its ocean-fresh taste from the vitamin-rich kombu sea vegetable and its creamy texture from pureeing part of the soup. Coarsely chopped oyster mushrooms make this soup reminiscent of a traditional New England clam chowder. Look for certified organic kombu and other sea vegetables at natural foods stores.

2 tablespoons olive oil

1 large onion, chopped

2 celery ribs, chopped

3 Yukon Gold potatoes, peeled and diced

4 cups vegetable broth

1 (2-inch-square) piece kombu sea vegetable

1 bay leaf

Salt

1 cup plain unsweetened nondairy milk

1 tablespoon mellow white miso paste dissolved in 2 tablespoons hot (not boiling) water

8 ounces oyster mushrooms, coarsely chopped

½ teaspoon Old Bay seasoning

1. Heat 1 tablespoon of the oil in a large pot over medium heat. Add the onion and celery, cover, and cook until softened, about 5 minutes. Add the potatoes, broth, kombu, bay leaf, and salt to taste. Bring to a boil, then reduce the heat to medium-low and simmer until the vegetables are soft, 20 to 30 minutes. Remove the kombu and bay leaf.

2. Carefully transfer about 2 cups of the soup solids and ¼ cup of the broth to a food processor or blender and process until smooth, then return the mixture to the pot. Alternatively, you can use an immersion blender to puree a portion of the chowder right in the pot. Stir in the nondairy milk and dissolved miso. Keep the soup warm over low heat, being careful not to boil.

3. Heat the remaining 1 tablespoon oil in a large skillet over medium heat. Add the mushrooms and cook, stirring constantly, until softened, 3 to 5 minutes. Sprinkle with the Old Bay seasoning, stirring to coat. Stir the cooked mushrooms into the chowder and serve hot.

Serves 4 to 6

Farmhouse Vegetable Soup

This is a good old-fashioned vegetable soup that can be made with just about any vegetables you have on hand. Kidney beans boost the protein, making this a great one-dish meal when served with a loaf of warm crusty bread.

1 tablespoon olive oil or ¼ cup water

1 large onion, chopped

2 carrots, cut into ¼-inch-thick slices

1 celery rib, chopped

3 small red potatoes, unpeeled and diced

½ small red bell pepper, seeded and chopped

4 ounces green beans, trimmed and cut into 1-inch pieces

2 small zucchini or yellow squash, diced

3 garlic cloves, minced

6 cups vegetable broth

1½ cups cooked dark red kidney beans or 1 (15-ounce) can beans, rinsed and drained

1 teaspoon dried basil

½ teaspoon dried marjoram

Salt and freshly ground black pepper

2 tablespoons chopped fresh parsley

Heat the oil or water in a large pot over medium heat. Add the onion, carrots, and celery. Cover and cook until softened, about 5 minutes. Add the potatoes, bell pepper, green beans, zucchini, and garlic and cook for 5 minutes. Add the broth, increase the heat to high, and bring to a boil. Reduce the heat to low, add the kidney beans, basil, and marjoram. Season with salt and pepper to taste, and simmer until the vegetables are tender and the flavors have developed, 30 to 40 minutes. Stir in the parsley, then taste and adjust the seasonings. Serve hot.

Serves 4 to 6

Sassy Vegetable Gumbo

Gumbo, a thick soup served over rice, is synonymous with spicy Cajun cooking. Since the word *gumbo* means "okra," it is included among the ingredients. But if you don't like it, don't use it—there'll be plenty of other vegetables in the pot, including the New Orleans vegetable "trinity" of onions, celery, and green bell pepper, as well as tomatoes and corn. This soup is made "sassy" with the addition of a smoky chipotle chile and a generous sprinkling of ground sassafras leaves, known as filé powder. The filé, along with the okra, helps thicken the soup and adds traditional flavor. The optional barley miso, though nontraditional, enriches the broth and deepens its color.

1 tablespoon olive oil or ¼ cup water

1 large onion, diced

1 medium-size green bell pepper, seeded and diced

½ cup chopped celery

2 garlic cloves, minced

6 cups vegetable broth or water

1 (14.5-ounce) can diced tomatoes, undrained

1½ cups fresh or frozen sliced okra

1½ teaspoons filé powder

1 teaspoon dried thyme

Salt and freshly ground black pepper

1 tablespoon barley miso paste (optional)

1 cup fresh or frozen corn kernels

1 chipotle chile in adobo, minced

1 teaspoon Tabasco sauce, or to taste

2 to 3 cups freshly cooked long-grain white or brown rice

1. Heat the oil or water in a large pot over medium heat. Add the onion, bell pepper, celery, and garlic. Cover and cook until softened, about 5 minutes. Add the broth, tomatoes and juice, okra, filé, thyme, and salt and pepper to taste. Reduce the heat to low and simmer for 30 minutes, stirring occasionally.

2. Place the miso, if using, in a small bowl. Add 2 tablespoons of the hot broth and stir to thin the miso, then add it to the gumbo along with the corn, chipotle, and Tabasco. Taste and adjust the seasonings, then cook for 10 minutes.

3. To serve, spoon about ½ cup of the cooked rice into each soup bowl and top with the gumbo. Serve hot.

Serves 4 to 6

A Soup by Any Other Name

- *Stock:* A clear, flavorful liquid made by simmering ingredients (such as vegetables for vegetable stock) with water to release the flavor of the ingredients. The strained liquid is used to make soups, stews, and sauces.

- *Broth:* Stock that is served on its own as a soup.

- *Consommé:* Stock that has been reduced to intensify the flavor and then filtered for clarity.

- *Bisque:* Traditionally made with shellfish, but the term also can refer to any smooth, creamy soup. To make a vegan bisque, vegetables are cooked in liquid and then pureed. For added creaminess, nondairy- milk may be added near the end of the cooking time.

- *Chowder:* A hearty, chunky soup usually associated with seafood and dairy. A vegan chowder can be made with vegetables such as corn or potatoes.

- *Gumbo:* A traditional Cajun dish, gumbo is a spicy, thick, stew-like soup that is served over rice. Usually thickened with okra (the word gumbo means "okra") and filé powder (ground sassafras leaves), gumbo may be made with a variety of vegetables instead of the traditional meat and seafood. (Tip: Chunks of browned soy sausage added at the end of the cooking time are delicious.)

Ribollita

This flavorful cabbage and bean soup from Tuscany is made thick by spooning it over a slice of toasted Italian bread. To me, it's the ultimate in simple, economical comfort food that nourishes both body and soul. Canned borlotti beans can be found in Italian markets and some supermarkets. If unavailable, use cannellini beans.

1 tablespoon olive oil or ¼ cup water

1 medium-size onion, chopped

1 medium-size carrot, halved lengthwise and cut into ¼-inch-thick half-moons

3 garlic cloves, minced

1 small head green cabbage, quartered, cored, and cut into ½-inch-wide strips

2 small white potatoes, peeled and diced

⅓ cup tomato paste blended with 1 cup warm water

5 cups vegetable broth or water

1 teaspoon dried oregano

2 bay leaves

Salt and freshly ground black pepper

1½ cups cooked borlotti or cannellini beans or 1 (15-ounce) can beans, rinsed and drained

4 to 6 slices Italian bread, toasted

1. Cut the cabbage into ½-inch-wide strips and set aside.

2. Heat the oil or water in a large pot over medium heat. Add the onion, carrot, and garlic. Cover and cook until softened, about 5 minutes. Add the cabbage, potatoes, diluted tomato paste, broth, oregano, bay leaves, and salt and pepper to taste. Bring to a boil, then reduce the heat to low and simmer until the vegetables are soft, about 45 minutes. Add the beans and cook for 20 minutes. Remove the bay leaves, then taste and adjust the seasonings.

3. To serve, place a slice of toasted bread in the bottom of each bowl and ladle the soup over the bread. Serve hot.

Serves 4 to 6

Italian Wedding Soup

In the ever-evocative Italian language, minestrone is often called wedding soup. There are infinite variations of this classic vegetable soup—the only requirement is a variety of vegetables. My mother often added tiny meatballs (which you can do by thawing frozen veggie burgers, breaking off small pieces, rolling them into balls, and browning in a skillet) just before serving. In this version, I use the traditional borlotti beans, available at Italian markets, but you may use chickpeas or cannellini beans instead. For additional substance, add some cooked small pasta a few minutes before serving—just long enough to warm the pasta.

1 tablespoon olive oil or ¼ cup water

1 medium-size onion, minced

1 large carrot, chopped

1 celery rib, chopped

3 garlic cloves, minced

1 cup trimmed green beans cut into 1-inch pieces

1 (14.5-ounce) can diced tomatoes, undrained

6 cups vegetable broth or water

Salt and freshly ground black pepper

1 medium-size zucchini, diced

1½ cups cooked borlotti beans, chickpeas, or cannellini beans or 1 (15-ounce) can beans, rinsed and drained

1 tablespoon minced fresh parsley

¼ cup Basil Pesto (page 142) or purchased pesto, for garnish (optional)

1. Heat the oil or water in a large pot over medium heat. Add the onion, carrot, celery, and garlic. Cover and cook until softened, about 5 minutes. Add the green beans, tomatoes and juice, broth, and salt and pepper to taste. Bring to a boil, reduce the heat to low, and simmer for 30 minutes.

2. Add the zucchini, borlotti beans, and parsley and cook for 15 minutes. Serve hot, garnished with a small spoonful of the vegan pesto, if desired.

Serves 4 to 6

Potato-Watercress Soup with Sesame

Buttery Yukon Gold potatoes combine with the peppery flavor of watercress to make a luxurious soup accented by a touch of toasted sesame oil.

1 tablespoon neutral vegetable oil or ¼ cup water

4 large shallots, chopped

4 cups vegetable broth

1½ pounds Yukon Gold potatoes, peeled and diced

Salt

½ cup plain unsweetened nondairy milk

Cayenne

2 bunches watercress, tough stems removed, finely chopped

1 tablespoon toasted sesame oil

1 tablespoon sesame seeds, toasted (page 171), for garnish

1. Heat the vegetable oil or water in large pot over medium heat. Add the shallots, cover, and cook until softened, about 5 minutes. Add the broth and potatoes and bring to a boil. Reduce the heat to low, season to taste with salt, and simmer until the potatoes are soft, about 30 minutes.

2. Pass the potato mixture through a food mill into a large bowl. Stir in the nondairy milk and season to taste with cayenne. Return to the pot and keep warm over low heat.

3. Heat the sesame oil in a medium-size skillet over medium heat. Add the watercress and stir-fry until just wilted, about 2 minutes. Add the watercress and sesame oil to the soup, stirring to combine. Serve hot, garnished with the sesame seeds.

Serves 4 to 6

Udon Noodles in Shiitake-Ginger Broth

Udon noodles and shiitake mushrooms swim in a broth flavored with ginger and a hint of toasted sesame oil. Once the miso has been added to the broth, be sure the broth does not return to a boil, as boiling will destroy the beneficial enzymes in the miso.

8 ounces udon noodles

1 teaspoon toasted sesame oil

6 cups vegetable broth

4 ounces fresh shiitake mushrooms, stems removed and caps thinly sliced

1 tablespoon grated fresh ginger

4 scallions, minced

2 tablespoons low-sodium tamari

1 tablespoon mellow white miso paste

1 tablespoon minced fresh parsley, for garnish

1. Cook the udon in a pot of boiling salted water until just tender, 6 to 8 minutes. Drain and transfer to a large bowl. Add the sesame oil and toss to coat. Set aside.

2. Place the broth, shiitakes, ginger, scallions, and tamari in a large pot over medium heat. Bring to a boil, reduce the heat to low, and simmer until the shiitakes soften, about 5 minutes.

3. In a small bowl, blend the miso with ¼ cup of the hot broth. Stir into the soup and add the noodles. Serve immediately, garnished with the parsley.

Serves 4 to 6

Did You Know?

Ginger is known for its healing properties as well as its fragrant spiciness. It is said to have a positive effect on the heart and blood circulation and is also used to prevent nausea. Hot ginger tea is sometimes used to relieve symptoms of the common cold.

Sherry-Laced Garlic Soup with Pasta Stars

Both garlic and soup have long been used as home remedies for colds, so combining them would seem to be a sure-fire cure. Long, slow simmering helps mellow the flavor of the garlic. Tiny pasta stars, called stelline, add substance to this restorative soup.

10 garlic cloves, crushed

2 tablespoons olive oil

5 cups vegetable broth

Salt

Cayenne

½ cup stelline or other tiny pasta

2 tablespoons dry sherry

1. Place the garlic and olive oil in a blender or food processor and process until smooth. Transfer to a large pot and cook over medium heat until very fragrant, about 3 minutes, being careful not to let the garlic brown. Stir in the broth and season to taste with salt and cayenne. Bring to boil, reduce the heat to medium-low, and simmer for 30 minutes.

2. Meanwhile, cook the pasta in a pot of boiling salted water, stirring occasionally, until al dente, about 5 minutes. Drain and divide among 4 soup bowls.

3. When ready to serve, add the sherry to the soup, ladle into the bowls, and serve at once.

================= *Serves 4 to 6* =================

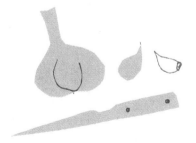

Barley Soup with Porcini and Dill

Barley soups are especially popular in eastern European cultures, where they often contain mushrooms. Here dried porcinis add a rich, woodsy element, while minced dill heightens the flavor. Using vegetable broth will yield a fine soup, but mushroom broth will produce a more pronounced mushroom flavor.

½ cup dried porcini mushrooms, soaked in 1 cup very hot water for 20 minutes

1 tablespoon olive oil or ¼ cup water

1 large onion, chopped

1 large carrot, minced or grated

2 garlic cloves, minced

1 cup pearl barley

5 cups vegetable broth or Mushroom Broth (page 59)

Salt and freshly ground black pepper

2 tablespoon minced fresh dill or 2 teaspoons dried dill

1. Remove the porcinis from the soaking liquid and strain the liquid. Thinly slice the porcinis and return to the strained liquid. Set aside.

2. Heat the oil or water in a large pot over medium heat. Add the onion, carrot, and garlic. Cover and cook, stirring a few times, until softened and lightly caramelized, about 10 minutes. Add the barley and broth and bring to a boil. Season to taste with salt and pepper, reduce the heat to medium-low, and simmer for 20 minutes. Add the porcinis and their soaking liquid and half the dill. Cook until the barley is tender, about 10 minutes. Serve hot, garnished with the remaining dill.

Serves 4 to 6

Did You Know?

Mushrooms are a good source of potassium and riboflavin. These flavorful fungi are also extremely low in calories and are credited with having medicinal qualities, from antibiotic to aphrodisiac.

Tuscan Spelt Soup

Also known as farro, emmer, or German wheat, spelt is an ancient grain (it is mentioned twice in the Bible). A type of wheat with large grains that resemble brown rice, it has a chewy texture and hearty flavor and is popular in soups, especially in Tuscany and the Provence region of France. Like its cousin kamut, spelt can often be tolerated by those with wheat allergies. This recipe was inspired by one contained among the writings of Apicius, a first-century food writer credited with writing the first cookbook.

¾ cup spelt

1 tablespoon olive oil or ¼ cup water

1 large onion, chopped

1 large carrot, chopped

1 celery rib, chopped

3 garlic cloves, minced

1 teaspoon minced fresh or dried thyme

5 cups vegetable broth or water

1½ cups cooked cannellini or other white beans or 1 (15-ounce) can beans, rinsed and drained

Salt and freshly ground black pepper

1. Soak the spelt in a bowl with cold water to cover for 12 hours to soften. Drain and set aside.

2. Heat the olive oil or water in a large pot over medium heat. Add the onion, carrot, celery, garlic, and thyme. Cover and cook until the vegetables soften, about 5 minutes. Add the broth and bring to a boil. Add the spelt and reduce the heat to low. Cover and simmer until the spelt is tender, 1½ to 2 hours. Add more broth or water if the soup becomes too thick.

3. Add the beans and season to taste with salt and pepper. Simmer for 30 minutes to allow the flavors to blend. Serve hot.

Serves 4

Salads & Slaws

Salads have come a long way since that crunchy wedge of iceberg lettuce drowning in bottled dressing that many of us grew up with. These days salad greens abound, with choices ranging from the usual romaine, butter, and leaf lettuces to arugula, chicory, and baby spinach. And the greens are just the beginning. Look for them topped with anything from grilled vegetables to marinated bean and grain medleys. Main-dish salads are featured entrées on many restaurant menus, and a salad course is an important part of many dinner parties. Marinated salads are great choices for picnics and potlucks, and some of the more substantial salads can be an entire meal.

Vegetarians and vegans alike are sometimes jokingly called "salad eaters," but with salads such as the ones in this chapter, that's not necessarily a bad label. Consider the elegance of *Eggplant Salad Towers* or *Artichoke Salad Parfaits*, or the rustic goodness of two different bread salads, *Panzanella* from Tuscany and Lebanese *Fattoush*. A selection of slaws and potato salads, a variety of grain salads such as *Five-Spice Moroccan Couscous Salad* and *Quinoa Tabbouleh*, and some Asian salads such as *Thai-Style Papaya Salad* and *Asian Noodle Salad with Spicy Peanut Sauce* help round things out.

Eight Great Health Reasons to Go Vegan

As most vegans will tell you, a diet without animal products is not only good for your health, but it feels good, too. It is estimated that nearly 50 percent of the vegans in the United States made the choice for health reasons. Here's why:

1. A vegan diet reduces the risk of heart disease, stroke, cancer, adult-onset diabetes, and osteoporosis. Cornell University's long-term diet study, the China Project, showed that 80 to 90 percent of cardiovascular disease, cancer, and other forms of degenerative illness may be prevented by adopting a plant-based diet.
2. The *Journal of the American Medical Association* reported that a vegan diet can prevent 97 percent of coronary obstructions.
3. Dairy consumption has been linked to heart disease, cancer (especially breast cancer), allergies, sinus trouble, migraines, and psoriasis.
4. Dairy foods can create excess mucus in the body, which can host cold and virus germs in the respiratory tract.
5. More than 90 percent of the toxic chemical residues found in foods consumed by Americans come from animal products.
6. The antibiotics fed to livestock result in a diminished effectiveness of antibiotics when used in humans.
7. Meat contains bovine growth hormone, which can cause early puberty in children.
8. A plant-based diet can increase your life expectancy by 7 to 15 years.

Goddess of Kale Salad

To boost the protein and make it a meal, add some baked tofu (page 8) or roasted chickpeas (page 259) when ready to serve.

2 scallions, chopped

2 tablespoons chopped fresh parsley

1 large garlic clove, crushed

¼ cup firm silken tofu

2 tablespoons fresh lemon juice

2 tablespoons rice vinegar

2 tablespoons water

1 tablespoon almond butter

2 teaspoons low-sodium tamari

2 teaspoons agave nectar

½ teaspoon salt

¼ teaspoon freshly ground black pepper

1 bunch kale, leaves torn, washed and dried well (about 6 cups)

8 cherry or grape tomatoes, halved lengthwise

1 large ripe Hass avocado (optional), peeled, pitted, and diced

¼ cup kalamata olives, halved and pitted

1 tablespoon sunflower seeds

1. In a blender or food processor combine the scallions, parsley, and garlic and process until finely minced. Add the tofu, lemon juice, vinegar, water, almond butter, tamari, agave, salt, and pepper and process until smooth and well blended.

2. Place the kale in a large bowl. Drizzle with about ¼ cup of the dressing and massage it into the leaves. Set aside for 5 minutes. Add the tomatoes, avocado (if using), olives, and sunflower seeds and toss to coat, adding a little more of the dressing, if needed. Transfer the remaining dressing to a tightly covered jar and refrigerate for another use.

Serves 4

Asian Pear and Spinach Salad with Warm Walnut Dressing

Asian pears are increasingly available in supermarkets and can be found in Asian markets as well. If they're unavailable, you may substitute another variety of pear.

¾ cup walnut pieces

3 tablespoons neutral vegetable oil

2 tablespoons fresh lemon juice

½ teaspoon natural sugar

Salt and freshly ground black pepper

6 cups baby spinach leaves

2 Asian pears, peeled, cored, and thinly sliced

1. Place the walnuts in a dry skillet over medium heat and toast, stirring or shaking a few times, until fragrant and lightly browned, about 3 minutes. Be careful not to let burn.

2. Remove about ½ cup of the walnuts from the skillet and set aside to cool. Add the oil to the remaining walnuts in the skillet and warm over low heat for 5 minutes. Add the lemon juice, sugar, and salt and pepper to taste. Transfer to a blender and process until smooth. Return to the saucepan and keep warm over very low heat.

3. Place the spinach and all but 12 of the pear slices in a large bowl. Add as much of the dressing as needed and toss to coat. Divide the salad among 4 plates. Arrange the remaining pear slices on top of the spinach and drizzle with any remaining dressing. Scatter the reserved walnuts on top and serve immediately.

Serves 4

Thai-Style Papaya Salad

Inspired by the classic green papaya salads often served in Thai restaurants, this refreshing salad is sweet, hot, tangy, and crunchy all at the same time—typical of the complex flavors of Thai cuisine. I created this version to enjoy at home since most restaurants make theirs with fish sauce and shrimp. Look for green papayas in Asian markets. The best way to shred them is with a mandoline—I like the Benriner, a less expensive Japanese version.

2 garlic cloves, minced

2 to 3 teaspoons natural sugar

1 teaspoon grated fresh ginger

½ to 1 teaspoon Asian chili paste or sriracha

¼ cup fresh lime juice

2 tablespoons low-sodium tamari

1 or 2 green papayas (about 1½ pounds)

1 carrot

½ cup chopped unsalted dry-roasted peanuts

4 large Boston lettuce leaves

12 very thin cucumber slices, for garnish

4 cherry tomatoes, for garnish

1. In a small bowl, combine the garlic, sugar, ginger, and chili paste. Slowly stir in the lime juice and tamari, blending well. Set aside.

2. Peel the papayas, halve lengthwise, and seed. Use a mandoline or similar slicer to cut the papayas into long, thin shreds. Alternatively, use a box grater, food processor with a shredding disk, or sharp knife to achieve the same kind of shreds. Place in a large bowl. Shred the carrot the same way and add to the papayas.

3. Pour the dressing over the papayas and carrot, add the peanuts, and toss to combine well.

4. To serve, place a lettuce leaf on each of 4 salad plates, top with a mound of papaya salad, and garnish each plate with 3 cucumber slices and a cherry tomato.

Serves 4

Walnut-Crusted Apple-Cranberry Salad Pie

In this recipe, elements of the classic Waldorf salad—tasty bits of apples, celery, and walnuts—are transformed into a salad "pie" with dried cranberries and soy mayonnaise. Who says we can't begin our meal with dessert? The choice of apple is up to you—if you like a sweeter apple, use Delicious or perhaps Fuji or Gala. If you like a slightly tart, crisp taste, go for Granny Smith.

½ cup dates, pitted and soaked in hot water to cover until soft

2 cups walnut pieces

4 apples (see headnote)

1 tablespoon fresh lemon juice

½ cup sweetened dried cranberries

1 cup minced celery

2 scallions, minced

½ cup vegan mayonnaise, homemade (page 125) or purchased

½ teaspoon natural sugar

¼ teaspoon salt

1. Lightly oil a 9-inch pie plate. Drain the dates and set aside.

2. In a food processor, combine 1½ cups of the walnuts with the drained dates and process into a sticky paste. Press the mixture evenly into the bottom and sides of the prepared pie plate and set aside.

3. Peel, core, and shred the apples or cut into very thin slices and place in a large bowl. Add the lemon juice and toss to coat to prevent discoloration. Drain any liquid from the apples, then add the cranberries, celery, scallions, mayonnaise, sugar, and salt. Stir gently to combine. Taste and adjust the seasonings, then transfer to the prepared pie plate. Spread the mixture evenly, pressing it into the crust and smoothing the top. Sprinkle the remaining ½ cup walnuts on top.

4. Cover and refrigerate for at least 30 minutes or up to 2 hours before serving. Cut into wedges and serve.

Serves 6

Indonesian-Style Vegetable Salad

The pleasing crunch of cabbage, carrots, and jicama against the backdrop of a creamy, peanutty dressing makes for a tasty salad combination and a nice change from the usual raw vegetable salads. Toss this with cold rice or noodles for a substantial one-dish meal. The coconut milk adds a rich finish to the sauce, but water will work if you want to reduce the fat.

1 tablespoon neutral vegetable oil
or ¼ cup water

½ cup chopped shallots

2 garlic cloves, minced

2 teaspoons peeled and grated fresh ginger

½ cup peanut butter

3 tablespoons fresh lemon juice

2 tablespoons low-sodium tamari

1 teaspoon natural sugar

¼ teaspoon cayenne

1 cup unsweetened coconut milk
or water, or as needed

1 small head green cabbage,
cored and finely shredded

1 small carrot, shredded

1 cup peeled and shredded jicama

⅓ cup chopped unsalted dry-roasted peanuts

¼ cup raisins

½ cup fresh bean sprouts

1. Heat the oil or water in a medium-size skillet over medium heat. Add the shallots, garlic, and ginger. Cover and cook until softened, about 5 minutes. Stir in the peanut butter, lemon juice, tamari, sugar, cayenne, and as much coconut milk as necessary to make a thick sauce. Reduce the heat to low and simmer for 5 minutes, stirring a few times.

2. Transfer to a blender or food processor and process until smooth.

3. Place the cabbage, carrot, jicama, peanuts, and raisins in a large serving bowl. Pour in the sauce and toss to combine. Sprinkle the bean sprouts on top and serve immediately.

Serves 4

Sprouting Up All Over

Loaded with concentrated flavor and nutrition, a wide variety of fresh sprouts are available in supermarkets and natural foods stores. In addition to the familiar mung bean sprouts common in Asian cooking and the popular fluffy salad garnish sprouted from alfalfa seeds, we now have radish sprouts, broccoli sprouts, lentil sprouts, soybean sprouts, and numerous other types grown from various vegetable and herb seeds, beans, and grains. When buying sprouts, be sure they are very firm and fresh. Most sprouts will keep well in the refrigerator for several days.

Here's My Heart Salad
with Raspberry Vinaigrette

Valentine's Day was my inspiration for this heartwarming salad made with four kinds of vegetable "hearts." A blushing raspberry vinaigrette adds a touch of pink, which is picked up by the sliced beets and radishes. If you want to go all out, cut beet slices into heart shapes for a garnish. The white wine vinegar combines with the raspberry jam to create an economical alternative to the pricey raspberry vinegars available in specialty food shops.

2 hearts of romaine lettuce

1 (9-ounce) package frozen artichoke hearts, cooked according to package directions, drained, and thinly sliced

1 (14-ounce) can hearts of palm, drained and thinly sliced

½ cup minced celery hearts

2 red radishes, thinly sliced

2 tablespoons white wine vinegar

1 small shallot, minced

1 teaspoon fruit-sweetened raspberry jam

Salt and freshly ground black pepper

3 tablespoons olive oil

½ cup sliced cooked or canned beets

1. Tear the romaine into bite-size pieces and place in a large bowl. Add the artichoke hearts, hearts of palm, celery, and radishes. Set aside.

2. In a small bowl, combine the vinegar, shallot, raspberry spread, and salt and pepper to taste. Whisk in the olive oil until blended. Pour the dressing over the salad.

3. If using plain sliced beets, add them now and toss the salad to combine. If using heart-shaped beets, toss the salad first, then divide among 4 plates, garnishing each salad with the beet slices.

Serves 4

Did You Know?

The greener the lettuce, the more nutritious it is. Dark green lettuce varieties such as romaine contain more vitamins and minerals than pale varieties such as iceberg.

Artichoke Salad Parfaits

The ingredients in these salad "parfaits" can be varied according to personal preference. Presentation is the key—ice-cream sundae glasses are best, but large wineglasses or even martini glasses can be used instead.

3 tablespoons olive oil

1½ tablespoons rice vinegar

1 teaspoon minced fresh basil or ½ teaspoon dried basil

½ teaspoon minced garlic

½ teaspoon salt

⅛ teaspoon freshly ground black pepper

1 small red bell pepper, seeded and chopped

1 small cucumber, peeled, seeded, and chopped

1 small carrot, grated

Romaine lettuce, cut into thin strips

1 (9-ounce) jar marinated artichoke hearts, drained and chopped

2 tablespoons pine nuts, lightly toasted (page 203)

4 pitted kalamata olives

1. In a small bowl, combine the olive oil, vinegar, basil, garlic, salt, and pepper, whisking until blended. Set aside.

2. Place the bell pepper, cucumber, and carrot in separate small bowls and drizzle a little dressing on each. Toss to coat.

3. Arrange the salad ingredients in layers in 4 glasses (see headnote), beginning with a layer of romaine lettuce, followed by bell pepper, cucumber, carrot, and artichoke hearts, adding more lettuce if there is room in the glass.

4. Drizzle with a little of the remaining dressing, top each salad with pine nuts and an olive, and serve.

Serves 4

Pseudo Caesar Salad

This salad is great for those who enjoy the crunchy goodness of romaine lettuce tossed with fresh croutons and a garlicky dressing but want to avoid the raw eggs and anchovies found in a classic Caesar salad.

4 thick slices Italian bread, crusts removed, cut into 1-inch cubes

3 garlic cloves, crushed

¼ cup olive oil

2 tablespoons nutritional yeast

2 tablespoons fresh lemon juice

1 tablespoon tahini

1 tablespoon mellow white miso paste

1 teaspoon low-sodium tamari

¼ teaspoon vegan Worcestershire sauce (optional)

Salt and freshly ground black pepper

1 head romaine lettuce

1. Preheat the oven to 325°F. Spread the bread cubes on a baking sheet. Bake, turning occasionally, until lightly toasted on all sides, about 20 minutes. Set aside to cool.

2. In a food processor or high-speed blender, combine the garlic, olive oil, nutritional yeast, lemon juice, tahini, miso, tamari, and Worcestershire (if using), until blended. Taste and adjust the seasonings, adding salt and pepper to taste. Set aside.

3. Tear the lettuce leaves into bite-size pieces and place in a large serving bowl. Pour the dressing over the salad and toss until evenly coated. Add the croutons, toss again, and serve immediately.

Serves 4

Watercress-Fennel Salad
with Pecans and Orange Vinaigrette

The vibrant colors, complementary flavors, and contrasting textures in this salad create a sparkling combination that will make it a favorite.

1 navel orange, peeled

2 large fennel bulbs, trimmed

2 bunches watercress, tough stems removed, leaves coarsely chopped

½ cup pecan halves, toasted (page 203)

2 tablespoons rice vinegar

1½ tablespoons frozen orange juice concentrate, thawed

1½ tablespoons water

1 teaspoon Dijon mustard

½ teaspoon salt

¼ teaspoon freshly ground black pepper

2 tablespoons olive oil

1. Remove the white pith from the orange. Cut sections of orange from between the membranes and set aside.

2. Halve each fennel bulb lengthwise, then cut crosswise into paper-thin slices. Place in a large serving bowl. Add the watercress, orange sections, and pecans.

3. In a small bowl, combine the vinegar, orange juice concentrate, water, mustard, salt, and pepper. Whisk in the olive oil until blended and pour the dressing over the salad. Toss gently to coat evenly and serve immediately.

Serves 4

Eggplant Salad Towers

A stacked salad makes a striking first course. Instead of the eggplant slices, you can substitute slices of grilled portobello mushroom caps, if you prefer.

1 large roasted red bell pepper (page 129), minced

½ cup fresh or thawed frozen green peas

⅓ cup minced red onion

1 garlic clove, minced

2 tablespoons olive oil

1 tablespoon balsamic vinegar

1 tablespoon fresh lemon juice

Salt and freshly ground black pepper

1 medium-size eggplant

4 slices Italian bread, crusts removed

1 large ripe tomato

4 Boston lettuce leaves

1 tablespoon minced fresh parsley

1. Preheat the oven to 400°F. Lightly oil a baking sheet and set aside. In a medium-size bowl, combine the bell pepper, peas, onion, and garlic. Add the olive oil, vinegar, lemon juice, and salt and pepper to taste. Toss to combine and set aside.

2. Cut the middle section of the eggplant into twelve ¼-inch-thick slices and place on the prepared baking sheet. Season with salt and pepper to taste and bake until soft, turning once, 12 to 15 minutes total.

3. Toast the bread in the oven at the same time (or in a toaster oven) to make 4 large croutons. Set aside.

4. Cut four ¼-inch-thick slices from the tomato and set aside.

5. Set out 4 salad plates and place 1 lettuce leaf on each. Top each leaf with a large crouton. Using a slotted spoon, place an eggplant slice on top of the crouton. Top with a spoonful of the marinated salad, followed by another eggplant slice and then a tomato slice. Repeat with the remaining marinated salad and top with the remaining eggplant slice. Sprinkle with the parsley and drizzle with any extra dressing from the marinated vegetables. Serve at once.

Serves 4

Chili Taco Salad

This recipe is a refreshing way to stretch a small amount of chili into a satisfying lunch for six and is great served in bowls made from tortillas.

6 cups shredded lettuce

3 cups of your favorite vegan chili
(pages 290–301), heated

1 cup Fresh Tomato Salsa
(page 157) or purchased salsa

1 cup vegan sour cream, homemade
(page 126) or purchased

1 cup shredded vegan cheddar cheese
or Cheesy Sauce (page 128)

1 small red bell pepper, seeded and chopped

1 large ripe Hass avocado,
peeled, pitted, and diced

¼ cup pitted and sliced
brine-cured black olives

Tortilla chips, for serving

1. Place a bed of lettuce on each of 6 salad plates. Top with the chili, dividing it evenly among the plates.

2. In a small bowl, combine the salsa and vegan sour cream until well mixed, then spoon over the chili. Top each serving with the vegan cheese and scatter the bell pepper, avocado, and olives evenly over the top. Serve with the tortilla chips.

Serves 6

Carrot-Mung Bean Salad

In addition to being rich in protein and complex carbohydrates, this flavorful salad is also very low in fat. Yellow split mung beans can be found in natural foods stores and Indian markets. For variation, chopped fresh mango may be substituted for the apple.

¼ cup yellow split mung beans, picked over and rinsed

1 large carrot, grated

½ Granny Smith apple, cored and chopped

½ red bell pepper, seeded and chopped

1 teaspoon grated fresh ginger

2 tablespoons fresh lemon juice

1 tablespoon neutral vegetable oil

½ teaspoon black mustard seeds

1 small, fresh hot green chile, seeded and minced

1 tablespoon chopped fresh cilantro

Salt

1. Soak the beans in water to cover for at least 2 hours or up to 8 hours.

2. Drain the beans and place them in a large serving bowl. Add the carrot, apple, bell pepper, ginger, and lemon juice. Set aside.

3. Heat the oil in a small saucepan over medium heat. Add the mustard seeds, cover, and cook until the seeds start popping. When the popping stops, add the chile and stir for 30 seconds to bring out the flavor. Add the mustard seeds and chile to the salad mixture.

4. Just before serving, add the cilantro and salt to taste, tossing gently to combine.

Serves 4

Watercress and White Bean Salad

This is one of my favorite salads. I love the combination of flavors and textures, from the creamy white beans and peppery watercress to the crunchy pecans and chewy sweet cranberries.

1½ cups cooked cannellini beans or 1 (15-ounce) can beans, rinsed and drained

1 carrot, shredded

1 celery rib, chopped

1 cup grape tomatoes, halved lengthwise

½ cup fresh or thawed frozen peas

⅓ cup toasted pecans or almonds (page 203)

2 scallions, chopped

1 bunch watercress leaves, coarsely chopped (about 2 cups)

⅓ cup dried sweetened cranberries

¼ cup chopped fresh tarragon or basil

2 tablespoons almond butter

2 tablespoons fresh lemon juice

2 teaspoons agave nectar

½ teaspoon prepared mustard

Salt and freshly ground pepper to taste

1. In a large bowl, combine the beans, carrot, celery, tomatoes, peas, pecans, scallions, watercress, cranberries, and tarragon. Set aside.

2. In a small bowl, combine the almond butter, lemon juice, agave, mustard, and salt and pepper to taste. Mix until well blended. Add a little water, if needed, to reach the desired consistency. Add the dressing to the salad and toss gently to combine. Taste and adjust the seasonings, if needed.

Serves 4

Gold and Black Bean Salad

Black beans, corn, and yellow bell peppers make for a striking contrast in this salad with a southwestern accent. Serve as is, or toss with a cup or so of cold rice or other grain and spoon over torn salad greens for a more substantial dish.

3 cups cooked black beans or 2 (15-ounce) cans beans, rinsed and drained

2 cups cooked fresh or frozen corn kernels

1 small yellow bell pepper, seeded and chopped

2 shallots, minced

2 tablespoons fresh lime juice

½ teaspoon salt

¼ teaspoon ground cumin

⅛ teaspoon cayenne

¼ cup olive oil

2 tablespoons minced fresh cilantro

1. In a large serving bowl, combine the beans, corn, and bell pepper. Set aside.

2. In a small bowl, combine the shallots, lime juice, salt, cumin, and cayenne. Whisk in the olive oil until blended.

3. Pour the dressing over the salad and toss lightly to coat. Taste and adjust the seasonings. Sprinkle with the cilantro and serve at room temperature.

Serves 4 to 6

Lima Bean and Tomato Salad

Frozen lima beans are economical and simple to prepare. They also happen to look and taste great in this main-dish salad. Grape tomatoes tend to be much sweeter than cherry tomatoes, but if you can't find them, feel free to use cherry tomatoes instead.

3 cups frozen lima beans, cooked according to package directions and cooled

2 cups grape tomatoes, cut in half

⅓ cup minced scallions

¼ cup minced fresh parsley

¼ cup chopped basil

¼ cup kalamata olives, pitted and thinly sliced

2 tablespoons fresh lemon juice

2 tablespoons olive oil

½ teaspoon salt

¼ teaspoon freshly ground black pepper

In a large serving bowl, combine the cooked lima beans, tomatoes, scallions, parsley, basil, and olives. Add the lemon juice, olive oil, salt, and pepper. Toss gently to combine, then serve.

Serves 4

Tomato and White Bean Salad with Watercress

Sweet ripe tomatoes combine with creamy white beans and refreshing crisp watercress for a lovely salad combination that tastes as good as it looks. Add a loaf of warm crusty bread, and you have a delicious light meal.

1 shallot, halved

1 garlic clove, crushed

3 tablespoons olive oil

2 tablespoons fresh lemon juice

1 teaspoon Dijon mustard

½ teaspoon salt

¼ teaspoon freshly ground black pepper

1½ cups cooked cannellini or other white beans or 1 (15-ounce) can beans, rinsed and drained

2 bunches watercress, tough stems removed, leaves coarsely chopped

12 grape or cherry tomatoes, cut in half

8 kalamata olives, pitted

2 tablespoons chopped fresh basil

1. Place the shallot and garlic in a food processor and process to a paste. Add the olive oil, lemon juice, mustard, salt, and pepper. Process until well blended and set aside.

2. In a large serving bowl, combine the beans, watercress, tomatoes, olives, and basil. Pour the dressing over the salad and toss gently to combine. Serve immediately.

Serves 4

Panzanella (Tuscan Bread Salad)

I know firsthand how thrifty Italians can be—my grandmother once saved three peas left over from dinner to be used the next day. So this luscious salad, traditionally made with stale bread, comes as no surprise to me. The bread absorbs the surrounding flavors and becomes the focal point of the dish. I don't know about your house, but around my kitchen, good Italian bread doesn't last long enough to go stale, so I begin with a fresh loaf.

1 loaf Italian bread, crust removed, cut into ¾-inch cubes (about 5 cups)

1 shallot, halved

2 garlic cloves, crushed

2 tablespoons red wine vinegar

1 teaspoon chopped fresh oregano or ½ teaspoon dried oregano

½ teaspoon natural sugar

½ teaspoon salt

¼ teaspoon freshly ground black pepper

3 tablespoons olive oil

2 cups grape or cherry tomatoes, cut in half

½ large yellow bell pepper, seeded and chopped

½ cup kalamata olives, pitted and halved

¼ cup minced fresh flat-leaf parsley

Salad greens, to serve

1. Preheat the oven to 325°F. Spread the bread cubes on a baking sheet and bake until lightly toasted, turning occasionally, 15 to 20 minutes.

2. In a blender or food processor, combine the shallot, garlic, vinegar, oregano, sugar, salt, and pepper. Process until smooth. With the machine running, slowly add the olive oil in a steady stream through the feed tube, processing until blended.

3. In a large serving bowl, combine the bread cubes, tomatoes, bell pepper, olives, and parsley. Pour the vinaigrette over the salad and toss to combine. Let stand at room temperature for 15 to 20 minutes to let the flavors develop before serving over salad greens.

Serves 6

Fattoush (Lebanese Bread Salad)

Not to be outdone by the Italians, the Lebanese have their own delicious bread salad, which they make with stale pita bread. I use whole-wheat pita for added flavor and nutrition. The addition of chickpeas and tahini is a departure from the traditional, but they add lots of protein and turn this refreshing salad into a one-dish meal.

⅓ cup fresh lemon juice

3 tablespoons olive oil

2 teaspoons tahini

2 garlic cloves, mashed into a paste

½ teaspoon salt

Pinch of cayenne

2 large or 4 small pita breads

1 cup cooked or canned chickpeas, rinsed and drained

1 large cucumber, peeled, seeded, and chopped

1 large ripe tomato, seeded and chopped

½ small green bell pepper, seeded and chopped

½ cup minced red onion

⅓ cup chopped fresh parsley

⅓ cup chopped fresh mint

2 cups shredded romaine lettuce

1. Preheat the oven to 350°F. In a small bowl, whisk together the lemon juice, olive oil, tahini, garlic, salt, and cayenne until blended. Set aside.

2. Place the pitas on a baking sheet and bake until lightly toasted, turning once, 10 to 12 minutes. Remove from the oven, cut or tear into bite-size pieces, and place in a large bowl. Add the chickpeas, cucumber, tomato, bell pepper, onion, parsley, mint, and as much of the dressing as needed to coat. Toss well to combine, then let sit for 10 to 15 minutes to let the flavors develop.

3. Divide the lettuce among 4 salad plates, top with the salad, and serve.

Serves 4

Close to Mom's Potato Salad

My mom's potato salad always included diced hard-cooked eggs and sliced pimiento-stuffed green olives. I keep the olives in as a nod to nostalgia, but I'll pass on the eggs. This has all the great taste of a classic potato salad, but it's better for you because it's made with vegan mayonnaise. Look for vegan mayonnaise at natural foods stores or well-stocked supermarkets, or make it yourself.

2 pounds red or white waxy potatoes

1 celery rib, minced

1 carrot, grated

2 scallions, minced

¼ cup sliced pimiento-stuffed green olives

¾ cup vegan mayonnaise, homemade (page 125) or purchased

2 tablespoons rice vinegar

1 teaspoon Dijon mustard (or more to taste)

1 teaspoon salt

½ teaspoon freshly ground black pepper

Paprika

1. Place the potatoes in a large saucepan with salted water to cover. Bring to a boil over medium-high heat and continue to boil until tender, about 30 minutes. Drain and allow to cool.

2. Peel the potatoes, cut into bite-size chunks, and place in a large serving bowl. Add the celery, carrot, scallions, and olives. Set aside.

3. In a small bowl, combine the mayonnaise, vinegar, mustard, salt, and pepper. Mix well and add to the potato mixture, stirring gently to combine. Sprinkle the top with paprika. Serve right away or cover and refrigerate until ready to serve. This is best eaten within a day or two of being made.

Serves 4 to 6

Less-Dressed Potato Salad with Fennel and Chives

Sometimes less is more. Potatoes share the bowl with fennel in this salad that is lightly dressed in a simple lemony vinaigrette to let the flavors of the vegetables come through. As a variation, add some cooked green beans cut into 1-inch pieces.

2 pounds small red potatoes

1 cup minced fennel bulb

¼ cup niçoise olives, pitted

¼ cup chopped fresh chives

3 tablespoons olive oil

1½ tablespoons fresh lemon juice

1 teaspoon Dijon mustard

1 shallot, minced

½ teaspoon salt

¼ teaspoon freshly ground black pepper

2 tablespoons chopped fresh tarragon, dill, or basil

1. Place the potatoes in a large saucepan with salted water to cover. Bring to a boil over medium-high heat and continue to boil until tender, about 30 minutes. Drain and cut into halves or quarters, depending on the size. Transfer to a large serving bowl and add the fennel, olives, and chives. Set aside.

2. In a small bowl, whisk together the olive oil, lemon juice, mustard, shallot, salt, and pepper until blended. Pour the dressing over the potato mixture and toss gently to combine. Taste and adjust the seasonings. Serve right away or cover tightly and refrigerate until ready to serve. When ready to serve, sprinkle on the tarragon and toss to combine. This salad will keep in a tightly covered container in the refrigerator for up to 3 days.

Serves 4 to 6

Red Flannel Coleslaw

The term *coleslaw* comes from the Dutch, *koolsla*, for "cabbage salad." The vibrant red colors from the cabbage, bell pepper, radishes, and beets make this a pretty "cool" slaw in more ways than one.

2 medium-size beets

1 small head red cabbage, cored and shredded

½ small red bell pepper, seeded and minced

3 red radishes, shredded

2 tablespoons olive oil

2 tablespoons fresh orange juice

1 tablespoon fresh lemon juice

½ teaspoon natural sugar

½ teaspoon salt

¼ teaspoon celery salt

¼ teaspoon freshly ground black pepper

⅛ teaspoon Tabasco sauce

1. Place the beets in a medium-size saucepan, cover with water, and bring to a boil. Reduce the heat to low, cover, and simmer until just tender, about 30 minutes. Drain and rinse under cold running water, then peel and cut into matchsticks. Place in a large serving bowl along with the cabbage, bell pepper, and radishes. Set aside.

2. In a small bowl, whisk together the olive oil, orange juice, lemon juice, sugar, salt, celery salt, pepper, and Tabasco until blended. Pour the dressing over the vegetables and stir to coat. Taste and adjust the seasonings.

3. Cover and refrigerate for at least 1 hour before serving. Serve chilled.

===== *Serves 6 to 8* =====

Asian Coleslaw

Fragrant ginger and cilantro are just two of the great flavor elements in this Asian-style slaw. You can use napa cabbage, if you like, but I prefer regular green cabbage because it has a crunchier texture. Daikon is a large, white radish available in many supermarkets and Asian grocery stores.

3 cups shredded green cabbage	1 tablespoon toasted sesame oil
1 cup peeled and grated daikon radish	1 tablespoon neutral vegetable oil
1 large carrot, grated	2 teaspoons grated fresh ginger
2 scallions, minced	1 teaspoon low-sodium tamari
2 tablespoons chopped fresh cilantro	½ teaspoon natural sugar
2 tablespoons rice vinegar	½ teaspoon salt
1 tablespoon fresh lime juice	¼ teaspoon freshly ground black pepper

1. In a large serving bowl, combine the cabbage, daikon, carrot, scallions, and cilantro. Set aside.

2. In a small bowl, whisk together the vinegar, lime juice, sesame oil, vegetable oil, ginger, tamari, sugar, salt, and pepper until well blended. Pour the dressing over the vegetables and toss gently to coat well. Taste and adjust the seasonings.

3. Refrigerate, covered, until ready to serve. This slaw will keep for up to 3 days, although the flavors will get stronger the longer it sits. Serve chilled.

Serves 4

"Cool" Slaw

Coleslaw has a long history in America, having arrived in the 1620s with Dutch immigrants, who called it koolsla, which means "cabbage salad." Originally made with shredded cabbage and a boiled dressing, it now exists in many variations, including those made with vegetables other than cabbage.

Quinoa Tabbouleh

This classic Middle Eastern salad is normally made with bulgur, tomato, and loads of chopped parsley and mint. Here it is given a new twist with quinoa, the protein-rich "super grain" of the Incas, and yellow tomatoes, although red tomatoes may be substituted if yellow are unavailable. Be sure to rinse the quinoa well before using to remove the bitter white coating called saponin. Fresh cilantro replaces the mint, and tiny red adzuki beans are added for substance, although chickpeas make a fine substitute if adzuki beans are unavailable.

1 cup quinoa	¼ cup minced red onion or scallions
2 cups water	1 cup minced fresh parsley
Salt	3 tablespoons chopped fresh cilantro
2 medium-size ripe yellow tomatoes, chopped	3 tablespoons olive oil
1 cup cooked or canned adzuki beans, rinsed and drained	2 tablespoons fresh lemon juice
	Freshly ground black pepper

1. Wash the quinoa thoroughly to remove any trace of the bitter white coating, then rinse and drain.

2. Bring the water to a boil in a medium-size saucepan. Add salt to taste and the quinoa. Reduce the heat to low, cover, and simmer until all of the water is absorbed, about 15 minutes. Blot the quinoa with paper towels to remove excess moisture.

3. Place the quinoa in a large serving bowl and set aside to cool. Once cool, add the tomatoes, adzuki beans, onion, parsley, and cilantro.

4. In a small bowl, whisk together the olive oil, lemon juice, and salt and pepper to taste until blended. Pour the dressing over the salad and toss well to combine.

5. Cover and refrigerate for at least 1 hour before serving. For the best flavor, this salad should be served the day it is made. Serve chilled.

Serves 4 to 6

Three-Green Tabbouleh

This hearty grain salad gets a nutrition—and flavor—boost with three kinds of greens.

1½ cups water

¾ cup medium-grind bulgur

1 cup watercress leaves

1 cup arugula leaves

1 cup baby spinach leaves

½ cup parsley leaves

5 scallions, coarsely chopped

2 garlic cloves, crushed

4 tablespoons fresh lemon juice

2 tablespoons olive oil

Salt and freshly ground black pepper

1½ cups cooked chickpeas or 1 (15-ounce) can chickpeas, rinsed and drained

1 cup grape or cherry tomatoes, quartered

1. Combine the water and bulgur in a saucepan and bring to a boil. Salt the water and reduce the heat to a simmer. Cover and cook for 5 minutes, or until all of the liquid is absorbed. Set aside.

2. In a food processor, combine ½ cup each of the watercress, arugula, and spinach. Add the parsley, scallions, and garlic and pulse until finely chopped. Add the lemon juice, oil, and salt and pepper to taste. Pulse until combined. Place the remaining greens in a bowl and toss to combine.

3. Stir the finely chopped greens mixture into the cooked bulgur. Add the chickpeas and tomatoes and toss to combine. Taste and adjust the seasonings, if needed. Divide the reserved greens among 4 shallow bowls or serving plates and top with the bulgur mixture.

Serves 4

Ancient Grains on Wild Greens

Kamut, a large-grain member of the wheat family, is said to have its origins in ancient Egypt, while quinoa, a small protein-rich grain with a faintly popcorn-like aroma, is called "the mother grain" by the Incas. Together, they are tossed in a light vinaigrette and served on a bed of mesclun or mixed baby greens for a hearty salad that is visually appealing and full of great taste and nutrition.

3 tablespoons olive oil

1½ tablespoons balsamic vinegar

1 garlic clove, minced

1 teaspoon Dijon mustard

½ teaspoon salt

¼ teaspoon freshly ground black pepper

6 cups mesclun salad mix

1½ cups cooked kamut (page 198)

1½ cups cooked quinoa (page 198)

1 cup cherry or grape tomatoes, halved

½ English cucumber, peeled, halved lengthwise, and thinly sliced

1 large carrot, shredded

⅓ cup chopped toasted pecans or walnuts (page 203)

3 scallions, minced

1. In a small bowl, whisk together the olive oil, vinegar, garlic, mustard, and salt and pepper to taste until blended. Set aside.

2. Place the salad greens in a large bowl. Add about half the dressing and toss gently to coat lightly. Divide the dressed greens among 4 salad plates.

3. In the same bowl, combine the kamut, quinoa, tomatoes, cucumber, carrot, pecans, and scallions. Add the remaining dressing and toss gently to combine. Divide the grain mixture among the salad plates, mounding it in the center of each salad plate on top of the greens. Serve immediately.

Serves 4

Asian Noodle Salad
with Spicy Peanut Sauce

Crisp vegetables play nicely against the chewy noodles and creamy sauce. The salad components may be made ahead, covered, and refrigerated. When ready to serve, bring the sauce to room temperature, thinning with additional water, if necessary. Udon noodles are thick Japanese wheat noodles. If they're unavailable, linguine may be substituted.

⅓ cup peanut butter

¼ cup low-sodium tamari

2 tablespoons rice vinegar

1 teaspoon Asian chili paste or sriracha

2 garlic cloves, minced

1 teaspoon grated fresh ginger

½ teaspoon natural sugar (optional)

½ cup water

8 ounces udon noodles or rice noodles

1 tablespoon toasted sesame oil

1 large carrot, shredded

2 cups finely shredded napa cabbage

1 small red bell pepper, seeded and cut into matchsticks

1 bunch scallions, minced

1. In a medium-size bowl, combine the peanut butter, tamari, vinegar, chili paste, garlic, ginger, and sugar, if using. Stir to blend well. Add the water, stirring to make a creamy sauce. Set aside.

2. Cook the noodles in large pot of boiling water according to package directions. Drain and rinse the noodles under cold running water, then transfer to a large serving bowl. Toss with the sesame oil to coat.

3. Add the carrot, cabbage, bell pepper, and scallions to the noodles. Add just enough of the peanut sauce to coat, tossing gently to combine. Serve at room temperature.

Serves 4

Five-Spice Moroccan Couscous Salad

Heady Moroccan spices add an exotic touch to this colorful salad bursting with flavor. Although couscous is often thought of as a grain, it is actually bits of dried semolina.

2 tablespoons neutral vegetable oil

¼ teaspoon turmeric

¼ teaspoon ground cinnamon

¼ teaspoon ground ginger

¼ teaspoon ground cumin

¼ teaspoon cayenne

1½ cups instant couscous

2½ cups vegetable broth or water

3 tablespoons fresh orange juice

½ teaspoon natural sugar

Salt

1½ cups cooked chickpeas or 1 (15-ounce) can chickpeas, rinsed and drained

1 small red onion, finely chopped

½ large red bell pepper, seeded and cut into ¼-inch pieces

⅓ cup dates, pitted and chopped

¼ cup golden raisins

2 tablespoons minced fresh cilantro, for garnish

2 tablespoons chopped unsalted dry-roasted peanuts, for garnish

1. Heat 1 tablespoon of the oil in a medium-size saucepan over medium heat. Add the turmeric, cinnamon, ginger, cumin, cayenne, and couscous. Cook, stirring, until fragrant, about 2 minutes, being careful not to burn. Stir in the broth and bring to a boil. Reduce the heat to very low, cover, and cook until all of the liquid is absorbed, about 5 minutes. Remove from the heat and let stand for 5 minutes.

2. Transfer the couscous to a large serving bowl, using a fork to fluff it up. Set aside.

3. In a small bowl, combine the remaining 1 tablespoon oil, orange juice, sugar, and salt to taste. Stir to blend well and set aside.

4. To the couscous, add the chickpeas, onion, bell pepper, dates, and raisins. Add the dressing and toss gently to combine well. Garnish with the cilantro and peanuts and serve.

Serves 4

Springy Tarragon Pasta Salad
with White Beans and Roasted Asparagus

"Springy" because of the pencil-thin asparagus plentiful at that time of year, but also for the rotini pasta "springs" that are used in the salad. Fresh tarragon adds a sweetly aromatic accent.

1 pound thin asparagus, trimmed

8 ounces rotini

Salt and freshly ground black pepper

3 tablespoons olive oil

2 tablespoons fresh lemon juice

½ medium-size yellow bell pepper, seeded and chopped

2 shallots, minced

1 large ripe yellow tomato, seeded and diced

1½ cups cooked cannellini beans
or 1 (15-ounce) can beans, rinsed and drained

2 tablespoons minced fresh tarragon

1. Preheat the oven to 425°F. Lightly oil a baking sheet. Place the asparagus on the baking sheet and season to taste with salt and pepper. Roast until soft and lightly browned, about 10 minutes. Set aside to cool.

2. Meanwhile, cook the pasta in a pot of boiling salted water, stirring occasionally, until al dente, 8 to 10 minutes. Drain and rinse under cold running water. Transfer to a large bowl and set aside.

3. In a small bowl, combine the olive oil, lemon juice, and salt and pepper to taste. Pour the dressing over the pasta. Add the bell pepper, shallots, tomato, beans, and tarragon and toss to combine well. Divide among 4 individual plates and top with the asparagus. Serve immediately.

Serves 4

Fresh Herbs

Fresh herbs can work like magic to elevate an ordinary dish to the extraordinary. A sprinkling of minced fresh parsley, basil, tarragon, or chives can brighten almost any salad, grain, or vegetable dish in the same way a little thyme, oregano, or sage can do wonders for soups, stews, and stuffings. Because most fresh herbs are expensive and highly perishable, it is a wise and rewarding investment to plant your own. Whether grown in a few small pots on the windowsill or in a garden full of lush plants, a variety of fragrant herbs can be an indispensable tool for the creative cook.

Pasta Salad Niçoise

Classic *salade niçoise* ingredients team up with penne pasta for a great-tasting Mediterranean fusion salad perfect for al fresco dining. Accompany with grilled portobello mushrooms and crusty bread for a terrific meal.

8 ounces penne

2 cups green beans, trimmed and cut into 2-inch pieces

1½ cups cooked cannellini or other white beans or 1 (15-ounce) can beans, rinsed and drained

1 cup cherry or grape tomatoes, cut in half

⅓ cup niçoise or kalamata olives, pitted

2 tablespoons minced fresh parsley

2 tablespoons chopped basil

2 tablespoons white wine vinegar

1 garlic clove, minced

1 teaspoon Dijon mustard

½ teaspoon salt

¼ teaspoon freshly ground black pepper

Pinch of natural sugar

3 tablespoons olive oil

Salad greens, to serve

1. Cook the penne in a pot of boiling salted water, stirring occasionally, until al dente. During the last 3 or 4 minutes of cooking time, add the green beans to the pot. Drain the pasta and green beans and rinse under cold running water. Transfer to a large bowl and add the cannellini beans, tomatoes, olives, parsley, and basil. Toss gently to combine.

2. In a small bowl, combine the vinegar, garlic, mustard, salt, pepper, and sugar. Whisk in the olive oil and add to the pasta and vegetables. Toss gently to coat evenly. Taste and adjust the seasonings.

3. Divide the salad greens among 4 individual plates, top with the pasta salad, and serve.

Serves 4

Lighten Up Macaroni Salad

When I crave the old-fashioned macaroni salad I grew up with, I "lighten up" and make it with heart-healthy vegan ingredients. Serve it alongside grilled veggie burgers for a healthful cookout with all the trimmings.

8 ounces elbow macaroni

1 celery rib, minced

1 carrot, grated

⅓ cup fresh or thawed frozen baby peas

2 to 3 scallions, minced

½ cup vegan mayonnaise, homemade (page 125) or purchased

2 tablespoons plain unsweetened nondairy milk

1 tablespoon fresh lemon juice

1 tablespoon rice vinegar

1 tablespoon sweet pickle relish or 1 teaspoon natural sugar

½ teaspoon salt

¼ teaspoon freshly ground black pepper

1. Cook the macaroni in a pot of boiling salted water, stirring occasionally, until just tender. Drain, rinse under cold running water, and transfer to a large serving bowl. Add the celery, carrot, peas, and scallions. Set aside.

2. In a medium-size bowl, combine the mayonnaise, nondairy milk, lemon juice, vinegar, relish, salt, and pepper. Mix well. Add the dressing mixture to the pasta and mix well to coat evenly. Taste and adjust the seasonings.

3. Cover and refrigerate for at least 1 hour before serving. Stir before using. Taste and adjust the seasonings, if needed. Serve chilled.

Serves 4

Summer Sunshine Pasta Salad

Evocative of a summer day, seashell and butterfly pasta combine with broccoli florets and sunflower seeds for a whimsical ray of sunshine any time of year. If serving as an entrée, add cooked chickpeas or kidney beans to the salad.

8 ounces farfalle

¼ teaspoon turmeric

8 ounces small pasta shells

2 cups broccoli florets

Juice and grated zest of 1 orange

2 tablespoons fresh lemon juice

Salt

Cayenne

¼ cup olive oil

1 small yellow bell pepper, seeded and cut into thin strips

1 small red onion, chopped

1 cup cherry or grape tomatoes, cut in half

¼ cup hulled raw sunflower seeds

1. Cook the farfalle in a pot of boiling salted water, stirring occasionally, until al dente, 8 to 10 minutes. While the farfalle is cooking, add the turmeric to the water to turn the pasta a bright yellow color.

2. At the same time, cook the pasta shells in a separate pot of boiling salted water, stirring occasionally, until al dente, about 8 minutes. During the last 2 minutes of cooking time, add the broccoli. Drain both pastas and broccoli and rinse under cold running water. Transfer to a large serving bowl and set aside.

3. In a small bowl, combine the orange juice and zest, lemon juice, and salt and cayenne to taste. Whisk in the olive oil until blended, then pour the dressing over the pasta and broccoli. Add the bell pepper, onion, and tomatoes and toss to coat evenly with the dressing. Sprinkle on the sunflower seeds right before serving.

Serves 4 to 6

Pasta Salad: The Rinse Cycle

When cooking pasta for salad, be sure to rinse it after it's cooked. This will stop the cooking process and wash away the outer coating of starch, which would otherwise make your pasta gummy, sticking to itself and the other ingredients.

Pasta Salad with Jalapeño Pesto

Cumin, jalapeños, and lime juice add a piquant touch to this substantial salad, making it a nice change from the usual pasta salads. I usually go for penne pasta, but any bite-size pasta may be used. For less heat, use only one jalapeño.

3 tablespoons olive oil

1 teaspoon ground cumin, or to taste

8 ounces penne

1½ cups cooked pinto beans or 1 (15-ounce) can beans, rinsed and drained

1 large carrot, shredded

3 scallions, chopped

1½ cups grape tomatoes, halved

2 jalapeños, halved and seeded

2 garlic cloves, crushed

⅓ cup coarsely chopped fresh parsley

⅓ cup coarsely chopped fresh cilantro

2 tablespoons fresh lime juice

1 teaspoon chili powder

½ teaspoon natural sugar

½ teaspoon salt

Salad greens

1. Heat 1 tablespoon of the olive oil in a small skillet over medium heat. Add the cumin and stir until fragrant, about 30 seconds. Remove from the heat and set aside.

2. Cook the pasta in a pot of boiling salted water, stirring occasionally, until al dente, 8 to 10 minutes. Drain, rinse under cold running water, and place in a large bowl. Add the cumin-scented oil, along with the pinto beans, carrot, scallions, and tomatoes, and toss to combine. Set aside.

3. To make the pesto, process the jalapeños and garlic in a food processor until minced. Add the parsley, cilantro, lime juice, chili powder, sugar, and salt. With the machine running, add the remaining 2 tablespoons olive oil and process to form a smooth paste. If the pesto is too thick, add some water, a tablespoon or two at a time. Add the pesto to the pasta mixture and toss gently to coat.

4. Line 4 to 6 individual plates with the salad greens. Divide the pasta salad among the plates and serve at room temperature.

Serves 4 to 6

Tropical Pasta Salad
with Fresh Fruit and Coconut

Juicy fresh fruit and creamy coconut milk add a taste of the tropics to this colorful salad. Try it on a warm summer night served with jerk-spiced tempeh cooked on the grill. For a spectacular presentation, serve in hollowed-out pineapple shells (cut in half lengthwise).

8 ounces small pasta shells

2 cups fresh pineapple chunks

1 medium-size ripe mango, peeled, pitted, and cut into ½-inch pieces

1 navel orange, peeled, white pith removed, and cut into 1-inch chunks

1 small red bell pepper, seeded and cut into thin strips

⅓ cup minced celery

2 tablespoons minced scallions

2 tablespoons chopped fresh mint

½ cup unsweetened coconut milk

2 tablespoons fresh orange juice or pineapple juice

Juice and grated zest of 1 lime

½ teaspoon natural sugar, or to taste

⅛ teaspoon ground allspice or cinnamon

⅛ teaspoon cayenne

Salt

Salad greens, to serve

¼ cup unsweetened shredded coconut, toasted (page 453)

1. Cook the pasta in a pot of boiling salted water, stirring occasionally, until al dente, about 8 minutes. Drain, rinse under cold running water, and place in a large bowl. Add the pineapple, mango, orange, bell pepper, celery, scallions, and mint and set aside.

2. In a small bowl, combine the coconut milk, orange juice, lime juice and zest, sugar, allspice, cayenne, and salt to taste. Mix well. Pour the dressing over the pasta salad and toss gently to coat evenly.

3. Arrange the salad greens on 4 individual plates. Divide the pasta salad among the plates, sprinkle with the toasted coconut, and serve.

Serves 4 to 6

Sauces & Dressings

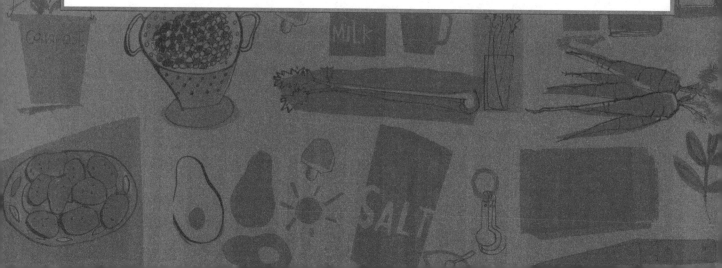

> "While we ourselves are the living graves of murdered beasts, how can we expect any ideal conditions on this earth?"
>
> —GEORGE BERNARD SHAW

From a simple vinaigrette to the temperamental hollandaise, the world of dressings and sauces is vast. Used to enhance and even define many salads, vegetables, pastas, and desserts, sauces can be the most important flavor elements of numerous dishes.

Included in the sweeping category of dressings and sauces are the roux-thickened brown and béchamel sauces, as well as egg-based hollandaise and mayonnaise, characteristic of the classic European kitchen. Thanks to the innovations of nouvelle cuisine in the 1970s, however, lighter sauces also have become popular. Although many traditional sauces are made with butter, cream, and eggs, as you will see in this chapter, even these can be made without dairy products, using soy products, nut butters, and bean purees instead. As an added benefit, sauces made with these protein-rich ingredients are low in fat and cholesterol-free.

Also included in this chapter are Asian soy-based sauces, oil-based dressings, tomato sauces, and many tempting toppings made with vegetable and fruit purees, ground herbs, beans, and seeds.

Many of the sauces presented here require no cooking, making them simple to whip up in a blender or food processor.

Vegan Mayonnaise

This is a low-fat, cholesterol-free version of the versatile condiment. Use it in any way you'd use the original—from sandwich spread to salad dressing. If you prefer the convenience of purchased, vegan mayonnaise is available commercially in natural foods stores and some supermarkets.

6 ounces soft silken tofu, drained

2 tablespoons rice vinegar

2 tablespoons neutral vegetable oil

1 teaspoon agave nectar

1 teaspoon salt

¼ teaspoon dry mustard powder

1. Combine all of the ingredients in a food processor or blender and process until smooth. Taste and adjust the seasonings, if needed.

2. Transfer to a glass jar or other container with a tight-fitting lid. Cover and refrigerate until ready to use, up to 5 days.

Makes about 1 cup

Vegan Sour Cream

This sour cream alternative couldn't be easier. Blend in some minced chives and try it on a baked potato, or use it in any recipe calling for sour cream.

6 ounces soft tofu, well drained and blotted dry

2 tablespoons rice vinegar

2 teaspoons tahini

½ teaspoon salt

Combine all of the ingredients in a blender or food processor and process until completely smooth. Taste and adjust the seasonings if needed. Transfer to a container with a tight-fitting lid. Cover and refrigerate until ready to use, up to 4 days.

Makes about 1 cup

Vegan Cream Cheese

Easy to make at home, this vegan cream cheese is more economical than buying it ready-made. You can use this in any recipe calling for vegan cream cheese.

1 cup raw cashews, soaked for at least 3 hours or up to overnight, then drained

1½ tablespoons fresh lemon juice

1½ tablespoons apple cider vinegar

1 teaspoon mellow white miso paste

1 teaspoon agave nectar

6 ounces firm silken tofu, drained and blotted dry

½ teaspoon salt

Combine the drained cashews, lemon juice, vinegar, miso, and agave in a food processor or high-speed blender and process until smooth. Add the tofu and salt and process until completely smooth and well blended. Transfer to a container with a tight-fitting lid, cover, and refrigerate until needed. Properly stored, it will keep well for up to 4 days.

Makes about 2 cups (about 10 ounces)

Cashew Cream

I love to use cashew cream to thicken soups, stews, and sauces; as a base for a creamy pasta sauce or sauce for vegetables; or as a dessert topping or filling. This recipe makes a basic cashew cream. To add a bit of tartness, add 1 tablespoon fresh lemon juice; to add sweetness, blend in 1 tablespoon natural sugar or pure maple syrup.

1 cup raw cashews, soaked for at least 3 hours or up to overnight, then drained

½ cup water, plus more as needed

¼ teaspoon sea salt (optional)

In a high-speed blender or food processor, combine the soaked and drained cashews with the water and salt (if using), and blend until completely smooth and creamy. For a thinner cream, add more water or a little plain unsweetened nondairy milk. This will keep, tightly covered, in the refrigerator for up to 4 days or in the freezer for up to 3 months.

Makes about 1½ cups

Easy Vegan Hollandaise

Healthful hollandaise may sound like an oxymoron, but with this eggless, butter-free version, you can literally dip your asparagus to your heart's content. Add the turmeric if you want a brighter yellow color.

⅔ cup vegan mayonnaise, homemade (page 125) or purchased

2 to 3 teaspoons fresh lemon juice

½ to 1 teaspoon Dijon mustard

Pinch of cayenne

Pinch of turmeric (optional)

Pinch of salt

Place all of the ingredients in a food processor or blender and process until smooth. This will keep, tightly covered, in the refrigerator for up to 3 days.

Makes about 1 cup

Cheesy Sauce

This all-purpose sauce can be used to top casseroles, vegetables, or tacos. It can also be blended with cooked pasta for mac and cheese.

1 cup raw cashews, soaked for at least 3 hours or up to overnight, then drained

1 cup water or plain unsweetened nondairy milk

½ cup nutritional yeast

2 tablespoons fresh lemon juice

1 teaspoon Dijon mustard

½ teaspoon garlic powder

½ teaspoon onion powder

½ teaspoon paprika

½ teaspoon vegetable broth powder

½ teaspoon salt

Combine all of the ingredients in a food processor or high-speed blender and process until smooth. Taste and adjust the seasonings if needed. This will keep, tightly covered, in the refrigerator for up to 3 days.

Makes about 2 cups

Nutritional Yeast

Nutritional yeast is an inactive yeast that is used as a food supplement and seasoning. It is yellow and has a distinctive, some say "cheesy," flavor. Because it has no leavening power, it cannot be used in baking. Nutritional yeast is extremely high in protein, B vitamins, and folic acid and very low in fat and sodium. Perhaps its greatest merit is that it provides vegans with a reliable, nonanimal source of vitamin B_{12}. Nutritional yeast will keep indefinitely if stored in a tightly closed container. It is widely available at natural foods stores and online under the Red Star label, as well as from other brands.

Red Bell Pepper and Caper Mayonnaise

The many mayonnaise-based sauces in French cooking can be used in all sorts of ways. Among the most versatile (and flavorful) are rémoulade, made with fresh herbs and capers, and andalouse, made with tomato and red bell pepper. I've combined elements of the two using vegan mayonnaise, resulting in a flavorful sauce that can be used on veggie burgers, on grilled or steamed vegetables, or as a binder for chopped vegetable salads.

1 cup vegan mayonnaise, homemade (page 125) or purchased

1 tablespoon tomato paste

¼ teaspoon Tabasco sauce

⅓ cup chopped roasted red bell pepper (recipe follows)

1 tablespoon capers, drained and minced

1 tablespoon minced fresh parsley

Salt

In a small bowl, combine the mayonnaise, tomato paste, and Tabasco. Stir in the roasted pepper, capers, parsley, and salt to taste. Blend thoroughly, then cover and refrigerate until ready to use, up to 5 days. Serve chilled.

Makes about 1¼ cups

ROASTED RED BELL PEPPERS

Roasting bell peppers gives them a deep, rich flavor, which may account for their amazing popularity on everything from salads and sandwiches to entrées and pizza. Although you can buy roasted red peppers in the supermarket, try making them yourself with fresh peppers. They are much more flavorful.

2 large red bell peppers

1. Hold the peppers over an open flame with a pair of tongs or place on a baking sheet under a preheated broiler until the skin is blackened on all sides.

2. Place the charred peppers in a paper bag and let stand for 5 minutes to steam. Remove from the bag and scrape off the charred skin. Cut the peppers open and remove the stem, seeds, and white ribs. The peppers are now ready to use in recipes.

3. Roasted peppers will keep for up to 1 week in the refrigerator if properly stored. For best results, place them in a tightly sealed container (a glass jar is ideal) and cover with olive oil.

Makes about 1½ cups

Rouille Redux

Try this egg-free version of the garlicky red mayonnaise from France on grilled or steamed vegetables or as a dipping sauce for crudités. It's also delicious as a spread on sandwiches or veggie wraps.

2 or 3 garlic cloves, crushed

⅓ cup jarred pimientos or coarsely chopped roasted red peppers, drained

1 cup vegan mayonnaise, homemade (page 125) or purchased

Pinch of cayenne

Salt

1. Place the garlic and pimientos in a blender or food processor and process until smooth. Add the vegan mayonnaise, cayenne, and salt to taste and process again until smooth.

2. Transfer to a tightly covered container and store in the refrigerator for up to 5 days.

Makes about 1¼ cups

Did You Know?

The shallot was considered an aphrodisiac in ancient Rome. One wonders if this was because the subtle-tasting shallot, unlike its odoriferous relatives, garlic and onions, does not cause bad breath.

Choron Sauce

Many years ago, I worked in a restaurant that served Choron sauce, an opulent variation of hollandaise that combined chopped tomato in a tangy béarnaise (a hollandaise flavored with a white wine, shallot, and tarragon reduction). Here's my vegan version, which tastes amazingly like the original. It's delicious served with grilled or steamed vegetables or sautéed seitan. I especially like it with the roasted cauliflower on page 179.

⅓ cup dry white wine

2 shallots, minced

1½ teaspoons minced fresh tarragon or ½ teaspoon dried tarragon

⅔ cup vegan mayonnaise, homemade (page 125) or purchased

Pinch of cayenne

Pinch of turmeric (optional)

Salt

1 large ripe tomato, peeled, seeded, and finely chopped

1. Place the wine, shallots, and tarragon in a small saucepan over medium-high heat and boil until the liquid is reduced by half.

2. Place the reduced wine mixture in a food processor or blender along with the vegan mayonnaise, cayenne, turmeric (if using), and salt to taste and process until smooth. Add the tomato and pulse to combine. Taste and adjust the seasonings if needed. Use immediately or transfer to a tightly covered container and refrigerate until needed. This will keep in the refrigerator for up to 3 days.

Makes about 1 cup

Vegan Béchamel Sauce

This rich white sauce is protein-rich, dairy-free, and utterly delicious. Use it anytime you want a creamy white sauce without the cream.

1 tablespoon neutral vegetable oil or ¼ cup water

1 small onion, chopped

1 tablespoon dry white wine

¾ cup raw cashews, soaked for at least 3 hours or up to overnight, then drained

1½ cups plain unsweetened nondairy milk

Pinch of freshly grated nutmeg

Salt and freshly ground black pepper

1. Heat the oil or water in a small skillet over medium-low heat. Add the onion, cover, and cook until softened, about 5 minutes. Do not brown. Stir in the wine and set aside.

2. Place the drained cashews and 1 cup of the nondairy milk in a high-speed blender or food processor and process until smooth. Add the onion mixture and the remaining ½ cup nondairy milk and process until thoroughly smooth.

3. Transfer to a medium-size saucepan over low heat. Season with the nutmeg and salt and pepper to taste. Serve hot.

Makes about 2½ cups

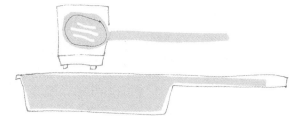

Vegan Mornay Sauce

Classic Mornay sauce is made by adding grated Gruyère or a similar cheese to a basic béchamel or white sauce. Thanks to the popularity of lighter sauces, you don't see this heavy, high-fat sauce all that much anymore. This creamy, cheesy sauce is great in mac and cheese and other casseroles or as a creamy adornment for steamed broccoli. Nutritional yeast is available at natural foods stores—it adds a "cheesy" flavor to recipes.

1 cup cooked or canned cannellini or other white beans, rinsed and drained

1 tablespoon chopped onion

2 tablespoons tahini

1 tablespoon mellow white miso paste

3 tablespoons nutritional yeast

½ cup plain unsweetened nondairy milk

2 tablespoons fresh lemon juice

½ teaspoon prepared yellow mustard

½ teaspoon salt

Pinch of cayenne

1. Place the beans, onion, tahini, miso, and nutritional yeast in a blender or food processor and process until smooth. Add the milk, lemon juice, mustard, salt, and cayenne, and process until creamy.

2. Use as is in casserole recipes. To use as a sauce for vegetables, warm in a saucepan over low heat, stirring constantly, being careful not to boil. Store leftovers in a covered container in the refrigerator for up to 4 days.

Makes about 1½ cups

Basic Brown Sauce

Instead of the traditional roux thickener (butter or oil and flour), this sauce is thickened with cornstarch. Additions to this infinitely versatile sauce include minced herbs, sautéed shallots, or a splash of wine. It also can be transformed into a creamy gravy with the addition of ¼ cup plain unsweetened nondairy milk. Use it like a gravy over mashed potatoes, rice, vegan meatloaf or burgers, stuffed portobellos, or sautéed seitan.

2 cups vegetable broth

2 tablespoons low-sodium tamari

1 tablespoon cornstarch dissolved in 2 tablespoons water

Salt and freshly ground black pepper

Combine the broth and tamari in a small saucepan over high heat and bring to a boil. Reduce the heat to low, whisk in the cornstarch mixture, and stir until the sauce thickens, 2 to 3 minutes. Season to taste with salt and pepper and serve hot. Store leftovers in a covered container in the refrigerator for up to 5 days.

Makes about 2 cups

Double Mushroom Sauce

Fresh and dried mushrooms deepen the flavor of this sauce, which can be used in the same ways as Basic Brown Sauce (page 134) but provides more texture and flavor. Die-hard mushroom lovers might want to use Mushroom Broth (page 59) instead of vegetable broth for a triple layering of mushroom flavor.

½ cup dried porcini or other dried mushrooms, soaked in 1 cup very hot water for 20 minutes

1 tablespoon olive oil or ¼ cup water

3 shallots, minced

1 cup sliced white mushrooms

1½ cups vegetable broth

1 tablespoon low-sodium tamari

Salt and freshly ground black pepper

1½ tablespoons cornstarch dissolved in 3 tablespoons water

1. Drain the soaked mushrooms, reserving the soaking liquid. Strain the liquid and set aside. Chop the mushrooms.

2. Heat the olive oil or water in a medium-size saucepan over medium heat. Add the shallots, cover, and cook until softened, about 5 minutes. Add all of the mushrooms and cook for 2 minutes. Stir in the broth, tamari, and reserved mushroom soaking liquid and season to taste with salt and pepper. Bring to a boil, then reduce the heat to low. Whisk in the cornstarch mixture and cook, stirring, until thickened, 2 to 3 minutes. Serve hot. Store leftovers in a covered container in the refrigerator for up to 4 days.

Makes about 2 cups

Summertime Tomato Sauce

For many of us, the window of opportunity for making sauce with fresh, ripe tomatoes is woefully brief, but if you have a bumper crop and want to dress your pasta with the fresh taste of summer, this is the way to go. You can also make a raw version of this sauce— just combine the ingredients, leaving the garlic whole but crushed. Let the sauce stand in a covered bowl at room temperature for one hour, then remove the garlic before tossing the sauce with hot pasta. In addition to pasta, I like to serve this simple, fresh-tasting sauce with steamed green beans or as a dipping sauce for fried potato sticks.

3 pounds ripe tomatoes

1 tablespoon olive oil or ¼ cup water

3 garlic cloves, minced

Salt and freshly ground black pepper

1 tablespoon chopped fresh parsley

1 tablespoons chopped fresh basil

1 teaspoon minced fresh oregano or ½ teaspoon dried oregano

1. Bring a large pot of water to a boil and prepare an ice water bath. Core the tomatoes by cutting out the stem end. Score a small X in the bottom of each tomato and plunge them into the boiling water for 30 seconds. Remove from the water and plunge into the ice water to stop the cooking process. Peel off the skins—they will come off easily. Cut each tomato in half crosswise and remove the seeds. Coarsely chop the tomatoes and set aside.

2. Heat the olive oil or water in a large saucepan over medium heat. Add the garlic and cook until fragrant, about 30 seconds. Add the tomatoes, season to taste with salt and pepper, and simmer for 20 minutes to reduce the liquid and thicken the sauce. Add the parsley, basil, and oregano, then taste and adjust the seasonings. This sauce can be frozen, but to fully appreciate the flavor of the fresh tomatoes, it's best to enjoy it within a day or two of making it.

Makes about 3 cups

Tomato Sauce in Winter

Actually, this is a good tomato sauce to serve in the spring, fall, and most of the summer, too—virtually anytime you don't have fresh, ripe tomatoes. Be sure you buy San Marzano tomatoes (available under various brand names at Italian markets and gourmet shops) for the best-tasting canned tomatoes. Omit the red pepper flakes if you prefer to delete the heat.

1 tablespoon olive oil or ¼ cup water

1 small onion, minced

1 large garlic clove, minced

2 tablespoons tomato paste

¼ teaspoon red pepper flakes (optional)

¼ cup dry red wine

1 (28-ounce) can crushed tomatoes

Salt and freshly ground black pepper

1 tablespoon chopped fresh parsley

Heat the olive oil or water in a large saucepan over medium heat. Add the onion and garlic and cook, stirring, until fragrant, about 1 minute, being careful not to burn the garlic. Stir in the tomato paste and red pepper flakes (if using) and cook, stirring, for 1 minute to heat through. Add the wine, blending until smooth. Stir in the crushed tomatoes and bring to a simmer. Reduce the heat to low, season to taste with salt and pepper, and cook for about 15 minutes to thicken the sauce, stirring occasionally. Stir in the parsley, taste and adjust the seasonings, and serve hot. This sauce freezes well.

Makes about 3½ cups

Bourbon-Spiked Barbecue Sauce

Use this sauce to make the tempeh recipe on page 317 or combine it with shredded seitan or vegan burger crumbles for a delicious meatless barbecue. To make this sauce kid-friendly, omit the chiles and substitute apple juice for the bourbon.

1 small onion, cut into quarters

2 garlic cloves, crushed

1 tablespoon olive oil or ¼ cup water

1 or 2 chipotle chiles in adobo, chopped

1 (6-ounce) can tomato paste

¾ cup water

¼ cup bourbon

¼ cup light or dark unsulphured molasses (not blackstrap)

¼ cup low-sodium tamari

2 tablespoons pure maple syrup

2 tablespoons cider vinegar

1 teaspoon dry mustard

Salt and freshly ground black pepper

1. Place the onion and garlic in a blender and process until smooth. Heat the olive oil or water in a large skillet over medium heat. Add the onion and garlic puree and cook, stirring a few times, to mellow the flavor, about 5 minutes.

2. Place the chipotles in the blender and process until smooth. Add to the onion-garlic puree along with the tomato paste, water, bourbon, molasses, tamari, maple syrup, vinegar, and mustard. Bring to a boil, then reduce the heat to low. Season to taste with salt and pepper and simmer, stirring occasionally, until the sauce thickens slightly and the flavor develops, about 15 minutes. This sauce will keep for several days, tightly covered, in the refrigerator. It also freezes well.

Makes about 2 cups

Marvelous Molasses

A byproduct of the sugar-refining process, molasses is a syrupy liquid that can vary in sweetness and color depending on what phase, or "boiling," it is extracted from. The finest-quality molasses is unsulphured molasses from the first boiling, which is quite sweet and light in color, especially compared to blackstrap molasses, which is dark, aromatic, and slightly bitter. Nutritionally, however, blackstrap shines. It is extremely high in iron and calcium and for that reason is more of a nutritional supplement than a sweetener, although some people enjoy its distinctive flavor in dark breads, baked beans, and spice cookies. Whether you choose light or dark molasses, be sure it is labeled "unsulphured." Sulphured molasses is made from immature green sugar cane that has been treated with sulfur fumes during the sugar-extracting process. The residue of this sulfur can remain in the molasses.

Gloria's Glorious Garlic Sauce

Necessity is often the mother of invention, and it was certainly true with this sauce. When her favorite brand of garlic sauce was no longer available, my friend and recipe tester Gloria Siegel wanted to develop a sauce to replace it. After much tinkering, we've come up with a versatile sauce that can be used on steamed or grilled vegetables or to perk up sauces and stews. I've even thinned it a little and used it as a salad dressing.

1 head garlic, top ½ inch sliced off	1 tablespoon cider vinegar
3 tablespoons olive oil, plus more for drizzling	1 tablespoon water, or more as needed
2 tablespoons blanched almonds	½ teaspoon salt

1. Preheat the oven to 350°F. Place the garlic head, with the skins still on, in a small baking dish. Drizzle with a bit of olive oil, cover tightly with aluminum foil, and bake until soft, about 45 minutes.

2. Squeeze the garlic cloves out of their skins into a blender or food processor. Add the almonds and process until smooth. Add the olive oil, vinegar, water, and salt and process until well blended. Add a little more water if a thinner consistency is desired.

3. Transfer to a container with a tight-fitting lid and refrigerate until ready to use, up to several days.

Makes about ⅔ cup

Avocado-Wasabi Sauce

My favorite sushi roll is made with creamy avocado strips and fiery wasabi paste. Although these two ingredients are the same color, their flavors couldn't be more different. Here this odd couple joins forces to make a lovely green sauce with an Asian accent. Use it to dress salads, to spread on sandwiches, or as a dipping sauce for fried tofu.

1 medium-size ripe Hass avocado, peeled and pitted

1 scallion, minced

½ cup vegan mayonnaise, homemade (page 125) or purchased

2 tablespoons fresh lemon juice

1 tablespoon chopped fresh cilantro or parsley

2 teaspoons wasabi paste

1 teaspoon toasted sesame oil

1 teaspoon low-sodium tamari

1. Combine all of the ingredients in a food processor or blender and process until smooth.

2. Transfer to a tightly covered container and refrigerate. This sauce is best used within an hour or so after it is made. Serve chilled or at room temperature.

Makes about 1½ cups

Mango Sunburst Sauce

This easy-to-make sauce boasts a gorgeous golden orange color and fresh mango flavor. Use it as a dipping sauce for spring rolls, samosas, or fried tofu. If you omit the rice vinegar and sriracha, you can transform it into a dessert sauce and serve it with cut fruit or sliced teacakes.

1 large ripe mango, peeled, pitted, and cut into chunks

Juice of 1 orange

1 teaspoon rice vinegar

½ teaspoon sriracha or other Asian chili paste

½ teaspoon natural sugar

1. Place the mango flesh in a blender or food processor with the remaining ingredients and process until smooth.

2. Transfer to a container, cover tightly, and refrigerate until ready to use. For best flavor, use this sauce within 24 hours of making it.

Makes about 1 cup

Yellow Pepper Coulis

This smooth puree of sweet yellow bell peppers is especially good with grilled or steamed vegetables, but it can also be used to add flavor and color to soups, salad dressings, or other sauces.

1 tablespoon olive oil or ¼ cup water

1 small onion, chopped

3 medium-size yellow bell peppers, seeded and chopped

¼ cup water

Salt and freshly ground black pepper

1. Heat the olive oil or water in a large skillet over medium heat. Add the onion and bell peppers, cover, and cook, stirring a few times, until softened, about 5 minutes. Add the water, season to taste with salt and pepper, and cook until the vegetables are very soft, about 15 minutes.

2. Transfer the cooked vegetables to a food processor or blender and process until smooth.

3. Push the mixture through a fine-mesh strainer into a small saucepan and heat over low heat. Use immediately or allow to cool, then refrigerate in a tightly sealed container for up to 3 days. Reheat over low heat.

Makes about 2 cups

Basil Pesto

Pesto isn't just for pasta. You can use it to flavor salad dressings, swirl it into soups at serving time, or serve it with grilled vegetables or sliced ripe tomatoes. But the variations don't end there. Experiment with the ingredients themselves for different taste sensations. Try parsley and walnuts, or mint and almonds, instead of the usual basil and pine nuts. Pesto will keep in the refrigerator for several weeks. Before refrigerating it in a tightly sealed container, spread a thin layer of olive oil on top to prevent it from discoloring.

3 garlic cloves, crushed

⅓ cup pine nuts or other nuts (see headnote), toasted (page 203)

½ teaspoon salt

3 cups loosely packed fresh basil or other herb (see headnote)

3 tablespoons olive oil

Finely grind the garlic, pine nuts, and salt together in a food processor or blender. Add the basil and process until minced. With the machine running, slowly add the olive oil in a steady stream through the feed tube until the pesto is blended into a paste. Transfer to a bowl, cover tightly, and refrigerate until ready to use. Add a little water to thin the pesto as desired.

Makes about 1½ cups

Black Bean Sauce
with Jalapeños and Cilantro

If you can't take the heat, eliminate the jalapeños, and the sauce will still be delicious. Use it over grain dishes, polenta, sautéed tofu slices, or burgers.

1 tablespoon olive oil or ¼ cup water

3 garlic cloves, chopped

1 or 2 jalapeños, seeded and chopped

1½ cups black beans or 1 (15-ounce) can beans, rinsed and drained

1 tablespoon low-sodium tamari

½ teaspoon ground cumin

½ teaspoon ground coriander

¼ teaspoon dried oregano

⅓ cup water, or more as needed

1 teaspoon fresh lime juice

2 tablespoons minced fresh cilantro

Salt and freshly ground black pepper

1. Heat the oil or water in a large skillet over medium heat. Add the garlic and jalapeños and cook for 1 minute. Stir in the beans, tamari, cumin, coriander, and oregano and simmer for 5 minutes to blend the flavors.

2. Transfer the mixture to a blender or food processor, add the water and lime juice, and process until smooth.

3. Transfer to a medium-size saucepan and add the cilantro and more water, if necessary, to get the consistency you prefer. Season to taste with salt and pepper. Heat over low heat, stirring, until hot.

Makes about 2 cups

Harissa

Use this Tunisian hot sauce in the traditional manner—to enliven vegetable tagines and similar stews from that part of the world—or use your imagination and let it spice up your life in unexpected ways: as a condiment for sautéed tofu or veggie burgers or as an addition to vegan mayonnaise or any sauce where you want a bit of flavorful heat.

½ cup dried chiles, seeded, cut into small pieces, and soaked in very hot water to cover for 30 minutes

1 tablespoon caraway seeds

2 teaspoons coriander seeds

3 small, fresh hot chiles, seeded

5 garlic cloves, crushed

½ teaspoon salt

¼ cup water

2 tablespoons olive oil

1 tablespoon white wine vinegar

1. Drain the dried chiles and set aside.

2. Place the caraway and coriander seeds in a small skillet over low heat and toast them until fragrant, 1 to 2 minutes, stirring frequently so they don't burn. Remove from the heat and grind finely in a spice grinder.

3. In a food processor, grind the fresh chiles, garlic, ground spices, and salt. Add the dried chiles to the processor along with the water, olive oil, and vinegar. Process into a smooth paste. Harissa will keep, tightly covered, in the refrigerator for several weeks.

Makes about 1 cup

Spicy Peanut Dipping Sauce

Serve this delicious and extremely versatile sauce with steamed vegetables or spring rolls (page 38), or toss with hot or cold cooked noodles.

⅓ cup peanut butter

¼ cup water, or more as needed

3 tablespoons low-sodium tamari

1 tablespoon rice vinegar

1 teaspoon minced garlic

1 teaspoon Asian chili paste

½ teaspoon natural sugar

2 tablespoons finely chopped fresh cilantro

1. In a small bowl or food processor, combine the peanut butter, water, tamari, vinegar, garlic, chili paste, and sugar until well blended. Taste and adjust the seasonings. Add more water if the sauce is too thick.

2. Use at once, or cover and refrigerate until ready to use. Stir in the cilantro just before using. Stored properly, this sauce will keep for up to 5 days.

Makes about 1 cup

Ginger-Lime Dipping Sauce

This light and refreshing sauce is ideal with the scallion pancakes on page 52. It can also be used to dress a salad.

1 scallion, finely chopped

1 garlic clove, minced

2 teaspoons grated fresh ginger

¼ cup low-sodium tamari

2 tablespoons fresh lime juice

1 tablespoon rice vinegar

1 tablespoon toasted sesame oil

½ teaspoon red pepper flakes

½ teaspoon natural sugar

1. In a small bowl, combine the scallion, garlic, and ginger. Stir in the tamari, lime juice, vinegar, sesame oil, red pepper flakes, and sugar. Blend well.

2. Cover tightly and refrigerate until ready to use. This sauce will keep for several days, but the flavors will intensify the longer it is kept.

Makes about ½ cup

Garlicky Herb Marinade

I especially like to use this marinade for tofu or portobello mushrooms. Sometimes I'll feature one herb prominently, and other times I'll include a pinch of virtually every herb in my garden. Feel free to vary the type and amount of herbs according to personal preference and availability—you'll need ¼ cup of minced fresh herbs in total.

3 large garlic cloves, chopped

½ cup low-sodium tamari

¼ cup olive oil

¼ cup white wine vinegar

¼ teaspoon salt

2 tablespoons minced fresh tarragon

1 tablespoon minced fresh basil

1 tablespoon minced fresh chervil

In a small bowl, combine the garlic, tamari, olive oil, vinegar, and salt. Whisk until well blended. Stir in the tarragon, basil, and chervil. Cover and refrigerate until ready to use. Be sure to use this marinade the same day you make it to ensure the fresh taste of the herbs.

Makes about 1 cup

Fresh Herb and Scallion Dressing

This creamy dressing is bursting with the flavors of fresh herbs, which can be varied according to personal taste and availability. Use it to dress romaine lettuce, sliced ripe tomatoes, or a cucumber salad. It also makes a flavorful topping for baked potatoes.

3 scallions, minced

½ cup Cashew Cream (page 127)

2 tablespoons fresh lemon juice

1 tablespoon cider vinegar

½ teaspoon Dijon mustard

⅛ teaspoon Tabasco sauce

Salt and freshly ground black pepper

¼ cup chopped fresh parsley

2 tablespoons minced fresh basil, tarragon, or dill

1. In a food processor, combine the scallions, cashew cream, lemon juice, vinegar, mustard, Tabasco, and salt and pepper to taste and process until smooth.

2. Transfer to a small bowl and stir in the fresh herbs. Stir in a little water, if desired, for a thinner dressing. Refrigerate, covered, until ready to use, up to 3 days.

Makes about 1 cup

Balsamic Vinaigrette with Garlic and Sun-Dried Tomatoes

The addition of heady garlic and smoky sun-dried tomatoes adds an assertive note to the traditional oil and vinegar pairing. This dressing can also be made in a bowl or a jar with a tight-fitting lid. Simply chop the tomatoes and garlic before combining them with the rest of the ingredients. Then whisk or shake well. It can be used on almost any salad, and it stands up well to strong-flavored greens.

3 oil-packed or rehydrated sun-dried tomatoes

2 garlic cloves, crushed

¼ teaspoon natural sugar

¼ teaspoon salt

⅓ cup olive oil

2 tablespoons balsamic vinegar

Freshly ground black pepper

Place the tomatoes, garlic, sugar, and salt in a blender or food processor and process until smooth. Add the olive oil, vinegar, and pepper to taste and blend well. This will keep, tightly covered, in the refrigerator for up to 1 week.

Makes about ¾ cup

Dressed for Success

The dressing can make or break a salad. No matter how crisp your lettuce, if the dressing you use is bitter, bland, or just plain blah, the entire salad will suffer. A good dressing doesn't have to be complicated—it just needs to enhance the flavors of the salad ingredients. It can be a simple vinaigrette consisting of nothing more than a good oil and vinegar blended in just the right amounts. Add a touch of salt and a grinding of pepper, and you can approach salad perfection. Extra-virgin olive oil is standard, but other flavored oils, such as hazelnut, walnut, or sesame oil, may be used. The choice of vinegar can range from the deeply flavored balsamic, to lighter-tasting vinegars such as sherry, wine, or champagne, to those infused with fresh herbs or fruits. Remember to toss your salads with the dressing just before serving to keep the greens from wilting.

Chutneys, Salsas, & Other Condiments

Like sauces, condiments such as chutneys and salsas can be the crowning glory of a meal, often providing the flavor that defines the dish with which it is served.

Condiments not only add their special flavors to vegan foods, but they also can provide the link to make foods taste like familiar family favorites. Slather ketchup on a veggie burger, and you've got a great-tasting burger. Serve cranberry sauce or relish with a seitan roast and mashed potatoes, and it's suddenly Thanksgiving.

This chapter traverses the globe to deliver a selection of delectable condiments to enliven your next meal. Choose from a number of fresh salsas, from refreshing *Cilantro–Green Tomato Salsa* to vibrant *Summer Sunshine Salsa*, made with a variety of yellow vegetables. Tangy chutneys include *Fresh Plum Chutney with Two Gingers*, *Five-Spice Pear Chutney*, and tasty *Fresh Mint Chutney*, which looks more like pesto than a typical chutney. All-American favorites with a twist include *Roasted Corn Relish with Smoked Chile Strips*, *Tangy Tomato Ketchup*, and dazzling *Cranberry-Walnut Relish*. Sophisticated condiments such as *Three-Onion Confit* and *Fennel Compote with Black Olives and Pine Nuts* can elevate even the simplest fare.

Eight Environmental Reasons to Go Vegan

Animal agriculture takes a heavy toll on the environment. Here are some of the consequences.

1. Since 1967, forests have been destroyed at a rate of 1 acre every 5 seconds to create grazing land for beef cattle to ensure the supply of inexpensive meat for our fast-food restaurants.
2. Runoff from animal waste is linked to a 7,000-square-mile "dead zone" in the Gulf of Mexico that no longer supports aquatic life.
3. At the present rate, many rain forests—a natural resource on which we rely for everything from lifesaving medicines to the very air we breathe—will be gone in 30 years.
4. Livestock produces 7 trillion tons of manure every year, and it all finds its way into our water systems.
5. Sixty percent of all water used in America is used for meat production.
6. It takes 16 pounds of grain and 2,500 gallons of water to produce 1 pound of meat. Yet 16 people can be fed on the grain it takes to produce that pound of meat. Growing that amount of grain requires only 250 gallons of water.
7. Countries such as Ethiopia and some Central American countries use their farmland to supply the United States with cheap burgers instead of growing healthful grain foods for their own starving people.
8. The livestock population of the United States consumes enough grain and soybeans to feed more than five times its human population.

Fresh Plum Chutney with Two Gingers

Fresh plums team up with two kinds of ginger in this fruity chutney, best made when plums are plentiful. Use underripe or barely ripe fruit for best results. You may use peaches instead of plums, if you prefer.

1½ pounds ripe plums

4 dates, pitted and chopped

3 shallots, finely chopped

½ small red bell pepper, seeded and minced

1 small, fresh hot chile, seeded and finely chopped

½ cup water

3 tablespoons natural sugar

2 tablespoons balsamic vinegar

1 tablespoon minced fresh ginger

1 tablespoon chopped crystallized ginger

⅛ teaspoon salt

1. Bring a large saucepan of water to a boil and prepare an ice water bath. Cut a small X in the bottom of each plum and place in the boiling water for about 30 seconds. Drain and transfer to the ice water. Peel the skins from the plums, then pit and coarsely chop.

2. Place the chopped plums in a medium-size saucepan over medium heat. Add the remaining ingredients and bring to a boil. Reduce the heat to low and simmer, stirring occasionally, until the fruit and vegetables have softened and most of the liquid has evaporated, about 30 minutes. Taste and adjust the seasonings. Let cool to room temperature before serving.

3. If not serving right away, cover and refrigerate until ready to serve. Bring back to room temperature for the best flavor. This chutney is best used within 3 days.

===== *Makes about 2 cups* =====

Three-Fruit Chutney

I like the balance of flavors here, with the tart apples, sweet pears, and dried apricots, but other fruits may be used, such as pineapple or peaches.

1 pound Granny Smith apples, peeled, cored, and chopped

1 pound ripe pears, peeled, cored, and chopped

1 cup dried apricots, chopped

1 small onion, minced

1 small, fresh hot red chile, seeded and minced

¾ cup natural sugar

¾ cup cider vinegar

2 tablespoons minced fresh ginger

1 tablespoon grated lemon zest

1 teaspoon ground cinnamon

½ teaspoon ground allspice

½ teaspoon salt

1. Place all of the ingredients in a large saucepan over medium heat and bring to a boil, stirring occasionally. Reduce the heat to low and simmer until the mixture is very thick, stirring frequently toward the end of the cooking time to prevent burning, about 45 minutes.

2. Let cool to room temperature, then refrigerate in a tightly sealed container (a glass jar is best) until ready to serve. This chutney will keep for several weeks in the refrigerator. Bring to room temperature before serving for the best flavor.

Makes about 3 cups

Five-Spice Pear Chutney

This chutney highlights the sweet taste of ripe pears complemented by the fragrant blend of five flavorful spices. I like to use a firmer pear, such as Anjou, for this recipe.

3 large ripe pears, peeled, cored, and coarsely chopped

1 small, fresh hot red chile, seeded and minced

½ cup minced onion

½ cup natural sugar

½ cup rice vinegar

¼ cup golden raisins

¼ teaspoon ground allspice

¼ teaspoon ground ginger

¼ teaspoon ground coriander

¼ teaspoon ground cloves

¼ teaspoon ground cardamom

1. Place all of the ingredients in a medium-size saucepan over medium heat and bring to a boil. Reduce the heat to low and simmer, stirring occasionally, until the pears and onion are soft and the liquid is syrupy, about 30 minutes.

2. Remove from the heat and let cool. This chutney will keep, tightly covered, in the refrigerator for several days. Serve at room temperature.

Makes about 2 cups

The Charm of Chutney

One of the most alluring things about chutney is its versatility. Traditionally thought of as an accompaniment to curries and other Indian meals, chutney has grown beyond expectations and can be used with a variety of dishes from sandwiches to stews. Chutney is especially delicious with vegan foods because it adds zest to grain and bean dishes. The possibilities for using chutney are as varied as the ingredients that can be used to make it. At once sweet and savory, chutney can be mild or hot and made with ingredients such as fresh or dried fruits, hot chiles, crystallized ginger, onions, and spices. Add some vinegar, sugar, and water, then simply simmer for a while until the liquid reduces and you have a thick consistency, and you have chutney. After you've made your first batch, you'll be hooked. Not only does the flavor of homemade chutney far surpass most store-bought varieties, but making your own chutney can be economical as well.

Dried Fruit Chutney

This easy, spur-of-the-moment chutney is made with pantry ingredients. Add raisins or dried cranberries, if you like.

1 cup dried apricots	½ cup natural sugar
½ cup chopped dried apples	½ cup cider vinegar
½ cup chopped pitted prunes	½ cup water
¼ cup dates, pitted and chopped	1 tablespoon minced fresh ginger
1 small onion, minced	1 teaspoon ground allspice
1 small dried chile, seeded and chopped	⅛ teaspoon salt

1. Soak the apricots in boiling water to cover for 15 minutes. Drain and chop the apricots, then place in a medium-size saucepan over medium heat. Add the remaining ingredients and bring to a boil. Reduce the heat to low and simmer, stirring frequently, until the chutney is thick, 30 to 40 minutes.

2. Let cool to room temperature. Store in the refrigerator in a tightly sealed container, where it will keep for several weeks. Serve at room temperature.

Makes about 2 cups

Fresh Mint Chutney

I've always enjoyed the fresh mint chutney at my favorite Indian restaurant, where they were kind enough to divulge the ingredients. When last summer yielded a bumper crop of fresh mint—it actually took over my garden—it was time to retrieve the ingredient list and concoct my own version of the fragrant condiment. It actually looks more like pesto than a traditional chutney, but it goes well with virtually any Indian dish. I've even used it as a dipping sauce for samosas.

2 large shallots, coarsely chopped

1 small, fresh hot green chile, seeded and coarsely chopped

1 teaspoon natural sugar

¼ teaspoon salt

2 cups tightly packed fresh mint

¼ cup water, or more as needed

1 tablespoon fresh lemon juice

1. Place the shallots, chile, sugar, and salt in a food processor and process until minced. Add the mint, water, and lemon juice and process until smooth, adding more water if a thinner consistency is desired.

2. Transfer to a small bowl, cover, and refrigerate for 30 minutes. Taste and adjust the seasonings before serving. Although this chutney will keep in the refrigerator for a day or so, I like to serve it shortly after making it, when the bright green color of the mint is at its best.

Makes about 1 cup

Summer Sunshine Salsa

This mild, sunny salsa comprises vibrant yellow vegetables, making it a striking topping for soups, stews, and chilis or a colorful addition to a taco bar. I especially like the way it looks as a garnish for black bean soup. For a hot version, add a minced fresh jalapeño or serrano chile. A little minced cilantro will add flavor and a touch of contrasting color.

1 pound ripe yellow tomatoes, peeled, seeded, and chopped

¼ cup chopped onion

1 small yellow bell pepper, seeded and chopped

Juice of 1 lemon

¼ teaspoon salt, or more to taste

2 tablespoons minced fresh cilantro (optional)

1. In a medium-size bowl, combine the tomatoes, onion, bell pepper, lemon juice, and salt. Cover and refrigerate until ready to serve.

2. When ready to serve, stir in the cilantro, if using. This salsa will keep, tightly covered, in the refrigerator for up to 5 days.

Makes about 2½ cups

Cooking in the Raw

As people become more aware that fresh fruits and vegetables are essential for good health, the raw, or "living," foods diet is gaining increased attention, especially from vegetarians and many nutrition professionals. The raw foods diet consists mainly of fresh fruits, leafy greens and other vegetables, soaked nuts and seeds, and occasionally soaked or sprouted beans and grains.

The main reason advocates of living foods eat raw foods is that they believe that cooking foods destroys the enzymes and most of the vitamins. They also believe that the human body is better suited to eating and assimilating plant foods rather than animal foods.

Although the stove may fall into disuse when you "go raw," your blender, food processor, or juicer will be humming as you prepare raw appetizers, entrées, and desserts. If you have a food dehydrator, you can make yummy pizzas, breads, cookies, and crackers with soaked grains, seeds, and nuts. It's easy to include more raw foods at meals and as between-meal snacks by eating more fresh fruits, raw vegetables, and salads.

Green Apple Salsa

The sweet-tart taste of Granny Smith apples is punctuated by the bite of jalapeños in this unusual salsa. Try it with grilled vegetables or as an accompaniment to grain dishes, stews, and sandwiches.

2 large Granny Smith apples, peeled, cored, and coarsely chopped

1 jalapeño, seeded and minced

⅓ cup minced scallions

Juice of 1 lime

Salt and freshly ground black pepper

¼ cup minced fresh mint

1. Place the apples in a medium-size bowl. Add the jalapeños, scallions, lime juice, and salt and pepper to taste and toss to combine. Cover and refrigerate until ready to use.

2. Just before serving, stir in the mint. Taste and adjust the seasonings, then serve. This salsa is best served within a few hours after it is made.

Makes about 2½ cups

Peeling and Seeding Tomatoes

When fresh tomatoes are used for cooking, the skin and seeds are often removed for a more appetizing appearance.

To peel tomatoes: Use a small knife to cut out the core or stem end of each tomato, then cut an X in the bottom of the tomato and place it in boiling water for 20 to 30 seconds. Using a slotted spoon, transfer the tomato to a bowl of ice water. The skin will peel off easily.

To seed tomatoes: Cut the peeled tomato in half crosswise and use your finger or a spoon to remove the seeds. The peeled and seeded tomato is now ready to use in recipes.

Fresh Tomato Salsa

This is an easy salsa to make when ripe tomatoes are plentiful. Omit the chile if you prefer a mild salsa or add a second one if you like it extra-hot.

3 large ripe tomatoes, peeled, seeded, and chopped

1 small, fresh hot chile (optional), seeded and minced

4 scallions, minced

1 garlic clove, minced

1 tablespoon fresh lime juice

¼ cup minced fresh cilantro

Salt and freshly ground black pepper

1. Combine the tomatoes, chile (if using), scallions, and garlic in a large bowl. Add the lime juice and cilantro, season to taste with salt and pepper, and stir to combine.

2. Cover and let stand at room temperature for 1 hour before serving. If not using right away, store in the refrigerator, tightly covered, where it will keep for up to 5 days. Bring back to room temperature before serving.

Makes about 2½ cups

Cilantro-Green Tomato Salsa

Green tomatoes give this salsa a refreshing piquancy that is missing from salsas made with ripe tomatoes.

1 pound green tomatoes, peeled, seeded, and chopped

¼ cup chopped onion

2 scallions, chopped

1 or 2 small, fresh hot chiles (optional), seeded and chopped

2 teaspoons fresh lime juice

¼ teaspoon salt

¼ cup minced fresh cilantro

1. Combine all of the ingredients in a medium-size bowl.

2. Cover and let stand at room temperature for 1 hour before serving. If not using right away, store in the refrigerator, tightly covered, where it will keep for up to 5 days. Bring back to room temperature before serving.

Makes about 2½ cups

Cranberry-Walnut Relish

Walnuts add crunch to this colorful no-cook cranberry relish flavored with citrus. Use as a condiment with sandwiches, veggie burgers, grain dishes, or stews, as well as a refreshing alternative to traditional cranberry sauce on Thanksgiving. Chopped pecans or almonds may be used instead of the walnuts.

1 orange, peeled, white pith removed

1 (12-ounce) bag fresh cranberries, picked over

¾ cup natural sugar

3 tablespoons orange marmalade

Juice of 1 lime

½ cup chopped walnuts

1. Remove the orange flesh from the membranes and place in a food processor. Add the cranberries, sugar, marmalade, and lime juice and process until coarsely chopped.

2. Transfer the mixture to a bowl and stir in the walnuts. Taste and adjust the seasonings. Let stand for at least 30 minutes to develop the flavors before serving. Serve cold or at room temperature. Stored tightly covered in the refrigerator, this relish will keep well for up to 5 days.

Makes about 3 cups

Roasted Corn Relish
with Smoked Chile Strips

The corn may be grilled instead of roasted, if you prefer. Cooked frozen corn kernels may be used when fresh corn is not in season, although you will not have that fresh-roasted flavor.

3 ears corn or 2 cups frozen corn kernels, cooked and drained

1 dried chipotle chile, soaked in very hot water to cover for 30 minutes

⅓ cup minced red onion

3 tablespoons olive oil

2 tablespoons minced fresh cilantro

1½ tablespoons fresh lemon juice

Salt and freshly ground black pepper

1. Preheat the oven to 450°F. If using fresh corn, peel back the husks from the corn, remove the corn silk, and pull the husks back up to cover the kernels. Place the ears on a baking sheet and roast until the outer husks begin to brown and the corn is fragrant, about 30 minutes. Remove from the oven and set aside to cool. Remove the husks. Using a sharp knife, cut the kernels from the cobs into a large bowl. Discard the cobs and husks.

2. Drain the chile and cut into thin strips. Add the chile, onion, olive oil, cilantro, lemon juice, and salt and pepper to taste to the corn. Mix well to combine, then cover and set aside to allow the flavors to blend, 15 to 20 minutes. Serve at room temperature. This relish will keep, tightly covered, in the refrigerator for a few days, but it is best eaten the same day it is made.

Makes about 3 cups

Carole's Chow-Chow

At the end of each summer, my sister, Carole, uses bushels of fresh produce to make 30 quarts of chow-chow, a delicious mixed-vegetable relish with Pennsylvania Dutch origins. I've managed to scale down her ambitious recipe to just 3 quarts for those who prefer to make smaller batches. The flavor of the chow-chow improves if it's allowed to marinate for several days before use. Properly stored, it will keep for several months in the refrigerator.

2 medium-size carrots	½ head cauliflower
2 celery ribs	Salt
1 large onion	1½ cups prepared yellow mustard
1 small red bell pepper, seeded	1½ cups cider vinegar
4 ounces green beans	1¼ cups natural sugar
½ small head green cabbage	2 cups frozen lima beans

1. Peel, trim, and/or core all the fresh vegetables as needed, then cut into bite-size pieces. Place in a large bowl and salt well. Cover and let stand at room temperature for several hours or overnight.

2. In a large bowl, combine the mustard, vinegar, and sugar and blend until smooth. Set aside.

3. Drain the vegetables well and place them in a large pot with just enough water to cover. Bring to a boil, then reduce the heat to medium and add the lima beans. Pour off about 2 cups of the cooking liquid, add the mustard sauce, and simmer until the vegetables are crisp-tender, about 20 minutes.

4. Let cool, then transfer the vegetables and sauce to containers with tight-fitting lids (pint- or quart-size glass jars are ideal) and store in the refrigerator until ready to use.

Makes about 3 quarts

Fennel Compote
with Black Olives and Pine Nuts

Serve this flavorful condiment over golden fried tofu, or double the recipe, add a little extra olive oil, and use it as a pasta sauce.

1 large fennel bulb, trimmed and diced	¼ cup pine nuts, toasted (page 203)
3 tablespoons fresh lemon juice	3 tablespoons chopped fresh parsley
2 shallots, minced	2 tablespoons pitted and halved black olives
2 teaspoons grated lemon zest	3 tablespoons olive oil
Salt and freshly ground black pepper	

In a medium-size bowl, toss the fennel with the lemon juice. Stir in the shallots, lemon zest, and salt and pepper to taste. Add the pine nuts, parsley, and olives. Drizzle with the olive oil and stir to combine. Taste and adjust the seasonings, then serve at once to fully appreciate the fresh taste and color of the ingredients.

Makes about 2 cups

Knife Knowledge

No matter how many fancy kitchen gadgets you may have, a good set of knives is among the most important. A well-equipped cook can get by with only a few carefully chosen knives for most jobs: a small paring knife, a medium-size paring knife, a 10-inch chef's knife, and a serrated knife will do the trick. Many home cooks prefer stainless steel knives because they don't rust or react chemically with food, but many professional chefs prefer high-carbon steel knives because they are easy to keep well sharpened. It is important, however, to wash and dry them immediately after each use. Another option is a set of Japanese ceramic knives, which stay sharp and are good for delicate work. A sharp knife can actually be safer than a dull one, as it keeps you from forcing the knife and possibly losing your grip. In addition, a well-sharpened knife can make short work of almost any cutting job.

Three-Onion Confit

A confit is traditionally made with ingredients that are cooked slowly in animal fat. This version uses flavorful and heart-healthy olive oil to cook three kinds of onions. Use this confit as an accompaniment to sautéed seitan, or serve with hearty grain and bean dishes. It also makes a sophisticated condiment for veggie burgers.

¼ cup olive oil

1 large red onion, chopped

3 shallots, chopped

5 to 6 scallions, chopped

1 teaspoon cider vinegar

1 teaspoon natural sugar

Salt and freshly ground black pepper

1. In a medium-size saucepan, combine the olive oil, onion, shallots, and scallions. Cover and cook over low heat until the onions begin to soften, about 10 minutes. Stir in the vinegar, sugar, and salt and pepper to taste. Continue to cook until the mixture is thick and syrupy, about 30 minutes. Stir occasionally to make sure it doesn't stick to the bottom of the pan.

2. Taste and adjust the seasonings, then set aside to cool. Serve at once, or cover and refrigerate until ready to use. Bring back to room temperature before serving. If not using right away, cover and store in the refrigerator, where it will keep for several days.

Makes about 2 cups

Roasted Garlic and Lemon Marmalade

The mellow flavor of the garlic is accented by the fresh taste of lemons. Enjoy this unusual condiment with fried tofu or grilled vegetables.

2 heads garlic

1 tablespoon olive oil

⅓ cup water

Juice and grated zest of 2 lemons

½ cup natural sugar

½ teaspoon salt

⅛ teaspoon freshly ground black pepper

1. Preheat the oven to 375°F. Place the garlic in a shallow baking pan and drizzle with the olive oil. Add the water to the pan and cover tightly with aluminum foil. Bake until the garlic is soft, about 1 hour. Allow to cool.

2. Squeeze the garlic cloves from their skins into a medium-size saucepan, mashing them slightly. Add the remaining ingredients, cover, and cook over low heat until the mixture cooks down and becomes syrupy, about 20 minutes. Stir occasionally to make sure it doesn't stick to the bottom of the pan.

3. Taste and adjust the seasonings. Let cool to room temperature, then refrigerate in a tightly sealed container until ready to use. This marmalade will keep well for up to 5 days. Serve at room temperature.

Makes about 1 cup

Quick Kimchi

Made with the requisite cabbage, garlic, and chiles, this piquant Korean condiment is a good accompaniment to stir-fries and Asian-style rice dishes.

1 medium-size head napa cabbage, cored and coarsely chopped

1 medium-size carrot, cut into thin diagonal slices

5 to 6 scallions, cut into thin diagonal slices

⅓ cup rice vinegar

2 garlic cloves, mashed into a paste

2 tablespoons toasted sesame oil

2 tablespoons low-sodium tamari

1 tablespoon grated fresh ginger

½ teaspoon natural sugar

1 teaspoon red pepper flakes, or more to taste

½ teaspoon salt

1. In a large bowl, combine the cabbage, carrot, and scallions and set aside.

2. In a small bowl, combine the remaining ingredients with ½ cup water and blend well.

3. Pour the sauce over the vegetables and stir to combine. Cover and let marinate at room temperature for at least 30 minutes before serving. If not using right away, cover and store in the refrigerator, where it will keep for several days. Serve at room temperature.

Makes about 6 cups

Cucumber-Mint Raita

Cooling cucumber raita is a refreshing way to tone down the heat of a spicy Indian meal.

1 cup plain vegan yogurt

1 English cucumber, peeled, seeded, and chopped

Salt and freshly ground black pepper

¼ cup chopped fresh mint

Place the yogurt in a medium-size bowl. Add the cucumber and season to taste with salt and pepper. Cover and refrigerate for 30 minutes. When ready to serve, stir in the mint. Serve chilled. Leftovers don't keep very well because the cucumbers release their liquid and the mint gets very limp, so try to use it on the same day that it's made.

Serves 4

Tangy Tomato Ketchup

Homemade ketchup not only tastes better than bottled, but it also can be customized to suit your palate. This recipe is much less sweet than purchased ketchup and the flavor is more complex.

1 ancho or other dried chile, soaked in very hot water to cover for 30 minutes

1 tablespoon olive oil or ¼ cup water

1 small onion, chopped

1 garlic clove, chopped

3 cups diced fresh tomatoes

¼ cup tomato paste

3 tablespoons natural sugar

1 teaspoon salt

1 teaspoon ground allspice

½ teaspoon paprika

½ teaspoon dry mustard

Cayenne

½ cup cider vinegar

1. Drain, seed, and chop the chile. Set aside.

2. Heat the olive oil or water in a medium-size saucepan over medium heat. Add the onion and garlic, cover, and cook until softened, about 5 minutes. Stir in the tomatoes, tomato paste, and chile and simmer for 15 minutes.

3. Put the mixture through a food mill or puree in a food processor, then push through a fine-mesh strainer back into the saucepan. Add the sugar, salt, allspice, paprika, mustard, and cayenne to taste. Cook over medium heat, stirring occasionally, until thick, about 30 minutes. Stir in the vinegar and cook, stirring occasionally, until thick, about 15 minutes. Allow to cool.

4. Refrigerate in a tightly sealed container until ready to use. The ketchup will keep for 2 weeks in the refrigerator or for several months in the freezer.

Makes about 2 cups

Veggies in the Middle

> "Non-violence leads to the highest ethics, which is the goal of all evolution. Until we stop harming all other living beings, we are still savages."

—THOMAS A. EDISON

It has always amazed me how, with one sweeping expression, our society has relegated vegetables to a culinary afterthought with the phrase "a side of vegetables," as if to say that vegetables by definition have less importance than the meaty entrée. Few would argue that Americans would be a healthier lot if they started enjoying their vegetables "in the middle" rather than "on the side."

With the huge variety of vegetables available today, it can be a simple matter to eat the USDA-recommended "five per day"—and then some. Vegetables prepared simply, especially at the peak of their season, can be the best way for you to enjoy their true flavor—lightly steamed, grilled, or roasted, with little or no adornment beyond a grinding or two of pepper and a squeeze of lemon. What could be easier or better tasting? Or more nutritious, since raw or lightly cooked vegetables retain the most enzymes and other nutrients.

When you consider the versatility and range of vegan ingredients, it becomes clear that there is a place for vegetables on the side, in the middle, and everywhere in between. By preparing vegetables using different cooking methods and seasonings, you can experience the full spectrum of textures and flavors. For example, *Szechuan String Beans* can be served as an entrée over rice or as an accompaniment to fried tofu or braised tempeh. Mashed potatoes can be served alongside a vegan meat loaf or seitan roast as easily as they can become the anchor of a dazzling vegetable platter. Imagine a bed of mashed potatoes surrounded by lightly steamed asparagus, crisp roasted root vegetables, and wine-braised mushrooms, or a vegetable ragout served with a raw vegetable salad or relish.

The fact is, where vegetables are concerned, there are no rules. No longer limited by the meat-starch-vegetable trinity of the past, we are free to expand our repertoires and explore vegetable preparations the world over.

Of course, it's a good idea to purchase seasonal vegetables at their peak, for that is when they are most flavorful and most economically priced. I believe that the body responds to cycles, enjoying heavier, hot, slower-cooked foods in winter and lighter foods in summer. However, since most vegetables are now available year round, when you do get a craving for that springtime asparagus in the midst of winter, you can satisfy it.

I've included a broad sampling of vegetable recipes in this chapter to spur your imagination and show how particular cooking methods or ethnic nuances can transform everyday vegetables into exciting new flavor experiences. Although this chapter barely scratches the surface of ways to prepare vegetables, I hope it provides a springboard for you to explore the amazing choices at your disposal.

Roasted Vegetables
with Lemony White Bean Sauce

Although the vegetables are roasted together, each one retains its own unique flavor and texture, adding interest and variety to the dish. This recipe provides only one suggested combination, but you can substitute other vegetables according to your own taste. For example, try red onion instead of sweet onion, sweet potato instead of Yukon Gold, cauliflower instead of Brussels sprouts, and so on.

The sublime white bean sauce is rich-tasting but low in fat, and adds protein and other nutrients to your meal. The vegetables and sauce are delicious as is or served over rice, quinoa, or pasta. Sautéed sliced vegan sausage or toasted pecans or walnuts can be added as well, and a sprinkling of your favorite fresh herb just before serving adds a lovely flavor and color contrast.

VEGETABLES

1 sweet onion, diced

2 cups peeled and diced butternut or other winter squash

2 cups Brussels sprouts, halved lengthwise

2 carrots, cut diagonally into ½-inch slices

1 large Yukon Gold potato, peeled if desired, cut into 1-inch chunks

1 tablespoon olive oil

Salt and freshly ground black pepper

SAUCE

2 cups cooked or canned cannellini beans

½ cup vegetable broth

2 tablespoons fresh lemon juice

2 tablespoons nutritional yeast

½ teaspoon garlic powder

½ teaspoon salt, or more if needed

⅛ teaspoon cayenne

1 tablespoon minced fresh basil, parsley, tarragon, cilantro, chives, or sage (optional)

1. To make the vegetables: Preheat the oven to 425°F. Line a rimmed baking sheet with parchment paper or spray it with cooking spray. Combine the vegetables with the oil and salt and pepper to taste, tossing to coat. Arrange the vegetables in a single layer on the prepared baking sheet. Roast the vegetables until tender and slightly caramelized, about 45 minutes, turning them once about halfway through.

2. To make the sauce: While the vegetables are roasting, combine all of the sauce ingredients (except for the optional herbs) in a food processor or blender and process until smooth. The amount of salt needed will depend on the saltiness of your broth. Transfer the sauce to a small saucepan and heat until hot, stirring so it doesn't stick. Keep warm. To serve, transfer the vegetables to a large serving bowl and drizzle with the sauce. Sprinkle with your herb of choice, if using. Serve hot.

Serves 4

Szechuan String Beans

My version of this classic Chinese vegetable dish is made with considerably less oil than the original, but it still has loads of flavor. Make it with regular green beans, or use Chinese long beans (also called yard-long beans), if you can find them.

1½ pounds green beans, trimmed	3 shallots, minced
3 tablespoons low-sodium tamari	2 garlic cloves, minced
1 tablespoon toasted sesame oil	3 tablespoons minced scallions
1 tablespoon mirin	2 teaspoons grated fresh ginger
½ teaspoon natural sugar	½ to 1 teaspoon red pepper flakes
1 tablespoon neutral vegetable oil	

1. Lightly steam the green beans over boiling water until just tender, about 5 minutes. Rinse under cold running water to stop the cooking process and set the color. Drain and set aside.

2. In a small bowl, combine the tamari, sesame oil, mirin, and sugar and set aside.

3. Heat the oil in a wok or large skillet over medium-high heat. When the oil is hot, add the beans, a handful at a time, and stir-fry for 30 seconds, transferring the cooked beans with a slotted spoon to a platter, until all of the beans are cooked.

4. Let the oil reheat, then add the shallots, garlic, scallions, ginger, and red pepper flakes and stir-fry for 10 seconds. Return the beans to the wok and stir-fry for 30 seconds. Add the tamari mixture and stir-fry until the beans are hot and coated with sauce, about 30 seconds. Serve immediately.

Serves 4

Mahogany Eggplant

Tender slices of Japanese eggplant are steeped in a flavorful tamari broth, which imbues it with a rich mahogany color. I like to use small Japanese eggplants, but regular eggplants may be substituted, if necessary. To prepare this dish on the grill, brush the eggplant slices with a small amount of the sauce, then heat the remaining sauce separately to top the grilled eggplant.

2 tablespoons neutral vegetable oil

3 Japanese eggplants, cut into ¼-inch-thick diagonal slices

3 scallions, chopped

2 garlic cloves, minced

2 teaspoons grated fresh ginger

¼ cup water

3 tablespoons low-sodium tamari

2 tablespoons sake or dry white wine

1 teaspoon Asian chili paste

½ teaspoon natural sugar

1. Heat 1 tablespoon of the oil in a large skillet over medium-high heat. Add the eggplant in batches and cook until browned on both sides, about 10 minutes total. Transfer to a plate and set aside.

2. Heat the remaining 1 tablespoon oil in the same skillet over medium heat. Add the scallions, garlic, and ginger and cook, stirring, until fragrant, about 30 seconds. Stir in the water, tamari, sake, chili paste, and sugar and simmer for 2 to 3 minutes, stirring to blend. Return the eggplant to the pan, tossing to coat it with the sauce. Cover and simmer until tender, about 10 minutes. Serve hot.

Serves 4

Roasted Sesame Asparagus

Once you begin roasting asparagus, you'll wonder why you ever prepared it any other way. Toasted sesame seeds and sesame oil give this recipe a decidedly Asian accent. For a Western approach, leave the spears whole and roast them with a small amount of olive oil instead of vegetable oil, then omit the sesame.

1½ to 2 pounds thin asparagus, trimmed
1½ tablespoons neutral vegetable oil
Salt and freshly ground black pepper

2 tablespoons sesame seeds, toasted (see below)
1 tablespoon toasted sesame oil

1. Preheat the oven to 450°F. Cut the asparagus diagonally into 2-inch pieces and place in a bowl. Drizzle with the vegetable oil and season to taste with salt and pepper. Toss to coat, then spread on a baking sheet in a single layer.

2. Roast the asparagus until just tender, 6 to 8 minutes, depending on the thickness.

3. Transfer to a bowl, sprinkle with the sesame seeds, and drizzle with the sesame oil. Toss to coat and serve hot.

Serves 4

Toasted Sesame Seeds

Toasting brings out the nutty flavor of sesame seeds. Because they are so small, it is best to toast them in a skillet on top of the stove, where you can keep a close eye on them, rather than in the oven.

Place the sesame seeds in a skillet over medium heat and toast, stirring once or twice, until fragrant and lightly browned, 2 to 4 minutes. Once the seeds are toasted to your liking, remove them from the skillet so they don't continue to brown from the residual heat in the pan.

Crispy Kale Strips

This is a foundational recipe with lots of room for variation. I prefer strips, but you can cut or tear your kale into squarish shapes if you prefer. You can also season however you like—toss with nutritional yeast, your favorite herbs, or a spice blend such as curry or Jamaican jerk seasoning.

1 bunch kale   Salt

1 tablespoon olive oil

1. Preheat the oven to 325°F. Remove any thick stems from the kale. After washing the kale leaves, dry them well in a salad spinner or in a clean dishtowel—they should be very dry in order to get crispy. Stack the leaves and cut them into thin strips.

2. Transfer to a bowl and drizzle with the olive oil, tossing to coat. Transfer the kale strips to a baking sheet in a single layer. Bake for 15 minutes, remove any pieces that are crisp and flip any pieces that are not, and return to the oven until crisp, about 10 minutes longer. Remove from the oven and sprinkle with salt to taste.

Makes about 5 cups

Sautéed Green Beans
with Tomatoes and Garlic

This colorful sauté goes well with a variety of dishes. As a "side," it makes a nice pairing for sautéed tofu, tempeh, or seitan. If you cut the beans into 1- to 2-inch lengths, the recipe can be used as a topping for baked potatoes or rice or tossed with pasta.

1 pound green beans, trimmed

1 tablespoon olive oil or ¼ cup water

1 small red onion, chopped

3 garlic cloves, minced

1 (14.5-ounce) can diced tomatoes, drained

Salt and freshly ground black pepper

1 tablespoon chopped fresh basil

1. Lightly steam the green beans over boiling water until just tender. Rinse under cold running water to set the color and stop the cooking process. Drain and set aside.

2. Heat the oil or water in a large saucepan over medium heat. Add the onion, cover, and cook until softened, about 5 minutes. Add the garlic and cook until fragrant, about 30 seconds. Add the green beans, tomatoes, and salt and pepper to taste. Simmer, stirring occasionally, until the vegetables are hot and the flavors are well combined, about 10 minutes. Add the basil and toss to combine. Serve hot.

Serves 4

Orange-Roasted Beets and Shallots with Orange Gremolata

I prefer to make this dish with small, sweet beets, but if the larger ones are all you can find, cut them into quarters to reduce the cooking time. If you prefer to omit the gremolata, you can garnish the beets with chopped fresh parsley or mint and a little grated orange zest.

2 tablespoons frozen orange juice concentrate, thawed

1 tablespoon olive oil

8 small beets, trimmed, well scrubbed, and halved

4 large shallots, halved

Salt and freshly ground black pepper

2 tablespoons Orange Gremolata (recipe follows), for garnish

1. Preheat the oven to 450°F. Lightly oil a baking dish. In a small bowl, combine the orange juice concentrate and oil, stirring to blend.

2. Place the beets and shallots in the prepared baking dish and add the orange juice mixture, stirring to coat. Spread out in a single layer and season to taste with salt and pepper.

3. Cover the baking dish tightly and roast until the beets are soft and the shallots are caramelized, about 50 minutes, stirring halfway through. Remove the beet peels—they should come off easily.

4. Serve hot, garnished with a sprinkling of the gremolata.

Serves 4

ORANGE GREMOLATA

This variation on traditional gremolata is made with oranges and mint and uses shallots instead of garlic. It's a great garnish for black bean soup and roasted vegetables, but it can be used anytime you want to punch up the flavor of a dish with the sweet-fresh taste of orange and mint.

Grated zest of 1 orange

1 large shallot, chopped

⅓ cup chopped fresh mint

Mince the orange zest, shallot, and mint together until well combined. Place in a tightly sealed container and refrigerate until ready to use. It is best used the same day it is made, although it will keep, tightly covered, in the refrigerator for a day or two.

===== *Makes about ⅓ cup* =====

Kitchen Timesavers

Too busy to cook? Here are some great ways to save time in the kitchen.

1. Plan ahead. It can be easier than it sounds. List your family's favorite dishes and rotate them regularly—use a calendar, if it's easier. When you plan your meals in advance, you can schedule easy dishes such as veggie burgers, stir-fries, or make-ahead one-dish meals for busy nights.
2. Keep your pantry, refrigerator, and freezer organized and well stocked with a variety of healthy "convenience" foods, such as canned beans, couscous, quick-cooking pasta, frozen vegetarian burger crumbles, and an arsenal of condiments for last-minute inspirations.
3. Give leftovers a makeover. Make a double recipe, serving it one way the first time, then transforming it into something else for a future meal. For instance, you can turn leftover roasted vegetables into a soup, stew, or potpie or combine them with beans and pasta or rice.
4. Once a week, have a cooking marathon, where you prepare several dishes for the week. Once you put on a pot of chili and a hearty soup, they cook themselves. While they simmer, put together a casserole, stuffed peppers, or maybe a rice dish.
5. Cook double recipes of beans, grains, and other dishes and freeze half for later use.
6. Double up on your oven time. If you're baking a casserole, also bake a few potatoes or some long-cooking vegetables such as winter squash, carrots, and onions to use the next day.

Piccata-Style Cauliflower Steaks

Serve this cauliflower with pasta, rice, or polenta, and a green vegetable such as broccoli rabe, spinach, or Tuscan kale sautéed with white beans and garlic.

1 head cauliflower, cored

Olive oil, for cooking

Salt and freshly ground black pepper

2 shallots, finely minced

1 cup sliced mushrooms (optional)

⅓ cup dry white wine

3 tablespoons fresh lemon juice

1 to 2 tablespoons capers, drained

4 very thin lemon slices

¼ cup minced fresh parsley

2 teaspoons chilled vegan butter (optional)

1. Preheat the oven to 425°F. Lightly oil two baking sheets. Place the cauliflower on a cutting board, cored side down, and cut it into ½-inch-thick slices, as if you were cutting a loaf of bread.

2. Arrange the cauliflower slices in a single layer on the prepared baking sheets and season to taste with salt and pepper. Drizzle with a little olive oil and roast until tender and nicely browned, about 30 minutes, turning once with a large metal spatula about halfway through. While the cauliflower is roasting, make the sauce.

3. Heat 2 teaspoons oil in a skillet over medium heat. Add the shallots and sauté for 3 minutes, then stir in the mushrooms, if using, and cook 2 minutes longer. Add the wine, lemon juice, and capers and cook, stirring, until the liquid reduces slightly. Just before serving, add the lemon slices and parsley, then the vegan butter (if using), stirring to melt it into the sauce.

4. To serve, arrange the cauliflower on plates and spoon the hot sauce on top. Serve hot.

Serves 4

Hoisin-Braised Baby Bok Choy and Shiitake Mushrooms

Slow cooking over low heat allows the flavors of the sauce to permeate the bok choy and shiitakes, resulting in a satisfying and flavorful dish that is delicious over rice.

3 tablespoons hoisin sauce

1 tablespoon low-sodium tamari

1 tablespoon sake

1 tablespoon water

1 tablespoon neutral vegetable oil or ¼ cup water

2 dried chiles

1 teaspoon minced fresh ginger

1 teaspoon minced garlic

4 small baby bok choy, trimmed and halved lengthwise

4 ounces fresh shiitake mushrooms, stems removed and caps thinly sliced

2 tablespoons thinly sliced scallions

1. In a small bowl, combine the hoisin, tamari, sake, and water and set aside.

2. Heat the oil or water in a wok or large skillet over medium-high heat. When the oil is hot, add the chiles and stir-fry for about 30 seconds. Discard the chiles. Add the ginger and garlic and stir-fry until the garlic is fragrant, about 30 seconds. Add the bok choy, mushrooms, scallions, and sauce and stir-fry to coat the vegetables, 2 to 3 minutes.

3. Reduce the heat to low, cover, and simmer until the vegetables are tender, about 15 minutes. Serve hot.

Serves 4

Sesame-Broccoli Stir-Fry

Like most of the recipes in this chapter, this fragrant broccoli dish can fill the role of side dish or entrée. For a complete, well-balanced meal, add some diced firm tofu to the stir-fry and serve over brown rice.

1 large head broccoli

¼ cup sesame seeds, toasted (page 171)

3 tablespoons toasted sesame oil

3 tablespoons low-sodium tamari

2 tablespoons hoisin sauce

1 tablespoon neutral vegetable oil

½ large red bell pepper, seeded and cut into matchsticks

2 garlic cloves, minced

1. Cut the broccoli into small florets and peel and thinly slice the stems. Steam the broccoli over boiling water until barely tender, about 3 minutes. Rinse under cold running water to set the color and stop the cooking process, then drain and set aside.

2. In a small bowl, combine the sesame seeds, sesame oil, tamari, and hoisin, and set aside.

3. Heat the vegetable oil in a wok or large skillet over medium-high heat. When the oil is hot, add the bell pepper and garlic and stir-fry to soften slightly, about 1 minute. Add the broccoli and sauce and stir-fry, coating the vegetables with the sauce, until the vegetables are cooked to the desired doneness, about 3 minutes. Serve hot.

Serves 4

Did You Know?

Broccoli is an excellent source of calcium, potassium, and folic acid and contains more vitamin C than oranges. In addition, like other crucifers, broccoli contains glucosinolates, which are known for their cancer-fighting effect.

Roasted Cauliflower with Choron Sauce

What were once considered a boring vegetable and an old-fashioned sauce are given new life in this updated preparation. Roasting the cauliflower gives it an entirely new character that is complemented by the rich-tasting Choron sauce.

1 head cauliflower, cored

2 tablespoons olive oil

Salt and freshly ground black pepper

1 recipe Choron Sauce (page 131), heated

1. Preheat the oven to 425°F. Lightly oil two baking sheets. Place the cauliflower on a cutting board, cored side down, and cut it into ½-inch-thick slices, as if you were cutting a loaf of bread.

2. Toss the cauliflower slices with the olive oil and arrange in a single layer on the prepared baking sheets. Season to taste with salt and pepper. Roast until just tender, about 30 minutes, turning once halfway through. Remove from the oven and transfer to a shallow serving platter.

3. Serve topped with the sauce, or serve the sauce on the side for dipping.

Serves 4

Balsamic-Glazed Carrots and Kale

Why eat plain boiled carrots and greens? Give them a lift with this piquant balsamic glaze.

6 medium-size carrots, thinly sliced on the diagonal

1 bunch kale, thick stems removed, leaves coarsely chopped

1 tablespoon olive oil or ¼ cup water

2 tablespoons balsamic vinegar

2 teaspoons low-sodium tamari

½ teaspoon natural sugar

⅛ teaspoon cayenne

1. Bring a large pot of salted water to a boil. Add the carrots and kale and cook until the carrots soften slightly and the kale turns bright green, 3 to 4 minutes. Drain well and set aside.

2. Heat the oil or water in a large skillet over medium heat. Add the carrots and kale along with the remaining ingredients. Bring to a simmer, then reduce the heat to low and cook, stirring occasionally, until all the liquid evaporates, about 10 minutes. Serve hot.

Serves 4

Cajun-Style Collards

Collard greens are popular in the southern states, where they are often boiled with a ham hock for what seems like forever. Here they have new appeal, with a different, but still southern, approach. Try this "mess of greens" with Not-So-Dirty Rice (page 210).

1½ pounds collard greens

1 tablespoon olive oil or ¼ cup water

1 small onion, minced

1 celery rib, minced

½ large green bell pepper, seeded and minced

2 garlic cloves, minced

1 (14.5-ounce) can diced tomatoes, drained

1 teaspoon dried thyme

¼ teaspoon filé powder

¼ teaspoon cayenne

Salt and freshly ground black pepper

1. Bring a large pot of salted water to a boil and cook the collards until tender, 20 to 30 minutes. Drain, then coarsely chop and set aside.

2. Heat the oil or water in a large skillet over medium heat. Add the onion, celery, bell pepper, and garlic. Cover and cook until softened, about 7 minutes. Stir in the tomatoes, thyme, filé, and cayenne. Add the collards, season to taste with salt and pepper, and stir to coat the collards with the onion mixture. Simmer until the flavors are blended, about 10 minutes. Serve hot.

Serves 4

Chipotle Mashed Potatoes

Pureed chipotle chiles add a smoky heat to these mashed potatoes, which can liven up the most basic meal. I like to serve them with a vegan meatloaf or grilled seitan and sautéed greens.

2 pounds Yukon Gold or russet potatoes, peeled and cut into 2-inch chunks	⅓ cup plain unsweetened nondairy milk, heated
1 or 2 chipotle chiles in adobo, finely minced	1 tablespoon olive oil
	Salt

1. Place the potatoes in a large saucepan with cold salted water to cover. Bring to a boil over medium-high heat and cook the potatoes until tender, about 20 minutes.

2. Drain the potatoes, return them to the saucepan, and mash with a potato masher. Mix in the chipotle chiles, nondairy milk, olive oil, and salt to taste. Continue to mash until all of the ingredients are well mixed and the potatoes are smooth. Serve hot.

Serves 4

Chipotles: Smokin' Good

The popularity of smoky hot chipotle chiles is spreading like wildfire. Their distinctive, earthy flavor adds spice to salsas and dips, chilis and stews, and even breads and potatoes. At one time, these dried jalapeños were found only in ethnic markets, either plain or canned in adobo sauce (a rich tomato sauce). These days, chipotles can be found on many supermarket shelves. The McIlhenny Company of Tabasco fame even makes a chipotle sauce.

Mashed Potatoes and Company

Buttery Yukon Gold potatoes team up with sweet potatoes and parsnips for an unusual variation on traditional mashed potatoes. Experiment with other additions such as carrots or turnips—just be sure they're cooked until soft so they incorporate well with the potatoes.

1½ pounds Yukon Gold potatoes, peeled and quartered

1 small sweet potato, peeled and quartered

2 small parsnips, peeled and sliced

2 garlic cloves, crushed

⅓ to ½ cup plain unsweetened nondairy milk, heated

Salt and freshly ground black pepper

1. Place the potatoes, sweet potato, parsnips, and garlic in a large saucepan with cold salted water to cover. Bring to a boil over medium-high heat and cook until tender, about 30 minutes.

2. Drain and return the vegetables to the saucepan. Add ⅓ cup of the nondairy milk. Using a potato masher or ricer, mash the vegetables until smooth, adding more milk if necessary. Season to taste with salt and pepper.

Serves 4

Rosemary-Lemon Potatoes
with Kalamata Olives and Sun-Dried Tomatoes

Small red potatoes offer a perfect backdrop for a wide range of Mediterranean flavors, from fragrant rosemary and refreshing lemon to the salty depth of black olives and the smoky richness of sun-dried tomatoes.

1½ pounds small red potatoes

1 tablespoon olive oil

2 shallots, minced

2 tablespoons fresh lemon juice

1 teaspoon chopped fresh rosemary

½ teaspoon salt

¼ cup kalamata olives, pitted and halved

¼ cup oil-packed or rehydrated sun-dried tomatoes, chopped

1. Place the potatoes in a large saucepan with salted cold water to cover. Bring to a boil over medium-high heat and cook the potatoes until tender, about 30 minutes. Drain well. Cut the potatoes into halves or quarters, depending on their size, place in a large bowl, and set aside.

2. Heat the olive oil in a large skillet over medium heat. Add the shallots, cover, and cook until softened, 3 to 5 minutes. Add the potatoes and cook until browned, 5 to 7 minutes. Sprinkle with the lemon juice, rosemary, and salt, then add the olives and sun-dried tomatoes and stir gently to combine. Serve hot.

Serves 4

Grilled Radicchio and Fennel

It's no wonder grilled vegetables have become so popular—the flavor is incredible. I like to experiment with grilling different vegetables just to see how delicious the results might be, and I haven't been disappointed yet. Fennel and radicchio might be considered two unusual choices for the grill, but they are commonly grilled in Italy—a country where cooks know how to coax the most flavor out of their ingredients. If you don't have a grill, use the broiler instead.

2 medium-size fennel bulbs, trimmed

Olive oil

2 large heads radicchio, wilted outer leaves removed

Salt and freshly ground black pepper

Chopped fresh herbs, for garnish (optional)

Lemon wedges, for serving (optional)

1. If using a gas or electric grill or a broiler, preheat it until it is hot (about 500°F). If using charcoal, let the fire burn until the coals are hot and covered with white ash. You will want to cook your vegetables about 4 inches from the heat source.

2. Cut the fennel into wedges, toss with enough olive oil to coat, and grill on both sides until soft and lightly browned, about 10 minutes per side.

3. Meanwhile, cut the radicchio heads into quarters, cutting through the root end, and place them in a bowl of cold water for 5 minutes.

4. Coat the radicchio with olive oil and place on the grill, turning frequently and brushing with more oil, if necessary. Watch carefully to be sure it does not burn. Grill until soft and browned, about 10 minutes total.

5. Serve the fennel and radicchio hot, sprinkled with salt and pepper to taste and a drizzle of olive oil, if desired. Garnish with chopped herbs and serve with lemon wedges, if you like.

Serves 4

Indian Cauliflower and Mushrooms

Lightly fried cauliflower and mushrooms make an exceptional accompaniment to a flavorful dal and basmati rice. For a variation, use broccoli florets and sliced carrots.

½ cup unbleached all-purpose flour

½ teaspoon salt

½ teaspoon ground coriander

¼ teaspoon ground cumin

¼ teaspoon cayenne

⅛ teaspoon baking soda

⅛ teaspoon baking powder

⅔ cup water, or more if needed

Neutral vegetable oil, for frying

2½ cups small cauliflower florets, steamed until just tender and blotted dry

1½ cups small button mushrooms, lightly steamed and blotted dry

Plain vegan yogurt

Mint or tamarind chutney (optional)

1. In a medium-size bowl, combine the flour, salt, coriander, cumin, cayenne, baking soda, and baking powder. Stir in as much of the water as needed to make a thin batter.

2. Heat a thin layer of oil in a large nonstick skillet over medium-high heat. Dip the cauliflower and mushrooms in the batter, one piece at a time, and add to the hot skillet. Do not crowd. Cook until crisp on both sides, turning once, about 4 minutes per side. Repeat until all of the cauliflower and mushrooms are cooked. Arrange the vegetables on a plate and drizzle with yogurt. Serve hot, with chutney, if desired.

Serves 4

Broccoli Rabe
with Figs, Garlic, and Pine Nuts

Southern Italian cooking often combines bitter greens such as broccoli rabe, also known as rapini, with dried fruits such as figs or raisins. The garlic and olive oil add depth, and the pine nuts provide a bit of crunch. Use fresh figs when they are in season; otherwise, dried are fine.

2 bunches broccoli rabe, stems trimmed, leaves coarsely chopped

1 tablespoon olive oil

3 garlic cloves, minced

⅓ cup coarsely chopped fresh or dried figs

¼ cup pine nuts

Salt and freshly ground black pepper

1. Bring a large pot of salted water to a boil. Add the broccoli rabe and cook for 5 minutes. Drain well and set aside.

2. Heat the olive oil in a large skillet over medium heat. Add the garlic and cook until fragrant, about 30 seconds. Add the figs and pine nuts and cook until the pine nuts are lightly toasted, about 1 minute. Stir in the broccoli rabe and season to taste with salt and pepper. Cook, stirring occasionally, until tender, about 5 minutes. Serve hot.

Serves 4

Brandy-Glazed Winter Squash with Apple-Pecan Topping

I like to make this dish just for the lovely aroma that permeates the house while it bakes.

1 large winter squash, such as buttercup or butternut

1 small onion, chopped

⅓ cup brandy

2 tablespoons natural sugar

2 tablespoons olive oil

1 tablespoon water

Salt and freshly ground black pepper

1 large Granny Smith apple, peeled, cored, and chopped

½ cup chopped pecans

1. Preheat the oven to 400°F. Lightly oil a large baking dish. Halve, seed, and peel the squash, then cut into 2-inch chunks. Place in a single layer in the prepared baking dish.

2. Sprinkle the onion over the squash and pour on the brandy. Add 1 tablespoon of the sugar, 1 tablespoon of the olive oil, and the water. Season to taste with salt and pepper. Cover tightly and bake until soft, 30 to 40 minutes. Gently turn the squash at least once during cooking for even browning.

3. In a bowl, combine the apple, pecans, the remaining 1 tablespoon olive oil, and the remaining 1 tablespoon sugar. Sprinkle the apple mixture over the squash, return to the oven, and bake, uncovered, until the top is bubbly and golden brown, about 15 minutes. Serve hot.

Serves 4

Watercress-Walnut Stir-Fry

Infused with the flavors of ginger, garlic, and walnuts, the watercress is cooked just long enough to lose its raw taste while retaining its texture and freshness. I like to think of this as a cooked salad and often use it as a bed for sautéed portobello mushroom or seitan strips.

2 teaspoons neutral vegetable oil

1 teaspoon grated fresh ginger

1 garlic clove, minced

2 bunches watercress, tough stems removed, leaves coarsely chopped

½ cup chopped walnuts

1 tablespoon low-sodium tamari

¼ teaspoon red pepper flakes

2 teaspoons walnut oil (optional)

1. Heat the vegetable oil in a large skillet or wok over medium-high heat. When the oil is hot, add the ginger and garlic and cook until fragrant, about 30 seconds. Add the watercress, walnuts, tamari, and red pepper flakes and stir-fry until just wilted, about 3 minutes.

2. Serve hot, drizzled with the walnut oil, if desired.

Serves 4

Golden Ratatouille

Using the many golden-hued vegetables now available gives a new lift to this classic vegetable stew from the Provence region of France. Fresh herbs provide a green color accent. If you want to turn this into a glowing main course, add a 15-ounce can of chickpeas, rinsed and drained, and serve over rice that has been cooked with a pinch of turmeric.

1 tablespoon olive oil or ¼ cup water

1 small onion, diced

1 small yellow bell pepper, seeded and cut into ½-inch dice

1 small eggplant, peeled and cut into ½-inch dice

2 garlic cloves, minced

Salt and freshly ground black pepper

2 small yellow squash, cut into ½-inch-thick rounds

4 large ripe yellow tomatoes, peeled, seeded, and chopped

1 tablespoon minced fresh thyme

1 tablespoon chopped fresh parsley

1. Heat the olive oil or water in a large saucepan over medium heat. Add the onion, cover, and cook until softened, about 5 minutes. Add the bell pepper, eggplant, garlic, and salt and pepper to taste and stir gently to combine. Cover and cook until the vegetables are slightly softened, about 10 minutes. Stir in the squash, tomatoes, and thyme. Cover and cook, stirring occasionally, until all of the vegetables are tender, about 20 minutes.

2. Sprinkle with the parsley and serve hot.

Serves 4 to 6

Did You Know?

Bell peppers are a good source of potassium and vitamins A and C. In fact, they contain more vitamin C than oranges.

Maple-Baked Root Vegetables

Oven baking and root vegetables were made for each other, especially during the chilly winter months when their warm fragrance fills the house. Cutting the vegetables into similar-size pieces helps ensure even cooking, and a small amount of maple syrup brings out their natural sweetness.

4 medium-size carrots, cut into 1-inch chunks

2 medium-size parsnips, peeled and cut into 1-inch chunks

2 small turnips, peeled and cut into 1-inch chunks

1 small rutabaga, peeled and cut into 1-inch chunks

6 shallots, halved

2 tablespoons olive oil

2 tablespoons pure maple syrup

1 teaspoon dried thyme

½ teaspoon smoked paprika (optional)

Salt and freshly ground black pepper

1. Preheat the oven to 450°F. Lightly oil a roasting pan or baking dish. Place the carrots, parsnips, turnips, rutabaga, and shallots in a large bowl. Add the olive oil, maple syrup, thyme, paprika (if using), and salt and pepper to taste and toss to combine well.

2. Transfer the vegetables to the prepared baking dish and bake until soft on the inside and caramelized on the outside, about 1 hour, stirring gently every 20 minutes to ensure even browning. Serve hot.

===== *Serves 4* =====

Rootin' for Root Vegetables

In addition to the ever-popular carrots, root vegetables include turnips, beets, rutabagas, celery root (celeriac), parsley root, and parsnips. Root vegetables make wonderful additions to soups, stews, and vegetable medleys. In addition, they are delicious glazed, pureed, or roasted. Carrots are especially rich in vitamin A and potassium, beets are loaded with iron, and parsley root is high in B vitamins. Parsnips, celery root, rutabagas, and turnips are all high in potassium and vitamin C.

Shredded Vegetable Fritters

You can vary the vegetables and seasonings in these fritters according to your preference. A dash of curry powder or cumin will change their character, as will substituting cilantro for the parsley or adding some minced hot chile. Serve with vegan sour cream, applesauce, chutney, or salsa. Use a hand grater or the shredding disk of a food processor to shred the vegetables. If you don't have oat flour on hand, you can grind it yourself in a food processor using rolled oats.

1 small red onion, shredded	1 teaspoon baking powder
1 large sweet potato, peeled and shredded	½ teaspoon ground coriander
1 carrot, shredded	½ teaspoon salt
3 scallions, minced	¼ teaspoon freshly ground black pepper
1 tablespoon minced fresh parsley	¼ teaspoon ground cumin
½ cup oat flour	Neutral vegetable oil for frying

1. Preheat the oven to 250°F. Combine the shredded onion, sweet potato, and carrot in a colander. Press out the liquid and transfer the vegetables to a large bowl. Stir in the scallions, parsley, flour, baking powder, coriander, salt, pepper, and cumin and mix well. If the mixture is too dry, stir in a small amount of plain unsweetened nondairy milk. If the mixture is too wet, sprinkle on a little more flour.

2. Pour a thin layer of oil in a large nonstick skillet and heat over medium-high heat. Scoop out a large spoonful of the vegetable mixture and press against it with your hand to tightly pack. Place the fritter in the hot pan and cook until golden brown on both sides, about 4 minutes per side. Drain the cooked fritter on paper towels, then transfer to the oven to keep warm. Repeat until all of the vegetable mixture is used, adding more oil to the pan as needed. Serve hot.

Serves 4

Autumn Roasted Vegetables

Roasting vegetables deepens their flavor and brings out their natural sweetness.

1 large red onion, cut into ½-inch pieces

3 large carrots, cut into ¼-inch slices

8 ounces Brussels sprouts, trimmed and halved

2 parsnips, peeled and cut into ¼-inch slices

½ small head cauliflower, cut into 1-inch florets

1 tablespoon pure maple syrup

1 tablespoon low-sodium tamari

1 tablespoon olive oil

1 tablespoon rice vinegar

1 teaspoon Dijon mustard

1 teaspoon dried thyme

¼ teaspoon ground rosemary

¼ teaspoon ground dried sage

3 tablespoons water

Salt and freshly ground black pepper

1. Preheat the oven to 400°F. Lightly oil a 9 x 13-inch baking dish. Arrange the vegetables in a single layer in the prepared baking dish.

2. In a small bowl, combine the maple syrup, tamari, olive oil, vinegar, mustard, thyme, rosemary, and sage. Stir until well blended, then stir in the water, and pour over the vegetables. Season to taste with salt and pepper. Cover the baking dish tightly and bake for 30 minutes, then stir the vegetables gently and continue baking, uncovered, until the vegetables are tender when pierced with a fork, about 20 minutes longer. Serve hot.

Serves 4

Roasted Sweet Potatoes with Shallots

This delectable dish, streaked with orange, green, brown, and red, is a vision of autumn colors that tastes as good as it looks. Serve these roasted sweet potatoes alone, with the kale, or decked out for the holidays with the addition of nuts and cranberries.

1½ pounds sweet potatoes, peeled and cut into ½-inch dice

3 medium-size shallots, halved lengthwise and thinly sliced crosswise

½ teaspoon dried oregano

Salt and freshly ground black pepper

Olive oil

6 large kale leaves, tough stems removed and discarded, leaves washed and dried

⅓ cup toasted walnut or pecan pieces (page 203)

⅓ cup sweetened dried cranberries

1. Preheat the oven to 425°F. Lightly oil two rimmed baking sheets. Place the sweet potatoes, shallot, and oregano in a large bowl. Season to taste with salt and pepper, drizzle about 1 tablespoon olive oil over the mixture, and toss to coat.

2. Spread the mixture in a single layer on one of the prepared baking sheets and bake until the potatoes are tender and lightly browned, about 30 minutes, turning once about halfway through.

3. Meanwhile, stack the kale leaves and roll them into a tight roll, then cut crosswise into thin ribbons. Transfer to a bowl, drizzle with a little olive oil and season to taste with salt and pepper. Spread the kale on the second baking sheet and place in the oven when the sweet potatoes are about halfway done roasting. Bake the kale until it is crisp and lightly browned, about 15 minutes.

4. To serve, transfer the sweet potatoes to a bowl and season with a few grinds of black pepper. Add the walnuts and cranberries and toss to combine. Top with the kale. Serve hot.

Serves 4 to 6

> "Custom will reconcile people to any atrocity; and fashion will drive them to acquire any custom."
>
> —GEORGE BERNARD SHAW

Grains are finally receiving the attention they deserve, as basmati and jasmine rice now occupy shelves where only Uncle Ben's once stood, and ancient grains such as quinoa and kamut appear on trendy restaurant menus. Until recent years, the only exposure to grains for many Americans, beyond the occasional serving of white rice, was in the form of processed breakfast cereals, breads, and pasta.

Many people now enjoy nutritious whole grains as the foundation of a well-balanced meal. Spoon some brown rice or quinoa onto a plate, top it with a generous serving of a bean and vegetable stew, and dinner is served. Grains can also be used to make everything from soups to desserts and to add substance to burgers, loaves, and stuffings.

This chapter offers recipes using several varieties of rice, including brown, basmati, and jasmine. You will also find recipes that use cornmeal (polenta), quinoa, barley, and millet, as well as couscous—that great grain impostor that is actually milled semolina wheat. These and other grains, such as spelt, amaranth, and kamut, which are extremely high in protein and loaded with flavor, provide immense versatility in menu planning. Best of all, you can now find these formerly exotic grains in natural foods stores and many large supermarkets.

A world of exciting flavors awaits you with each grain you try. I encourage you to experiment with some of the whole grains used in this chapter and to explore further by substituting grains or perhaps making a grain medley, using two or more grains in the same recipe. Although quinoa, kamut, and even millet might be unfamiliar to you, they are staple grains elsewhere in the world. Their widely divergent textures and generally neutral flavors make them fun to incorporate into your cooking repertoire.

Grains

Grains are an economical source of high-quality nutrition. Whole grains are rich in protein, B vitamins, vitamin E, and other nutrients and are good sources of fiber and carbohydrates. Refined grains are less nutritious because they have had part or all of the germ and bran removed. To compensate, many refined grain products are enriched with vitamins and minerals.

Here is a list of the some of the grains in the world's pantry.

- **AMARANTH:** Considered a sacred grain of the Incas, this tiny grain is high in lysine, which boosts its value as a protein source. It has a distinctive, nutty flavor and can be used in baking or as a hot breakfast cereal.

- **BARLEY:** A flavorful, chewy grain, barley is frequently used in soups, pilafs, and salads or cooked as a breakfast cereal. Pearl barley, which has had its hard outer layers removed, is less nutritious than unrefined whole barley.

- **BUCKWHEAT:** A traditional ingredient in eastern Europe, buckwheat groats, or kasha, as they are called when cooked, have a deep, nutty flavor that combines well with other grains.

- **BULGUR:** Sometimes called cracked wheat, bulgur is partially cooked whole-grain wheat that has been dried and cracked. It comes in small, medium, and coarse grinds and has a nutty flavor and a fluffy texture when cooked. Bulgur is used to make tabbouleh salad.

- **CORN:** Often treated as a vegetable, corn is in reality a grain that can be ground into different textures, called cornmeal or grits, and used to make breakfast porridge and polenta, as well cornbread and other baked goods.

- **COUSCOUS:** Usually classified as a grain, couscous is actually a tiny pasta made from semolina wheat. But since it looks and acts like a grain, it is included here. Popular in North African and Middle Eastern cooking, couscous is most widely available in a precooked, or instant, form and takes just five minutes to cook.

- **KAMUT:** This ancient member of the wheat family has its origins in Egypt. Its grains are extremely large, chewy, and dense when cooked. Kamut is an interesting and nutritious addition to grain medleys. Because of its large size, kamut benefits from soaking overnight to reduce its long cooking time.

- **MILLET:** A tiny, nutritious grain, millet is high in protein and rich in iron, calcium, B vitamins, and potassium. This highly digestible grain

cooks fairly quickly and works well in stuffings, patties, and pilafs.

- **OATS:** Available steel-cut, rolled, or quick-cooking, oats are predominantly used as a breakfast cereal in the United States, and their flour is used in baking. Oats contain calcium, iron, and B vitamins and are a good source of protein and carbohydrates.

- **QUINOA:** Pronounced "KEEN-wah," this small, quick-cooking grain is extremely high in protein and has a good balance of amino acids. It also contains calcium, B vitamins, vitamin E, and iron. This sand-colored, disk-shaped grain is from the Andes, where it is known as "the mother grain." Quinoa has a mild, nutty flavor and fluffy texture when cooked.

- **RICE:** See page 198.

- **SPELT:** Also called farro, spelt is one of the oldest cultivated grains. Related to wheat, it has a mild, nutty flavor and is usually tolerated well by people with wheat allergies. As is the case with kamut, because of its large size and long cooking time, spelt benefits from soaking overnight.

- **TEFF:** This grain is so small that several uncooked teff kernels can fit on the head of a pin. Cooked teff has a sweet flavor and a somewhat gelatinous consistency. It is best used in puddings and baked goods. The Ethiopian flatbread called *injera* is made with teff.

Rice

There's more to rice than the refined, starchy white variety, and many of the more exotic varieties are also more nutritious. Here are the main varieties widely available in supermarkets and natural, ethnic, and specialty food stores.

- **Arborio rice:** A short-grain rice from Italy's Po Valley, Arborio rice is the star ingredient in creamy risottos.

- **Basmati rice:** This aromatic long-grain rice from India comes in white and brown varieties. It has long grains that remain separate and firm when cooked.

- **Brown rice:** This whole-grain form of rice is available in short-, medium-, and long-grain varieties. It is nutritionally superior to white rice because it has not been stripped of its nutrients through polishing.

- **Jasmine rice:** This fragrant Thai favorite has a delicate, flowery bouquet. Its texture is slightly sticky when cooked.

- **Sticky rice:** This short-grain rice is used to make Asian dishes and desserts and is also called glutinous rice. Japanese sticky rice is used to make sushi and is sometimes sold as sushi rice.

- **White rice:** This is brown rice that has been stripped of its nutrients through polishing, which removes the hull, bran, and germ. Because of this, white rice is often enriched with vitamins and minerals. Long-grain white rice is the most widely used variety.

- **Wild rice:** Not really a rice but the seed of a tall, aquatic grass of North America, wild rice is high in amino acids and B vitamins and has double the protein of white rice. It is often paired with other grains in pilafs.

Storing and Cooking Grains

Most whole grains can be stored, unrefrigerated, in tightly covered containers away from heat, light, and humidity. Grains that have been ground, cracked, or flaked should be refrigerated, as the natural oils in the grains have been exposed and are more prone to becoming rancid. As a general rule, however, I store all grains in the refrigerator or freezer.

Although soaking grains is not necessary, it can significantly reduce their cooking times. In all cases, grains should be rinsed before using to remove loose hulls, dust, and other impurities.

To intensify the flavor of grains, you can lightly toast them in a dry skillet before cooking.

Most grains can be cooked in a pot with about two times as much water as grain, or more, depending on the cooking time. Bring the water to a boil, cover, reduce the heat to low, and simmer until tender. The water will be absorbed into the grain. For 1 cup of uncooked grain, the average yield will be about 3 cups of cooked grain. Besides cooking on top of the stove, grains may be baked in the oven in a tightly covered pot. To do this, bring the water to a boil on top of the stove, then add the grain, cover tightly, and bake in a preheated 325°F oven for approximately the same amount of time as for stovetop cooking. Longer-cooking grains benefit from cooking in a pressure cooker, while grains with shorter cooking times taste great prepared pilaf style, which begins with sautéing the grains in oil, then adding liquid to finish the cooking.

Following is a table of average cooking times for several (unsoaked) grains using the stovetop cooking method. Be sure to salt the water after it comes to a boil. Let the grains stand, covered, for 5 minutes after cooking, then fluff with a fork before serving.

Stovetop Cooking Times for Grains

Grain (1 cup)	Water	Cooking Time
Amaranth	2 cups	20 minutes
Barley (pearl)	3 cups	30 minutes
Basmati rice	1¾ cups	30 minutes
Brown rice (long-grain)	2 cups	30 to 40 minutes
Brown rice (short- or medium-grain)	3 cups	45 minutes
Buckwheat (kasha)	2 cups	20 minutes
Bulgur	2 cups	15 minutes
Couscous	1¼ cups	5 minutes
Kamut	4 cups	2 hours
Millet	2 cups	30 minutes
Quinoa	2 cups	15 to 20 minutes
Spelt	2¾ cups	1 hour
Teff	3 cups	15 minutes
White rice (long-grain)	1¾ cups	20 minutes
Wild rice	3¾ cups	45 minutes

Baked Polenta with Red Beans and Fresh Tomato Salsa

The polenta may be made a few days ahead and refrigerated until needed. Then simply cut it into serving-size portions and finish in the oven. If you prefer, you may pan-fry the polenta in a little olive oil instead of baking it.

3½ cups water

1 teaspoon salt, plus more for seasoning

1 cup medium-ground yellow cornmeal

2 tablespoons minced fresh cilantro

3 tablespoons olive oil

Freshly ground black pepper

4 scallions, chopped

1½ cups cooked dark red kidney or other red beans or 1 (15-ounce) can beans, rinsed and drained

1 cup Fresh Tomato Salsa (page 157) or purchased salsa

1. Bring the water to a boil in a large saucepan over high heat. Reduce the heat to medium, add the salt, and slowly whisk in the cornmeal, stirring constantly. Reduce the heat to low and continue to cook, stirring frequently, until thick, 30 to 40 minutes. Stir in 1 tablespoon of the cilantro and 1 tablespoon of the olive oil and season to taste with salt and pepper.

2. Lightly oil a shallow 10-inch square baking dish. Spoon the polenta into the dish and spread it evenly over the bottom. Set aside to cool to room temperature for a few minutes, then cover and refrigerate until firm, about 30 minutes

3. Heat 1 tablespoon of the olive oil in a medium-size skillet over medium heat. Add the scallions and cook until slightly softened, about 1 minute. Stir in the beans, the remaining 1 tablespoon cilantro, and the salsa. Season to taste with salt and pepper. Simmer until the mixture is hot and the flavors are blended, about 5 minutes. Keep warm over very low heat.

4. Preheat the oven to 375°F. Lightly oil a baking sheet. Cut the polenta into 4 squares and place on the baking sheet. Brush the tops with the remaining 1 tablespoon olive oil and bake until hot and golden brown, about 20 minutes.

5. To serve, transfer the polenta to individual plates, spoon some of the warm beans and salsa on top, and serve hot.

Serves 4

Pesto Polenta with Sautéed Portobello Slices

Slices of juicy portobello mushrooms complement the pesto-infused polenta for an intriguing flavor. This is a great company dish because the polenta may be made a day or so in advance and then cut and baked when needed.

3½ cups water

1 teaspoon salt, plus more for seasoning

1 cup medium-ground yellow cornmeal

¼ cup Basil Pesto (page 142) or purchased vegan pesto

2 tablespoons olive oil

Freshly ground black pepper

2 garlic cloves, chopped

4 large portobello mushroom caps, gills scraped out, cut into ¼-inch-thick slices

1. Bring the water to a boil in a large saucepan over high heat. Reduce the heat to medium, add the salt, and slowly whisk in the cornmeal, stirring constantly. Reduce the heat to low and continue to cook, stirring frequently, until thick, about 30 minutes. Near the end of the cooking time, thin the pesto with 1 tablespoon hot water and stir it into the polenta. Season to taste with salt and pepper.

2. Lightly oil a shallow 10-inch square baking dish. Spoon the polenta into the dish and spread it evenly over the bottom. Set aside to cool to room temperature for a few minutes, then cover and refrigerate until chilled, about 30 minutes.

3. Heat 1 tablespoon of the olive oil in a large skillet over medium heat. Add the garlic and cook until fragrant, about 30 seconds. Add the mushroom slices, season to taste with salt and pepper, and cook until the mushrooms are tender, about 5 minutes. Keep warm over very low heat.

4. Preheat the oven to 375°F. Lightly oil a baking sheet. Cut the polenta into 4 squares and place on the baking sheet. Brush the tops with the remaining 1 tablespoon olive oil and bake until hot and golden brown, about 30 minutes.

5. To serve, transfer the polenta to individual plates, spoon some of the mushrooms on top, and serve hot.

Serves 4

Barley Risotto
with Wild Mushrooms and Fresh Herbs

Both fresh and dried mushrooms are used to amplify the woodsy mushroom flavor, which is complemented by the barley and fresh herbs. Another layer of mushroom flavor is added with the mushroom broth, but you may use vegetable broth instead, if you prefer. Although Arborio rice is traditionally used to make risotto, barley provides a hearty change of pace.

¼ cup dried porcini mushrooms, soaked in 1 cup very hot water for 20 minutes

4 cups Mushroom Broth (page 59) or vegetable broth

½ cup dry white wine

1 tablespoon olive oil or ¼ cup water

¼ cup minced shallots

1 large garlic clove, minced

1 cup pearl barley

2 cups chopped cremini mushrooms

2 teaspoons minced fresh parsley

2 teaspoons minced fresh chives

1 teaspoon minced fresh marjoram, thyme, or oregano

Salt and freshly ground black pepper

1. Drain the porcinis, reserving the soaking liquid. Strain the liquid and set aside. Chop the mushrooms and set aside.

2. Combine the broth, reserved mushroom liquid, and wine in a medium-size saucepan over medium heat and bring to a simmer.

3. In a large skillet or saucepan, heat the olive oil or water over medium heat. Add the shallots and garlic and cook, stirring, until fragrant and slightly softened, about 1 minute. Add the barley and both kinds of mushrooms and stir until coated with oil.

4. Add ½ cup of the hot liquid and simmer, stirring frequently, until the liquid is almost absorbed. Continue adding the broth mixture ½ cup at a time, stirring until the liquid is absorbed, until the barley is tender, about 30 minutes. You may not need to use all of the broth mixture.

5. About 5 minutes before the risotto is finished, stir in the parsley, chives, marjoram, and salt and pepper to taste. Spoon the risotto into shallow bowls and serve hot.

Serves 4

Chickpea and Bulgur Pilaf

Also called cracked wheat, bulgur is a quick-cooking grain with a hearty, nut-like flavor that is used to make the popular Middle Eastern salad tabbouleh. It also makes a terrific pilaf when combined with chickpeas, tomatoes, and shallots. Serve with a cooked green vegetable such as string beans or sautéed spinach for a satisfying meal.

2 cups vegetable broth or water

1 cup medium-grind bulgur

1 tablespoon olive oil or ¼ cup water

4 shallots, finely chopped

2 cups chopped fresh or canned tomatoes

1½ cups cooked chickpeas or 1 (15-ounce) can chickpeas, rinsed and drained

Salt and freshly ground black pepper

2 tablespoons toasted pine nuts or walnut pieces (see below)

2 tablespoons chopped fresh mint, parsley, or basil

1. Bring the vegetable broth to a boil in a small saucepan. Remove from the heat and stir in the bulgur. Set aside until the liquid is absorbed and the bulgur is softened, about 20 minutes.

2. Heat the olive oil or water in a large skillet over medium heat. Add the shallots and cook until softened, about 3 minutes. Stir in the bulgur, tomatoes, chickpeas, and season to taste with salt and pepper. Cook, stirring, until hot, about 5 minutes. Stir in the pine nuts and mint. Serve hot.

Serves 4

Toasting Nuts

Toasting brings out the flavor in nuts. For small quantities of nuts (less than a cup), it is easy to toast them in a dry skillet over medium heat, shaking or stirring constantly until toasted. When toasting larger amounts, however, the oven works better.

Preheat the oven to 350°F. Spread the nuts on a baking sheet and bake until lightly browned and dry. Walnuts can take up to 25 minutes; pecans and hazelnuts, about 15 minutes; and almonds and pine nuts, about 10 minutes. Be sure to remove the toasted nuts from the hot baking sheet or skillet, or they will continue to cook.

Allow the nuts to cool completely and store in an airtight container until ready to use. They are best eaten within a few days.

Saffron Couscous Cake
with Spring Vegetable Sauté

Whether this dish is saffron flavored or saffron colored will depend on your budget. Made with either saffron or turmeric, it's lovely served for a spring lunch or light supper. To serve as a first course, you can cut the couscous cake into smaller wedges or place the couscous mixture into small ring molds or individual tart pans instead of the large springform pan. You can vary the types of vegetables according to availability or personal preference.

2 tablespoons olive oil, plus more for brushing

2 large shallots, minced

2 cups instant couscous

3 cups hot vegetable broth

Pinch of ground saffron or turmeric

1/8 teaspoon cayenne

Salt

1 small yellow bell pepper, seeded and cut into matchsticks

8 ounces thin asparagus, trimmed and cut diagonally into 1-inch pieces

1 large carrot, shredded

4 scallions, minced

2/3 cup fresh or thawed frozen baby peas

1 cup grape or cherry tomatoes, cut in half

Freshly ground black pepper

2 tablespoons minced fresh parsley or other herb

1. Heat 1 tablespoon of the olive oil in a medium-size saucepan over medium heat. Add the shallots, cover, and cook until softened, about 5 minutes. Add the couscous and stir to coat with the oil. Stir in the hot broth and bring to a boil. Reduce the heat to low and stir in the saffron, cayenne, and salt to taste. Cover and cook until all of the liquid is absorbed, 5 to 7 minutes.

2. Transfer the couscous to a lightly oiled 9-inch springform pan. Lightly press the couscous into the pan and smooth the top. Refrigerate until firm, at least 1 hour or up to 4 hours.

3. Preheat the oven to 350°F. Lightly oil a baking sheet. Remove the cake from the refrigerator, release the springform pan, and cut the cake into 6 wedges. Place on the prepared baking sheet and brush lightly with olive oil. Bake until just hot, 12 to 15 minutes.

4. Meanwhile, heat the remaining 1 tablespoon olive oil in a large skillet over medium heat. Add the bell pepper and asparagus and cook, stirring, until slightly softened, about 5 minutes. Add the carrot, scallions, peas, tomatoes, and salt and pepper to taste. Cook, stirring, until the vegetables are tender, about 3 minutes. Stir in the parsley.

5. Arrange the couscous wedges on individual plates, top with a large spoonful of the vegetables, and serve immediately.

===== *Serves 6* =====

Eight Compelling Ethical Reasons to Go Vegan

A vegan lifestyle is one of compassion, nonviolence, and respect for all sentient life. The process of bringing animal meat to market is rife with extraordinary cruelties imposed on them. Going vegan can help end the needless suffering and deaths of thousands of animals.

1. Food animals are not protected by the Animal Welfare Act. With virtually no laws to protect these animals, cruelty and abuse on farms go unchecked.
2. Lack of enforcement of the Humane Slaughter Act allows cattle, pigs, horses, and sheep to be shackled and throat-slit without first being stunned. Animals often are skinned, boiled, and butchered alive.
3. Factory-farm hens are forced to live in "battery" cages—stacked in rows four cages high—by the thousands. Each hen is confined to a tiny space, where it ends up suffering from blisters, bare wings, torn feet, and bloody combs. "Spent" birds are sometimes ground up while alive to be used as feed for the next flock.
4. A factory-farm dairy cow must endure a painfully swollen udder and spend her entire life in a stall, being milked up to 3 times a day. She is kept pregnant most of her life, and her young are usually taken from her at birth.
5. Egg producers can force spent hens to lay again by starving them for up to 14 days. No U.S. law prevents this practice.
6. Sick or crippled animals, called downers, are not protected from cruelty by federal law. These animals are bulldozed or dragged by chains and may be left to starve or freeze to death.
7. Mutilation occurs throughout animal agriculture. Animals are branded, ear-notched, and tail-docked. Birds are debeaked to reduce stress-related violence. Bulls, calves, and piglets are routinely castrated.
8. Veal calves—byproducts of the dairy industry—are locked up in stalls and chained by the neck so they cannot turn around their entire lives. They are kept in darkness and fed a diet without iron or roughage in order to produce tender, milky white meat.

Quinoa and Pan-Fried Corn with Orange Zest and Basil

The sweetness of the corn, accented by the orange zest, complements the nutty flavor of the quinoa.

3 cups vegetable broth

1½ cups quinoa, rinsed and drained

1 tablespoon olive oil or ¼ cup water

2 cups fresh or thawed frozen corn kernels

5 scallions, minced

1 tablespoon grated orange zest

Salt and freshly ground black pepper

2 tablespoons chopped fresh basil leaves

1. Bring the broth to a simmer in a large saucepan over medium heat. Stir in the quinoa, cover, and reduce the heat to low. Simmer until all of the water is absorbed, 12 to 15 minutes.

2. Heat the olive oil or water in a medium-size skillet over medium heat. Add the corn and scallions and cook, stirring, until fragrant, about 3 minutes. Add the contents of the skillet to the quinoa. Stir in the orange zest and salt and pepper to taste. Set aside for 5 minutes so the flavors can blend. Add the basil and toss to combine. Serve hot.

Serves 4

Indian-Spiced Quinoa
with Raisins and Pine Nuts

Despite the fact that quinoa hails from South America, it adapts deliciously to the flavors of Indian spices and the Middle Eastern pilaf-style cooking method. Quinoa is available in natural foods stores and many large supermarkets.

1 tablespoon olive oil or ¼ cup water

2 large shallots, minced

1 teaspoon minced fresh ginger

1½ cups quinoa, rinsed and drained

½ teaspoon ground cardamom

½ teaspoon ground coriander

¼ teaspoon ground cumin

⅛ teaspoon cayenne

3 cups hot vegetable broth or water

Salt and freshly ground black pepper

⅓ cup golden raisins

¼ cup pine nuts, toasted (page 203)

2 tablespoons minced fresh parsley

1. Heat the olive oil or water in a large skillet over medium heat. Add the shallots and ginger and cook, stirring, until the shallots are slightly softened, about 1 minute. Add the quinoa along with the cardamom, coriander, cumin, and cayenne and stir to coat with the oil. Stir in the hot broth and bring to a boil. Reduce the heat to low and season to taste with salt and pepper. Cover and cook until all of the water is absorbed, 12 to 15 minutes.

2. Remove from the heat and stir in the raisins, pine nuts, and parsley. Serve hot.

Serves 4

Savory Amaranth Porridge

This ancient grain of the Aztecs has a strong flavor that is at once sweet and savory—some say "nutty"—and that people seem to either love or hate. Extremely high in protein, iron, and calcium, the tiny amaranth grains cook up slightly gelatinous and are often ground into flour and combined with other flours to make baked goods such as muffins, cookies, and quick breads. This porridge is similar in texture to a restorative Chinese congee and may be eaten at any time of day, including breakfast. To prepare this as a more traditional hot breakfast cereal, omit the last four ingredients and top as you would oatmeal—with nondairy milk, sweetener, and a sprinkling of granola or raisins.

1 cup amaranth

3 cups water or vegetable broth

Salt

3 scallions, minced

1 tablespoon low-sodium tamari

1 teaspoon dark sesame oil

2 tablespoons roasted pumpkin seeds

1. In a medium-size saucepan over medium-high heat, combine the amaranth and water and bring to a boil. Reduce the heat to low, add salt to taste, and simmer until the water is absorbed, about 30 minutes. During the last 5 minutes of cooking time, stir in the scallions, tamari, and sesame oil.

2. Spoon the porridge into serving bowls, sprinkle with the pumpkin seeds, and serve hot.

Serves 4

Walnut-Crusted Millet and Celery Root Croquettes

These croquettes can be served as a side dish or light entrée and are a delicious way to enjoy millet, a very nourishing grain that is an infrequent visitor to dinner tables in the United States. Celery root, or celeriac, is an often overlooked vegetable that resembles a large, dusky brown knob. It tastes like regular celery but with a subtler flavor. For an elegant presentation, serve these croquettes in a pool of Basic Brown Sauce (page 134) or Yellow Pepper Coulis (page 141).

1 cup millet	Salt and freshly ground black pepper
1 small celery root, peeled and shredded	1 cup ground walnuts
1 medium-size onion, minced	½ cup dry bread crumbs
3 cups water	Olive oil for frying

1. Combine the millet, celery root, and onion in a medium-size saucepan. Add the water and bring to a boil over medium-high heat. Reduce the heat to low, salt the water, cover, and simmer until the ingredients are soft and all of the water is absorbed, about 30 minutes.

2. Transfer the millet mixture to a medium-size bowl. Season to taste with salt and pepper. Set aside to cool to room temperature for a few minutes, then cover and refrigerate until chilled, about 1 hour.

3. In a shallow bowl, combine the walnuts and bread crumbs. Shape the millet mixture into 4 patties and coat evenly with the walnut mixture.

4. Heat 2 tablespoons of the olive oil in a large skillet over medium heat. Working in batches if necessary, add the croquettes and cook until well browned on both sides, about 4 minutes per side. Add more oil as needed. Serve immediately.

Serves 4

Not-So-Dirty Rice

Traditional dirty rice is so named because the white rice is flecked with brown pieces of chopped chicken livers. In this version, your choice of chopped mushrooms, seitan, or tempeh are combined with onion, bell pepper, garlic, and spices.

1 tablespoon olive oil or ¼ cup water

1 medium-size onion, finely chopped

1 small green bell pepper, seeded and finely chopped

2 garlic cloves, minced

2 cups chopped mushrooms, seitan, or steamed tempeh (page 10)

1 teaspoon Tabasco sauce

1 teaspoon dried thyme, crumbled

½ teaspoon salt

⅛ teaspoon cayenne

3 cups freshly cooked long-grain white rice

Heat the olive oil or water in a large saucepan over medium heat. Add the onion and bell pepper, cover, and cook until softened, about 5 minutes. Add the garlic, mushrooms, Tabasco, thyme, salt, and cayenne. Stir to combine and heat through, about 5 minutes. Stir in the rice and cook until hot, 5 to 7 minutes. Taste and adjust the seasonings, then serve hot.

Serves 4

Caribbean Rice with Red Beans and Chiles

As in many other areas of the world, rice and beans are a popular combination in the Caribbean islands, where cooks often jazz things up with hot chiles and fragrant spices. If you have a jerk spice blend on hand, you can substitute it for the spices in this recipe. For a colorful taste of the tropics, garnish with the optional mango.

1 tablespoon olive oil or ¼ cup water

1 small red onion, minced

1 red bell pepper, seeded and chopped

1 or 2 small, fresh hot chiles, seeded and minced

2 garlic cloves, minced

½ teaspoon grated fresh ginger

1 cup basmati rice

½ teaspoon natural sugar

½ teaspoon salt

½ teaspoon ground allspice

¼ teaspoon dried thyme

¼ teaspoon freshly grated nutmeg

2 cups hot water

1½ cups cooked dark red kidney or other red beans or 1 (15-ounce) can beans, rinsed and drained

3 tablespoons chopped fresh cilantro

1 ripe mango (optional), peeled, seeded, and chopped

1. Heat the olive oil or water in a saucepan over medium heat. Add the onion, bell pepper, chiles, garlic, and ginger. Cover and cook, stirring, until the onion is softened, about 5 minutes. Stir in the rice to coat with the oil. Add the sugar, salt, allspice, thyme, and nutmeg, stirring to combine. Stir in the water, reduce the heat to medium-low, cover, and cook until the rice is tender, 30 to 40 minutes.

2. Stir in the beans and cook until hot, about 5 minutes. Taste and adjust the seasonings, if needed. Serve hot, sprinkled with cilantro and mango, if using.

Serves 4

Spicy Jasmine Rice
with Carrots and Cashews

In this quick and easy dish, fragrant jasmine rice is stir-fried with vegetables, fresh ginger, and minced hot chile pepper. If you like, add some green peas for a color accent. The sweet crunch of cashews adds textural contrast, and the Thai basil, with its anise-like flavor, is stirred in at the end.

1 tablespoon neutral vegetable oil or ¼ cup water

1 red onion, finely chopped

1 small, fresh hot red chile, seeded and minced

1 large carrot, grated

2 garlic cloves, minced

2 teaspoons grated fresh ginger

3 scallions, minced

2 tablespoons low-sodium tamari

½ teaspoon natural sugar

3 cups cold cooked jasmine rice, broken up into small clumps

½ cup chopped fresh Thai basil or ¼ cup chopped fresh cilantro

½ cup chopped unsalted dry-roasted cashews

1. Heat the oil or water in a large skillet or wok over medium-high heat. Add the onion and stir-fry until softened, about 5 minutes. Add the chile, carrot, garlic, ginger, and scallions and stir-fry until soft and fragrant, about 2 minutes.

2. Add the tamari, sugar, and rice and stir-fry until the ingredients are blended and the rice is heated through, about 10 minutes. Stir in the basil.

3. To serve, transfer the rice to a shallow bowl, sprinkle with the chopped cashews, and serve immediately.

Serves 4

Indonesian-Style Rice with Tempeh

Inspired by the spicy-sweet Indonesian fried rice dish called *nasi goreng*, this can be made using alternative ingredients. For example, omit the tempeh, use broccoli and bell pepper instead of carrot and cabbage, or garnish with bean sprouts or diced tomato instead of cucumber and peanuts. The traditional accompaniment is *sambal,* a hot and spicy condiment that can be found in Asian markets.

3 shallots, trimmed and halved or 1 small onion, trimmed and quartered

1 or 2 small, fresh hot red chiles, seeded

1 garlic clove, crushed

¼ teaspoon salt

1 tablespoon neutral vegetable oil

1 large carrot, shredded

2 cups finely chopped napa cabbage

1 cup crumbled steamed tempeh (page 10)

3 tablespoons low-sodium tamari

1 teaspoon natural sugar

3 cups cold cooked basmati or other long-grain white or brown rice, broken up into small clumps

1 medium-size cucumber, peeled, seeded, and shredded, for garnish

½ cup chopped unsalted dry-roasted peanuts, for garnish

1. In a food processor or blender, combine the shallots, chiles, garlic, and salt and process until smooth. Set aside.

2. Heat the oil in a large skillet or wok over medium heat. Add the carrot and cabbage and stir-fry until slightly softened, about 1 minute. Add the tempeh, 1½ tablespoons of the tamari, and the sugar and cook until the tempeh is lightly browned, about 2 minutes. Stir in the reserved shallot mixture and cook until fragrant, about 30 seconds. Add the rice and the remaining 1½ tablespoons tamari and stir-fry to combine all of the ingredients and heat through, about 10 minutes.

3. To serve, place the rice mixture in a shallow serving bowl or on a large platter and garnish with the cucumber and peanuts.

Serves 4

Rice and Chickpeas with Broccoli Rabe

This nourishing and wholesome recipe makes a great one-dish meal that you can put together in minutes when you start with cooked rice and canned chickpeas. Broccoli rabe, also called rapini, looks sort of like "skinny" broccoli, with long slender stems, tiny buds, and leaves. It has a pleasant, slightly bitter flavor and is available in well-stocked supermarkets.

2 bunches broccoli rabe, stems trimmed

1 tablespoon olive oil or ¼ cup water

1 small onion, finely chopped

2 garlic cloves, minced

3 cups cold cooked brown rice, broken up into small clumps

1½ cups cooked chickpeas or 1 (15-ounce) can chickpeas, rinsed and drained

Salt and freshly ground black pepper

1. Bring a large pot of salted water to a boil over high heat. Cook the broccoli rabe until tender, about 5 minutes. Drain and coarsely chop. Set aside.

2. Heat the olive oil or water in a large skillet over medium heat. Add the onion and garlic, cover, and cook until softened, about 5 minutes. Add the broccoli rabe and cook for 2 minutes, stirring to combine. Stir in the rice, chickpeas, and salt and pepper to taste. Cook, stirring, until heated through, about 10 minutes. Serve hot.

Serves 4

Spicy Teff Griddle Cakes

This tiniest of grains is used to make *injera*, the traditional Ethiopian flatbread. High in protein and calcium, teff can be enjoyed as a breakfast cereal or used in baked goods. Serve these griddle cakes with any of a variety of sauces, including Choron Sauce (page 131) and Spicy Peanut Dipping Sauce (page 145). If you'd like to try these cakes for breakfast, omit the scallions and cayenne and top with pure maple syrup. Look for teff in natural foods stores.

½ cup teff

3 cups water, or as needed

1 cup unbleached all-purpose flour

½ cup minced scallions

1 teaspoon baking powder

⅛ teaspoon cayenne, or to taste

Salt

1. In a medium-size saucepan over medium heat, combine the teff and 1½ cups of the water. Cover and bring to a boil. Reduce the heat to low and simmer, stirring occasionally, until all of the water is absorbed, about 15 minutes.

2. Transfer the teff to a large bowl and add the flour, scallions, baking powder, cayenne, and salt to taste. Stir in as much of the remaining 1½ cups water as needed to make a batter and mix until smooth.

3. Preheat the oven to 200°F. Lightly oil a griddle or large skillet and place over medium-high heat. For each cake, ladle about ¼ cup of the batter onto the hot griddle and cook until it is browned on both sides, 3 to 4 minutes per side. Repeat until all of the batter is used, re-oiling the griddle as needed and keeping the cooked cakes warm in the oven.

Serves 4

Lemony Green Pea Risotto

The sparkling taste of fresh lemon makes this risotto ideal springtime fare. I like to accompany it with roasted asparagus and warm crusty bread.

5 cups vegetable broth

1 tablespoon olive oil

1½ cups Arborio rice

½ cup minced scallions

1 cup fresh or thawed frozen baby peas

2 teaspoons fine lemon zest

3 tablespoons fresh lemon juice

½ to 1 teaspoon salt

¼ teaspoon freshly ground black pepper

1. Bring the broth to a simmer in a medium-size saucepan over medium heat. Reduce the heat to low and continue to simmer.

2. In a large skillet or saucepan, heat the oil over medium heat. Add the rice and scallions and stir until coated with oil. Add ½ cup of the hot broth and simmer, stirring frequently, until the liquid is almost absorbed. Continue adding the broth ½ cup at a time, stirring until the liquid is absorbed, until the rice is tender but firm and the mixture is thick and creamy, about 25 minutes. You may not need to use all of the broth.

3. About 10 minutes before the risotto is finished, stir in the peas, lemon zest, lemon juice, salt (the amount needed will depend on the saltiness of your broth), and pepper. Taste and adjust the seasonings, if needed. Spoon into shallow bowls and serve hot.

Serves 4

Universal Pasta

"People often say that humans have always eaten animals, as if this is a justification for continuing the practice. According to this logic, we should not try to prevent people from murdering other people, since this has also been done since the earliest of times."

—ISAAC BASHEVIS SINGER

Everyone loves pasta. What's not to like? It's delicious and versatile, fun to eat, and easy to prepare. Pasta is an especially popular choice for vegan meals because of the seemingly endless variety of plant-based toppings. From the traditional tomato marinara sauce to basil pesto to the vegetable showcase pasta primavera, you could eat a different pasta meal every night. Add the international noodle dishes to pasta's repertoire, and your pasta world becomes a pasta universe.

You may already be familiar with naturally vegan pasta dishes—sauces that do not include meat or dairy. But there are easy ways to transform favorite meat- and dairy-based sauces into vegan originals. In this chapter, you will discover *Alfredo-Style Fettuccine,* made creamy with almonds and soy, and *Mac UnCheese* casserole, which works magic using tofu,

miso, and nutritional yeast. Veggie crumbles, eggplant, and mushrooms provide meaty substance in several tomato-based sauces. There's also a selection of hearty Eastern European recipes, including *Potato Pierogi and Cabbage with Pear and Dried Plum Compote,* as well as a number of flavorful Asian dishes that pair soba, udon, and rice sticks with vegetables, soy foods, and exotic seasonings.

Vegans, take note: Whereas most dried pasta is made without eggs, most fresh pasta is made with them. However, a few brands of fresh vegan pasta can be found in some natural foods stores and through mail-order sources. (This goes for egg-free "egg" noodles as well.) It is also possible to make fresh pasta at home without using eggs. The simplest approach, however, is to rely on dried pasta.

Penne and Butternut Squash with Kale Pesto

The pairing of butternut squash with kale is a longtime personal favorite, so I had no doubt that I would love the combination in this pasta dish.

8 ounces penne

½ small butternut squash, peeled, seeded, and cut into 1-inch dice (about 2 cups)

2 garlic cloves, minced

2 cups chopped kale leaves

¼ cup walnut pieces

2 tablespoons fresh lemon juice

2 tablespoons olive oil

¼ teaspoon salt

1 small red onion, finely chopped

1. Bring a medium-size pot of salted water to a boil over high heat. Add the pasta, and when the water returns to a boil, stir in the squash. Cook the pasta and squash together until just tender. Drain well, reserving ½ cup of the pasta water. Return the pasta and squash to the pot; cover to keep warm.

2. While the pasta and squash are cooking, make a kale pesto. In a food processor, combine the garlic, kale, walnuts, lemon juice, 1 tablespoon of the oil, and the salt. Process for 2 minutes until a paste forms. Add the reserved pasta water and continue to process until incorporated.

3. Heat the remaining 1 tablespoon oil in a large nonstick skillet over medium heat. Add the onion and cook for 5 minutes to soften. Add the pesto and cook, stirring, until fragrant. Combine the sauce with the pasta and squash, tossing to combine. Heat through if needed. Serve hot.

Serves 4

Eat Your Greens: Collards and Kale

Sturdy, dark leafy greens such as collards and kale are high in vitamins A and C, iron, calcium, and potassium. These hardy greens keep well in the refrigerator for a week or longer and are especially delicious boiled, steamed, or braised. They go well with grains and can be added to casseroles and stews. Pair collards or kale with carrots, sweet potatoes, or kidney beans for a colorful combination that is full of flavor and nutrition.

Pesto Paglia e Fieno
with Green and Yellow Squash

Tuscany's "straw and hay" pasta dish is so named for its green and yellow noodles. This recipe elaborates on the theme with the addition of green and yellow squash, cut into long strips with a mandoline, sharp knife, or vegetable peeler.

8 ounces spinach linguine

8 ounces regular linguine

1 tablespoon olive oil

1 medium-size zucchini, cut lengthwise into thin strips

1 medium-size yellow summer squash, cut lengthwise into thin strips

Salt and freshly ground black pepper

⅓ cup Basil Pesto (page 142) or purchased vegan pesto

1. Bring a large pot of salted water to a boil over high heat. Cook both types of linguine, stirring occasionally, until al dente.

2. While the pasta is cooking, heat the olive oil in medium-size skillet over medium heat, add the squash, and cook until softened, 3 to 4 minutes. Season to taste with salt and pepper. Reduce the heat to low. Add about ½ cup of pasta water to the cooked squash and stir in the pesto. Keep warm.

3. Drain the pasta and place in a large, shallow serving bowl. Add the squash and pesto mixture and toss gently to combine. Serve at once.

Serves 4

Linguine and Oyster Mushrooms with Gremolata

Gremolata is a zesty mixture of garlic, lemon, and parsley that brings out the slightly sweet flavor of the oyster mushrooms in this recipe. A garnish often sprinkled on Italian stews such as osso buco, this Milanese seasoning is paired here with pasta to good effect.

1 pound linguine	2½ cups sliced oyster mushrooms
2 tablespoons olive oil	Salt and freshly ground black pepper
¼ cup minced shallots	⅓ cup Gremolata (recipe follows)

1. Bring a large pot of salted water to a boil over high heat. Cook the linguine, stirring occasionally, until al dente.

2. While the pasta is cooking, heat the oil in a large skillet over medium heat. Add the shallots, cover, and cook until softened, about 5 minutes. Add the mushrooms and cook, stirring frequently, until they begin to soften, about 3 minutes. Season to taste with salt and pepper. Stir in about ½ cup of the hot pasta water and the gremolata.

3. Drain the pasta and place in a large, shallow serving bowl. Add the mushroom and gremolata mixture and toss gently to combine. Serve at once.

Serves 4

GREMOLATA

Gremolata is a flavorful garnish made with lemon, garlic, and parsley. It can be used to enhance certain stews, pastas, and sautéed dishes. I sometimes add 2 tablespoons of ground nuts or seeds for extra flavor and substance.

⅓ cup chopped fresh parsley	Grated zest of 1 lemon
2 large garlic cloves, chopped	

Mince the parsley, garlic, and lemon zest together until well combined. Cover tightly and refrigerate until ready to use. For the best flavor, use the gremolata the same day it is made, but it will keep for a day or so in the refrigerator.

Makes about ⅓ cup

Gemelli with Artichokes and Yellow Pepper Rouille

A rouille is a thick Provençal sauce usually made with roasted red peppers and thickened with bread. This version uses yellow peppers that are sautéed rather than roasted, resulting in a much lighter flavor.

2 tablespoons olive oil

2 large yellow bell peppers, seeded and coarsely chopped

1 slice firm white bread

½ teaspoon salt

⅛ teaspoon cayenne

8 to 12 ounces gemelli or other bite-size pasta

4 garlic cloves, minced

1 (15-ounce) can artichoke hearts, drained and quartered

2 tablespoons chopped fresh basil

1. Heat 1 tablespoon of the olive oil in a large skillet over medium-low heat. Add the bell peppers, cover, and cook until soft, about 15 minutes. Remove from the heat.

2. Trim the crust from the bread and soak in water to cover for 5 minutes. Squeeze out the water and place the bread in a food processor along with the cooked bell peppers, salt, and cayenne. Process until smooth, then set the rouille aside.

3. Bring a large pot of salted water to a boil over high heat. Cook the gemelli, stirring occasionally, until al dente.

4. While the pasta is cooking, heat the remaining 1 tablespoon olive oil in a medium-size skillet over medium heat. Add the garlic and cook until fragrant, about 30 seconds. Add the artichoke hearts and cook, stirring to coat with the garlic and oil, until heated through, about 5 minutes.

5. Drain the pasta and place in a large, shallow serving bowl. Add the artichokes and toss to combine. Top with the rouille, sprinkle with the basil, and serve immediately.

Serves 4

Ziti, Artichokes, and Olives with Spicy Tomato Sauce

Plum tomatoes are a good choice for making tomato sauce because they are meatier than regular tomatoes, with less water and seeds. Canned tomatoes may be used if fresh ones are unavailable or out of season.

1 tablespoon olive oil or ¼ cup water

1 medium-size onion, chopped

3 garlic cloves, chopped

2 tablespoons tomato paste

2 pounds ripe plum tomatoes, chopped, or 1 (28-ounce) can diced tomatoes, drained

1 (9-ounce) package frozen artichoke hearts, cooked according to package directions and drained

2 tablespoons dry red wine

½ teaspoon red pepper flakes

½ cup kalamata or other brine-cured black olives, pitted and chopped

Salt and freshly ground black pepper

1 pound ziti

¼ cup chopped fresh basil or parsley

1. Heat the olive oil or water in a large saucepan over medium heat. Add the onion, cover, and cook until softened, about 5 minutes. Stir in the garlic and tomato paste and cook, stirring, until the garlic is fragrant, about 30 seconds. Add the tomatoes, artichokes, wine, and red pepper flakes. Reduce the heat to low and stir in the olives. Season to taste with salt and pepper and simmer while you cook the ziti.

2. Bring a large pot of salted water to a boil over high heat. Cook the ziti, stirring occasionally, until al dente. Drain the pasta and place in a large, shallow serving bowl. Add the sauce and basil and toss to combine. Serve hot.

Serves 4

Fusilli with Roasted Asparagus, Sun-Dried Tomatoes, and Pine Nuts

The smoky flavor of sun-dried tomatoes teams with roasted asparagus and toasted pine nuts against a backdrop of chewy fusilli tossed in garlicky olive oil for a wonderful combination of textures and flavors.

12 ounces thin asparagus, trimmed and cut diagonally into 2-inch pieces

3 tablespoons olive oil

1 pound fusilli

3 garlic cloves, minced

½ cup oil-packed or rehydrated sun-dried tomatoes, cut into ¼-inch-wide strips

Salt and freshly ground black pepper

¼ cup chopped fresh basil or parsley

3 tablespoons pine nuts, toasted (page 203)

1. Preheat the oven to 450°F. Lightly oil a baking sheet. Toss the asparagus with 1 tablespoon of the olive oil and place on the baking sheet. Roast until just tender, 6 to 8 minutes. Remove from the oven and set aside.

2. Bring a large pot of salted water to a boil over high heat. Cook the fusilli, stirring occasionally, until al dente.

3. While the pasta is cooking, heat the remaining 2 tablespoons olive oil in a large skillet over medium heat. Add the garlic and cook, stirring, until fragrant, about 30 seconds. Add the roasted asparagus, tomatoes, and salt and pepper to taste. Reduce the heat to low and keep warm.

4. Drain the pasta and place in a large, shallow serving bowl. Add the asparagus mixture, basil, and pine nuts. Toss to combine. Serve hot.

===== *Serves 4* =====

Linguine with Pesto-Kissed Tomato Sauce

Basil pesto is swirled into the tomato sauce just before serving to add an extra dimension of flavor. For a heartier sauce, add some chopped seitan or cooked lentils or cannellini beans near the end of the cooking time.

1 tablespoon olive oil or ¼ cup water

1 small onion, chopped

2 garlic cloves, minced

¼ cup tomato paste

1 (28-ounce) can crushed tomatoes

Salt and freshly ground black pepper

¼ cup Basil Pesto (page 142) or purchased vegan pesto

1 pound linguine

1. Heat the olive oil or water in a large skillet over medium heat. Add the onion, cover, and cook until softened, about 5 minutes. Add the garlic and cook, stirring, until fragrant, about 30 seconds. Stir in the tomato paste, crushed tomatoes, and salt and pepper to taste. Reduce the heat to low and simmer to reduce slightly and blend the flavors, 10 to 15 minutes.

2. As the sauce simmers, bring a large pot of salted water to a boil over high heat. Cook the linguine, stirring occasionally, until al dente.

3. Drain the pasta and place in a large, shallow serving bowl. Blend the pesto into the sauce, add it to the pasta, and toss to coat evenly. Serve hot.

Serves 4

Penne Puttanesca

The name of this piquant pasta sauce means "streetwalker style," supposedly because ladies of the evening often prepared it at the end of a long night's work. Flavorful gaeta olives are available in Italian markets and well-stocked supermarkets and are especially good in this sauce. If unavailable, substitute another high-quality black olive such as kalamata.

2 tablespoons olive oil

3 to 5 garlic cloves, minced

1 (28-ounce) can crushed tomatoes

½ cup pitted and sliced black gaeta olives

¼ cup pitted and sliced green olives

2 tablespoons capers, drained and chopped

½ teaspoon red pepper flakes

Salt and freshly ground black pepper

1 pound penne

2 tablespoons minced fresh parsley

1. Heat the olive oil in a large saucepan over medium heat. Add the garlic and cook, stirring, until fragrant, about 30 seconds. Stir in the tomatoes, black and green olives, capers, red pepper flakes, and salt and pepper to taste. Reduce the heat to low and simmer, stirring occasionally, for 10 to 15 minutes to blend the flavors.

2. While the sauce is simmering, bring a large pot of salted water to a boil over high heat. Cook the penne, stirring occasionally, until al dente.

3. Drain the pasta and place in a large, shallow serving bowl. Add the sauce and toss gently to combine. Sprinkle with the parsley and serve hot.

Serves 4

Pappardelle Cacciatore

As a child, when my mom made chicken cacciatore, I'd skip the chicken and enjoy the tender stewed vegetables and wide ribbon pasta that went with it. Now I enjoy Mom's recipe made with tempeh and still savor the pasta and vegetables. If pappardelle is unavailable, use fettuccine instead.

2 tablespoons olive oil

8 ounces tempeh, steamed (page 10) and cut into 1-inch pieces

½ cup dry white wine

1 celery rib, coarsely chopped

1 carrot, coarsely chopped

1 green bell pepper, seeded and coarsely chopped

3 garlic cloves, minced

1 (28-ounce) can diced tomatoes, undrained

1 teaspoon minced fresh rosemary or ½ teaspoon dried rosemary

1 teaspoon minced fresh marjoram or ½ teaspoon dried marjoram

½ teaspoon salt

¼ teaspoon freshly ground black pepper

1 pound pappardelle or fettuccine

1. Heat 1 tablespoon of the olive oil in a large skillet over medium heat. Add the tempeh and cook, stirring, until lightly browned on all sides, about 5 minutes. Remove from the skillet and set aside.

2. Deglaze the pan with the wine, stirring to scrape up any browned bits of tempeh from the bottom. Reduce the wine by half and set aside.

3. Heat the remaining 1 tablespoon olive oil in a large saucepan over medium heat. Add the celery, carrot, bell pepper, and garlic. Cover and cook until softened, about 10 minutes. Add the tomatoes and their juice, rosemary, marjoram, salt, and pepper and simmer for 15 minutes. Add the reserved tempeh and reduced wine and simmer for 15 minutes to blend the flavors. Reduce the heat to low and keep warm.

4. Bring a large pot of salted water to a boil over high heat. Cook the pappardelle, stirring occasionally, until al dente. Drain and divide among 4 individual plates or shallow bowls. Top with the sauce and serve at once.

Serves 4

Tuscan-Style Pasta with Chickpeas, Zucchini, and Rosemary

Beans are so prevalent in Tuscan cooking that the people of Tuscany are called bean eaters. For variety, fresh basil or another fragrant herb may be substituted for the rosemary.

2 tablespoons olive oil

2 small zucchini, halved lengthwise and cut into ¼-inch-thick half-moons

3 garlic cloves, minced

1½ cups cooked chickpeas or 1 (15-ounce) can chickpeas, rinsed and drained

1 (14.5-ounce) can diced tomatoes, drained

1 tablespoon chopped fresh rosemary

¼ teaspoon red pepper flakes

Salt and freshly ground black pepper

1 pound penne

1. Heat the olive oil in a medium-size saucepan over medium heat. Add the zucchini and cook until slightly softened, about 2 minutes. Add the garlic and cook until fragrant, about 30 seconds. Stir in the chickpeas, tomatoes, rosemary, red pepper flakes, and salt and pepper to taste. Cook, stirring occasionally, for 10 minutes to blend the flavors.

2. Meanwhile, bring a large pot of salted water to a boil over high heat. Cook the penne, stirring occasionally, until al dente. Drain and place in a large, shallow serving bowl. Add the sauce and toss gently to combine. Serve at once.

Serves 4

Pasta: Fresh versus Dried

Both fresh and dried pasta are enjoyed for their unique tastes and textures. Although both can produce delicious results, commercially made fresh pasta is generally not vegan, since it is usually prepared with eggs, which are combined with all-purpose flour to make a soft dough that is then rolled through a pasta machine. By contrast, dried pasta is made by an extrusion process using semolina flour and water—no eggs. The good news is that if you really prefer fresh pasta, you can easily make fresh egg-free pasta at home. In addition, a few commercial egg-free brands are available in natural foods stores or from mail-order outlets.

Dried pasta takes longer to cook than fresh, usually 3 to 15 minutes, depending on the shape, and the preferred outcome is al dente, or "firm to the bite." Fresh pasta cooks in 2 to 3 minutes, with more tender results. Dried pasta will keep for up to a year when stored in a tightly sealed container in a cool, dry place. Fresh pasta will keep in the refrigerator for up to 1 week or in the freezer for up to 1 month.

Fettuccine with Red Lentil Sauce

Although lentils are more prominent in Indian and Middle Eastern cooking, they are also used in Italian cuisine. This thin, lens-shaped legume is rich in protein, calcium, iron, and B vitamins. Use red lentils if you can find them; otherwise, brown are fine. Since lentils do not require soaking and cook quickly in 30 minutes, this recipe doesn't require a lot of planning to get dinner on the table.

¾ cup dried red or brown lentils, picked over and rinsed

2 carrots, cut into thin diagonal slices

1 celery rib, diced

2 tablespoons olive oil

1 garlic clove, minced

1 (6-ounce) can tomato paste

Salt and freshly ground black pepper

1 pound fettuccine

2 tablespoons chopped fresh flat-leaf parsley

1. Bring a medium-size pot of salted water to a boil over high heat. Add the lentils, carrots, and celery, reduce the heat to medium-low, and simmer until tender, about 30 minutes. Drain, reserving 2 cups of the cooking liquid. Toss the lentil mixture with 1 tablespoon of the olive oil and set aside.

2. Heat the remaining 1 tablespoon oil in a large skillet over medium heat. Add the garlic and cook until fragrant, about 30 seconds. Stir in the tomato paste and cook for 2 minutes to mellow the flavor of the paste. Stir in the reserved lentil cooking liquid, blending until smooth. Add the lentil mixture and season to taste with salt and pepper. Reduce the heat to low and simmer to blend the flavors while you cook the pasta. If too much liquid evaporates, add some water.

3. Bring a large pot of salted water to a boil over high heat. Cook the fettuccine, stirring occasionally, until al dente. Drain and divide among 4 individual plates or shallow bowls. Top with the sauce, sprinkle with the parsley, and serve at once.

Serves 4

Linguine with Sage and White Bean Sauce

Cannellini beans flavored with sage are a popular Tuscan combination. Here they are pureed into a creamy pasta sauce enlivened with a splash of balsamic vinegar, a slightly sweet and syrupy aged vinegar from Modena, Italy.

1 tablespoon olive oil

1 small onion, minced

¼ cup torn fresh sage leaves

1½ cups cooked cannellini beans
or 1 (15-ounce) can beans, rinsed and drained

2 teaspoons balsamic vinegar

½ teaspoon salt

¼ teaspoon freshly ground black pepper

½ cup hot vegetable broth
or water, or more as needed

1 pound linguine

Whole fresh sage leaves, for garnish

1. Heat the oil in a large skillet over medium heat. Add the onion, cover, and cook until softened, about 5 minutes. Add the torn sage leaves and cook for 1 minute. Add the beans, vinegar, salt, and pepper. Stir to blend the flavors.

2. Transfer the mixture to a food processor or blender, add the broth, and process until smooth, adding more broth, if necessary. Transfer to a small saucepan and keep warm over low heat, adding more broth if the sauce is too thick.

3. Bring a large pot of salted water to a boil over high heat. Cook the linguine, stirring occasionally, until al dente. Drain and place in a large, shallow serving bowl. Add the sauce and toss to combine. Garnish with the whole sage leaves and serve at once.

Serves 4

Alfredo-Style Fettuccine

Inspired by the Roman classic made with grated cheese and heavy cream, this version relies on cashew cream and cannellini beans to create a delicious, protein-rich sauce.

1 tablespoon olive oil or ¼ cup water

1 small onion, chopped

2 garlic cloves, minced

2 tablespoons dry white wine

1 cup cooked or canned cannellini beans, rinsed and drained

½ cup Cashew Cream (page 127)

¼ cup nutritional yeast

1 tablespoon lemon juice

2 cups plain unsweetened nondairy milk, or as needed

½ teaspoon salt, or more to taste

Pinch of freshly grated nutmeg

Pinch of cayenne

12 ounces fettuccine

2 tablespoons minced fresh parsley or basil

Freshly ground black pepper

1. Heat the olive oil or water in a small skillet over medium heat. Add the onion and garlic, cover, and cook until softened, about 5 minutes. Stir in the wine and cook for 1 minute longer.

2. In a high-speed blender or food processor, combine the onion mixture, beans, cashew cream, nutritional yeast, and lemon juice. Process until blended. Add the nondairy milk, salt, nutmeg, and cayenne and process until smooth.

3. Transfer to a medium-size saucepan and heat gently over low heat. Taste and adjust the seasonings and keep warm.

4. Bring a large pot of salted water to a boil over high heat. Cook the fettuccine, stirring occasionally, until al dente. Drain and place in a large, shallow serving bowl. Add the sauce and toss. Sprinkle with the parsley and freshly ground black pepper. Serve hot.

Serves 4

Mac UnCheese

Reminiscent of the baked macaroni and cheese my mother used to make, this version is made rich and creamy thanks to the addition of cooked cauliflower blended with cashew cream.

8 ounces elbow macaroni

2 tablespoons olive oil

1 large onion, chopped

2 cups plain unsweetened nondairy milk

1½ cups steamed cauliflower florets

1 cup Cashew Cream (page 127)

½ cup nutritional yeast

1½ tablespoons fresh lemon juice

1 teaspoon prepared yellow mustard

1 teaspoon smoked paprika

¼ teaspoon cayenne (optional)

Pinch of freshly grated nutmeg

Salt

¼ cup dry bread crumbs

¼ cup Parma-zen (recipe follows)

1. Lightly oil a 2½-quart baking dish and set aside.

2. Bring a medium-size pot of salted water to a boil over high heat. Cook the macaroni, stirring occasionally, until it is al dente. Drain well and transfer to the prepared baking dish. Preheat the oven to 375°F.

3. Heat 1 tablespoon of the olive oil in a medium-size skillet over medium heat. Add the onion, cover, and cook until softened, about 5 minutes.

4. Transfer the cooked onion to a blender or food processor. Add the nondairy milk, cauliflower, cashew cream, nutritional yeast, lemon juice, mustard, paprika, cayenne (if using), nutmeg, and salt to taste. Process until smooth. Pour the sauce over the macaroni and mix well.

5. In a small bowl, combine the bread crumbs and Parma-zen with the remaining 1 tablespoon olive oil, stirring to coat. Sprinkle the crumb mixture evenly over the macaroni mixture, cover, and bake until hot and bubbly, about 25 minutes. Uncover and bake until the top is lightly browned, about 10 minutes more. Remove from the oven and let sit for 5 minutes before serving.

Serves 4

PARMA-ZEN

This nutty alternative to Parmesan cheese combines a variety of nuts and seeds with nutritional yeast and a little salt, resulting in a flavor-packed topping that tastes great on pasta or grain dishes, salads, casseroles, or anything where you want a little cheesy crunch.

½ cup toasted walnuts (page 203)

½ cup raw almonds

2 tablespoons raw sesame seeds, pine nuts, or shelled sunflower seeds

3 tablespoons nutritional yeast

½ teaspoon salt

Combine the walnuts, almonds, and sesame seeds in a food processor or blender and process until finely ground. (Don't overprocess, or you will end up with nut butter.) Transfer to a bowl and add the nutritional yeast and salt. Mix to combine well. Transfer to a tightly covered container and store in the refrigerator.

===== *Makes about 1½ cups* =====

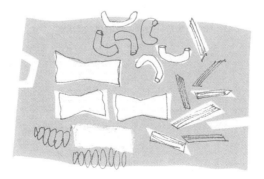

Easy Mac and Cheesy

This stovetop mac and cheese is quick to make and delicious. You can add your favorite cooked vegetable, such as broccoli or green peas, if you like.

8 ounces elbow macaroni

¾ cup nutritional yeast

¼ cup jarred pimientos or coarsely chopped roasted red bell pepper

2 tablespoons almond butter

2 tablespoons fresh lemon juice

2 tablespoons cornstarch

1 teaspoon mellow white miso

1 teaspoon salt

1 teaspoon onion powder

½ teaspoon garlic powder

½ teaspoon prepared yellow mustard

½ teaspoon paprika, preferably smoked

¼ teaspoon turmeric

¼ teaspoon ground black pepper

2 cups plain unsweetened nondairy milk

1 or 2 cups cooked broccoli, cauliflower, peas, or asparagus (optional)

1. Bring a medium-size pot of salted water to a boil over high heat. Cook the macaroni until it is al dente. Drain and return to the pot.

2. While the macaroni is cooking, combine the nutritional yeast, pimientos, almond butter, and lemon juice in a food processor or high-speed blender. Add the cornstarch, miso, salt, onion powder, garlic powder, mustard, paprika, turmeric, and pepper. Pour in 1 cup of the nondairy milk and blend until smooth. Add the remaining 1 cup nondairy milk and blend until completely smooth and creamy.

3. Add the sauce mixture to the pot containing the cooked and drained macaroni and cook, stirring, over medium heat until the sauce begins to thicken. Taste and adjust the seasonings, if needed. Stir in 1 or 2 cups of cooked vegetables, if desired. If the mixture becomes too thick, stir in a little extra nondairy milk or some vegetable broth. Serve hot.

Serves 4

Tahini Rotini with Broccoli and Lemon

Tahini, or sesame paste, is loaded with protein and calcium, while broccoli is a good source of calcium, vitamin C, and other nutrients. It's hard to believe that a dish that's so good for you could taste this rich and creamy. Typically used in Middle Eastern cuisine, tahini is available in well-stocked supermarkets, natural foods stores, and specialty food shops.

1 cup cooked or canned chickpeas, rinsed and drained

Juice and zest of 1 lemon

2 large garlic cloves, crushed

2 tablespoons tahini

2 tablespoons low-sodium tamari

⅛ teaspoon cayenne

1½ cups vegetable broth or water

8 ounces rotini

3 cups small broccoli florets

2 tablespoons sesame seeds, toasted (page 171)

1. In a food processor, combine the chickpeas, lemon juice (reserve the zest), garlic, tahini, tamari, and cayenne and process until smooth. Add 1 cup of the vegetable broth and process until smooth. Transfer the mixture to a medium-size saucepan over low heat. Stir in the remaining broth and heat until hot, stirring occasionally. Keep warm.

2. Bring a large pot of salted water to a boil over high heat. Cook the rotini, stirring occasionally, until al dente. During the last 2 or 3 minutes of cooking time (depending on how firm you like your broccoli), add the broccoli florets to the pot with the pasta.

3. Drain the pasta and broccoli and transfer to a large, shallow serving bowl. Add the warm tahini sauce and toss gently. Sprinkle with the reserved lemon zest and sesame seeds and serve at once.

Serves 4

Ravioli without Borders

This recipe is inspired by "open" ravioli, in which the pasta and stuffing are layered rather than sealed shut. Taking it a step further, these borderless ravioli use ingredients that traverse the globe. For a quicker version, top all of the ravioli with your favorite marinara sauce.

1 tablespoon olive oil or ¼ cup water

3 garlic cloves, minced

¼ cup minced onion

8 ounces fresh cremini mushrooms, finely chopped

8 ounces firm tofu, drained and crumbled

2 tablespoons nutritional yeast

½ large roasted red bell pepper, finely chopped

2 oil-packed or rehydrated sun-dried tomatoes, minced

½ teaspoon salt

¼ teaspoon freshly ground black pepper

24 vegan wonton wrappers, thawed if frozen, or 6 lasagna noodles (see Note)

24 baby spinach leaves, lightly steamed and kept warm

1 cup of your favorite marinara sauce, warmed

¼ cup Basil Pesto (page 142) or purchased vegan pesto

¼ cup black olive tapenade

Whole fresh basil leaves or minced fresh parsley, for garnish

1. Heat the olive oil or water in a large skillet over medium heat. Add the garlic, onion, and mushrooms. Cook, stirring, until softened, about 5 minutes. Stir in the tofu, nutritional yeast, roasted pepper, sundried tomatoes, salt, and pepper. Continue cooking until all of the liquid evaporates, then reduce the heat to low and keep warm.

2. Bring a large pot of salted water to a gentle boil over high heat. Working in batches, cook the wonton wrappers until they rise to the surface and are tender. Using a slotted spoon, transfer the cooked wonton wrappers to a dry kitchen towel to drain.

3. To serve, spread a small amount of marinara sauce on each of 4 plates, then arrange 3 wonton wrappers on top of the sauce on each plate in a spoke-like fashion. Top each wrapper with 2 spinach leaves. Top the spinach with a spoonful of the warm filling mixture and top the filling with the remaining wonton wrappers. Place a spoonful of the pesto on one of the assembled ravioli on each plate, a spoonful of the tapenade on another of the ravioli on each plate, and a spoonful of the marinara on the remaining ravioli on each plate. Garnish with the basil and serve hot.

Serves 4

NOTE: You can substitute lasagna noodles for the wonton wrappers. Just soften 6 noodles in hot water until pliable, then cut each into 4 squares.

Sweet Noodle Kugel
with Apples and Almonds

For convenience, you can assemble the kugel the day before and refrigerate it until needed. For best results, return it to room temperature before baking. Served with a salad, this makes a good lunch or brunch entrée.

8 ounces fettuccine, broken into thirds

1 large Delicious apple, peeled, cored, and shredded

½ cup golden raisins, soaked in boiling water to cover and drained

2 teaspoons fresh lemon juice

1 (12-ounce) package soft silken tofu, drained

2 cups plain unsweetened nondairy milk

½ cup plus 1 tablespoon natural sugar

¼ cup almond butter

2 teaspoons ground cinnamon

1 teaspoon pure vanilla extract

½ cup ground almonds

½ cup fresh bread crumbs

2 tablespoons neutral vegetable oil

1. Bring a large pot of salted water to a boil over high heat. Cook the fettuccine, stirring occasionally, until al dente. Drain and place in a large bowl. Add the apple, raisins, and lemon juice. Toss well to mix and set aside.

2. Preheat the oven to 350°F. Lightly oil a shallow 9 x 13-inch baking dish. In a food processor or blender, combine the tofu, nondairy milk, ½ cup of the sugar, the almond butter, 1 teaspoon of the cinnamon, and the vanilla and process until smooth. Stir into the noodle mixture and mix well.

3. Transfer to the prepared baking dish, cover, and bake for 30 minutes.

4. While the kugel is baking, combine the almonds, bread crumbs, oil, and remaining 1 tablespoon sugar and 1 teaspoon cinnamon in a small bowl.

5. Remove the kugel from the oven, top evenly with the almond-crumb mixture, and bake, uncovered, until lightly browned, about 10 minutes. Let stand for 15 minutes before serving. Serve warm or at room temperature.

Serves 6

Potato Pierogi and Cabbage with Pear and Dried Plum Compote

My mother always made three kinds of pierogi: potato, cabbage, and prune. It was then up to everyone in the family to discern his or her favorite by the slight color variation the different filling would impart through the dough. As luck would have it, I enjoyed all three. My updated and streamlined interpretation of Mom's recipe is for potato pierogi (most people's favorite), but I like to serve them with sautéed cabbage and a dried plum compote. That way, I can still enjoy the flavors of all three varieties.

FILLING
1½ pounds Yukon Gold potatoes

Salt and freshly ground black pepper

2 tablespoons olive oil

1 small onion, minced

DOUGH
3 cups unbleached all-purpose flour

1 cup water

1 tablespoon olive oil

1 teaspoon salt

CABBAGE
2 tablespoons olive oil

½ small head Savoy cabbage, cored and thinly sliced

Salt and freshly ground black pepper

1 to 1½ cups Pear and Dried Plum Compote (page 513)

1. To make the filling, peel the potatoes and cut them into 2-inch chunks. Place in a large pot with cold salted water to cover. Bring to a boil over medium-high heat and cook the potatoes until tender, about 20 minutes. Drain and mash, then season to taste with salt and pepper and set aside.

2. Heat the olive oil in a medium-size skillet over medium heat. Add the onion, cover, and cook until softened, about 5 minutes. Add the onion to the potatoes and set aside to cool completely.

3. To make the dough, place the flour in a large bowl and make a well in the center. Add the water, olive oil, and salt and mix until combined. Knead until smooth, then divide the dough in half.

4. On a floured work surface, roll out one piece of the dough into a rectangle about ⅛ inch thick. Cut into 4-inch-wide strips, then cut crosswise to make 4-inch squares.

5. To assemble the pierogi, place a heaping tablespoon of the filling on one half of each dough square. Moisten the edges and fold over into triangles. To seal, press the edges together with your fingers or the tines of a fork. Repeat with the remaining dough and filling.

6. Bring a large pot of salted water to a boil over high heat. Working in batches, cook the pierogi until they float, 2 to 3 minutes. Drain well and transfer to a plate. Repeat until all of the pierogi are cooked.

7. To make the cabbage, heat 1 tablespoon of the olive oil in a large skillet over medium heat. Add the cabbage and salt and pepper to taste. Cook, stirring occasionally, until tender, 8 to 10 minutes. Keep warm.

8. To fry the pierogi, heat the remaining 1 tablespoon olive oil in a large nonstick skillet over medium heat. Working in batches, cook the pierogi until lightly browned on both sides, about 3 minutes total.

9. To serve, arrange the cabbage on a serving platter and top with the pierogi. Serve with the compote on the side.

Serves 6

Did You Know?

If you add salt to the water when washing vegetables, it will help remove any insects, sand, and other particles.

Kasha with Buttons and Bow Ties

The eastern European favorite known as *kasha varnishkas* is made with buckwheat groats, or kasha, combined with bow-tie pasta, or farfalle. I like to add carrot "buttons" for color, as well as to further embellish the whimsical name. The homey nature of this naturally vegan dish makes it ideal winter fare. Look for kasha in well-stocked supermarkets and natural foods stores.

2 tablespoons olive oil

1 cup coarse buckwheat groats (kasha)

2 small carrots, cut into thin rounds

2 cups hot vegetable broth

8 ounces farfalle

1 small onion, chopped

Salt and freshly ground black pepper

2 tablespoons minced fresh parsley, for garnish

1. Heat 1 tablespoon of the olive oil in a medium-size saucepan over medium heat. Stir in the groats and carrots and cook for 2 minutes, stirring to coat with the oil. Add the broth and bring to a boil. Reduce the heat to low, cover, and simmer until the groats are cooked and the carrots are tender, about 15 minutes. Set aside.

2. Bring a large pot of salted water to a boil over high heat. Cook the farfalle, stirring occasionally, until al dente. Drain, combine with the groats and carrots, and set aside.

3. Heat the remaining 1 tablespoon olive oil in a small skillet over medium heat. Add the onion and cook, stirring, until tender and lightly browned, about 10 minutes. Stir the onion into the groats mixture and season to taste with salt and pepper. Set over low heat, stirring gently, to heat through, about 5 minutes. Garnish with the parsley and serve hot.

Serves 4

Pesto-Tossed Golden Potato Gnocchi

A bit of turmeric adds a light golden hue to the gnocchi to make a colorful contrast to the green pesto. For best results, make sure the potatoes are still warm when making the dough. Be judicious in your use of turmeric, using only enough to impart a light golden color—too much will turn the gnocchi bright yellow and add a slightly bitter flavor. If you won't be using the gnocchi right away, place the raw gnocchi on cookie sheets and freeze for several hours or overnight. Transfer them to plastic bags and store in the freezer, where they will keep for a month or so.

2 large baking potatoes

1 cup unbleached all-purpose flour, or more as desired

1 teaspoon salt

¼ teaspoon turmeric, or more as needed

½ cup Basil Pesto (page 142) or purchased vegan pesto, at room temperature

1. Preheat the oven to 400°F. Puncture the potatoes in a few places and bake until soft, about 1 hour. Reduce the oven temperature to 275°F.

2. Place the flour in a large bowl and sprinkle with the salt. Make a well in the center of the flour and set aside.

3. Peel the potatoes while they are still hot and mash them using a potato masher or ricer. Sprinkle on the turmeric, stirring gently to incorporate it. Place the potatoes in the center of the flour. Using a spoon, slowly draw the flour into the potatoes to form a slightly sticky dough, adding more flour, if necessary. If a deeper yellow color is desired, sprinkle on a little more turmeric. Knead the dough until smooth, 3 to 4 minutes. Divide the dough into 6 pieces.

4. On a floured work surface, use your palms to roll each piece of dough into a ½-inch-thick rope. Cut into ¾-inch pieces, then roll each piece briefly between your fingers to smooth the edges. Press the tines of a fork against one side of each gnocchi.

5. Bring a large pot of salted water to a boil over high heat. Working in batches, cook the gnocchi until they rise to the top, about 3 minutes. Remove with a slotted spoon and drain well. Transfer to a rimmed baking sheet and keep warm in the oven while you cook the rest.

6. Once all of the gnocchi are cooked, place in a large, shallow serving bowl, add the pesto, and toss gently to combine. Serve hot.

Serves 4

Vermicelli and Vegetables with Creamy Curry Sauce

In India, vermicelli noodles are often used to make a sweet pudding, but I prefer to prepare them with a savory curry sauce and lots of vegetables. At Indian markets, you can find a variety of curry seasoning blends in powder or paste form, from mild to extra-hot. If the Madras curry powder sold in supermarkets is all that is available, that will work, too. Accompany this dish with Three-Fruit Chutney (page 151) or another chutney of your choice.

1 tablespoon neutral vegetable oil or ¼ cup water

1 small onion, minced

1 small carrot, thinly sliced

1 small green or red bell pepper, seeded and chopped

2 garlic cloves, minced

2 tablespoons Indian curry powder or paste

1 (14.5-ounce) can diced tomatoes, undrained

1½ cups cooked chickpeas or 1 (15-ounce) can chickpeas, rinsed and drained

½ cup fresh or thawed frozen peas

1 (14-ounce) can unsweetened coconut milk

4 ounces soft silken tofu, drained

Salt and freshly ground black pepper

12 ounces vermicelli

½ cup chopped unsalted dry-roasted peanuts

2 scallions, minced

1. Heat the oil or water in a large skillet over medium heat. Add the onion, carrot, and bell pepper. Cover and cook until softened, about 5 minutes. Add the garlic and curry and stir to blend. Stir in the tomatoes and their juice, simmer to blend the flavors, and reduce the liquid by half, 5 to 7 minutes. Add the chickpeas and peas, reduce the heat to low, and keep warm.

2. In a food processor or blender, combine the coconut milk, tofu, and salt and pepper to taste. Process until smooth, then stir into the vegetable mixture and simmer gently.

3. Bring a large pot of salted water to a boil over high heat. Cook the vermicelli, stirring occasionally, until al dente. Drain and place in a large, shallow serving bowl. Add the vegetables and sauce and toss well to combine. Sprinkle with the peanuts and scallions and serve hot.

Serves 4

Udon-Shiitake Stir-Fry with Sake and Ginger

This noodle stir-fry features udon, the chewy noodles from Japan, combined with woodsy shiitake mushrooms and a flavorful sauce laced with sake and ginger. If sake is unavailable, dry white wine may be substituted. I like to precede this dish with an appetizer of edamame, fresh soybeans in the pod. Frozen edamame can be found in Asian markets and some supermarkets.

12 ounces udon noodles

2 teaspoons toasted sesame oil

3 tablespoons sake

3 tablespoons low-sodium tamari

1 tablespoon brown rice syrup or agave nectar

1 tablespoon neutral vegetable oil

2 shallots, finely chopped

8 ounces fresh shiitake mushrooms, stems removed and caps thinly sliced

1 tablespoon minced fresh ginger

1. Cook the udon noodles according to the package directions. Drain and place in a medium-size bowl. Add the sesame oil and toss to combine. Set aside.

2. In a small bowl, combine the sake, tamari, and brown rice syrup and stir until well blended. Set aside.

3. Heat the oil in a large skillet or wok over medium-high heat. Add the shallots, mushrooms, and ginger and stir-fry until the mushrooms are tender, about 3 minutes.

4. Stir in the sake mixture and udon noodles and cook, stirring, until heated through, 3 to 5 minutes. Serve hot.

Serves 4

Pad Thai

Slightly sweet and sour and mildly spiced, pad thai is the most popular Thai noodle dish in the West. For a colorful addition, add bite-size pieces of steamed broccoli or green beans.

8 ounces fresh or dried rice noodles

2 tablespoons plus 1 teaspoon neutral vegetable oil

8 ounces extra-firm tofu, drained and cut into ½-inch-wide strips

2 tablespoons low-sodium tamari

1 red bell pepper, seeded and cut into thin strips

6 scallions, chopped

2 or 3 garlic cloves, minced

1 cup cherry tomatoes, halved

2 tablespoons tamarind sauce

2 tablespoons rice vinegar

2 teaspoons natural sugar

½ cup fresh bean sprouts

¼ cup chopped unsalted dry-roasted peanuts

1. Prepare the rice noodles. If fresh, rinse under very hot water and place in a large bowl, separating them into individual strands. If dried, plunge into a large pot of boiling water to soften. Drain and place in a large bowl. Toss the noodles with 1 teaspoon of the oil and set aside.

2. Heat 1 tablespoon of the oil in a large skillet or wok over medium-high heat. Add the tofu and stir-fry until golden brown, about 7 minutes. Add 1 tablespoon of the tamari, stirring to coat. Transfer to a platter and set aside.

3. Heat the remaining 1 tablespoon oil in the same skillet or wok over medium heat. Add the bell pepper, scallions, and garlic and stir-fry until softened, about 5 minutes. Add the tomatoes, tamarind sauce, vinegar, sugar, and remaining 1 tablespoon tamari. Cook for 1 minute, then stir in the reserved noodles and tofu and toss gently to combine and heat through, about 5 minutes.

4. Divide among individual plates, sprinkle with the bean sprouts and peanuts, and serve at once.

Serves 4

Rice Noodles and Tofu with Asian Pesto

Fresh and dried rice noodles are available at Asian markets in a variety of sizes, from narrow vermicelli to ¼-inch-wide rice sticks. Some stores carry rice noodle sheets that you can cut to any width you prefer. As a flavor variation, you could use Thai basil or mint leaves instead of the cilantro.

2 large garlic cloves, crushed

1 small, fresh hot chile (optional), seeded

⅓ cup unsalted dry-roasted peanuts

1 teaspoon grated fresh ginger

1½ cups loosely packed fresh cilantro leaves

½ cup loosely packed fresh parsley leaves

2 tablespoons toasted sesame oil

1 tablespoon neutral vegetable oil

8 ounces extra-firm tofu, drained and cut into ½-inch dice

1 tablespoon low-sodium tamari

1 pound fresh or dried rice noodles

1. In a food processor, combine the garlic, chile (if using), peanuts, and ginger and process until minced. Add the cilantro and parsley and process into a paste. With the machine running, add the sesame oil through the feed tube and process until smooth. Set aside.

2. Heat the vegetable oil in a large skillet over medium-high heat. Add the tofu and cook until golden brown all over, about 5 minutes. Sprinkle with the tamari, tossing to coat. Reduce the heat to low and keep warm.

3. Prepare the rice noodles. If fresh, rinse under very hot water and place in a large, shallow serving bowl, separating them into individual strands. If dried, plunge into a large pot of boiling water to soften. Drain and place in a large, shallow serving bowl. Toss the noodles with the pesto to coat evenly. Top with the tofu and serve hot.

Serves 4

Sesame Soba Noodles

Soba, or Japanese buckwheat noodles, have a nutty flavor that matches well with the creamy sesame sauce, which is also rich in protein and calcium. Colorful vegetables add textural variety as well as nutrients.

⅓ cup tahini

3 garlic cloves, crushed

3 tablespoons low-sodium tamari

2 tablespoons toasted sesame oil

1 tablespoon brown rice vinegar

2 teaspoons natural sugar

½ to ¾ cup water, as needed

1 tablespoon neutral vegetable oil or ¼ cup water

1 large carrot, cut into small matchsticks

½ red bell pepper, seeded and cut into small matchsticks

½ cup fresh or thawed frozen peas

12 ounces soba noodles

1 tablespoon sesame seeds, toasted (page 171)

1. In a food processor or blender, process the tahini, garlic, tamari, 1 tablespoon of the sesame oil, the vinegar, sugar, and enough water to obtain a smooth, sauce-like consistency. Transfer the sauce to a small saucepan and heat over low heat, stirring until hot. Keep the sauce warm.

2. Heat the vegetable oil or water in a medium-size skillet over medium-high heat. Add the carrot and bell pepper and stir-fry until tender, 3 to 5 minutes. Add the peas and stir-fry until hot, about 1 minute. Reduce the heat to low and keep the vegetables warm.

3. Cook the soba noodles according to the package directions. Drain and place in a large, shallow serving bowl. Drizzle on the remaining 1 tablespoon sesame oil and toss to coat evenly. Add the vegetables and sauce and toss to combine. Sprinkle with the sesame seeds and serve hot.

Serves 4

Drunken Noodles

Some say this Thai dish is so named because it features hot chiles, which are believed to be a cure for hangovers. Whatever the reason for the name, it is one of my favorite dishes. The distinctive, licorice-like flavor of fresh Thai basil (available at Asian markets) is essential, but if Thai chiles are unavailable, any hot chile will do. Look for dark soy sauce, vegan oyster sauce, and palm sugar at Asian markets as well.

8 ounces fresh or dried rice noodles, about ¼-inch wide

1 tablespoon plus 1 teaspoon neutral vegetable oil

¼ cup dark soy sauce or low-sodium tamari

2 tablespoons vegan oyster sauce

1 teaspoon palm sugar or natural sugar

8 to 12 ounces extra-firm tofu, drained and cut into ½-inch dice

1 small red onion, halved and cut into thin half-moons

3 garlic cloves, minced

2 Thai chiles, or to taste, seeded and minced

2 cups broccoli florets, blanched for 1 minute in boiling water and drained

1½ cups loosely packed fresh Thai basil leaves

1. Prepare the noodles. If fresh, rinse under very hot water and place in a large bowl, separating them into individual strands. If dried, plunge into a large pot of boiling water to soften. Drain and place in a large bowl. Toss the noodles with 1 teaspoon of the oil and set aside.

2. In a small bowl, combine the dark soy sauce, oyster sauce, and sugar and set aside.

3. Heat the remaining 1 tablespoon oil in a large skillet or wok over medium-high heat. Add the tofu and cook, stirring, until golden, about 1 minute. Remove from the skillet and set aside.

4. Add the onion to the skillet and stir-fry to soften slightly, about 2 minutes. Add the garlic and chiles and stir-fry until fragrant, about 30 seconds. Add the sauce mixture, broccoli, noodles, tofu, and basil and stir-fry until hot, about 4 minutes. Taste and adjust the seasonings. Serve hot.

Serves 4

Three-Flavor Pancit

Although the recipe calls for a small amount of tofu, seitan, and tempeh, the dish is equally delicious if made with just 8 to 12 ounces of any of them either alone or in combination, so if you have small amounts of any of them on hand, this is a great way to use them up.

8 ounces wheat or rice vermicelli

2 teaspoons dark sesame oil

2 tablespoons neutral vegetable oil

6 ounces extra-firm tofu, drained, pressed (page 7), and cut into ½-inch dice

4 ounces seitan, cut into thin strips

1 cup crumbled steamed tempeh (page 10)

1 small onion, chopped

2 garlic cloves, minced

2 teaspoons grated fresh ginger

4 cups shredded cabbage

2 carrots, shredded

4 scallions, chopped

1 cup fresh or thawed frozen peas

4 tablespoons low-sodium tamari

1 tablespoon fresh lime or lemon juice

2 tablespoons minced fresh cilantro, for garnish

Lime or lemon wedges, to serve

1. Cook the vermicelli according to the package directions. Drain and transfer to a bowl. Toss with the sesame oil and set aside.

2. Heat 1 tablespoon of the vegetable oil in a large skillet over medium-high heat. Add the tofu and cook until golden brown, about 7 minutes. Transfer to a medium-size bowl. Add the seitan to the same skillet and cook until browned, about 5 minutes. Transfer to the bowl with the tofu. Add the tempeh and cook until browned, about 7 minutes. Transfer to the bowl with the tofu and seitan.

3. Heat the remaining 1 tablespoon vegetable oil in the same skillet over medium-high heat. Add the onion, garlic, ginger, cabbage, carrots, and scallions and cook, stirring, until softened, 5 to 7 minutes. Stir in up to ½ cup of water if the vegetables begin to stick. Add the peas and the reserved tofu, tempeh, and seitan. Add 1 tablespoon of the tamari and stir to coat. Add the noodles, lime juice, and the remaining 3 tablespoons tamari and cook until hot, about 5 minutes, tossing gently to combine. Garnish with the cilantro and serve hot with the lime wedges.

===== *Serves 4* =====

Vegetable Lo Mein with Tofu

Traditional Chinese lo mein noodles may contain eggs, so be sure to check the ingredient list before you buy them. Regular linguine is a good substitute.

12 ounces egg-free Chinese noodles or linguine

2 teaspoons toasted sesame oil

2 tablespoons neutral vegetable oil

8 ounces extra-firm tofu, drained and cut into ½-inch dice

4 scallions, chopped

2½ cups shredded napa cabbage or trimmed and shredded bok choy

1 small carrot, shredded

1½ cups snow peas, strings removed

1 garlic clove, minced

2 teaspoons grated fresh ginger

3 tablespoons low-sodium tamari

1. Cook the noodles according to the package directions. Drain and place in a large bowl. Add the sesame oil and toss to coat evenly. Set aside.

2. Heat 1 tablespoon of the vegetable oil in a large skillet or wok over medium-high heat. Add the tofu and stir-fry until golden brown all over, about 5 minutes. Remove from the skillet and set aside.

3. Reheat the skillet over medium-high heat with the remaining 1 tablespoon vegetable oil. Add the scallions and cabbage and stir-fry for 1 minute to soften slightly. Add the carrot, snow peas, garlic, and ginger and stir-fry for 1 minute. Add 1 tablespoon of the tamari and stir-fry until the vegetables are tender, about 3 minutes. Add the noodles, tofu, and remaining 2 tablespoons tamari, tossing to combine. Serve hot.

Serves 4

As a major protein source for much of the world, beans are among the most important ingredients on the planet. Countless varieties exist in a wide range of colors and sizes. In addition to being high in protein, beans are also chock-full of fiber and B vitamins and low in fat. Among the best known are black beans, black-eyed peas, chickpeas, kidney beans, lentils, split peas, lima beans, navy beans, pinto beans, and soybeans.

Bean dishes have long played key roles in the cuisines of many cultures, but the same has not been true in the United States. Thanks to the recent interest in global cuisines and healthy eating, all that is changing. More Americans are realizing what vegetarians and much of the world have known for centuries—that beans can be enjoyed as a versatile and economical protein source. As more people look for alternatives to meat, beans are finding their way onto restaurant menus and dinner tables throughout the United States.

Because of their importance in the vegan diet, beans are used in many of the chapters throughout this book, often to add protein and substance to recipes that would otherwise be lacking in both, such as soups or pasta dishes. This chapter features a selection of recipes in which beans play the starring role. Among the global delights that await preparation are *White Bean Cassoulet, Three-Bean Dal,* and *Black*

Bean Croquettes with Yellow Pepper Coulis. In many instances, beans combine with grains and vegetables to make well-balanced one-dish meals. Because of their versatility, beans can be an inspiration to the creative cook.

Soaking Beans

Soaking dried beans is an important step in the bean-cooking process, since it rehydrates the dried beans and shortens their cooking time. Because soaking helps dissolve some of the complex sugars in beans that cause digestive gas, it also aids digestion. Before soaking or cooking, dried beans must be picked over and washed to remove dust, small stones, and other debris. With the exception of lentils and split peas, all beans require soaking.

To soak beans, place them in a bowl and add water to cover by about 3 inches. Soak the beans overnight and drain before cooking.

For a quick-soak method, place the beans in a pot with water to cover by 2 or 3 inches and bring to a boil for 2 minutes. Remove the pot from the heat, cover, and let stand for 2 hours. Drain the beans before cooking.

Don't be deterred by the long soaking and cooking times required for dried beans. All you need is a little planning. To save time, however, you can cook beans in a pressure cooker or a slow cooker. The new generation of pressure cookers is safer and easier to use than the old-fashioned variety, and slow cookers are now available with larger capacity, variable heat settings, and built-in timers.

Cooking Beans

To cook beans, simmer them in a pot over low heat in about 3 cups of water per 1 cup of beans. Cook with the lid on, stirring occasionally. Salt and acidic foods such as tomatoes should be added midway through or near the end of the cooking time, as adding them during the earlier cooking stages will toughen the beans and lengthen the cooking time. Generally, 1 cup of dried beans will yield 2 to 2½ cups of cooked beans. Cooking times may vary depending on the type, quality, and age of the bean;

the altitude; and even the water quality. The following cooking times are provided for conventional stovetop cooking, since that is the method that the majority of people use.

To give you more options, most of the bean recipes in this book call for "cooked or canned" beans. While canned beans are great to keep on hand for sheer convenience, dried beans that you cook yourself taste better and are more economical. To give dried beans the same convenience as canned, cook up a large batch and then divide and freeze them for later use.

Know Beans About Beans

- Purchase dried beans that are of uniform size and brightly colored. Avoid beans that are dull, cracked, or have pinholes.

- Store dried beans in airtight containers in a cool, dry place.

- Cook beans until tender to aid in their digestion.

- A piece of kombu sea vegetable added to the cooking water helps tenderize beans and adds flavor and nutrients.

- To keep beans from toughening, add salt at the end of the cooking time.

- Add dried herbs to beans during the final 30 minutes of cooking. Add fresh herbs after the beans are cooked.

- Cool cooked beans in their cooking water to keep them moist.

- When cooking beans, make extra for another use. Cooked beans will keep in the refrigerator for up to 1 week or in the freezer for up to 6 months.

Stovetop Cooking Times for Soaked Beans

Beans (1 cup dried)	Water	Cooking Time
Adzuki	3 cups	50 minutes
Anasazi	3½ cups	1½ hours
Black	3½ cups	1½ to 2 hours
Black-eyed peas	3 cups	1 hour
Borlotti	3 cups	1½ hours
Cannellini	3½ cups	1½ to 2 hours
Chickpeas	4 cups	3 hours
Great Northern	3½ cups	1½ to 2 hours
Kidney	3½ cups	2 hours
Lentils*	3 cups	35 to 45 minutes
Navy	3½ cups	1½ to 2 hours
Pinto	3½ cups	2 hours
Split peas*	3 cups	45 minutes

*Note: Lentils and split peas do not require soaking.

Smoky Maple Black Beans and Kale

Smoked paprika and liquid smoke combine to deliver a smoky nuance to these beans and greens. Add the optional chipotle chile if you want to add some heat.

1 tablespoon olive oil or ¼ cup water

1 medium-size onion, chopped

3 garlic cloves, minced

6 cups coarsely chopped kale

Salt and freshly ground black pepper

3 cups cooked black beans or 2 (15-ounce) cans beans, rinsed and drained

3 tablespoons water

2 tablespoons tamari

2 tablespoons pure maple syrup

1 tablespoon cider vinegar

1 teaspoon liquid smoke

½ teaspoon smoked paprika

1 chipotle chile in adobo (optional), minced

1. Heat the oil or water in a large pot over medium heat. Add the onion and garlic, cover, and cook until softened, about 5 minutes. Add the kale and season to taste with salt and pepper. Cook, stirring, until softened, about 5 minutes.

2. Stir in the beans, then add the remaining ingredients, stirring to combine. Simmer for 10 minutes longer to blend the flavors. Taste and adjust the seasonings, if needed. Serve hot.

===== *Serves 4* =====

Did You Know?

Dark green vegetables should be cooked uncovered to prevent discoloration. Covering green vegetables while they cook causes a buildup of acids that react with the chlorophyll and turn the vegetables a brownish color.

Adzuki Beans and Winter Squash Sauté

The naturally sweet adzuki bean and winter squash complement each other in flavor and texture, while the deep burgundy color of the beans makes a striking contrast with the vivid orange squash. Adzuki beans are available at natural foods stores, but another red bean can be substituted if you can't find them. For a nourishing meal, serve over freshly cooked brown rice and an accompanying dark green vegetable such as kale.

1 medium-size winter squash, such as butternut, buttercup, or kabocha

1 tablespoon olive oil or ¼ cup water (or more as needed)

3 shallots, halved and sliced

1 tablespoon low-sodium tamari

1½ cups cooked adzuki beans or 1 (15-ounce) can beans, rinsed and drained

Salt and freshly ground black pepper

1. Halve, peel, and seed the squash. Cut into bite-size pieces and set aside.

2. Heat the olive oil or water in a large skillet over medium heat. Add the shallots and cook, stirring, until slightly softened, about 3 minutes. Add the squash, stirring to coat. Add the tamari and another ¼ cup of water if needed. Cover, and cook until the squash is tender, about 20 minutes.

3. Gently stir in the beans and season to taste with salt and pepper. Cook until the beans are hot, about 5 minutes. Serve hot.

Serves 4

Cuban-Style Black Beans

This flavorful bean dish is sometimes called "Moors and Christians" when served with white rice. It's also tasty served over cornbread.

1 tablespoon olive oil or ¼ cup water

1 red onion, finely chopped

1 green bell pepper, seeded and finely chopped

3 garlic cloves, minced

1 small hot chile, seeded and minced

1 teaspoon ground cumin

½ teaspoon dried oregano

1 (14.5-ounce) can petite diced tomatoes, drained

3 cups cooked black beans or 2 (15-ounce) cans beans, rinsed and drained

2 teaspoons red wine vinegar

½ teaspoon natural sugar

Salt and freshly ground black pepper

¼ cup minced scallions, for garnish

2 tablespoons chopped fresh cilantro, for garnish

1. Heat the oil or water in a large skillet over medium heat. Add the onion, bell pepper, garlic, and chile. Cover and cook until softened, about 7 minutes. Stir in the cumin, oregano, tomatoes, and beans. Stir in the vinegar and sugar, and season to taste with salt and pepper. Cover and simmer, stirring occasionally, until the vegetables are tender and the tomatoes are saucy, about 15 minutes. Taste and adjust the seasonings.

2. Serve hot, garnished with the scallions and cilantro.

Serves 4

Black Bean Croquettes with Yellow Pepper Coulis

You can change the character of these versatile croquettes by varying the herbs or spices or by accompanying them with a different sauce, such as chutney, salsa, or Spicy Peanut Dipping Sauce (page 145).

1½ cups cooked black beans or 1 (15-ounce) can beans, rinsed and drained

½ cup old-fashioned rolled oats

¼ cup walnuts or sunflower seeds

¼ cup grated onion

¼ cup grated carrot

2 tablespoons minced fresh parsley

1 teaspoon salt

½ teaspoon freshly ground black pepper

1 cup dry bread crumbs, for dredging

Olive oil, for sautéing

1 cup Yellow Pepper Coulis (page 141)

1. Combine the beans, oats, walnuts, onion, carrots, parsley, salt, and pepper in a food processor and process until well blended. Divide the mixture into 4 equal mounds and shape into round patties. Coat each evenly with the bread crumbs and set on a baking sheet. Refrigerate for 30 minutes.

2. Heat a thin layer of olive oil in a large skillet over medium heat. Cook the croquettes until golden brown all over, about 8 minutes total. Drain on paper towels and serve hot, surrounded by the coulis.

Serves 4

Simmered Borlotti Beans and Tomatoes

Dried or canned borlotti beans, also called cranberry or Roman beans, can be found in Italian markets. If unavailable, use pinto, cannellini, or fava beans. I like to serve this dish over noodles or rice. It is also terrific prepared with the addition of diced steamed potatoes.

1 tablespoon olive oil or ¼ cup water

3 shallots, chopped

2 garlic cloves, chopped

1 teaspoon dried marjoram

⅛ teaspoon cayenne

1½ cups cooked borlotti beans
or 1 (15-ounce) can beans, rinsed and drained

1 (14.5-ounce) can diced tomatoes, drained

Salt and freshly ground black pepper

3 tablespoons chopped fresh
parsley, for garnish

Heat the olive oil or water in a large saucepan over medium heat. Add the shallots, cover, and cook until softened, about 5 minutes. Add the garlic, marjoram, and cayenne and cook, stirring, until fragrant, about 1 minute. Stir in the beans, tomatoes, and salt and pepper to taste. Cover and cook until the flavors are blended and the tomatoes are saucy, about 10 minutes. To serve, transfer to a large serving bowl and garnish with the parsley.

===== *Serves 4* =====

Roasted Chickpeas

Roasted chickpeas, called "chichers" in my family, were one of my grandmother's favorite snacks. When I was a child, my father and I would go to the Italian market to purchase treats for her. Chichers were always at the top of the list. Much like roasted peas, a popular Asian snack food, roasted chickpeas are crunchy and nut-like and can be eaten out of hand or used as a salad garnish. We traditionally enjoy them seasoned only with salt and olive oil, but you can sprinkle them with your favorite spices, from chili powder to a jerk spice blend.

1½ cups cooked chickpeas or 1 (15-ounce) can chickpeas, rinsed and drained

2 tablespoons olive oil

Salt

1. Preheat the oven to 400°F. Place the chickpeas and olive oil in a shallow baking dish large enough to accommodate the chickpeas in a single layer. Toss gently to coat, then season to taste with salt.

2. Roast the chickpeas, stirring occasionally, until they begin to brown, about 30 minutes (or even longer if you prefer them crunchier). Remove from the oven and allow to cool. Sprinkle with a little more salt, if desired. Serve at room temperature.

Serves 4

Chickpea and Green Bean Tagine

A tagine is a delectable Moroccan stew redolent of fragrant fruits and spices. The word *tagine* refers to both the dish itself and the pot it is cooked in. Try it served over couscous, quinoa, or rice.

1½ cups mixed dried fruit

1 tablespoon olive oil or ¼ cup water

1 large onion, chopped

2 garlic cloves, minced

½ teaspoon ground cinnamon

¼ teaspoon turmeric

⅛ teaspoon ground allspice

8 ounces green beans, trimmed and cut into 1-inch pieces

1 (14.5-ounce) can diced tomatoes, undrained

1½ cups vegetable broth

½ teaspoon natural sugar

Salt and freshly ground black pepper

1½ cups cooked chickpeas or 1 (15-ounce) can chickpeas, rinsed and drained

¼ cup slivered blanched almonds

2 tablespoons minced fresh parsley

1 teaspoon grated lemon zest

1. Place the dried fruit in a small heatproof bowl. Add boiling water to cover and soak for 20 minutes to soften. Drain, coarsely chop, and set aside.

2. Heat the olive oil or water in a large saucepan over medium heat. Add the onion, cover, and cook until softened, about 5 minutes. Stir in the garlic, cinnamon, turmeric, and allspice and cook, stirring, for 30 seconds. Add the green beans, tomatoes and their juice, broth, sugar, and salt and pepper to taste. Reduce the heat to low and simmer until the green beans are tender, about 20 minutes.

3. Add the reserved fruit and the chickpeas and cook for 5 to 10 minutes to blend the flavors. Stir in the almonds, parsley, and lemon zest. Taste and adjust the seasonings, then serve hot.

Serves 4

Chickpea and Eggplant Kibbeh

Kibbeh is a traditional Lebanese dish usually made with bulgur and ground lamb. In this version, chickpeas and eggplant, two popular Middle Eastern ingredients, replace the meat. The result is a hearty one-dish meal that can be assembled ahead of time and baked just before serving. I like to serve this with a sesame sauce that is made by thinning hummus with a little nondairy milk.

½ cup fine bulgur

1 cup boiling water

1½ cups cooked chickpeas or 1 (15-ounce) can chickpeas, rinsed and drained

½ teaspoon ground cinnamon

½ teaspoon ground cumin

¼ teaspoon ground allspice

Salt and freshly ground black pepper

1 tablespoon olive oil or ¼ cup water

1 large onion, chopped

1 medium-size eggplant, peeled and chopped

⅓ cup pine nuts

1 teaspoon fresh lemon juice

1. Place the bulgur in a medium-size heatproof bowl. Add the boiling water and let stand for 20 minutes.

2. Transfer the bulgur to a large bowl. Coarsely chop the chickpeas and add to the bulgur. Add the cinnamon, cumin, allspice, and salt and pepper to taste. Stir to combine and set aside.

3. Heat the olive oil or water in a large skillet over medium heat. Add the onion, cover, and cook until softened, about 5 minutes. Add the eggplant and continue to cook, stirring a few times, until tender, 5 to 7 minutes. Stir in the pine nuts and lemon juice and season with salt and pepper to taste. Set aside.

4. Preheat the oven to 350°F. Lightly oil a 10-inch square baking dish. Press half of the bulgur-chickpea mixture into the bottom of the dish, smoothing the top. Add the eggplant mixture, then cover with the remaining bulgur-chickpea mixture, pressing down to smooth.

5. Bake until hot and lightly browned, about 30 minutes. Remove from the oven and let stand for 10 minutes before serving. Serve warm or at room temperature.

Serves 6

Lentils and Rice with Caramelized Shallots

The traditional Middle Eastern combination of lentils and rice flavored with shallots and fragrant spices makes a well-balanced meal when accompanied by a green vegetable or salad.

1 cup dried brown lentils,
picked over and rinsed

2 tablespoons olive oil

4 large shallots, chopped

1 teaspoon ground cumin

1 teaspoon ground coriander

½ teaspoon sweet paprika

Salt and freshly ground black pepper

1 cup basmati rice

3 cups water

1. Bring a medium-size saucepan of salted water to a boil over high heat. Partially cook the lentils for 15 minutes. Drain and set aside.

2. Heat 1 tablespoon of the olive oil in a large skillet over medium heat. Add the shallots and cook, stirring frequently, until lightly browned, about 10 minutes. Remove half of the shallots from the skillet and set aside.

3. Add the lentils to the skillet and stir in the cumin, coriander, paprika, and salt and pepper to taste. Add the rice and water, bring to a boil, and cook, uncovered, until the lentils are tender and the rice is cooked, about 30 minutes. Remove from the heat, cover, and set aside for 10 to 15 minutes while you finish cooking the reserved shallots.

4. Heat the remaining 1 tablespoon olive oil in a small skillet over medium heat. Add the reserved shallots and cook until browned and caramelized, about 5 minutes.

5. Place the rice and lentil mixture in a large serving bowl and top with the crisp shallots. Serve hot.

Serves 4

Smoke and Spice Refried Beans

Chipotle chiles add smoke and heat to these cumin-spiced refried beans. Gauge the number of chiles and the amount of cumin used according to your taste. Refried beans are traditionally cooked in lard, but this healthier version is cooked in olive oil. I like to serve it over rice or use it as a burrito filling.

1 tablespoon olive oil

1 small onion, minced

1 teaspoon ground cumin, or to taste

½ teaspoon smoked paprika

3 cups cooked pinto beans or 2 (15-ounce) cans beans, rinsed and drained

1 or 2 finely minced chipotle chiles in adobo

Salt and freshly ground black pepper

Heat the oil in a large skillet over medium heat. Add the onion, cover, and cook until softened, about 5 minutes. Add the cumin and paprika and stir to coat the onion. Add the beans, chipotle chiles, and salt and pepper to taste. Coarsely mash the beans, stirring to incorporate the other ingredients. Cook until heated through, about 10 minutes. Add a small amount of water if the mixture becomes too thick. Taste and adjust the seasonings, if needed. Serve hot.

Serves 4

Did You Know?

Most beans are more than 20 percent protein.

Three-Bean Dal

This is my version of a creamy dal recipe shared by Ashok Arora, owner of Nawab, an Indian restaurant in Virginia Beach. The original dish, called *dal makhani*, is made with three kinds of dried beans, and the preparation time is often more than I can spare. By using a combination of canned beans and dried split peas, I manage to achieve that creamy, slow-cooked flavor in a fraction of the time.

½ cup dried yellow split peas, picked over and rinsed

3 cups water

1 teaspoon turmeric

1½ cups cooked black beans or 1 (15-ounce) can beans, rinsed and drained

1½ cups cooked kidney or other red beans or 1 (15-ounce) can beans, rinsed and drained

Salt

1 tablespoon neutral vegetable oil

1 medium-size onion, chopped

2 garlic cloves, minced

2 teaspoons grated fresh ginger

1 teaspoon ground cumin

½ teaspoon ground coriander

½ teaspoon cayenne

¼ teaspoon ground cardamom

1 (14.5-ounce) can petite diced tomatoes, drained

2 tablespoons chopped fresh cilantro, for garnish

1. Place the split peas and water in a large saucepan over medium-high heat. Bring to a boil, reduce the heat to low, add the turmeric, and simmer, partially covered and stirring occasionally, for 20 minutes. Add the black and red beans, season to taste with salt, and simmer, uncovered, until the beans are very soft, about 20 minutes.

2. Heat the oil in a large skillet over medium heat. Add the onion, cover, and cook until softened, about 5 minutes. Add the garlic and ginger and cook, stirring, until fragrant, about 30 seconds. Add the cumin, coriander, cayenne, cardamom, and tomatoes, stirring constantly for about 30 seconds. Pour the contents of the skillet over the simmering bean mixture and stir well to combine. Taste and adjust the seasonings. Simmer for 5 minutes to blend the flavors. Serve hot, garnished with the chopped cilantro.

Serves 6

Red Bean and Sweet Potato Curry

Vibrant in color and flavor, this curry is delicious served over freshly cooked basmati rice, accompanied by a green salad and your favorite chutney.

1 tablespoon neutral vegetable oil or ¼ cup water

1 small onion, chopped

1 tablespoon curry powder

1 teaspoon ground coriander

¾ teaspoon ground cumin

½ teaspoon turmeric

¼ teaspoon cayenne

1 small green bell pepper, seeded and coarsely chopped

2 garlic cloves, minced

2 teaspoons grated fresh ginger

1¾ cups vegetable broth

1 (14.5-ounce) can diced tomatoes, undrained

1½ cups cooked dark red kidney beans or 1 (15-ounce) can beans, rinsed and drained

2 medium-size sweet potatoes, peeled and diced

Salt and freshly ground black pepper

1. Heat the oil or water in a large saucepan over medium heat. Add the onion, cover, and cook until softened, about 5 minutes. Stir in the curry powder, coriander, cumin, turmeric, and cayenne. Add the bell pepper, garlic, and ginger and cook, stirring, for 30 seconds. Add the broth and tomatoes and their juice and bring to a boil. Reduce the heat to low and add the beans and sweet potatoes. Season to taste with salt and pepper, cover, and simmer until the vegetables are tender, about 20 minutes.

2. For a thicker, creamier sauce, puree up to 2 cups of the mixture in a blender or food processor and stir back into the pot, or use an immersion blender to puree some of the curry right in the pot. Serve hot.

Serves 4

Red Bean Cakes
with Creamy Coconut Sauce

Red beans and rice are a popular pair in many regions of the world. Here they are blended with spicy seasonings and formed into cakes that are served with a rich coconut sauce.

2 tablespoons olive oil, divided

1 small red onion, chopped

1 small red bell pepper, seeded and chopped

½ cup chopped celery

1 large garlic clove, minced

½ teaspoon sweet paprika

½ teaspoon dried thyme

¼ teaspoon cayenne, or to taste

Salt and freshly ground black pepper

1½ cups cooked pinto, kidney, or other red beans or 1 (15-ounce) can beans, rinsed and drained

½ cup cold cooked white or brown rice

2 tablespoons minced fresh parsley

⅓ cup raw cashews, soaked for at least 3 hours or up to overnight, then drained

½ to ¾ cup unsweetened coconut milk

1. Heat 1 tablespoon of the olive oil in a large skillet over medium heat. Add the onion, bell pepper, celery, garlic, paprika, thyme, and cayenne. Cover and cook, stirring occasionally, until softened, about 10 minutes. Season to taste with salt and pepper.

2. In a food processor, combine the beans, rice, parsley, salt and pepper to taste, and all but ⅓ cup of the sautéed onion mixture. Set aside the ⅓ cup of onion mixture for the sauce. Pulse the bean and rice mixture to combine well, leaving some texture intact. Shape the mixture into 4 patties. If the mixture is too soft, add a small amount of oats, bread crumbs, or ground nuts.

3. Heat the remaining 1 tablespoon olive oil in a large skillet over medium heat. Add the bean cakes and cook, turning once, until browned on both sides, 7 to 10 minutes total. Reduce the heat to low and keep warm while you prepare the sauce.

4. In a blender or food processor, combine the drained cashews and the reserved ⅓ cup onion mixture and grind into a paste. Add ½ cup of the coconut milk and salt and pepper to taste and blend until smooth. If a thinner sauce is desired, add a little more coconut milk. Transfer to a small saucepan over low heat and cook, stirring, until hot. Transfer the hot bean cakes to a platter, pour the sauce over them, and serve.

Serves 4

Tuscan White Beans with Garlic and Sage

The people of Tuscany have a prolific bean preparation repertoire. Among their classic recipes is a simple sauté of white beans, garlic, and sage in olive oil. This is delicious as a topping for bruschetta or pasta. You may add cooked chopped greens such as escarole or broccoli rabe (rapini) to the sauté, if you like.

2 tablespoons olive oil

3 garlic cloves, minced

10 fresh sage leaves, minced,
or 1 teaspoon ground dried sage

3 cups cooked cannellini
or other white beans or 2 (15-ounce)
cans beans, rinsed and drained

Salt and freshly ground black pepper

1. Heat the olive oil in a large skillet over medium-low heat. Add the garlic and cook, stirring, until fragrant, about 30 seconds. Add the sage and cook, stirring, until fragrant, 30 seconds more.

2. Add the beans, stirring to coat. Simmer over low heat until hot, 10 to 15 minutes. Season to taste with salt and pepper. Serve hot.

Serves 4

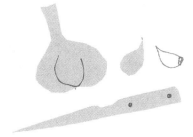

White Bean Cassoulet

This adaptation of a French country classic features white beans, an important component of the original meaty version. If you prefer to use dried beans (rather than canned), plan to soak and cook them in advance before proceeding with this recipe.

1 tablespoon olive oil or ¼ cup water

1 large onion, chopped

2 large carrots, thinly sliced

2 small parsnips, peeled and chopped

3 garlic cloves, minced

2 teaspoons Dijon mustard

1 tablespoon mellow white miso paste dissolved in 2 tablespoons hot (not boiling) water

1 teaspoon dried marjoram

1 teaspoon dried thyme

1 large bay leaf

½ teaspoon salt

¼ teaspoon freshly ground black pepper

3 cups cooked Great Northern, navy, or other white beans or 2 (15-ounce) cans beans, rinsed and drained

1 (14.5-ounce) can petite diced fire-roasted tomatoes, undrained

½ cup vegetable broth

½ to 1 teaspoon liquid smoke

½ cup dry bread crumbs

½ teaspoon smoked paprika

2 tablespoons chopped fresh parsley

1. Preheat the oven to 350°F. Lightly oil a shallow 2-quart baking dish and set aside. Heat the olive oil or water in a large skillet over medium heat. Add the onion, carrots, and parsnips. Cover and cook until slightly softened, about 5 minutes. Stir in the garlic and cook, stirring, until fragrant, about 30 seconds.

2. Blend the mustard into the miso mixture and stir it into the vegetables. Add the marjoram, thyme, bay leaf, salt, and pepper. Set aside.

3. Place the beans and tomatoes and their juice in the prepared baking dish. Add the vegetable mixture and the vegetable broth. Add the liquid smoke, and stir to mix well.

4. Cover tightly and bake until the vegetables are tender, about 1 hour. Uncover, remove and discard the bay leaf, and sprinkle the top with the bread crumbs and paprika. Return the cassoulet to the oven for 10 to 15 minutes to lightly toast the crumbs. Serve hot, sprinkled with the parsley.

Serves 4 to 6

Mediterranean Bean Ragout

Bean dishes can be found throughout the Mediterranean countryside. This one features creamy, meaty cannellini beans in a brothy ragout enriched with the sweet flavor of fennel. It is delicious served over freshly cooked flat noodles.

1 tablespoon olive oil or ¼ cup water

1 large onion, chopped

2 medium-size carrots, thinly sliced

2 Yukon Gold potatoes, peeled and diced

1 fennel bulb, trimmed and thinly sliced

3 garlic cloves, minced

2 cups vegetable broth

½ cup dry white wine

2 tablespoons tomato paste

1 teaspoon dried thyme

1 teaspoon dried marjoram

1 teaspoon dried basil

2 bay leaves

3 cups cooked cannellini
or other white beans or 2 (15-ounce)
cans beans, rinsed and drained

Salt

1. Heat the oil or water in a large saucepan over medium heat. Add the onion and carrots, cover, and cook until slightly softened, about 5 minutes. Add the potatoes, fennel, and garlic and cook, stirring, until the garlic is fragrant, about 30 seconds. Stir in the broth, wine, tomato paste, thyme, marjoram, basil, and bay leaves. Bring to a boil, then reduce the heat to low and simmer until the vegetables are tender, about 20 minutes.

2. Add the beans and salt to taste. Simmer until heated through and the flavors are blended, about 10 minutes. Remove and discard the bay leaves. If a thicker ragout is desired, puree about 1 cup of the mixture in a blender or food processor and stir back into the pot, or use an immersion blender to puree some of the stew right in the pot. Serve hot.

Serves 4 to 6

Za'tar-Spiced Bean Patties with Curry Sauce

My friend and former neighbor Samantha Ragan came up with this dish and brought over a plateful to share her creation. After one bite, I was hooked. The creamy richness of the sauce is an ideal complement to the spicy bean patties. You can vary the size of the patties according to your preference, from bite-size on up. You also can shape them into balls or logs, if you prefer, and serve them over basmati rice. Za'tar herb blend is usually made up of sumac, thyme, oregano, and hyssop and can be found in gourmet shops or specialty markets. The name also can refer to a wild oregano grown in the Middle East. If you cannot find za'tar, substitute a blend of dried thyme, mint, and oregano.

1 large Yukon Gold potato, peeled and diced

1 medium-size carrot, chopped

1 cup cooked or canned brown lentils, well drained

1 cup cooked or canned chickpeas, rinsed and drained

1 garlic clove, crushed

2 tablespoons dried za'tar (see headnote)

Salt

2 tablespoons olive oil, divided

1 small onion, chopped

1 tablespoon curry powder

½ teaspoon natural sugar

½ teaspoon cayenne

½ cup diced fresh or canned tomatoes, well drained

¾ to 1 cup plain unsweetened nondairy milk

1. Steam the potato and carrot over boiling water until tender, about 10 minutes. Set aside to cool. Blot dry.

2. Blot the lentils and chickpeas dry and place in a food processor. Add the potato and carrot, garlic, za'tar, and salt to taste. Pulse to combine, being careful not to overprocess, so that some of the texture remains. Shape into 4 large or 8 small patties. If the mixture is too soft, add a small amount of oats, bread crumbs, or ground nuts.

3. Preheat the oven to 275°F. Heat 1 tablespoon of the oil in a large nonstick skillet over medium-high heat. Working in batches, add the patties and cook, turning once, until they are browned on both sides, about 3 minutes per side. Place the browned patties on a baking sheet and keep warm in the oven.

4. Heat the remaining 1 tablespoon olive oil in a medium-size saucepan over medium heat. Add the onion, cover, and cook until softened, about 5 minutes. Stir in the curry powder, sugar, and cayenne, then add the tomatoes. Simmer until the tomatoes break up and become saucy, about 5 minutes.

5. Place the sauce mixture in a blender and process until smooth. Add as much of the nondairy milk as needed to achieve the desired consistency. Return the sauce to the saucepan and heat over low heat, then taste and adjust the seasonings, if needed. Serve the patties topped with the sauce.

Serves 4

The Facts About Vitamin B$_{12}$

- All vitamin B$_{12}$ comes from bacteria that live in the soil or in animal intestines.
- Animal products are a primary source of B$_{12}$ for humans.
- Vitamin B$_{12}$ is produced by bacteria in the human mouth and intestines.
- Humans store vitamin B$_{12}$ in their bodies for years.
- The human body requires only 2 micrograms of vitamin B$_{12}$ per day.
- Vitamin B$_{12}$ deficiency is not common among vegans.
- The best way for vegans to get vitamin B$_{12}$ is through fortified foods (such as breakfast cereals and nondairy milk), nutritional yeast, and supplements.

Old-Fashioned Baked Beans

The quintessential American bean dish drenched in a spicy-sweet tomato sauce can be enjoyed as more than a side dish for hot dogs. Try it as a main course, spooned over cornbread and accompanied by a salad or slaw.

1 tablespoon olive oil or ¼ cup water	1½ tablespoons low-sodium tamari
1 small onion, minced	1½ tablespoons cider vinegar
1 garlic clove, minced	1 tablespoon natural sugar
1 teaspoon chili powder	1 tablespoon prepared yellow mustard
⅛ teaspoon cayenne	Salt and freshly ground black pepper
1 (14.5-ounce) can tomato puree	3 cups cooked Great Northern or butter beans or 2 (15-ounce) cans beans, rinsed and drained
2 tablespoons molasses	

1. Preheat the oven to 350°F. Lightly oil a 1½-quart baking dish and set aside. Heat the olive oil or water in a medium-size saucepan over medium heat. Add the onion and garlic, cover, and cook until softened, about 5 minutes. Stir in the chili powder and cayenne. Add the tomato puree, molasses, tamari, vinegar, sugar, and mustard and bring to a boil. Reduce the heat to low and simmer until slightly reduced, about 15 minutes. Season to taste with salt and pepper.

2. Place the beans in the prepared baking dish. Add the sauce, stirring to combine. Cover and bake until hot and bubbly, about 20 minutes. Serve hot.

Serves 4

From the Stew & Chili Pot

Stews are one of my favorite choices for dinner. For one thing, they are easy to prepare—most stews require little more than combining several ingredients in a pot that simmers until done. This same ease of preparation is what helps build the rich, complex flavors of most stews, as the essence of the vegetables, seasonings, and other ingredients commingle into one delicious whole. When beans or soy products are added to the pot, a stew can become a delectable, well-balanced meal, especially when it is served over cooked whole grains.

In addition, stews can be economical and are a great way to stretch your dollar when cooking for a crowd. Among their other virtues, stews taste better when reheated, so leftovers become something to look forward to. Whether preparing a nourishing weeknight meal for the family or a sumptuous main course for guests, you can use stews ranging from humble to "haute" to fill the bill.

Is it any wonder that stews are enjoyed the world over? In this chapter, you will find recipes from virtually every corner of the globe—some authentically vegan stews and others made vegan with the change of a few ingredients. Sample such diverse dishes as *Indonesian-Inspired Tempeh Stew* and *Belgian-Style Seitan Stew with Dark Beer,* or choose from the wide variety of riffs on America's favorite stew—chili. Vegetarian chili is one of the most popular ways for vegans to enjoy a wholesome and hearty one-dish meal loaded with protein and flavor. If you've been making the same old chili recipe time and again, you're in luck—this chapter features a dozen different ways to make "a bowl of red."

Farm Stand Vegetable Stew with Basil Pesto

Although stews are more often enjoyed during the fall and winter months, don't overlook the opportunity to create a late-summer stew made with fresh seasonal vegetables. Prepare it early in the day, when the kitchen is still cool, and simply reheat it later on. Vary the vegetables according to your preference or what's plentiful. You may use chopped fresh herbs instead of the pesto, if you prefer. I like to serve this stew in shallow bowls accompanied by grilled bread.

2 ears corn

1 tablespoon olive oil or ¼ cup water

1 large red onion, chopped

1 small red bell pepper, seeded and cut into ¼-inch pieces

8 ounces green beans, trimmed and cut into 1-inch pieces

2 large ripe tomatoes, peeled, seeded, and chopped

2 cups vegetable broth, or more as needed

Salt and freshly ground black pepper

1 medium-size zucchini, diced

1 small yellow squash, halved lengthwise and cut into ¼-inch-thick half-moons

¼ cup Basil Pesto (page 142) or purchased vegan pesto

1. Using a sharp knife, cut the kernels from the corn and set aside.

2. Heat the oil or water in a large saucepan over medium heat. Add the onion, cover, and cook until softened, about 5 minutes. Add the bell pepper, green beans, tomatoes, broth, and salt and pepper to taste and bring to a boil. Reduce the heat to low and simmer, partially covered, until the vegetables are tender, about 20 minutes. Add the zucchini, yellow squash, and corn kernels and cook until tender, about 10 minutes, adding more broth if the stew becomes too dry.

3. When ready to serve, remove from the heat and stir in the pesto. Taste and adjust the seasonings, then serve.

Serves 4

Autumn Vegetable Stew

Each fall, when I feel that first nip in the air, I yearn for a fragrant pot of stew brimming with all of the colors and flavors of autumn. That's when I head to the nearest farmers' market, where summer's fragile offerings have been replaced by sturdy root vegetables, winter squash, collards, and other autumn produce. Dark red kidney beans add a lovely color accent, along with protein and substance, to this stew.

1 tablespoon olive oil or ¼ cup water

1 medium-size onion, finely chopped

1 large yellow turnip or small rutabaga, peeled and diced

1 large carrot, halved lengthwise and cut into ¼-inch-thick half-moons

1 large parsnip, peeled, halved lengthwise, and cut into ¼-inch-thick half-moons

1 large sweet potato, peeled and diced

2 cups peeled, seeded, and diced winter squash

2 cups vegetable broth, or more if desired

½ cup dry white wine

1 teaspoon chopped fresh thyme or ½ teaspoon dried thyme

1 teaspoon salt

¼ teaspoon freshly ground black pepper

2 cups chopped collard greens or other dark leafy greens, simmered in a pot of salted water until tender and drained

1½ cups cooked dark red kidney beans or 1 (15-ounce) can beans, rinsed and drained

2 tablespoons chopped fresh parsley

1. Heat the oil or water in a large saucepan over medium heat. Add the onion, turnip, carrot, parsnip, sweet potato, and squash. Cover and cook, stirring occasionally, until slightly softened, about 10 minutes. Stir in the broth, wine, thyme, salt, and pepper and bring to a boil. Reduce the heat to low and simmer until the vegetables soften and the liquid is reduced, about 30 minutes. If a thinner stew is desired, add more broth. If a thick stew is preferred, puree about 1½ cups of the stew in a blender or food processor and stir back into the pot, or use an immersion blender to puree some of the stew right in the pot.

2. Stir in the collards and kidney beans. Taste and adjust the seasonings. Simmer to heat through and allow the flavors to mingle, about 10 minutes. Sprinkle with the parsley and serve hot.

Serves 6

Portobello and Green Bean Ragout with Madeira

I especially like the way the mushrooms absorb the flavor of the Madeira, adding a lusty richness to the stew. If Madeira is unavailable, you could try another fortified wine such as Marsala or port, or use a regular dry red or white wine, if you prefer. Serve over rice, noodles, or mashed potatoes.

2 tablespoons olive oil

1 pound portobello mushrooms, stems and gills removed and caps cut into ½-inch dice

½ cup dry Madeira

3 shallots, chopped

1 celery rib, minced

2 cups vegetable broth, reduced over medium-high heat to 1 cup

Salt and freshly ground black pepper

8 ounces green beans, trimmed and cut into 1-inch pieces

1 tablespoon cornstarch dissolved in 2 tablespoons water (optional)

1 tablespoon minced fresh tarragon or parsley

1. Heat 1 tablespoon of the olive oil in a large skillet over medium heat. Add the mushrooms and cook until browned all over, about 5 minutes. Add ¼ cup of the Madeira, tossing to coat. Set aside.

2. Heat the remaining 1 tablespoon olive oil in a large saucepan over medium heat. Add the shallots and celery and cook, stirring occasionally, until tender, about 7 minutes. Stir in the remaining ¼ cup Madeira, the broth, and salt and pepper to taste and bring to a boil over medium-high heat. Add the green beans, reduce the heat to medium, and simmer until the beans are tender and the liquid is reduced slightly, about 20 minutes.

3. If a thicker sauce is desired, whisk in the cornstarch mixture and cook, stirring, until thickened, about 2 minutes. Add the mushrooms and tarragon, reduce the heat to low, and simmer for 5 minutes to blend the flavors. Serve hot.

Serves 4

Winter Squash and Burdock Root Stew

Burdock root is a long, slender root that is widely used in macrobiotic cooking to increase vitality. It is also considered a blood purifier. The plant grows wild throughout the United States, and the root is available in Asian markets and specialty food shops. It has a thin, edible skin and oxidizes quickly when cut. To prevent browning, soak cut burdock in water and lemon juice—this will also help eliminate its earthy, slightly bitter taste. Its texture is chewy and somewhat fibrous, but it softens when cooked. This gentle stew, which combines burdock with sweet-tasting kabocha squash and chewy shiitake mushrooms, is ideal winter fare served over brown rice or soba noodles.

Barley miso is made from barley, soybeans, and sea salt. One of the darker, saltier misos, it is aged longer and made with more soybeans than mellow white miso. As with all misos, don't let the stew boil after the miso is added, or all of its beneficial enzymes will be destroyed.

1 small kabocha or other winter squash, peeled, seeded, and diced

2 medium-size burdock roots, trimmed, well scrubbed, and thinly sliced

1½ cups diagonally sliced carrots

1 small onion, chopped

2½ cups vegetable broth

1 tablespoon barley miso paste

1 tablespoon low-sodium tamari

2 cups chopped napa cabbage

4 fresh shiitake mushrooms, stems removed and caps sliced

2 teaspoons toasted sesame oil

1. Place the squash, burdock, carrots, onion, and broth in a large saucepan and bring to a boil over medium-high heat. Reduce the heat to low, cover, and simmer until the vegetables begin to soften, about 20 minutes.

2. Remove about ¼ cup of the hot broth and place it in a small bowl. Add the miso and tamari and blend well, then stir the mixture back into the pot. Add the cabbage and mushrooms and simmer until the vegetables are tender, about 15 minutes.

3. Just before serving, drizzle the sesame oil into the stew. Taste and adjust the seasonings, then serve hot.

Serves 4

African Sweet Potato and Peanut Stew

If you've never had a dish that combined sweet potatoes and peanuts, you're in for a treat. Even people who claim not to like sweet potatoes enjoy this stew. Serve it over rice or couscous.

1 tablespoon olive oil or ¼ cup water

1 medium-size onion, chopped

1 medium-size green bell pepper, seeded and chopped

1 large garlic clove, minced

2 teaspoons natural sugar

1 teaspoon grated fresh ginger

½ teaspoon ground cumin

½ teaspoon ground cinnamon

¼ teaspoon cayenne

1½ pounds sweet potatoes, peeled and cut into ½-inch dice

1 (14.5-ounce) can crushed tomatoes

1½ cups vegetable broth

Salt

1½ cups cooked dark red kidney beans or 1 (15-ounce) can beans, rinsed and drained

2 tablespoons peanut butter

½ cup chopped unsalted dry-roasted peanuts

1. Heat the oil or water in a large saucepan over medium heat. Add the onion, cover, and cook until softened, about 5 minutes. Add the bell pepper and garlic, cover, and cook until softened, about 5 minutes. Stir in the sugar, ginger, cumin, cinnamon, and cayenne and cook, stirring, for 30 seconds. Add the sweet potatoes and stir to coat. Stir in the tomatoes, broth, and salt to taste. Bring to a boil, then reduce the heat to low and simmer until the vegetables are soft, about 30 minutes.

2. About 10 minutes before the end of the cooking time, stir in the kidney beans and simmer until heated through.

3. Remove about ¼ cup of the hot broth and place it in a small bowl. Blend in the peanut butter, stirring until smooth, then stir the mixture into the stew. If a thicker consistency is desired, puree about 1 cup of the stew in a blender or food processor and stir back into the pot, or use an immersion blender to puree some of the stew right in the pot.

4. Taste and adjust the seasonings. Sprinkle with the chopped peanuts and serve.

Serves 4 to 6

Marjoram-Scented Artichoke and Chickpea Stew

Two Mediterranean favorites, artichokes and chickpeas, come together in a flavorful stew redolent of fresh herbs. Frozen artichoke hearts and canned chickpeas make short work of the preparation, resulting in a dish special enough for company when served with a green salad and hearty bruschetta or focaccia.

1 tablespoon olive oil or ¼ cup water

1 large sweet onion, chopped

1 small red bell pepper, seeded and cut into 1-inch pieces

2 garlic cloves, minced

1 bay leaf

1½ teaspoons minced fresh marjoram or ¾ teaspoon dried marjoram

½ cup dry white wine

2 cups Super-Rich Vegetable Broth (page 60)

1 pound Yukon Gold potatoes, peeled and cut into 1-inch chunks

Salt and freshly ground black pepper

1 (9-ounce) package frozen artichoke hearts, cooked according to package directions and drained

1½ cups cooked chickpeas or 1 (15-ounce) can chickpeas, rinsed and drained

1. Heat the oil or water in a large skillet over medium heat. Add the onion, cover, and cook until softened, about 5 minutes. Add the bell pepper and garlic, cover, and cook until softened, about 5 minutes. Add the bay leaf and dried marjoram (if using). Stir in the wine. Add the broth and bring to a boil. Add the potatoes and salt and pepper to taste, reduce the heat to low, and simmer until the potatoes are fork tender, about 20 minutes.

2. Stir in the artichoke hearts, chickpeas, and fresh marjoram (if using). If a thicker stew is desired, puree about 1 cup of the mixture in a blender or food processor and stir back into the pot, or use an immersion blender to puree some of the stew right in the pot. Simmer gently until heated through, about 5 minutes.

Serves 4

Tuscan White Bean and Fennel Stew with Orange and Rosemary

Among other things, Tuscany is known for its olive oil, wine, and sun-ripened produce, as well as meaty beans such as the creamy cannellini. This stew incorporates many of these ingredients in a salute to the Tuscan countryside. A light, dry Pinot Grigio and some grilled Italian bread make ideal accompaniments.

1 tablespoon olive oil or ¼ cup water

1 large sweet onion, chopped

2 medium-size carrots, halved lengthwise and cut into ¼-inch-thick half-moons

2 garlic cloves, minced

1 large fennel bulb, trimmed and diced

½ cup dry white wine

1½ cups vegetable broth

1 pound small red potatoes, unpeeled and quartered

1 (14.5-ounce) can diced tomatoes, undrained

Salt and freshly ground black pepper

2 small zucchini, cut into ¼-inch-thick rounds

1½ cups cooked cannellini or other white beans or 1 (15-ounce) can beans, rinsed and drained

1 tablespoon minced orange zest

2 teaspoons minced fresh rosemary or 1 teaspoon dried rosemary

1. Heat the oil or water in a large saucepan over medium-high heat. Add the onion and carrots, cover, and cook until softened, about 5 minutes. Add the garlic and cook, stirring, for 30 seconds. Add the fennel and wine and bring to a boil. Reduce the heat to medium and simmer, stirring frequently, until the wine is reduced by half, about 5 minutes. Add the broth, potatoes, tomatoes and their juice, and salt and pepper to taste. Bring to a boil, then reduce the heat to low and simmer, stirring occasionally, until the potatoes soften, about 20 minutes.

2. Add the zucchini, beans, and salt and pepper to taste. Simmer until the ingredients are tender and the desired consistency is achieved, about 15 minutes. If a thicker stew is desired, puree about 1 cup of the stew in a blender or food processor and stir back into the pot, or use an immersion blender to puree some of the stew right in the pot. A few minutes before serving, stir in the orange zest and rosemary. Serve hot.

Serves 4 to 6

Moroccan-Spiced Fava Bean Stew

Fragrant spices and dried fruits lend a Moroccan accent to this hearty stew made with meaty fava beans. Fresh favas can be difficult to find and are time-consuming to prepare, since they need to be blanched and peeled before cooking. Dried, frozen, or canned fava beans may be found in specialty markets and some supermarkets. If favas are unavailable, substitute butter beans or lima beans. Serve over couscous or rice.

½ cup mixed dried fruit

¼ cup raisins or dried currants

1 tablespoon olive oil or ¼ cup water

1 large sweet onion, chopped

1 large carrot, diced

1 large garlic clove, minced

1 teaspoon ground cumin

1 teaspoon ground cinnamon

1 (14.5-ounce) can petite diced tomatoes, drained

8 ounces green beans, trimmed and cut into 1-inch pieces

2 cups vegetable broth

1½ cups cooked fava beans or 1 (15-ounce) can beans, rinsed and drained

½ cup fresh or thawed frozen peas

Salt and freshly ground black pepper

1 tablespoon minced fresh cilantro or parsley

1. Place the dried fruit and raisins in a small heatproof bowl. Add boiling water to cover and soak for 20 minutes to soften. Drain and set aside.

2. Heat the oil or water in a large saucepan over medium heat. Add the onion and carrot, cover, and cook until softened, about 5 minutes. Add the garlic, cumin, and cinnamon and cook, stirring, for 30 seconds. Add the tomatoes, green beans, and broth and bring to a boil. Reduce the heat to low, cover, and simmer until the vegetables are tender, about 20 minutes.

3. Add the favas, peas, fruit, and salt and pepper to taste. Simmer, uncovered, until the flavors are blended and the desired consistency is achieved, about 10 minutes.

4. Sprinkle with the cilantro and serve.

Serves 4

Curried Lentils with Carrots and Peas

Aromatic spices and coconut milk turn everyday lentils into a richly flavored stew. Serve over freshly cooked basmati rice.

1 large onion, cut into chunks

2 garlic cloves, crushed

1 teaspoon chopped fresh ginger

1 tablespoon olive oil

2 teaspoons curry powder or garam masala

1 teaspoon salt

½ teaspoon ground cumin

½ teaspoon ground coriander

¼ teaspoon dry mustard

¼ teaspoon freshly ground black pepper

¼ teaspoon cayenne

¼ teaspoon turmeric

⅛ teaspoon ground cardamom or cloves (optional)

4 cups water

1¼ cups dried brown lentils, picked over and rinsed

2 large carrots, halved lengthwise and cut into thin half-moons

¾ cup frozen green peas, thawed

1 cup unsweetened coconut milk

Hot cooked rice, to serve

1. In a food processor, puree the onion, garlic, and ginger.

2. Heat the olive oil in a large saucepan over medium heat. Add the onion puree, cover, and cook to mellow the flavor, about 5 minutes, stirring a few times to make sure it doesn't burn. Stir in all of the spices and cook, stirring, for 30 seconds. Add the water and bring to a simmer. Add the lentils, cover, and cook for 25 minutes. Add the carrots, cover, and continue to cook until tender, about 20 minutes more.

3. When the lentils and carrots are tender, stir in the peas and coconut milk. Taste and adjust the seasonings, if needed. Simmer, uncovered, to incorporate the flavors, about 10 minutes. Serve hot over rice.

Serves 4 to 6

Belgian-Style Seitan Stew with Dark Beer

This adaptation of the hearty Belgian stew *carbonnade à la flamande* is made with seitan, which absorbs all of the flavors of the rich sauce. Serve over noodles and wash it down with more of the beer that you used in the stew.

2 tablespoons olive oil

1 pound seitan, cut into thin strips

1 large onion, chopped

2 teaspoons natural sugar

2 tablespoons unbleached all-purpose flour

1 cup dark beer

1 tablespoon molasses

2 teaspoons Dijon mustard

2 teaspoons white wine vinegar

1 teaspoon dried thyme, crumbled

1 bay leaf

1 cup vegetable broth

Salt and freshly ground black pepper

1. Heat 1 tablespoon of the olive oil in a large skillet over medium-high heat. Add the seitan and cook until browned on all sides, about 10 minutes. Set aside.

2. Heat the remaining 1 tablespoon olive oil in a large saucepan over medium heat. Add the onion, cover, and cook until softened, about 5 minutes.

3. Stir in the sugar and cook, stirring frequently, until the onion is caramelized, about 10 minutes. Add the flour and cook, stirring, for 1 to 2 minutes to remove the raw taste. Stir in the beer, molasses, mustard, vinegar, thyme, and bay leaf. Add the broth, season to taste with salt and pepper, and simmer, stirring occasionally, until thickened, 10 to 15 minutes.

4. Add the seitan and simmer until the flavors are blended, about 10 minutes. Remove the bay leaf, and taste and adjust the seasonings. Serve hot.

Serves 4

Mushroom Stroganoff

Three types of mushrooms add texture and flavor to this creamy Eastern European classic made with vegan sour cream. Serve over wide noodles. For a variation, substitute seitan or reconstituted soy curls for a portion of the mushrooms.

2 tablespoons olive oil

3 large portobello mushroom caps, gills scraped out, cut into ¾-inch dice

2 tablespoons tomato paste

2 cups vegetable broth

1 large onion, chopped

1 large green bell pepper, seeded and chopped

8 ounces small white mushrooms, quartered

6 ounces shiitake mushrooms, stems removed and caps chopped

2 tablespoons unbleached all-purpose flour

1½ tablespoons sweet Hungarian paprika

Salt and freshly ground black pepper

½ cup vegan sour cream, homemade (page 126) or purchased

1. Heat 1 tablespoon of the olive oil in a large skillet over medium heat. Add the portobellos and brown on all sides, 7 to 8 minutes. Set aside.

2. In a small bowl, combine the tomato paste and ¼ cup of the broth, blending until smooth. Set aside.

3. Heat the remaining 1 tablespoon olive oil in a large saucepan over medium heat. Add the onion and bell pepper, cover, and cook until softened, about 5 minutes. Add the white mushrooms and shiitakes and cook, uncovered, until the liquid evaporates, about 3 minutes. Stir in the flour and paprika and cook, stirring, for about 1 minute to remove the raw taste from the flour. Add the tomato paste mixture, stirring until smooth. Stir in the remaining 1¾ cups broth and bring to a boil, then reduce the heat to low. Season to taste with salt and pepper and simmer until the flavors are blended and the sauce thickens somewhat, about 25 minutes.

4. Slowly whisk in the vegan sour cream until well blended. Add the reserved portobellos and simmer until heated through, about 5 minutes. Serve hot.

Serves 4

Vegetable Goulash

There are numerous variations on Hungarian goulash—this vegetable-centric version is just one of them. For a meatier version, add 8 ounces of diced seitan or reconstituted soy curls. This savory stew is especially good served over noodles.

1 tablespoon olive oil or ¼ cup water

1 large onion, chopped

1 carrot, chopped

1 small green bell pepper, seeded and chopped

3 garlic cloves, minced

2 Yukon Gold potatoes, diced

1 tablespoon sweet Hungarian paprika

1 tablespoon smoked paprika

½ teaspoon caraway seeds (optional)

2 cups diced mushrooms

1½ cups vegetable broth

¼ cup dry white wine (optional)

1 (14.5-ounce) can diced fire-roasted tomatoes, undrained

1½ cups cooked white beans or 1 (15-ounce) can beans, rinsed and drained

½ cup vegan sour cream, homemade (page 126) or purchased

Salt and freshly ground black pepper

1. Heat the oil or water in a large saucepan over medium heat. Add the onion and carrot, cover, and cook until softened, about 5 minutes. Stir in the bell pepper, garlic, potatoes, both kinds of paprika, and caraway seeds (if using) and cook for 1 minute. Stir in the mushrooms, broth, wine (if using) and bring to a boil.

2. Reduce the heat to a simmer and stir in the tomatoes and their juice and the beans. Cook, stirring occasionally, until the liquid is reduced and the flavors are blended, 20 to 30 minutes.

3. Remove about ⅓ cup of the hot broth and place it in a small bowl. Whisk in the vegan sour cream until blended, then stir the mixture back into the goulash. Season to taste with salt and pepper and simmer to blend the flavors, about 5 minutes. Serve hot.

Serves 4

Indonesian-Inspired Tempeh Stew

This flavorful stew is made with Indonesian ingredients, including tempeh, coconut milk, and pungent seasonings. Serve over freshly cooked rice.

2 tablespoons olive oil

8 ounces tempeh, steamed (page 10) and cubed

3 shallots, chopped

3 garlic cloves, minced

1 small, fresh hot chile, seeded and minced

1 teaspoon grated fresh ginger

1 large sweet potato, peeled and diced

1 cup water

1 (14.5-ounce) can crushed tomatoes

1 tablespoon low-sodium tamari

1 cup unsweetened coconut milk

Salt and freshly ground black pepper

2 tablespoons minced fresh cilantro

1 teaspoon minced lime zest

1. Heat 1 tablespoon of the olive oil in a large skillet over medium-high heat. Add the tempeh and brown on all sides, about 5 minutes. Set aside.

2. Heat the remaining 1 tablespoon olive oil in a large saucepan over medium heat. Add the shallots, garlic, chile, and ginger. Cook, stirring, until softened, about 5 minutes. Add the sweet potato, water, tomatoes, and tamari. Cover and cook, stirring occasionally, until the vegetables are tender, about 20 minutes. Uncover and reduce the heat to low. Add the coconut milk, salt and pepper to taste, and tempeh. Simmer, stirring occasionally, until thickened, about 10 minutes.

3. Just before serving, stir in the cilantro and lime zest. Serve hot.

Serves 4

Tempeh and Red Bean Jambalaya with Chipotle Chiles

The chipotle chiles add smoky heat to this spicy stew, which is best served over freshly cooked rice. Filé powder, made from sassafras leaves, thickens the stew and adds flavor. It can be found in specialty food shops and well-stocked supermarkets. For a milder version, decrease or omit the chiles.

2 tablespoons olive oil

8 ounces tempeh, steamed (page 10) and cut into ½-inch dice

1 large onion, chopped

1 large green bell pepper, seeded and chopped

2 garlic cloves, minced

1½ cups cooked dark red kidney beans or 1 (15-ounce) can beans, rinsed and drained

1 (28-ounce) can crushed tomatoes

2 chipotle chiles in adobo, minced

1 cup water

1 teaspoon filé powder

1 teaspoon dried thyme, crumbled

Salt

Cayenne

1. Heat 1 tablespoon of the olive oil in a large skillet over medium-high heat. Add the tempeh and cook, stirring occasionally, until browned on all sides, about 5 minutes. Set aside.

2. Heat the remaining 1 tablespoon olive oil in a large saucepan over medium heat. Add the onion and bell pepper, cover, and cook, stirring occasionally, until tender, about 10 minutes. Stir in the garlic and cook for 1 minute. Add the beans, tomatoes, chipotles, water, filé powder, thyme, and salt and cayenne to taste. Stir in the tempeh and simmer until the liquid cooks down and the flavors have blended, about 30 minutes. Serve hot.

Serves 4

Chickpeas Vindaloo

Vegetable vindaloo is a spicy favorite in Indian restaurants and is easy to make at home. In this version, chickpeas are prominent to add protein and substance. Serve over freshly cooked basmati rice.

1 tablespoon olive oil or ¼ cup water

1 large onion, chopped

1 green or red bell pepper, seeded and cut into ½-inch dice

1 serrano chile, seeded and minced

1 large sweet potato, peeled and cut into 1-inch dice

3 cups small cauliflower florets

3 garlic cloves, minced

2 teaspoons grated fresh ginger

2 teaspoons yellow curry powder

1 teaspoon ground coriander

½ teaspoon ground cumin

½ teaspoon ground cloves

½ teaspoon salt

¼ teaspoon cayenne

¼ teaspoon freshly ground black pepper

1 28-ounce can diced tomatoes, undrained

3 cups cooked chickpeas or 2 (15-ounce) cans chickpeas, rinsed and drained

2 to 3 tablespoons white wine vinegar

½ cup water, or more if needed

1 cup fresh or thawed frozen peas

Hot cooked rice, to serve

Heat the oil or water in a large pot over medium heat. Add the onion and cook until softened, about 5 minutes. Add the bell pepper, chile, sweet potato, cauliflower, garlic, and ginger. Cook, stirring occasionally, until slightly softened, about 5 minutes. Add the spices and cook, stirring, for 1 minute. Stir in the tomatoes and their juice, chickpeas, vinegar, and water and bring to boil. Reduce the heat to low, cover, and simmer until the vegetables are tender, about 15 minutes. Uncover, stir in the peas, then taste and adjust the seasonings, if needed. Cook uncovered for 10 minutes longer to blend the flavors. If the stew is too thick, add a little more water. Serve hot over rice.

Serves 4 to 6

Three-Bean Chili

Vegan chili is a great way to introduce meatless meals to nonvegans because it's hearty and robust—things many people do not usually associate with vegan cuisine. This version features three kinds of beans, but you may substitute chopped seitan, steamed tempeh, or reconstituted soy curls for some of the beans. Serve with crackers or cornbread, or ladled over rice or noodles.

1 tablespoon olive oil or ¼ cup water

1 large sweet onion, chopped

½ small green bell pepper, seeded and chopped

2 garlic cloves, minced

1 small, fresh hot chile (optional), seeded and minced

3 tablespoons tomato paste

2 tablespoons chili powder, or to your taste

1 (28-ounce) can crushed tomatoes

1½ cups cooked black beans or 1 (15-ounce) can beans, rinsed and drained

1½ cups cooked pinto beans or 1 (15-ounce) can beans, rinsed and drained

1½ cups cooked dark red kidney beans or 1 (15-ounce) can beans, rinsed and drained

1½ cups water

1 teaspoon salt

¼ teaspoon freshly ground black pepper

Heat the olive oil or water in a large saucepan over medium heat. Add the onion and bell pepper, cover, and cook, stirring occasionally, until tender, about 10 minutes. Add the garlic and chile (if using) and cook for 1 minute. Stir in the tomato paste, chili powder, and tomatoes until well blended. Add all of the beans, the water, salt, and pepper and simmer, stirring occasionally, until the liquid is reduced and the flavors are blended, about 45 minutes. Taste and adjust the seasonings, then serve hot.

Serves 6

Very Veggie Chili

This chili is loaded with a variety of vegetables that harmonize well with the zesty seasonings. For a change of pace, serve it over freshly cooked couscous or quinoa.

¼ cup tomato paste

1 tablespoon low-sodium tamari

2 teaspoons molasses

1 tablespoon olive oil or ¼ cup water

1 large red onion, chopped

1 celery rib, minced

1 medium-size eggplant, peeled and chopped

1 small red bell pepper, seeded and chopped

1 small, fresh hot chile (optional), seeded and minced

2 garlic cloves, minced

2 tablespoons chili powder

1 teaspoon ground coriander

1 teaspoon ground cumin

1 (14.5-ounce) can diced fire-roasted tomatoes, undrained

1½ cups cooked chickpeas or 1 (15-ounce) can chickpeas, rinsed and drained

1½ cups water

Salt and freshly ground black pepper

1. In a small bowl, combine the tomato paste, tamari, and molasses, stirring to blend. Set aside.

2. Heat the olive oil or water in a large saucepan over medium heat. Add the onion and celery, cover, and cook until softened, about 5 minutes. Add the eggplant, bell pepper, chile (if using), and garlic, then stir in the chili powder, coriander, and cumin. Cover and cook, stirring occasionally, until softened, about 10 minutes.

3. Stir in the tomato paste mixture. Add the tomatoes and their juice, chickpeas, water, and salt and pepper to taste. Simmer, uncovered, stirring occasionally, until the liquid is reduced and the vegetables are tender, 30 to 45 minutes. Serve hot.

Serves 6

Black Bean and Butternut Squash Chili

This chili recipe has become a tradition at Halloween parties because of the vivid color contrast between the black beans and bright orange squash. Serve it in a large, hollowed-out pumpkin to add to the festivities, accompanied by your choice of garnishes or toppings.

1 tablespoon olive oil or ¼ cup water

1 medium-size onion, chopped

1 garlic clove, minced

1 jalapeño (optional), seeded and minced

1 (14.5-ounce) can diced fire-roasted tomatoes, undrained

1 cup apple juice

¼ cup tomato paste

2 tablespoons chili powder, or to your taste

1 teaspoon salt

1 medium-size butternut squash, peeled, seeded, and cut into ½-inch dice

3 cups cooked black beans or 2 (15-ounce) cans beans, rinsed and drained

1. Heat the olive oil or water in a large pot over medium heat. Add the onion, garlic, and jalapeño (if using). Cover and cook until softened, about 5 minutes. Add the tomatoes and their juices, apple juice, tomato paste, chili powder, salt, and squash and stir to combine. Bring to a boil, then reduce the heat to low. Cover and simmer until the squash is tender, about 30 minutes.

2. Add the beans, then taste and adjust the seasonings. Simmer, uncovered, for about 15 minutes to blend the flavors. Serve hot.

Serves 6

Roasted Root Vegetable Chili

The rich, mellow flavor of roasted root vegetables makes this a perfect choice for a late autumn meal, accompanied by warm cornbread, fresh from the oven. You may peel or not peel the carrots, parsnips, and potato, but as with all vegetables, be sure to wash them thoroughly if left unpeeled.

1 large sweet onion, chopped

2 large carrots, diced

2 medium-size parsnips, peeled and diced

1 large Yukon Gold potato, diced

Salt and freshly ground black pepper

1 tablespoon olive oil or ¼ cup water

1 red or green bell pepper, chopped

3 garlic cloves, minced

1 jalapeño, seeded and minced

2 tablespoons tomato paste

2 tablespoons chili powder

1 teaspoon ground cumin

1 (14.5-ounce) can diced fire-roasted tomatoes, undrained

3 cups cooked pinto beans or 2 (15-ounce) cans beans, rinsed and drained

1 cup water or vegetable broth

1. Preheat the oven to 400°F. Generously oil a large shallow baking pan. Distribute the onion, carrots, parsnips, and potato in the pan. Sprinkle with salt and pepper, tossing to coat. Roast the vegetables, turning once, until softened and lightly browned, about 30 minutes.

2. Heat the olive oil or water in a large pot over medium heat. Add the bell pepper, garlic, and jalapeño and cook, stirring, until fragrant, about 1 minute. Stir in the tomato paste, chili powder, cumin, and ½ teaspoon of salt. Add the tomatoes and their juice, pinto beans, and ½ cup of the water and bring to a boil. Reduce the heat to a simmer and cook for 15 minutes.

3. When the roasted vegetables are tender, add them to the pot and simmer for 15 minutes to blend the flavors. Add additional water, if needed. Taste and adjust the seasonings, if needed. Serve hot.

Serves 6

Black Bean Chili with Cilantro Pesto

The Cilantro Pesto adds a special touch to this chili, but it's flavorful enough to stand on its own if you prefer to omit the pesto.

1 tablespoon olive oil or ¼ cup water

1 large onion, chopped

⅓ cup chopped celery

2 garlic cloves, minced

1 (14.5-ounce) can diced fire-roasted tomatoes, undrained

1 (6-ounce) can tomato paste

1 cup water

2 tablespoons chili powder

1 teaspoon ground cumin

Salt and freshly ground black pepper

1 tablespoon fresh lemon juice

3 cups cooked black beans or 2 (15-ounce) cans beans, rinsed and drained

⅓ cup Cilantro Pesto (recipe follows)

1. Heat the olive oil or water in a large pot over medium heat. Add the onion, celery, and garlic. Cover and cook until softened, about 5 minutes. Add the tomatoes and their juice, tomato paste, water, chili powder, cumin, and salt and pepper to taste. Reduce the heat to low and simmer for 30 minutes.

2. Add the lemon juice and beans and simmer for about 15 minutes. Taste and adjust the seasonings. Just before serving, swirl in the pesto.

Serves 6

CILANTRO PESTO

1 cup tightly packed fresh cilantro leaves

¼ cup raw almonds

2 large garlic cloves, crushed

½ teaspoon salt

3 tablespoons olive oil

Combine the cilantro, almonds, garlic, and salt in a food processor and process until smooth. With the machine running, add the olive oil through the feed tube and process into a smooth paste. Store, tightly covered, in the refrigerator with a thin layer of olive oil on top to prevent discoloration.

Makes about 1 cup

Anasazi Chili with Quinoa

The anasazi is a sweet, meaty bean, whose name means "ancient stranger" in the Navajo language. Paired with quinoa, the high-protein grain of the ancient Incas, it becomes a dish steeped in Native American heritage. If anasazi beans are unavailable, pinto or kidney beans may be used. Cook anasazi beans the same way you would cook pinto beans (see page 252).

1 tablespoon olive oil or ¼ cup water

1 medium-size onion, finely chopped

1 small red bell pepper, seeded and chopped

1 small, fresh hot chile (optional), seeded and minced

2 tablespoons chili powder

1 teaspoon ground cumin

1 teaspoon dried oregano

1 teaspoon smoked paprika

1 teaspoon salt

¼ teaspoon freshly ground black pepper

1 (28-ounce) can diced fire-roasted tomatoes, undrained

3 cups cooked anasazi beans or 2 (15-ounce) cans beans, rinsed and drained

½ to 1 cup water

4 cups freshly cooked quinoa (page 198)

1. Heat the olive oil or water in a large pot over medium heat. Add the onion, bell pepper, and chile (if using). Cover and cook until softened, about 5 minutes. Stir in the chili powder, cumin, oregano, paprika, salt, and pepper. Add the tomatoes and their juice, beans, and ½ cup water and stir to combine. Bring to a boil, reduce the heat to low, and simmer for 30 minutes, stirring occasionally. Add the remaining ½ cup water, if needed. Taste and adjust the seasonings.

2. To serve, spoon the chili over the quinoa.

Serves 4

Smoky Spicy Chili

I like to accompany this chili with brown basmati rice. The toasted almonds add an unexpected crunch.

1 tablespoon olive oil or ¼ cup water

1 large sweet onion, chopped

2 garlic cloves, minced

2 chipotle chiles in adobo, minced

2 tablespoons chili powder

1 teaspoon ground cumin

½ teaspoon ground cinnamon

1 teaspoon salt

1 teaspoon smoked paprika

1 (28-ounce) can diced fire-roasted tomatoes, undrained

¼ cup tomato paste

1½ cups water

3 cups cooked kidney beans or 2 (15-ounce) cans beans, rinsed and drained

2 cups finely chopped seitan, reconstituted soy curls, or reconstituted TVP

1 teaspoon liquid smoke

¼ cup smoked almonds, crushed, for garnish

Heat the olive oil or water in a large pot over medium heat. Add the onion, garlic, and chiles. Cover, and cook until softened, about 5 minutes. Stir in the chili powder, cumin, cinnamon, salt, and paprika. Add the tomatoes and their juice, tomato paste, water, and beans. Stir to combine and bring to a boil. Reduce the heat to low, stir in the seitan, and simmer for 30 minutes, stirring occasionally. Stir in the liquid smoke. Taste and adjust the seasonings. Serve hot, garnished with the almonds.

Serves 6

Tastes Like Mom's Chili

This chili is a vegan version of the chili my mother used to make, which she served over cooked elbow macaroni. Cooked green lentils replace the ground beef, although chopped seitan or reconstituted soy curls (or even TVP) can be used instead.

1 tablespoon olive oil or ¼ cup water

1 large onion, chopped

2 tablespoons chili powder, or to your taste

1 teaspoon dried oregano

1 teaspoon ground cumin

⅛ teaspoon cayenne

1 (28-ounce) can crushed tomatoes

1 cup water

2 cups cooked or canned green lentils, finely chopped seitan, or finely chopped reconstituted soy curls

3 cups cooked kidney beans or 2 (15-ounce) cans beans, rinsed and drained

Salt and freshly ground black pepper

1. Heat the olive oil or water in a large pot over medium heat. Add the onion, cover, and cook until softened, about 5 minutes. Stir in the chili powder, oregano, cayenne, tomatoes, and water. Bring to a boil, reduce the heat to low, cover, and simmer for 15 minutes.

2. Stir in the lentils, beans, and salt and pepper to taste. Simmer for about 30 minutes to blend the flavors. Serve hot.

Serves 6

California Chili

California olives and avocados, combined with vibrant fresh vegetables, contribute to the West Coast influence of this chili. To complete the picture, serve with a bottle of good California wine and some San Francisco sourdough bread. Be sure to prepare the avocado at the last minute to avoid discoloration.

1 tablespoon olive oil or ¼ cup water

1 medium-size onion, chopped

1 small red bell pepper, seeded and chopped

1 fresh hot chile (optional), seeded and minced

2 garlic cloves, minced

8 ripe plum tomatoes, diced

¼ cup tomato paste

2 tablespoons chili powder

1 teaspoon minced fresh oregano or ½ teaspoon dried oregano

1½ cups water

½ cup dry red wine

3 cups cooked kidney beans or 2 (15-ounce) cans beans, rinsed and drained

Salt and freshly ground black pepper

2 medium-size ripe Hass avocados, peeled, pitted, and diced, for serving

½ cup pitted and sliced brine-cured black olives, for serving

Heat the olive oil or water in a large pot over medium heat. Add the onion, bell pepper, chile (if using), and garlic. Cover and cook until softened, about 10 minutes. Add the tomatoes, tomato paste, chili powder, oregano, water, wine, beans, and salt and pepper to taste. Simmer until the flavors are blended and the desired consistency is achieved, 30 to 45 minutes. Serve hot, topped with the avocados and olives.

===== *Serves 4 to 6* =====

Did You Know?

Avocados are rich in potassium, folic acid, vitamin B_6, and other nutrients. Though high in fat, they contain enzymes that help break down fat in the body.

Backyard Barbecue Chili

The smoky sweetness of the barbecue sauce permeates this flavorful chili. To further promote the backyard barbecue spirit, serve it with coleslaw, corn chips, and other picnic fare, even if it's snowing outside.

1 tablespoon olive oil or ¼ cup water

1 large onion, chopped

1 red bell pepper, seeded and chopped

3 garlic cloves, minced

1 serrano chile (optional), seeded and minced

1 (28-ounce) can diced fire-roasted tomatoes, undrained

1 cup water

½ cup bottled spicy vegan barbecue sauce

2 tablespoons tomato paste

2 to 3 tablespoons chili powder

½ teaspoon natural sugar

Salt and freshly ground black pepper

2 cups cooked or canned green lentils or finely chopped seitan or 1 cup chopped reconstituted soy curls or reconstituted TVP

3 cups cooked kidney beans or 2 (15-ounce) cans beans, rinsed and drained

1. Heat the olive oil or water in a large pot over medium heat. Add the onion, bell pepper, garlic, and chile, if using. Cover, and cook until softened, about 5 minutes. Stir in the tomatoes and their juice, water, barbecue sauce, tomato paste, chili powder, sugar, and salt and pepper to taste. Bring to a boil, reduce the heat to low, cover, and simmer for 20 minutes, stirring occasionally.

2. Stir in the lentils and beans and cook for 15 minutes to blend the flavors. Add a little more water if the mixture becomes too dry. Serve hot.

Serves 6

Orange-Chipotle White Bean Chili

The combination of smoky hot chipotles, sprightly orange, and fresh thyme makes a delicious, if unexpected, white chili that is especially good served over basmati rice.

1 tablespoon olive oil or ¼ cup water

1 large onion, chopped

1 red bell pepper, seeded and chopped

1 or 2 chipotle chiles in adobo, minced

3 tablespoons chili powder

1 tablespoon minced fresh thyme
or 1 teaspoon dried thyme

1 teaspoon natural sugar

1 (14.5-ounce) can diced tomatoes, undrained

1 cup Fresh Tomato Salsa
(page 157) or purchased salsa

3 cups cooked cannellini
or other white beans or 2 (15-ounce)
cans beans, rinsed and drained

1½ cups cooked navy beans or 1 (15-ounce)
can beans, rinsed and drained

1 cup water

⅓ cup fresh orange juice

2 teaspoons grated orange zest

Salt and freshly ground black pepper

Orange slices and fresh thyme
sprigs, for garnish

1. Heat the olive oil or water in a large pot over medium heat. Add the onion and bell pepper. Cover and cook until softened, about 5 minutes. Stir in the chipotle chiles, chili powder, thyme, and sugar. Add the tomatoes and their juice, salsa, both kinds of beans, and water, and simmer for 45 minutes.

2. Stir in the orange juice, orange zest, and salt and pepper to taste. Cook for 10 minutes to blend the flavors. Serve hot, garnished with the orange slices and thyme sprigs.

Serves 6

Quick-as-Lightning Chili

This chili tastes as if it took all day to make, but it actually comes together in a flash with ingredients from your pantry. The vegetables in the chunky salsa add substance, making chopping vegetables unnecessary. A combination of pinto beans and lentils provide texture. Serve over pasta or rice, accompanied by your favorite toppings.

3 cups cooked pinto beans or 2 (15-ounce) cans beans, rinsed and drained

1½ cups cooked lentils or 1 (15-ounce) can lentils, rinsed and drained

1 (16-ounce) jar chunky salsa

1 (14.5-ounce) can diced fire-roasted tomatoes, undrained

½ cup water, or more as needed

2 tablespoons chili powder

1 teaspoon ground cumin

1 teaspoon dried marjoram

Salt and freshly ground black pepper

Combine all of the ingredients in a large pot over medium heat. Bring to a boil, then reduce the heat to low and simmer until the flavors are blended and the desired consistency is achieved, about 30 minutes. If the chili becomes too thick, add more water. Serve hot.

Serves 4 to 6

Whatever you're making for dinner, chances are good that you will use a skillet for all or part of the preparation. I can think of no other cooking vessel that commands such importance in the kitchen. A good skillet can become your best friend. The type of skillet you use is a matter of personal preference, whether it's Grandma's cast-iron frying pan or a shiny new wok. There are a wide variety of materials, sizes, and types of pans to choose from, but if I could have only one skillet, it would be a 12-inch sauté pan, for its versatility and ease of use.

From Asian stir-fries to French sautés to old-fashioned simmered dishes, the recipes in this chapter run the gamut of skillet-cooked entrées using tofu, tempeh, seitan, and vegetables. Many skillet dishes, especially stir-fries and sautés, can be ready in 15 minutes or less.

Even in oven-cooked dishes, a skillet is often used to partially cook or sear some of the ingredients to improve the flavor, texture, or color of the dish. At the same time, recipes that might normally be prepared in the oven are sometimes simmered on top of the stove to save time or to avoid heating up the kitchen by turning on the oven.

Having good skillet sense doesn't mean that you can't also enjoy the thrill of the grill. Many modern kitchens now have a grill built right into the stovetop for convenient grilling all year round. For that reason, this chapter includes suggestions for adapting certain recipes for the grill, as well as a few recipes designed specifically for grilling, whether indoors or out.

Grilled Portobellos
with Rosemary-Roasted Vegetables

This colorful dish is full of flavor, thanks to the plethora of diced roasted vegetables that make up the topping for the juicy portobello mushrooms. This is one of those recipes that can be adapted for stovetop, grill, or oven—or any combination. In this version, I grill the mushrooms and roast the vegetables for the topping, but the other cooking methods are interchangeable, with delicious results.

1 large red onion, chopped

1 large yellow bell pepper,
seeded and chopped

1 medium-size zucchini, chopped

⅓ cup olive oil

2 tablespoons coarsely chopped
fresh rosemary or other herb

Salt and freshly ground black pepper

1 large ripe tomato, chopped

4 large portobello mushroom
caps, gills scraped out

1. Preheat the oven to 425°F and heat your gas, charcoal, or stovetop grill. In a large bowl, combine the onion, bell pepper, zucchini, ¼ cup of the olive oil, the rosemary, and salt and pepper to taste. Toss to coat the vegetables with the oil, then spread them in a single layer on a rimmed baking sheet. Roast until tender and lightly browned, about 25 minutes.

2. Reduce the oven temperature to 275°F. Add the tomato to the roasted vegetables, stirring to combine, and return to the oven to keep warm.

3. Brush the mushrooms with the remaining olive oil and grill until tender and lightly charred on the outside, about 5 minutes per side.

4. To serve, arrange the portobello caps gill side down on 4 individual plates and top with the roasted vegetable mixture.

Serves 4

VARIATION: For a more substantial entrée, grill 4 vegan burgers or seitan cutlets along with the mushrooms. To serve, place a burger on each plate, top each with a mushroom cap, and top with the roasted vegetables.

Thrill of the Grill

Little compares with the flavor of vegetables cooked on the grill. Most vegetables can be grilled, as long as you account for their size and shape. For large pieces, simply place lightly oiled vegetables over hot coals and cook until slightly charred on the outside and tender on the inside. Smaller vegetables or cut vegetable pieces can be threaded onto bamboo skewers or placed on a mesh rack or in a perforated basket before grilling. Place longer-cooking vegetables, such as onions, on the grill first, then add the quick-cooking ones, such as tomatoes, later.

VEGAN "MEAT" ON THE GRILL

Like most vegetables, plant-based proteins such as seitan, tempeh, and tofu are great on the grill, as are commercial products such as burgers and hot dogs. For best results, keep these tips in mind.

1. Plant-based proteins contain little fat and are more delicate than meat, so it's important to start with a clean, well-oiled grill to ensure that they won't fall apart or stick to the grill.

2. Because of their naturally neutral flavors, tofu, tempeh, and seitan all take well to marinating and basting and are good choices for grilling. If you don't have time to marinate, be sure to brush them with a small amount of oil (or a mixture of oil and tamari) for easier grilling.

3. Vegan "meats" need very little time on the grill—just enough to heat them through and impart that great grilled taste and appearance. Cook for no more than 5 minutes per side over a medium-hot fire.

4. Tempeh, seitan, and tofu may be grilled in slices or slabs, or cut into bite-size pieces and threaded onto skewers or placed on a mesh rack or in a perforated basket (especially useful for the more delicate tofu).

5. To prepare tofu for the grill, use only extra-firm tofu and press out all the moisture (see page 7) before marinating or grilling.

6. As a rule, use ½ to ¾ cup marinade per pound of ingredients to be marinated—more if you plan to serve extra at the table. Marinate ingredients for about 1 hour, turning once. Following are some good marinade combinations. Note: Marinades that contain solid ingredients such as garlic or chiles should be pureed in a food processor or blender.

    - *Ragin' Cajun Marinade:* 2 chopped garlic cloves; ⅓ cup olive oil; 3 tablespoons white wine vinegar; 1 tablespoon tamari; 1 teaspoon dried thyme; ½ teaspoon cayenne; ½ teaspoon paprika; ¼ teaspoon celery salt; ¼ teaspoon salt

    - *Smoky Hot Southwest Marinade:* 2 chopped garlic cloves; 2 canned chipotle chiles in adobo; ⅓ cup fresh orange juice; 2 tablespoons fresh lime juice; 1 tablespoon tamari; ½ teaspoon ground cumin

- *Whatta Jerk Caribbean Marinade:* 1 seeded, chopped jalapeño; 3 chopped scallions; 1 chopped garlic clove; ¼ cup olive oil; 2 tablespoons tamari; ¼ cup fresh lime juice; 1 tablespoon natural sugar; 2 teaspoons dried thyme; 1 teaspoon ground allspice; ¼ teaspoon ground cinnamon; ¼ teaspoon dried oregano

- *Asian Barbecue Marinade:* 1 chopped garlic clove; 1 tablespoon minced fresh ginger; ¼ cup tamari; 2 tablespoons toasted sesame oil; 2 tablespoons hoisin sauce; 2 tablespoons rice vinegar

- *Tempting Teriyaki Marinade:* 2 chopped garlic cloves; 1 teaspoon grated fresh ginger; ¼ cup tamari; ¼ cup fresh orange juice; 2 tablespoons toasted sesame oil; 2 tablespoons rice vinegar; 1½ tablespoons natural sugar

- *Fragrant Thai Marinade:* 2 chopped garlic cloves; 1 teaspoon minced fresh ginger; 2 teaspoons minced fresh cilantro; ¼ cup tamari or dark soy sauce; ¼ cup vegetarian oyster sauce; 2 tablespoons fresh lime juice; 2 tablespoons palm sugar or other natural sugar

The following recipes can also be used as marinades or bastes for your favorite plant proteins or vegetables.

- Spicy Peanut Dipping Sauce (page 145)
- Ginger-Lime Dipping Sauce (page 145)
- Garlicky Herb Marinade (page 146)
- Mango Sunburst Sauce (page 140)
- Bourbon-Spiked Barbecue Sauce (page 138)
- Gloria's Glorious Garlic Sauce (page 139)

Jerk-Spiced Portobello Steaks

Zesty jerk seasonings enhance the meaty texture of the mushrooms. They are pan-fried in this recipe but are also delicious cooked on the grill or under the broiler. Green Apple Salsa (page 156) is a good accompaniment. These succulent 'shrooms can be served over rice or on toasted burger rolls.

2 teaspoons natural sugar

1 teaspoon ground cumin

1 teaspoon ground allspice

1 teaspoon dried oregano

1 teaspoon sweet paprika

1 teaspoon salt

½ teaspoon cayenne

¼ teaspoon freshly grated nutmeg

4 large portobello mushroom caps, gills scraped out

¼ cup olive oil

1. In a shallow bowl, combine the sugar, cumin, allspice, oregano, paprika, salt, cayenne, and nutmeg. Set aside.

2. Coat the mushroom caps with 2 tablespoons of the olive oil, then coat them evenly with the spice mixture. Heat the remaining 2 tablespoons olive oil in a large skillet over medium heat. Add the mushrooms and cook until tender, about 5 minutes per side. Serve hot.

Serves 4

Garlic and Herb-Marinated Vegetable Kabobs

If you're using wooden bamboo skewers, you'll need to soak them in water for 30 minutes before using to prevent them from burning. Cooking on an outdoor grill is ideal, but an indoor grill, broiler, or hot oven will do the job nicely as well. Serve over freshly cooked rice.

4 shallots, halved lengthwise

1 fennel bulb, trimmed, quartered, and separated into 8 pieces

1 large red bell pepper, seeded and cut into 8 pieces

2 small yellow squash or zucchini, cut into 8 chunks

8 small white mushrooms

1 cup Garlicky Herb Marinade (page 146)

1. Place all of the vegetables in a medium-size bowl. Pour the marinade over all, turning the vegetables to coat with the marinade. Set aside for 30 minutes to marinate, or cover and refrigerate for several hours or overnight.

2. Preheat the grill, broiler, or oven. Thread one piece of each vegetable on 8 skewers and cook on an indoor or outdoor grill, or place on a lightly oiled baking sheet and cook under the broiler or in a preheated 450°F oven. Cook until the vegetables are tender, about 10 minutes, turning once. Serve hot.

Serves 4

Pan-Fried Tofu and Watercress with Lemon-Caper Sauce

The piquant flavor of the lemon-caper sauce is absorbed by the crispy fried tofu and enhanced by the peppery bite of the watercress. Oven-browned potatoes make a particularly good accompaniment.

1 (12- to 16-ounce) package extra-firm tofu, drained and cut into ¼-inch-thick slices

Salt and freshly ground black pepper

2 tablespoons olive oil

¼ cup dry white wine

3 tablespoons fresh lemon juice

2 tablespoon capers, drained and chopped

1 large garlic clove, minced

2 bunches watercress, tough stems removed

1. Pat the tofu dry and season to taste with salt and pepper. Set aside.

2. Heat 1 tablespoon of the olive oil in a large skillet over medium-high heat. Add the tofu and cook in batches until golden brown on both sides, 2 to 4 minutes per side. Add the wine, lemon juice, and capers and simmer until the sauce is slightly reduced, about 2 minutes. Reduce the heat to low and keep warm.

3. Heat the remaining 1 tablespoon olive oil in a large skillet over medium heat. Add the garlic and cook, stirring, until fragrant, about 30 seconds. Add the watercress and cook, stirring, until just wilted, 2 to 3 minutes. Season to taste with salt and pepper.

4. Transfer the watercress to a serving platter or 4 individual plates and arrange the tofu on top. Drizzle the sauce over the tofu and serve hot.

Serves 4

Tofu with Almonds and Amaretto

I love to cook with wine and spirits—just a splash adds excitement and sophistication to a quick sauté. Amaretto, an almond-flavored liqueur, adds a decidedly decadent touch to thinly sliced tofu sautéed to a crisp golden brown. The crunch of toasted almonds amplifies the flavor of the liqueur. As an alternative, you could make this dish with hazelnuts and Frangelico, a hazelnut-flavored liqueur.

1 (12- to 16-ounce) package extra-firm tofu, drained, pressed (page 7), and cut into ¼-inch-thick slices

¼ cup unbleached all-purpose flour

Salt and freshly ground black pepper

2 tablespoons olive oil

4 shallots, thinly sliced lengthwise

½ cup vegetable broth

¼ cup amaretto or other almond-flavored liqueur

½ cup toasted slivered almonds (page 203)

1 tablespoon minced fresh parsley

1. Dredge the tofu in the flour, tapping off any excess. Season to taste with salt and pepper.

2. Heat the olive oil in a large nonstick skillet over medium-high heat. Add the tofu and cook until browned on both sides, 2 to 4 minutes per side. Remove from the skillet, transfer to a plate, and set aside.

3. Add the shallots to the skillet and cook until tender, 3 to 4 minutes. Add the broth and liqueur and heat almost to boiling. Reduce the heat to low, return the tofu to the pan, add the almonds and parsley, and simmer to infuse the tofu with the flavor of the sauce and to heat through, about 5 minutes. Serve hot.

Serves 4

How to Season Your Cast-Iron Skillet or Wok

The key to enjoying a long and happy relationship with your cast-iron skillet or wok is to condition it well. First, wash, rinse, and dry the pan. Next, generously oil the inside surface with a light, neutral-tasting cooking oil such as peanut oil. Then place the pan in a preheated 350°F oven for 1 hour. Turn the heat off and allow the pan to cool in the oven (this will take about 4 hours). Wipe out any excess oil, and your pan is ready to use. Do not wash your pan with detergent or scrub it with steel wool, and be sure to dry your pan well after each use to prevent rust.

Sesame-Encrusted Tofu with Spicy Broccoli

If you're looking for ways to get more calcium in your diet, this recipe is for you. Tofu, broccoli, and sesame seeds are loaded with calcium. Sesame lovers will delight in the three layers of sesame flavor—from the creamy tahini to the toasted sesame seeds and oil.

3 cups broccoli florets

¼ cup tahini

2 tablespoons low-sodium tamari

⅓ cup water, or as needed

1 cup sesame seeds

1 (12- to 16-ounce) package extra-firm tofu, drained and cut into ½-inch-wide x ½-inch-thick strips

2 tablespoons neutral vegetable oil

½ teaspoon red pepper flakes

2 teaspoons toasted sesame oil

1. Steam the broccoli over boiling water until crisp-tender, 2 to 3 minutes, then plunge into a bowl of ice water. Drain and set aside.

2. In a small, shallow bowl, combine the tahini, 1 tablespoon of the tamari, and enough water to make a smooth sauce. Place the sesame seeds on a plate. Dredge the tofu strips in the tahini mixture, then coat with the sesame seeds.

3. Heat 1 tablespoon of the vegetable oil in a large nonstick skillet over medium heat. Working in batches, add the tofu strips and cook until lightly browned on both sides, about 5 minutes total. Transfer to a serving platter and keep warm.

4. Heat the remaining 1 tablespoon vegetable oil in the same skillet over medium heat. Add the red pepper flakes and broccoli and stir-fry until hot, about 2 minutes. Splash with the remaining 1 tablespoon tamari and spoon the broccoli over the tofu. Drizzle the sesame oil over all and serve hot.

Serves 4

To-Fu Yung

Chinese and other Asian restaurants will often substitute tofu for meat or leave the egg out of some dishes when asked. But in dishes where eggs dominate, such as egg foo yung, it may be easier to make this vegan version at home.

BROWN SAUCE

1 cup vegetable broth

1 tablespoon low-sodium tamari

1 tablespoon dry sherry or rice vinegar

1 teaspoon grated fresh ginger

½ teaspoon natural sugar

1 tablespoon cornstarch dissolved in 2 tablespoons cold water

2 teaspoons toasted sesame oil

TO-FU YUNG

1 (12- to 16-ounce) package extra-firm tofu, drained

⅓ cup unbleached all-purpose flour

3 tablespoons nutritional yeast

2 tablespoons low-sodium tamari

1 teaspoon baking powder

1 tablespoon neutral vegetable oil or 2 tablespoons water

1 celery rib, chopped

8 white mushrooms or stemmed shiitake mushrooms, chopped

4 ounces finely chopped bok choy or Napa cabbage

6 scallions, chopped

1. To make the brown sauce: In a small saucepan, combine the broth, tamari, sherry, ginger, and sugar and bring to a boil. Reduce the heat to medium-high and add the cornstarch mixture, stirring until it thickens. Stir in the sesame oil. Keep warm.

2. To make the to-fu yung: Preheat the oven to 400°F. Generously oil two baking sheets and set aside. In a high-speed blender or food processor, combine the tofu, flour, nutritional yeast, tamari, and baking powder until well blended. Set aside.

3. Heat the oil or water in a large skillet over medium-high heat. Add the celery, mushrooms, bok choy, and 4 tablespoons of the scallions and stir-fry until tender, 3 to 5 minutes. Remove from the heat. Combine the tofu mixture with the vegetable mixture and stir to mix well.

4. Scoop ¼ cup of the mixture onto a prepared baking sheet to make a round pancake. Repeat with the remaining batter, arranging the pancakes on the baking sheets so they do not touch. Bake for 15 minutes, then gently flip them and bake for another 10 minutes or until browned.

5. Top with the sauce and garnish with the remaining 2 tablespoons scallions. Serve immediately.

Serves 4 to 6

The Entertaining Vegan

My husband and I love to entertain in our home, and the guests who share our table run the gamut from meat eaters to vegans. No one goes away hungry. My approach to vegan entertaining is to plan menus that are full of flavor and visually appealing—then relax and enjoy.

I don't usually "announce" that there's no meat or dairy on the table, because I believe that vegan food is a cuisine in its own right. Delicious food is delicious food—let it stand on its own without qualification. With nonvegans, I sometimes choose ethnic themes, pasta dishes, or one-pot vegetable and bean entrées, but I also like to expose my guests to the wonders of seitan and the versatility of soy.

Let the seasons, holidays, or other events provide inspirations for your menus. Do what many chefs do when planning their featured restaurant items: feature what's fresh and in season at the market. When planning a menu for company, try to find out whether your guests have any food allergies or aversions, say, to hot and spicy foods. If you know they have a favorite cuisine, consider choosing a theme they will enjoy.

Next, decide how many courses you want to make—from a casual one-dish supper to a formal seven-course dinner. Generally, three courses are enough, even for company. Begin with a soup, salad, or appetizer as a first course (you could do two or even all three if it is a very special meal and you have the time), then follow with a main course (with sides as appropriate) and dessert. It is important to balance the courses so that there is a variety of flavors, textures, and ingredients. Pay special attention to the use of garnishes and setting a lovely table. Those little touches can raise the dining experience to the next level.

The following menus are gleaned from the recipes in this book and are provided as a guide to spur your imagination. They can be easily adapted. For example, for menus that list a salad, appetizer, and soup, don't feel that you need to make all three—choose what feels comfortable. Feel free to substitute a different dessert or side dish, for example, according to your taste preferences. Do as much of the preparation ahead of time as possible. This will allow you to spend more time with your guests, feel more relaxed, and fix a mistake if something goes wrong. It's also a good idea to try a new recipe once before making it for company.

If you don't have the time or inclination for a multicourse dinner, many quick and easy one-dish recipes make great meals in themselves. Consider a thick soup served with good bread; a large salad made with raw and cooked vegetables, beans, and/or grains; a hearty stew, chili, or casserole; a quick stir-fry; or a pasta- or grain-based dish.

Use these ideas as a jumping-off point to create your own winning menu combinations for all reasons and all seasons.

MENUS FOR ALL OCCASIONS

SPRINGTIME LUNCHEON

Cool Cucumber Soup with Cilantro and Lime (page 61)

Watercress and White Bean Salad (page 103)

Tarragon-Scented Artichoke and Wild Mushroom Strudel (page 342)

Fresh Lime Cheesecake (page 453)

AUTUMN BRUNCH BUFFET

Tomato-Zucchini Frittata (page 498)

Pan-Seared Breakfast Mushrooms (page 505)

Spicy Sweet Potato Hash (page 503)

Couscous Breakfast Cake with Pear and Dried Plum Compote (page 512)

WINTER SUNDAY SUPPER

Orange and Chipotle–Kissed Butternut Squash Bisque (page 76)

Mushroom Stroganoff (page 285)

Mashed Potatoes and Company (page 183)

Balsamic-Glazed Carrots and Kale (page 180)

Chocolate Pudding Parfaits (page 468)

SUMMER AL FRESCO

Gazpacho *Verde* (page 63)

Garlic and Herb–Marinated Vegetable Kabobs (page 308)

Rosemary-Lemon Potatoes with Black Olives and Sun-Dried Tomatoes (page 184)

Fresh Peach Crisp with Almond Butter Cream (page 462)

COMPANY'S COMING

Walnut-Crusted Artichoke Hearts (page 30)

Goddess of Kale Salad (page 91)

Yuba-Wrapped Seitan and Vegetable Rolls (page 378)

Lemony Green Pea Risotto (page 216)

Tiramisu Cheesecake (page 451)

HOLIDAY DINNER

Wild Mushroom Pâté (page 47)

Asian Pear and Spinach Salad with Warm Walnut Dressing (page 92)

Seitan Roast with Chestnut and Cranberry Stuffing (page 380)

Orange-Roasted Beets and Shallots with Orange Gremolata (page 174)

Shredded Vegetable Fritters (page 192)

Brandy-Apple Pie (page 459)

THAI ONE ON

Thai-Style Coconut Soup (page 66)

Vegetable Spring Rolls with Spicy Peanut Dipping Sauce (page 38)

Drunken Noodles (page 247)

Thai-Style Papaya Salad (page 93)

Frozen Coconut "Thaiphoon" with Mango, Lime, and Peanuts (page 479)

Cajun Spice-Rubbed Tempeh

Spice rubs, popular in meat dishes, also work well for tofu, tempeh, and seitan, as well as vegetables such as portobello mushrooms and sliced eggplant. In addition to cooking in a skillet, spice-rubbed foods are terrific cooked on the grill. Serve with Not-So-Dirty Rice (page 210) and a side of slaw. Filé powder, made from ground sassafras leaves, is traditionally used to help thicken and season gumbo. It is available in gourmet shops and most well-stocked supermarkets.

1 teaspoon sweet paprika

1 teaspoon dried thyme

1 teaspoon garlic powder

1 teaspoon onion powder

1 teaspoon natural sugar

1 teaspoon salt

½ teaspoon cayenne

½ teaspoon filé powder (optional)

16 ounces tempeh, steamed (page 10) and cut into ½-inch-thick slices

2 to 3 tablespoons olive oil

1. Combine the paprika, thyme, garlic powder, onion powder, sugar, salt, cayenne, and filé powder in a small, shallow bowl and set aside.

2. Lightly brush the tempeh slices with some of the olive oil, then dredge them in the spice mixture, gently rubbing the spices into the tempeh with your hands.

3. Heat the remaining oil in a large skillet over medium-high heat. Cook the tempeh in batches until crisp and well browned, about 5 minutes per side. Serve hot.

Serves 4

Tempeh and Sweet Peppers
with Bourbon-Spiked Barbecue Sauce

This yummy sauce is a great way to make tempeh tempting. The sweet bell peppers add a delicious flavor and color accent. Serve as an entrée with oven-roasted potatoes, or spoon into crusty rolls for sandwiches.

1 tablespoon olive oil

8 ounces tempeh, steamed (page 10) and cut into ½-inch-dice

1 large red bell pepper, seeded and cut into ½-inch dice

1 small green bell pepper, seeded and cut into ½-inch dice

¾ cup Bourbon-Spiked Barbecue Sauce (page 138), or more as needed

1. Heat the olive oil in a large skillet over medium heat. Cook the tempeh in batches until browned on all sides, about 5 minutes. Remove from the skillet with a slotted spoon and set aside.

2. Add the bell peppers to the skillet. Cover and cook over medium heat until softened, about 5 minutes. Return the tempeh to the pan and reduce the heat to low. Add the barbecue sauce, stirring to coat the tempeh. Cook, stirring occasionally, for about 10 minutes to allow the tempeh to absorb the sauce. If the sauce becomes too thick, add a little water or more barbecue sauce. Serve hot.

Serves 4

Teriyaki-Glazed Tempeh

A sweet and savory teriyaki glaze gives the tempeh a lovely golden brown color while filling it with flavor. This sauce is also good on sautéed or grilled tofu, seitan, or eggplant. Or you can use it as a dipping sauce for vegetable tempura.

16 ounces tempeh, steamed (page 10) and cut into ½-inch dice

3 tablespoons low-sodium tamari

3 tablespoons fresh orange or pineapple juice

1 garlic clove, minced

1 teaspoon toasted sesame oil

1 tablespoon pure maple syrup

Salt and freshly ground black pepper

1 tablespoon neutral vegetable oil

1. Place the steamed tempeh in a large, shallow dish. Set aside.

2. In a small bowl, combine the tamari, orange juice, garlic, sesame oil, maple syrup, and salt and pepper to taste. Blend well, then pour over the tempeh and set aside for at least 1 hour, turning halfway through. If marinating for longer than 1 hour, cover and refrigerate.

3. Using a slotted spoon, transfer the tempeh to a platter, reserving the marinade.

4. Heat the vegetable oil in a large skillet over medium heat. Cook the tempeh in batches until browned all over, about 5 minutes per side. Add the reserved marinade and simmer until the tempeh is hot and well glazed, 10 to 15 minutes. Serve hot.

Serves 4

Tempeh and White Beans
with Tomatoes and Sauerkraut

Perhaps it's because they're both fermented foods, but tempeh and sauerkraut seem to be made for each other. Serve with a coarse, dark bread or spoon over wide noodles.

1 tablespoon olive oil

8 ounces tempeh, steamed (page 10) and cut into ½-inch dice

2 garlic cloves, minced

½ teaspoon smoked paprika

½ teaspoon salt

¼ teaspoon black pepper

1½ cups jarred sauerkraut, drained

1½ cups cooked cannellini beans or 1 (15-ounce) can beans, rinsed and drained

1 (14.5-ounce) can diced fire-roasted tomatoes, undrained

2 tablespoons minced fresh dill or parsley

1. Heat the olive oil in a large saucepan over medium heat. Add the tempeh and cook until browned all over, 8 minutes. Add the garlic and cook for 30 seconds, then sprinkle on the paprika, salt, and pepper, tossing to coat the tempeh.

2. Gently stir in the sauerkraut, beans, and tomatoes and their juice. Reduce the heat to low and simmer, stirring occasionally, until the flavors blend and the liquid reduces, about 15 minutes. Sprinkle with the dill and serve hot.

===== *Serves 4* =====

Pan-Seared Seitan
with Cremini Mushrooms and Red Wine

The red wine sauce is absorbed by both the seitan and the mushrooms, resulting in a full-flavored dish that goes well with noodles, rice, or potatoes.

1 tablespoon olive oil

1 pound seitan, cut into ½-inch-wide x ¼-inch-thick strips

2 to 3 shallots, minced

1 garlic clove, minced

8 ounces cremini mushrooms, sliced

½ cup dry red wine

1 cup vegetable broth

1 tablespoon vegan Worcestershire sauce

2 teaspoons tomato paste

1 teaspoon Dijon mustard

1 teaspoon minced fresh thyme or ½ teaspoon dried thyme

Salt and freshly ground black pepper

1. Heat the olive oil in a large skillet over medium-high heat. Add the seitan and cook until browned on all sides, about 5 minutes. Using a slotted spoon, transfer to a plate and set aside.

2. In the same skillet, cook the shallots, stirring, until softened, about 2 minutes. Add the mushrooms and wine and simmer, stirring, to reduce the liquid slightly, about 4 minutes. Using a slotted spoon, transfer the mushrooms to the plate with the seitan.

3. Add the broth, Worcestershire sauce, tomato paste, mustard, and thyme to the skillet, stirring to blend. Increase the heat to high, and bring to a boil. Reduce the heat to medium and simmer until the liquid is reduced by half, about 5 minutes. Return the seitan and mushrooms to the skillet and season to taste with salt and pepper. Cook until heated through, 2 to 3 minutes. Serve hot.

Serves 4

Shredded Seitan
with Green Beans and Shallots

A splash of sherry and tamari combines with a swirl of mustard to provide a flavorful backdrop for seitan and green beans sautéed with shallots. Serve over rice.

8 ounces green beans, trimmed and halved

2 tablespoons olive oil

2 large shallots, minced

1 large garlic clove, minced

1 pound seitan, shredded

Salt and freshly ground black pepper

⅓ cup dry sherry

1 tablespoon Dijon mustard

1 cup vegetable broth

2 tablespoons low-sodium tamari

1. Steam the green beans over boiling water until just tender, about 5 minutes. Rinse under cold running water to stop the cooking. Transfer to a large bowl and set aside.

2. Heat the olive oil in a large skillet over medium-high heat. Add the shallots, garlic, seitan, and salt and pepper to taste and cook until the seitan is browned all over, about 5 minutes. Using a slotted spoon, transfer the seitan to a plate and set aside.

3. Deglaze the skillet with the sherry, stirring to dislodge any browned bits from the pan. Stir in the mustard. Add the broth and tamari and bring to boil. Reduce the heat to low and simmer, uncovered, until the liquid is reduced, about 10 minutes. Add the seitan and green beans, stirring to heat through and coat with the sauce, about 5 minutes. Serve hot.

Serves 4

Hoisin-Drenched Garlic Seitan
with Baby Bok Choy

The sweet and sassy hoisin sauce permeates the seitan and enlivens the bok choy. Baby bok choy is more tender than the larger version and is visually appealing when served cut in half lengthwise. Look for it in Asian markets and well-stocked supermarkets. Serve over rice.

4 baby bok choy, trimmed
and halved lengthwise

1 tablespoon neutral vegetable oil

3 garlic cloves, minced

8 ounces seitan, thinly sliced

Salt and freshly ground black pepper

½ cup hoisin sauce blended with ¼ cup water

1. Lightly steam the bok choy over boiling water until just tender, 3 to 4 minutes. Transfer to a plate and set aside.

2. Heat the oil in a large skillet over medium heat. Add the garlic and seitan and cook until the seitan is browned all over, about 5 minutes. Season to taste with salt and pepper. Stir in the hoisin mixture. Add the bok choy and spoon the sauce over all to coat. Reduce the heat to low and simmer until tender, about 10 minutes. Serve hot.

Serves 4

> "The time will come when men such as I will look upon the murder of animals as they now look upon the murder of men."
>
> —LEONARDO DA VINCI

Throughout the world's cuisines can be found a variety of delicious oven-baked specialties, from gratins to casseroles to potpies. Some are naturally vegan, and those that are not can often be easily adapted by changing a few ingredients. Consider the quiche.

In its traditional state, a quiche is made with eggs, cream, and cheese. The *Provençal Vegetable Quiche* in this chapter uses tofu to replace those ingredients, resulting in a finished product that is every bit as delicious as its traditional counterpart. The same holds true for other classic recipes. Here you'll find a fresh take on old favorites such as shepherd's pie, eggplant parmigiana, and spanakopita. There are also intriguing new creations, such as *Tarragon-Scented*

Artichoke and Wild Mushroom Strudel and *Black Bean and Sweet Potato Enchiladas*.

Despite the fact that gratins often garner more respect than casseroles, the two have quite a lot in common. First, both the serving dish and the finished product have the same name. Second, both gratins and casseroles are usually topped with cheese or a bread crumb mixture. Whereas casseroles are thought of as home-style weekday fare and are decidedly heartier, gratins are often reserved for guests. Contrary to popular belief, neither has to be smothered in cheese or drowning in heavy cream to succeed. You'll be pleasantly surprised to find some light and lovely gratins and casseroles here that are completely vegan and thoroughly delicious.

Mushroom-Artichoke Quinoa Quiche

A rich filling made with artichokes, mushrooms, and white beans is nestled in a flavorful quinoa and walnut crust in this healthy and delicious quiche-inspired bake.

1 cup cooked or canned white beans, drained, rinsed, and blotted dry

3 tablespoons plain unsweetened nondairy milk

3 tablespoons nutritional yeast

2 tablespoons cornstarch

2 teaspoons almond butter

½ teaspoon onion powder

½ teaspoon salt, plus more for seasoning

¼ teaspoon freshly ground black pepper, plus more for seasoning

1½ cups cooked quinoa, blotted to remove any moisture

½ cup finely ground walnuts

1 tablespoon olive oil or ¼ cup water

1 small onion, minced

2 garlic cloves, minced

4 ounces sliced mushrooms (about 1¼ cups)

1 (14-ounce) can artichoke hearts, drained and chopped, or 2 cups frozen artichokes, cooked, drained, and chopped

1 plum tomato, sliced into very thin rounds

1. Preheat the oven to 350°F. Oil a 9-inch pie pan or spray it with cooking spray. Set aside.

2. In a food processor or high-speed blender, combine the white beans, nondairy milk, nutritional yeast, cornstarch, almond butter, onion powder, salt, and pepper. Process until smooth and well blended.

3. In a bowl, combine the quinoa and walnuts with 3 to 4 tablespoons of the bean mixture. Transfer the quinoa mixture to the prepared pie pan and press the mixture evenly into the bottom and up the sides of the pan. Bake for 8 minutes. Remove from the oven and set aside.

4. Heat the oil or water in a small skillet over medium heat. Add the onion and garlic and cook for 4 minutes. Add the mushrooms and cook, stirring, until softened, about 3 minutes longer. Stir in the artichokes and season to taste with salt and pepper. Cook, stirring, until most of the liquid has evaporated, another minute or two.

5. In the same bowl you used for the quinoa mixture, combine the vegetable mixture and the remaining bean mixture and mix well to combine. Spread the mixture evenly onto the crust. Smooth the surface and arrange the slices of tomato on top. Bake for 60 minutes. Let cool for about 10 minutes before cutting.

Serves 6

Broccoli Mac UnCheesecake

"Pure comfort food" is how recipe tester Lyndsay Orwig described this delicious mac and cheese variation. Baking it in a springform pan makes for an attractive and unusual presentation when unmolded.

8 ounces elbow macaroni

3 cups chopped broccoli florets

1½ cups cooked white beans or 1 (15-ounce) can beans, rinsed and drained

½ cup nutritional yeast

2 tablespoons low-sodium tamari

1 tablespoon fresh lemon juice

1 tablespoon almond butter

2 teaspoons prepared yellow mustard

1 teaspoon salt

1 teaspoon garlic powder

½ teaspoon smoked paprika

2 cups plain unsweetened nondairy milk

½ cup panko bread crumbs or ground walnuts

1 tablespoon olive oil

1. Preheat the oven to 350°F. Grease a 9-inch springform pan and set aside. Bring a medium-size pot of salted water to a boil over high heat and cook the macaroni until it is al dente. About 4 minutes before the macaroni is done cooking, add the broccoli. When the macaroni and broccoli are cooked, drain well, then return to the pot and set aside.

2. While the macaroni is cooking, combine the beans, nutritional yeast, tamari, lemon juice, almond butter, and mustard in a food processor or high-speed blender. Add the salt, garlic powder, paprika, and nondairy milk and process until smooth. Taste and adjust the seasonings if needed. Add the sauce to the macaroni and broccoli and stir to mix well. Pack the mixture into the prepared pan.

3. In a small bowl, combine the bread crumbs and oil, tossing to mix. Sprinkle the top of the macaroni mixture with the crumbs and cover tightly. Bake for 30 minutes, then uncover and bake about 10 minutes longer to brown the crumbs. To serve, remove the sides of the springform pan and cut into wedges.

Serves 6

Spring Vegetable Gratin

Roasting vegetables—even delicate spring vegetables such as asparagus—at high temperature brings out their full flavor. Here, instead of roasting individual vegetables, I combine them into a gratin that can be served as a light entrée or side dish. As an accompaniment, I like to serve bruschetta topped with garlicky white beans or another hearty topping.

2 tablespoons olive oil

5 scallions, chopped

2 garlic cloves, minced

2 tablespoons minced fresh dill, tarragon, or basil

1 pound small new red or white potatoes, unpeeled and thinly sliced

Salt and freshly ground black pepper

1 medium-size yellow summer squash, halved lengthwise and cut into ¼-inch-thick slices

1 cup cherry or grape tomatoes, cut in half

8 ounces thin asparagus, trimmed

¼ cup vegetable broth

½ cup fresh bread crumbs

¼ cup slivered or chopped almonds

1. Preheat the oven to 400°F. Heat 1 tablespoon of the olive oil in a large skillet over medium heat. Add the scallions and garlic and cook, stirring, until fragrant, about 30 seconds. Stir in 1 tablespoon of the minced dill and set aside.

2. Lightly oil a 2-quart gratin dish. Arrange the potato slices in the bottom of the dish. Season to taste with salt and pepper. Top with the scallion mixture. Add a layer of squash and a layer of tomatoes, then season to taste with salt and pepper.

3. Arrange the asparagus on top in a spoke-like fashion. Pour on the broth, sprinkle with the remaining 1 tablespoon dill, and season to taste with salt and pepper.

4. In a small bowl, gently blend the bread crumbs and the remaining 1 tablespoon olive oil with a fork to combine. Stir in the almonds and sprinkle the mixture evenly on top of the gratin.

5. Bake until the vegetables are tender and the top is golden brown, about 45 minutes. Let rest for 5 minutes before serving.

Serves 4

Artichoke and Root Vegetable Gratin

The artichokes provide texture and flavor in this satisfying gratin, while at the same time adding a sophisticated touch. Frozen artichoke hearts work fine and are more convenient than fresh.

1 pound Yukon Gold potatoes, peeled and thinly sliced

1 large carrot, thinly sliced

1 medium-size parsnip, peeled and thinly sliced

2 tablespoons olive oil

1 leek (white part only), washed well and thinly sliced

3 garlic cloves, minced

1 (9-ounce) package frozen artichoke hearts, cooked according to package directions, drained, and chopped

Salt and freshly ground black pepper

½ cup vegetable broth

2 teaspoons minced fresh thyme or 1 teaspoon dried thyme

½ cup fresh bread crumbs

½ teaspoon sweet Hungarian paprika

1. Preheat the oven to 375°F. Bring a large pot of salted water to a boil over high heat. Parboil the potato, carrot, and parsnip slices for 5 minutes. Drain well and set aside.

2. Heat 1 tablespoon of the olive oil in a large skillet over medium heat. Add the leek, garlic, artichokes, and salt and pepper to taste. Cover and cook, stirring occasionally, until the leek is tender, about 5 minutes. Stir in the broth and thyme and set aside.

3. Lightly oil a 2-quart gratin dish. Layer half of the potato, carrot, and parsnip slices in the bottom of the dish. Top with half of the artichoke mixture and season to taste with salt and pepper. Top with the remaining potato, carrot, and parsnip slices, the remaining artichoke mixture, and salt and pepper to taste.

4. In a small bowl, combine the bread crumbs, the remaining 1 tablespoon olive oil, and the paprika. Blend gently with a fork and sprinkle on top of the gratin.

5. Bake until the vegetables are tender and the top is golden brown, about 45 minutes. Let rest for 5 minutes before serving.

Serves 4

Basil-Scented Fennel and Tomato Gratin

Although this gratin is heavenly in the summer when fresh tomatoes and fennel are at their peak, I sometimes prepare it in the middle of winter when I crave the fresh flavors of the warmer months. Fennel can usually be found in supermarkets year round, but if the only fresh tomatoes available are rock hard and pink, use canned. Every year I try to freeze enough pesto to get me through the winter, but purchased vegan pesto (available at some natural foods stores) may be used if homemade is unavailable.

2 tablespoons olive oil

1 large onion, chopped

1 large or 2 small fennel bulbs, trimmed, halved lengthwise, then thinly sliced

2 garlic cloves, minced

¼ cup Basil Pesto (page 142) or purchased vegan pesto

¼ cup vegetable broth

3 large ripe tomatoes, thinly sliced, or 1 (28-ounce) can whole tomatoes, drained and sliced

Salt and freshly ground black pepper

½ cup bread crumbs

¼ cup ground walnuts

1. Preheat the oven to 375°F. Heat 1 tablespoon of the olive oil in a large skillet over medium heat. Add the onion, fennel, and garlic. Cover and cook until softened, about 5 minutes. Remove from the heat and set aside.

2. In a small bowl, combine the pesto and broth until blended. Set aside.

3. Lightly oil a 2-quart gratin dish. Arrange half of the fennel mixture in the bottom of the dish. Top with half of the tomato slices and season to taste with salt and pepper. Top with the remaining fennel mixture, the remaining tomato slices, and salt and pepper to taste. Pour the pesto mixture over the top.

4. In a small bowl, combine the bread crumbs, walnuts, and remaining 1 tablespoon olive oil. Blend gently with a fork and sprinkle on top of the gratin.

5. Bake until the vegetables are tender and the top is golden brown, about 40 minutes. Let rest for 5 minutes before serving.

Serves 4

Cheesy Potato-Chili Gratin

All this casserole needs as an accompaniment is a salad or green vegetable for a satisfying dinner. I prefer Yukon Gold potatoes for their buttery, rich flavor, but you may use another variety, if you wish.

3 large Yukon Gold potatoes, peeled and thinly sliced

1 small onion, thinly sliced

1 (4-ounce) can diced hot green chiles, drained

1 teaspoon salt

1 teaspoon dried basil

1 teaspoon chili powder

1/8 teaspoon cayenne

1 cup vegan sour cream, homemade (page 126) or purchased

2 cups of your favorite vegan chili (pages 290–301)

1 cup Cheesy Sauce (page 128) or shredded vegan mozzarella cheese

1. Preheat the oven to 375°F. Lightly oil a 9 x 13-inch baking dish.

2. Layer the potatoes, onion, and chiles in the prepared baking dish, sprinkling each layer with some of the salt, basil, chili powder, and cayenne. Cover and bake until the vegetables are tender, 30 to 40 minutes.

3. Remove from the oven and spread the vegan sour cream over the top. Spread the chili over the sour cream and sprinkle evenly with the cheesy sauce. Return to the oven and bake, uncovered, until heated through and bubbly, about 15 minutes. Serve hot.

Serves 6

Sweet Potato Gratin with Pineapple and Coconut Milk

This is a delicious way to prepare sweet potatoes around the holidays, especially for those finicky family members who say they don't like sweet potatoes. This opulent gratin, laced with coconut milk and pineapple, may just win them over.

1½ pounds sweet potatoes, peeled and thinly sliced

1 tablespoon olive oil or ¼ cup water

2 shallots, chopped

1 cup chopped fresh or canned pineapple

½ cup unsweetened coconut milk

½ teaspoon ground cardamom

⅛ teaspoon cayenne

Salt and freshly ground black pepper

½ cup ground unsalted dry-roasted peanuts

1. Preheat the oven to 375°F. Bring a large pot of salted water to a boil over high heat. Parboil the potato slices for 5 minutes, drain well, and set aside.

2. Heat the olive oil or water in a medium-size saucepan over medium heat. Add the shallots and cook until tender, about 5 minutes. Stir in the pineapple, coconut milk, cardamom, cayenne, and salt to taste. Set aside.

3. Lightly oil a 2-quart gratin dish. Arrange half of the sweet potatoes in the bottom of the dish. Season to taste with salt and pepper. Top with half of the pineapple mixture, followed by the remaining sweet potatoes, and then the remaining pineapple mixture. Sprinkle the peanuts on top.

4. Bake until the sweet potatoes are tender, about 40 minutes. Let rest for 5 minutes before serving.

Serves 4 to 6

Black Bean and Sweet Potato Enchiladas

Sweet potatoes can pop up in unusual places, such as this enchilada casserole made with black beans and spicy salsa. Easy to prepare ahead of time, this is a colorful and tasty way to enliven a weeknight meal. Roasting the sweet potatoes gives them a greater depth of flavor.

2 large sweet potatoes, peeled and diced

1 tablespoon olive oil or ¼ cup water

3 garlic cloves, minced

1 small, fresh hot chile, seeded and minced

1½ cups cooked black beans or 1 (15-ounce) can beans, rinsed and drained

1 (14.5-ounce) can diced tomatoes, drained

1 tablespoon chili powder

Salt and freshly ground black pepper

2 cups Fresh Tomato Salsa (page 157) or purchased salsa

8 large flour tortillas

¼ cup finely chopped red onion

1. Preheat the oven to 400°F. Lightly oil a baking sheet. Arrange the sweet potatoes in a single layer on the baking sheet and roast until tender, turning once, about 20 minutes. Remove from the oven and set aside. Reduce the oven temperature to 350°F.

2. Heat the olive oil or water in a large skillet over medium heat. Add the garlic and chile and cook, stirring, until fragrant, about 30 seconds. Add the beans, tomatoes, chili powder, and salt and pepper to taste. Stir in the sweet potatoes and simmer for 5 minutes. Set aside.

3. Lightly oil a 9 x 13-inch baking dish. Spread a thin layer of salsa over the bottom of the dish and set aside.

4. Place a tortilla on a flat work surface. Spoon a portion of the sweet potato mixture down the center of the tortilla and roll it up. Place the filled tortilla in the baking dish, seam side down, and repeat with the remaining tortillas and filling mixture. Spoon any remaining filling mixture on top of the enchiladas, top with the remaining salsa, and sprinkle with the chopped onion. Cover and bake until hot and bubbly, about 20 minutes. Serve hot.

Serves 8

Pistachio-Dusted Saffron Potatoes

The creamy white bean puree and crunchy pistachio topping provide added protein, making this a satisfying entrée as well as a side dish. As long as I have the oven on, I like to roast some asparagus to serve with it. If the pricey saffron is not within your culinary budget, substitute a pinch of turmeric to give the gratin a lovely golden color.

1 tablespoon olive oil or ¼ cup water

1 large onion, thinly sliced

1 medium-size yellow bell pepper, seeded and chopped

Salt and freshly ground black pepper

½ cup vegetable broth

Pinch of saffron threads or turmeric

1½ pounds Yukon Gold potatoes, peeled and thinly sliced

1½ cups cooked cannellini or other white beans or 1 (15-ounce can) beans, rinsed and drained

½ cup plain unsweetened nondairy milk

⅓ cup chopped unsalted dry-roasted pistachios

1. Preheat the oven to 400°F. Lightly oil a 2½-quart baking dish and set aside.

2. Heat the olive oil or water in a large skillet over medium heat. Add the onion and bell pepper and season to taste with salt and pepper. Cook until softened, about 5 minutes.

3. Heat the broth in a small saucepan over low heat and add the saffron. Remove from the heat.

4. Layer the potatoes and the onion mixture in the prepared baking dish. Season each layer to taste with salt and pepper.

5. In a food processor or blender, puree the beans. Add the nondairy milk and the reserved broth mixture and process until smooth. Pour the sauce over the potato mixture, cover, and bake until the potatoes are tender, about 1 hour.

6. Uncover, sprinkle with the pistachios, and bake for 10 minutes to lightly toast the pistachios. Let rest for 5 minutes before serving.

Serves 4

Italian Baked Eggplant

Eggplant parmigiana used to be one of my favorite dishes, so I was determined to make a vegan version that I could enjoy. As long as I was cutting out the cholesterol and fat of the cheese, I decided to make this dish even healthier by baking the eggplant slices rather than breading and frying them, resulting in a decidedly lighter dish than Mom used to make, but delicious nonetheless. You can use a vegan Parmesan cheese such as my Parma-zen if you like, or try some *gomasio*, a sesame seed and sea salt condiment that adds calcium as well as a great nutty-salty flavor.

1 large eggplant, cut into ¼-inch-thick slices

1 tablespoon olive oil or ¼ cup water

1 small onion, minced

3 garlic cloves, minced

4 ounces white mushrooms, finely chopped

1 (28-ounce) can crushed tomatoes

2 tablespoons minced fresh parsley

1 tablespoon minced fresh basil or 1½ teaspoons dried basil

1 teaspoon minced fresh oregano or ½ teaspoon dried oregano

Salt and freshly ground black pepper

¼ cup *Gomasio* (recipe follows) or Parma-zen (page 233)

1. Preheat the oven to 375°F. Lightly oil a baking sheet. Place the eggplant slices in a single layer on the baking sheet and bake until tender, 12 to 15 minutes, turning once. Remove from the oven and set aside. Leave the oven on.

2. Heat the olive oil or water in a large skillet over medium heat. Add the onion and garlic and cook until softened, about 5 minutes. Add the mushrooms and cook until softened, about 3 minutes, then stir in the tomatoes, herbs, and salt and pepper to taste. Simmer for 10 minutes to blend the flavors.

3. Spoon a layer of the tomato sauce over the bottom of a 2½-quart baking dish. Top with a layer of eggplant slices and sprinkle with a small amount of the *gomasio*. Continue layering until all of the eggplant slices are used. To finish, top with a layer of the sauce and sprinkle with the remaining *gomasio*. Bake until hot and bubbly, about 40 minutes. Let rest for 5 minutes before serving.

Serves 4

GOMASIO

Gomasio is a Japanese condiment made with ground sesame seeds and sea salt that imparts a delicious salty-nutty flavor to vegetable, grain, and pasta dishes. It can be purchased ready-made in Asian markets and natural foods stores or made easily at home. I like to keep some *gomasio* in a shaker to sprinkle on pasta instead of Parmesan cheese.

7 tablespoons sesame seeds, toasted (page 171)

1 tablespoon sea salt

Place the sesame seeds and sea salt in a food processor or blender and process until well ground but with some texture remaining. Transfer to an airtight container and store in the refrigerator, where it will keep for several weeks.

===== *Makes ½ cup* =====

Winter Vegetable Potpie

Potpies are old-fashioned comfort food at its best, and this version, made with chewy seitan and a variety of vegetables, is as comforting as they come. Feel free to vary the filling ingredients according to your preference or what you have on hand. For example, you could use corn instead of peas, or tofu or steamed tempeh in place of the seitan.

FILLING

1 large russet potato, peeled and chopped

1 large carrot, chopped

1 parsnip, peeled and chopped

1¼ cups Super-Rich Vegetable Broth (page 60)

2 tablespoons low-sodium tamari

1 tablespoon cornstarch dissolved in 2 tablespoons water

1 tablespoon olive oil

1 large onion, chopped

8 ounces seitan, coarsely chopped

Salt and freshly ground black pepper

¾ cup fresh or thawed frozen peas

CRUST

1¼ cups unbleached all-purpose flour

¼ teaspoon salt

⅓ cup chilled neutral vegetable oil

2 tablespoons ice water

1. To make the filling, bring a large pot of salted water to a boil over high heat. Cook the potato, carrot, and parsnip until tender, about 10 minutes. Drain, rinse, and set aside.

2. In a small saucepan, bring the broth and tamari to a boil over medium-high heat. Reduce the heat to low and whisk in the cornstarch mixture. Simmer, stirring, until thickened, 2 to 3 minutes. Remove from the heat and set aside.

3. Lightly oil a 2-quart casserole dish. Heat the olive oil in a medium-size skillet over medium heat. Add the onion, cover, and cook until softened, about 5 minutes. Using a slotted spoon, transfer the onion to the prepared dish.

4. Reheat the skillet and add the seitan. Season to taste with salt and pepper and cook, stirring, until browned, about 5 minutes. Transfer to the casserole dish. Stir in the peas, potato-carrot-parsnip mixture, and sauce and set aside.

5. Preheat the oven to 350°F.

6. To make the crust, in a food processor, combine the flour and salt, pulsing to blend. Add the cold oil and process until the mixture is crumbly. With the machine running, slowly add the ice water and process until the mixture forms a ball. On a lightly floured surface, roll out the dough until it is slightly larger than the casserole dish. Place the crust over the casserole and crimp the edges.

7. Bake until the filling is hot and bubbly and the crust is browned, about 45 minutes. Let rest for 5 minutes before serving.

===== *Serves 6* =====

Vegetables "Fall" into Winter

Long after the last tomato of summer has been picked from the vine, autumn vegetables take the spotlight, pleasing the eye as well as the palate. Whether it's the sturdy winter squash in one of its many brilliant hues, the lush green collards and kale, or the rugged earthiness of freshly dug potatoes, fall vegetables call us home to supper and gently nurture us as the weather turns colder. The very sight of them can make us crave simmering stews and the smell of fragrant casseroles baking in the oven.

It is widely known that fresh, locally grown produce tastes better and is more nutritious than that trucked or shipped in from somewhere else. In this age when supermarkets carry South American grapes, Australian oranges, and pencil-thin asparagus in the dead of winter, it's hard to tell what is in season and what is not. For that kind of information, go to the source: patronize your local farmers' markets and roadside stands. When you do, chances are you'll come home with a carload of culinary inspiration. And getting there can be half the fun. Little compares to driving down a country road on a cool autumn day to a produce stand where rows of field pumpkins stand at attention and the sweet scent of freshly picked apples perfumes the air. Filling your kitchen with fall vegetables—from cabbage to collards, potatoes to pumpkins—is a delicious way to make the transition into winter.

Ultimate Shepherd's Pie

Leftover mashed potatoes are often the inspiration for making a shepherd's pie, although the extra-rich Mashed Potatoes and Company (page 183) are so good, you may want to make a special batch just for this recipe.

1 tablespoon olive oil or ¼ cup water

1 large onion, chopped

1 large carrot, chopped

6 ounces white mushrooms, chopped

1 cup vegetable broth

2 tablespoons low-sodium tamari

1 tablespoon tomato paste

1 teaspoon minced fresh thyme
or ½ teaspoon dried thyme

1 teaspoon minced fresh marjoram
or ½ teaspoon dried marjoram

Salt and freshly ground black pepper

1 tablespoon cornstarch dissolved
in 2 tablespoons water

2 cups cooked or canned lentils

¾ cup fresh or thawed frozen peas

¾ cup fresh or thawed frozen corn kernels

¼ cup ground walnuts

3 cups mashed potatoes (see headnote)

¼ teaspoon sweet Hungarian paprika

1. Preheat the oven to 375°F. Heat the olive oil or water in a large skillet over medium heat. Add the onion and carrot and cook until tender, about 5 minutes. Add the mushrooms and cook, stirring occasionally, for 3 minutes. Stir in the broth, tamari, tomato paste, thyme, marjoram, and salt and pepper to taste. Stir in the cornstarch mixture and simmer to thicken slightly, about 1 minute.

2. Lightly oil a 2½-quart baking dish. Spoon the vegetable mixture into the dish. Stir in the cooked lentils, peas, corn, and walnuts. Taste and adjust the seasonings. Spread the mashed potatoes over the top. Sprinkle with the paprika. Bake until the potatoes are hot and bubbly and the top is golden brown, about 45 minutes. Serve hot.

Serves 4

Chili-Couscous Pie

This casserole can be assembled in advance and popped in the oven less than an hour before serving. While it bakes, you can make a salad and set the table—and suddenly dinner's ready. I like to put out bowls of salsa and sliced black olives as toppings. Sweet and Spicy Chili (page 296) is especially good in this recipe.

2¼ cups water

1½ cups instant couscous

1 teaspoon olive oil

½ teaspoon salt

1 cup shredded vegan cheddar cheese or Cheesy Sauce (page 128)

3 cups of your favorite vegan chili (pages 290–301)

⅓ cup minced onion

1 (4-ounce) can diced hot green chiles, drained

1. Preheat the oven to 350°F. Lightly oil a 10-inch baking dish or pie plate.

2. Bring the water to a boil in a large saucepan over high heat. Stir in the couscous, olive oil, and salt. Cover and remove from the heat. Let stand for 10 minutes, then spread the couscous over the bottom of the prepared baking dish.

3. Sprinkle the couscous with ½ cup of the vegan cheese, then top with the chili. Sprinkle evenly with the onion, chiles, and remaining ½ cup cheese. Bake until bubbly, about 30 minutes. Let rest for 5 minutes before serving.

Serves 4 to 6

Hot Tamale Vegetable Pie

Studded with chiles, corn, and pimientos, this colorful casserole is a crowd pleaser and easy to make to boot. Top with salsa, as recommended here, or use as a zesty base for your favorite chili.

2 cups fresh or thawed frozen corn kernels

1 (4-ounce) can diced hot green chiles, drained

¼ cup minced red onion

3 tablespoons chopped jarred pimientos

1½ cups cooked white beans or 1 (15-ounce) can beans, rinsed and drained

¼ cup medium-ground yellow cornmeal

2 tablespoons unbleached all-purpose flour

1 teaspoon chili powder

¾ teaspoon salt

¾ teaspoon baking powder

½ teaspoon natural sugar

Freshly ground black pepper

Fresh Tomato Salsa (page 157) or purchased salsa, for serving

1. Preheat the oven to 375°F. Lightly oil a 10-inch pie plate.

2. In a large bowl, combine the corn, chiles, onion, and pimientos. Set aside.

3. In a blender or food processor, combine the white beans, cornmeal, flour, chili powder, salt, baking powder, sugar, and black pepper to taste and process until smooth. Fold into the vegetable mixture, stirring to combine. Transfer to the prepared pie plate and smooth the top.

4. Bake until firm and golden brown on top, 30 to 35 minutes. Let rest for 5 minutes before cutting into wedges. Serve topped with the salsa.

Serves 4 to 6

Provençal Vegetable Quiche

Silken tofu is used instead of eggs and cream in this light and luscious quiche. Mediterranean-spiced vegetables and a flaky crust make it a good choice for a light lunch or supper entrée served with a crisp green salad.

CRUST
1 cup unbleached all-purpose flour

¼ cup chilled neutral vegetable oil

¼ teaspoon salt

1 tablespoon ice water, or more as needed

FILLING
1 tablespoon olive oil or ¼ cup water

1 leek (white part only), washed well and chopped

1 garlic clove, minced

1½ cups chopped zucchini

1 cup chopped white mushrooms

1 cup finely chopped fresh or canned tomatoes, well drained

¼ cup pitted black olives, chopped

1 teaspoon minced fresh marjoram

1 teaspoon minced fresh basil

1 teaspoon minced fresh tarragon

1 teaspoon minced fresh parsley

Salt and freshly ground black pepper

¼ cup Parma-zen (page 233; optional)

2 cups drained and crumbled firm silken tofu

1 cup plain unsweetened nondairy milk

1 tablespoon Dijon mustard

⅛ teaspoon cayenne

1. To make the crust, combine the flour, cold oil, and salt in a food processor and pulse until crumbly. With the machine running, add the ice water and process until the mixture forms a ball. Flatten the dough, wrap in plastic, and refrigerate for at least 30 minutes. On a lightly floured work surface, roll out the dough to fit into a 10-inch quiche pan or pie plate. Line the pan or plate with the dough and trim the edges.

2. Preheat the oven to 375°F. To make the filling, heat the olive oil or water in a large skillet over medium heat. Add the leek, garlic, zucchini, mushrooms, and tomatoes and cook, stirring occasionally, until the vegetables soften and the liquid evaporates, 8 to 10 minutes. Stir in the olives, herbs, and salt and pepper to taste. Spoon the vegetable mixture into the crust and sprinkle with the Parma-zen, if using.

3. In a food processor or blender, combine the tofu, nondairy milk, mustard, cayenne, and salt to taste. Blend well. Pour the tofu mixture over the vegetables in the crust, distributing it evenly.

4. Bake until the filling is set and the top is golden brown, about 45 minutes. Let rest for 5 minutes before cutting.

Serves 4 to 6

Tarragon-Scented Artichoke and Wild Mushroom Strudel

This elegant dish makes a terrific entrée for a special meal, preceded by a crisp green salad and served with grilled asparagus or tomatoes. A dry white wine is a good beverage choice.

1 tablespoon olive oil or ¼ cup water, plus more oil for brushing

3 shallots, chopped

2 garlic cloves, minced

8 ounces cremini or other mushrooms, chopped

Salt and freshly ground black pepper

8 ounces extra-firm tofu, drained and crumbled

1 (9-ounce) package frozen artichoke hearts, cooked according to package directions, drained, and coarsely chopped

2 tablespoons chopped fresh tarragon

1 (16-ounce) package phyllo pastry, thawed overnight in the refrigerator

1 cup Double Mushroom Sauce (page 135)

1. Heat the olive oil or water in a large skillet over medium heat. Add the shallots and garlic and cook, stirring, until tender, about 5 minutes. Add the mushrooms and salt and pepper to taste. Cook, stirring occasionally, until the mushrooms release their liquid. Continue cooking until the liquid has evaporated, about 5 minutes. Set aside to cool.

2. Place the tofu in a large bowl. Add the artichokes, tarragon, and mushroom mixture. Season to taste with salt and pepper and stir well to combine. Set aside.

3. Preheat the oven to 375°F. Lightly oil a large baking sheet. Remove 6 phyllo pastry sheets from the package. Tightly seal the remaining sheets and reserve for another use. Place 1 sheet on a flat work surface with a long side facing you and brush lightly with olive oil. Lay another sheet on top and brush with oil. Repeat the layering with the remaining 4 sheets.

4. Spoon the artichoke mixture evenly on top of the stack of phyllo sheets, leaving a 3-inch border around the edges. Fold the short ends over the filling, then roll lengthwise into a cylinder to encase the filling. Place the strudel, seam side down, on the prepared baking sheet and brush the top with oil.

5. Bake until hot inside and golden brown outside, 30 to 40 minutes. While the strudel bakes, heat the mushroom sauce in a small saucepan over medium heat. If serving family style, pass the sauce on the side. If serving on plates, spoon the sauce onto each plate and top with a slice of strudel.

Serves 4 to 6

Layered Polenta-Chili Casserole

The natural marriage of cornmeal and chili will make this casserole a family favorite. Instant polenta, as well as packaged cooked polenta, is available at specialty food stores or in the gourmet section of many supermarkets, if you prefer a quick alternative to making polenta from scratch.

4 cups water

1 tablespoon neutral vegetable oil

1½ teaspoons salt

1½ cups medium-ground yellow cornmeal

2½ cups of your favorite vegan chili (pages 290–301)

1 cup Fresh Tomato Salsa (page 157) or purchased salsa

1 cup shredded vegan mozzarella cheese or Cheesy Sauce (page 128)

1. In a large saucepan, combine the water, oil, and salt over high heat and bring to a boil. Reduce the heat to medium and gradually whisk in the cornmeal, stirring constantly to avoid lumps. Cook, stirring, until the polenta begins to pull away from the sides of the pan, about 20 minutes.

2. Preheat the oven to 350°F. Lightly oil a 9 x 13-inch baking dish. Spoon half of the polenta into the dish and smooth the surface with a wet rubber spatula. Spread the chili on top. Spoon the remaining polenta on top of the chili, top with the salsa, and sprinkle evenly with the vegan mozzarella. Bake until hot, about 30 minutes.

Serves 4 to 6

Mushroom Pastitsio

This fresh take on the classic Greek casserole uses mushrooms and tofu instead of ground meat. The special noodles used to make pastitsio can be found in ethnic markets, but I prefer a more unconventional shape, such as radiatore ("little radiators"). Like many of the recipes in this chapter, you can assemble it ahead of time and bake just before serving. A crisp green salad is all you need for a complete meal.

12 ounces radiatore or other small pasta

1 tablespoon olive oil or ¼ cup water

1 large onion, chopped

3 garlic cloves, chopped

1 (12- to 16-ounce) package firm tofu, drained and finely crumbled

8 ounces white mushrooms, chopped

½ teaspoon dried oregano

½ teaspoon ground cinnamon

Salt and freshly ground black pepper

¼ cup dry red wine

2 cups homemade or jarred marinara sauce

¼ cup chopped fresh parsley

¾ cup raw cashews, soaked for at least 3 hours or up to overnight, then drained

1 cup plain unsweetened nondairy milk

Pinch of freshly grated nutmeg

¼ cup *Gomasio*, homemade (page 335) or purchased, or vegan Parmesan cheese

1. Bring a large pot of salted water to a boil over high heat. Cook the pasta, stirring occasionally, until al dente. Drain and set aside.

2. Heat the olive oil or water in a large skillet over medium heat. Add the onion and cook until softened, about 5 minutes. Stir in the garlic, tofu, mushrooms, oregano, cinnamon, and salt and pepper to taste. Add the wine and simmer to reduce a bit, about 5 minutes. Stir in the marinara sauce and parsley, reduce the heat to low, and cook to reduce the liquid and blend the flavors, about 10 minutes.

3. Preheat the oven to 375°F. In a high-speed blender or food processor combine the drained cashews with the nondairy milk, ½ teaspoon salt, ¼ teaspoon black pepper, and the nutmeg. Process until very smooth.

4. Lightly oil a 9 x 13-inch baking dish. Spread half of the pasta over the bottom of the dish and sprinkle with half of the *gomasio*. Spread all of the tomato mixture over the pasta and layer the remaining pasta on top. Spread the cashew sauce over the pasta and sprinkle with the remaining *gomasio*. Bake until hot and bubbly and lightly browned on top, about 45 minutes. Let rest for 10 to 15 minutes before serving.

Serves 6

Chili-Macaroni Bake

A variation on the "chili mac" popular in Kansas City, this dish combines chili with everyone's favorite, macaroni and cheese. I like to use Three-Bean Chili (page 290) in this recipe.

12 ounces elbow macaroni

1 tablespoon olive oil

½ cup minced onion

2 tablespoons unbleached all-purpose flour

2 cups plain unsweetened nondairy milk, heated

1 teaspoon salt

⅛ teaspoon cayenne

1 cup Cheesy Sauce (page 128) or shredded vegan cheddar cheese

3 cups of your favorite vegan chili (pages 290–301)

1. Bring a large pot of salted water to a boil over high heat. Cook the macaroni, stirring occasionally, until al dente, about 8 minutes. Drain and set aside. Preheat the oven to 375°F.

2. Heat the olive oil in a medium-size saucepan over medium heat. Add the onion, cover, and cook until softened, about 5 minutes. Add the flour and cook, stirring, for 1 minute. Reduce the heat to low and slowly whisk in the nondairy milk. Continue to cook, stirring, until the mixture thickens, about 2 minutes. Add the salt and cayenne and transfer to a large bowl.

3. Add the pasta and ½ cup of the cheesy sauce to the bowl and stir to combine. Spoon the mixture into a 9 x 13-inch baking dish and spread the chili on top. Sprinkle the remaining ½ cup cheesy sauce over the chili and bake until hot and bubbly, about 30 minutes.

Serves 6

Linguine Tetrazzini

Based on the early 20ᵗʰ-century gratin made with turkey and noodles, this version uses tofu with the requisite sherry and almonds and adds green beans to make it a one-dish meal. Although it is named for the famous opera star Luisa Tetrazzini, most authorities agree that it is doubtful she ever tasted the dish.

8 ounces linguine, broken in halves or thirds

6 ounces fresh green beans, trimmed and cut into 1½-inch pieces

2 tablespoons olive oil

1 large onion, minced

3 garlic cloves, minced

1 (12- to 16-ounce) package firm tofu, drained and cut into ½-inch dice

8 ounces white mushrooms, sliced

¼ cup dry sherry

2 tablespoons minced fresh parsley

1 teaspoon dried basil

½ teaspoon salt

¼ teaspoon freshly ground black pepper

¾ cup toasted almonds, ground (page 203)

2 cups Vegan Béchamel Sauce (page 132)

½ cup dry bread crumbs

1. Bring a large pot of salted water to a boil over high heat. Cook the linguine, stirring occasionally, until al dente. During the last 3 or 4 minutes of cooking time, add the green beans to the pot. Drain the pasta and green beans and return to the pot. Set aside. Preheat the oven to 375°F. Lightly oil a 9 x 13-inch baking dish and set it aside.

2. Heat the olive oil in large skillet over medium heat. Add the onion and garlic and cook until softened, about 5 minutes. Add the tofu and mushrooms and cook until the tofu is lightly browned and the mushrooms are softened, about 5 minutes. Add the sherry, parsley, basil, salt, and pepper, stirring for 1 minute. Add the tofu mixture to the pot with the pasta and green beans. Add ½ cup of the almonds, stir in the béchamel sauce, and mix well. Taste and adjust the seasonings, if needed.

3. Transfer the mixture to the prepared baking dish. Sprinkle the top with the bread crumbs and remaining ¼ cup almonds. Bake until hot and bubbly, about 30 minutes.

Serves 6

Lasagna Primavera

When you see "primavera" in a recipe title, you know it means lots of colorful spring vegetables, and this lasagna won't disappoint. Layers of chewy noodles and a tofu-vegetable filling are blanketed with a creamy vegan white sauce topped with garlicky ground walnuts and bread crumbs. For variety, broccoli or asparagus may be substituted for the zucchini.

12 ounces lasagna noodles

2 tablespoons olive oil

1 medium-size onion, chopped

1 medium-size red bell pepper, chopped

1 large zucchini, chopped

4 ounces white mushrooms, chopped

½ cup fresh or thawed frozen peas

Salt and freshly ground black pepper

2 (12- to 16-ounce) packages firm tofu, drained and crumbled

¼ cup minced fresh parsley

3 cups Vegan Béchamel Sauce (page 132)

1 garlic clove, minced

¼ cup ground walnuts

½ cup bread crumbs

1. Bring a large pot of salted water to a boil over high heat. Cook the lasagna noodles, stirring occasionally, until al dente. Drain the noodles and spread out on a work surface to prevent them from sticking together. Preheat the oven to 350°F.

2. Heat 1 tablespoon of the olive oil in a large skillet over medium heat. Add the onion and bell pepper and cook until softened, about 5 minutes. Add the zucchini and mushrooms and cook, stirring occasionally, until softened, about 5 minutes. Stir in the peas and season to taste with salt and pepper. Set aside to cool.

3. In a large bowl, combine the tofu, parsley, sautéed vegetables, 1 teaspoon salt, and ¼ teaspoon black pepper. Mix well.

4. Spread a thin layer of béchamel sauce over the bottom of a 9 x 13-inch baking dish. Add a layer of noodles and top with half of the tofu-vegetable mixture, spreading it evenly. Repeat the layering with the sauce, noodles, and remaining tofu-vegetable mixture, and end with a final layer of sauce.

5. Heat the remaining 1 tablespoon olive oil in a small skillet over medium heat. Add the garlic and ground walnuts and cook, stirring, until fragrant, about 30 seconds. Remove from the heat, add the bread crumbs, and season to taste with salt and pepper. Toss to coat. Sprinkle on top of the lasagna. Bake until hot and bubbly, about 45 minutes. Let rest for 10 minutes before serving.

Serves 6 to 8

Butternut Squash and Wild Mushroom Lasagna

Flavorful mushrooms, butternut squash, and pecans make this out-of-the-ordinary lasagna extraordinary. Use a variety of fresh wild mushrooms, if available, or include a small amount of reconstituted dried porcinis or morels for extra flavor. Cremini or portobello mushrooms may be used as well. When assembled ahead of time, this makes a great weeknight supper. Serve with steamed broccoli or another green vegetable.

12 ounces lasagna noodles

¼ teaspoon turmeric

1 tablespoon olive oil or ¼ cup water

1 small onion, minced

1 small butternut squash, peeled, seeded, and coarsely grated

1 garlic clove, minced

3 cups mixed sliced wild mushrooms, such as chanterelle, shiitake, and oyster mushrooms

1 teaspoon dried thyme

Salt and freshly ground black pepper

1 (12- to 16-ounce) package soft tofu, drained

1 cup plain unsweetened nondairy milk

½ cup chopped pecans, toasted (page 203)

½ cup shredded vegan mozzarella cheese or Cheesy Sauce (page 128)

¼ cup minced fresh flat-leaf parsley

1. Preheat the oven to 375°F. Bring a large pot of salted water to a boil over high heat. Add the turmeric to the water and cook the lasagna noodles, stirring occasionally, until al dente. Drain the noodles and spread out on a work surface to prevent them from sticking together.

2. Heat the olive oil or water in a large saucepan over medium heat. Add the onion, squash, and garlic. Cover and cook, stirring occasionally, until softened, about 10 minutes. Add the mushrooms, thyme, and salt and pepper to taste and cook until softened, about 5 minutes. Transfer to a large bowl and set aside.

3. Combine the tofu, nondairy milk, and salt to taste in a food processor and process until smooth.

4. Spread a thin layer of the tofu mixture over the bottom of a 9 x 13-inch baking dish. Add a layer of noodles and top with half of the squash mixture. Sprinkle with half of the pecans. Repeat the layering with the remaining squash, noodles, and tofu. Top with the vegan cheese and remaining pecans.

5. Bake until hot and bubbly, about 30 minutes. Let rest for 5 minutes. Garnish with the parsley and serve.

Serves 8

"Say 'Cheese'" Alternatives

A number of vegan alternatives to cheese and other dairy products are available at natural foods stores and many large supermarkets. Vegan cheese can be used instead of Parmesan or mozzarella, and crumbled tofu can replace ricotta cheese in lasagna and other recipes. Also available are vegan cream cheese, vegan yogurt, and vegan sour cream. You can make your own (there are recipes for homemade vegan cream cheese, sour cream, and, parmesan in this book, along with an all-purpose cheesy sauce). There are also books devoted to making different varieties of vegan cheese. However, if you prefer to buy ready-made products, be sure to read the labels carefully to make certain they do not contain casein, whey, or other animal ingredients. Even if it says "vegetarian" on the package, unless it specifically indicates that it's vegan, check the ingredients.

Tomato-Basil Lasagna Spirals

Here lasagna noodles are used to create spirals of pasta for a lovely presentation. Serve with a salad or roasted asparagus and warm focaccia.

2 tablespoons olive oil or ¼ cup water

1 garlic clove, minced

4 shallots, minced

1 (12- to 16-ounce) package firm tofu, drained and crumbled

3 oil-packed or rehydrated sun-dried tomatoes, chopped

¼ cup Basil Pesto (page 142) or purchased vegan pesto

⅓ cup fresh bread crumbs

1 teaspoon salt

⅛ teaspoon cayenne

2 tablespoons tomato paste

¼ cup dry red wine

1 (14.5-ounce) can petite diced tomatoes, drained

Salt and freshly ground black pepper

¼ cup minced fresh basil

12 lasagna noodles

Whole fresh basil leaves, for garnish

1. Heat 1 tablespoon of the olive oil or 2 tablespoons of the water in a small skillet over medium heat. Add the garlic and half of the shallots, cover, and cook until softened, about 5 minutes. Transfer to a food processor and add the tofu, sun-dried tomatoes, pesto, bread crumbs, salt, and cayenne. Process until smooth. Transfer to a medium-size bowl, cover, and refrigerate for 30 minutes.

2. Meanwhile, heat the remaining 1 tablespoon olive oil or 2 tablespoons water in a medium-size saucepan over medium-low heat. Add the remaining shallots and cook for 5 minutes, stirring frequently. Stir in the tomato paste, then add the wine, tomatoes, and salt and pepper to taste. Simmer for 10 minutes, then stir in the minced basil. Reduce the heat to low and keep warm.

3. Bring a large pot of salted water to a boil over high heat. Cook the lasagna noodles, stirring occasionally, until al dente, about 10 minutes. Drain the noodles and spread out on a work surface to prevent them from sticking together. Pat dry.

4. Preheat the oven to 350°F. Lightly oil a shallow baking dish. Divide the chilled filling among the noodles, spreading it evenly over the surface of each noodle. Roll each up tightly into a spiral-shaped roll. Place the rolls, seam sides down, in the prepared baking dish. Lightly nap the pasta rolls with 1 cup of the warm sauce. Cover with aluminum foil and bake until hot, about 20 minutes.

5. To serve, spread a small amount of warm sauce on each individual plate and stand 2 or 3 of the rolls upright on the sauce, seam sides touching. Spoon the remaining sauce over the rolls and garnish with the whole basil leaves.

Serves 4 to 6

Love from the Oven

I hate to admit it, but I think there may be something to that old TV jingle "Nothing says lovin' like something from the oven"—especially during the cold winter months when any excuse for extra heat is appreciated. But it's more than that. When we bake foods in the oven, the fragrance broadcasts comfort throughout the house. Whether it's a slow-cooking entrée or a quick batch of cookies, the cozy warmth emanating from the kitchen sets the tone in the house. I find myself planning oven-baked meals just so I can experience the nurturing feeling they provide.

Eggplant and Spinach Lasagna

Adding cooked chopped eggplant to the tomato sauce gives this dish substantial texture. Since vegan mozzarella doesn't melt well, I make it an optional ingredient. Other topping ideas include Parma Zen (page 233) or a sprinkling of *Gomasio* (page 335).

12 ounces lasagna noodles

1 tablespoon olive oil or ¼ cup water

1 medium-size eggplant, peeled and chopped

3 cups tomato sauce, homemade (pages 136–137) or purchased

2 (12- to 16-ounce) packages firm tofu, drained and crumbled

1 (10-ounce) package frozen chopped spinach, cooked according to package directions and well drained

Salt and freshly ground black pepper

½ cup shredded vegan mozzarella cheese (optional)

1. Preheat the oven to 350°F. Bring a large pot of salted water to a boil over high heat. Cook the lasagna noodles, stirring occasionally, until al dente. Drain the noodles and spread out on a work surface to keep them from sticking together.

2. Heat the olive oil or water in a large skillet over medium heat. Add the eggplant and cook, stirring occasionally, until tender, about 10 minutes. Stir in the tomato sauce and set aside.

3. In a large bowl, combine the tofu and spinach, blending well. Season to taste with salt and pepper. Set aside.

4. Spread a thin layer of the eggplant-tomato sauce over the bottom of a 9 x 13-inch baking dish. Add a layer of noodles and top with half of the tofu mixture, spreading it out evenly. Top with another layer of noodles, a layer of sauce, and the remaining tofu mixture. Finish with a layer of noodles and the remaining sauce.

5. Bake for 30 minutes. Remove from the oven and sprinkle with the vegan cheese, if using. Continue to bake until hot and bubbly, about 15 minutes more. Let rest for 10 to 15 minutes before serving.

Serves 6 to 8

Tempeh and Eggplant Moussaka

This traditional Greek casserole made with eggplant lends itself well to a vegan interpretation.

1 large or 2 medium-size eggplants, peeled and cut into ¼-inch slices

2 tablespoons olive oil

8 ounces tempeh, steamed (page 10) and finely chopped

1 large onion, chopped

3 garlic cloves, minced

1 tablespoon minced fresh oregano or 1 teaspoon dried oregano

½ teaspoon ground nutmeg

¼ teaspoon ground cinnamon

1 (14.5-ounce) can crushed tomatoes

½ cup dry white wine

Salt and freshly ground black pepper

1 cup crumbled soft tofu *or* cooked or canned cannellini beans

¾ cup plain unsweetened nondairy milk

¾ cup vegetable broth

1 tablespoon fresh lemon juice

¼ cup dry bread crumbs or ground walnuts

1. Preheat the oven to 400°F. Lightly oil a baking sheet. Place the eggplant slices in a single layer on the sheet and bake until softened, about 15 minutes, turning once. Set aside. Reduce the oven temperature to 375°F.

2. Heat 1 tablespoon of the oil in a large skillet over medium heat. Add the tempeh and cook until golden, about 10 minutes. Remove from the skillet and set aside.

3. Heat the remaining 1 tablespoon oil in the same skillet over medium heat. Add the onion, cover, and cook until softened, about 10 minutes. Add the garlic, oregano, nutmeg, and cinnamon. Stir in the crushed tomatoes and wine. Add the reserved tempeh and season to taste with salt and pepper. Simmer until the mixture thickens slightly and the flavors are blended, 10 to 15 minutes. Set aside.

4. In a blender or food processor, combine the tofu, nondairy milk, vegetable broth, lemon juice, ½ teaspoon salt, and ¼ teaspoon black pepper. Process until smooth and set aside.

5. Arrange a layer of one-third of the reserved eggplant slices in the bottom of a 10-inch square baking dish, then top with half of the reserved tempeh mixture. Layer another one-third of the eggplant, then the remaining tempeh mixture, and finally the remaining eggplant slices. Pour the sauce over all and sprinkle with the bread crumbs.

6. Bake until hot and bubbly, about 40 minutes. Let rest for at least 10 minutes before serving.

Serves 4 to 6

Kale Spanakopita

This variation on the classic spanakopita is made with calcium-rich kale and firm tofu instead of the traditional spinach and feta cheese. Olive oil is used instead of butter to brush the layers of flaky pastry.

1 pound kale, stems removed

1 tablespoon olive oil, plus more for brushing

1 large onion, minced

3 garlic cloves, minced

1 (12- to 16-ounce) package firm tofu, drained and crumbled

1½ tablespoons fresh lemon juice

2 teaspoon fresh minced dill or 1 teaspoon dried dill

1 teaspoon fresh minced oregano or ½ teaspoon dried oregano

1 teaspoon salt

¼ teaspoon freshly ground black pepper

Pinch of freshly grated nutmeg

1 (16-ounce) package phyllo pastry, thawed overnight in the refrigerator

1. Bring a large pot of salted water to a boil over high heat. Cook the kale until tender, about 15 minutes. Drain well, squeezing out any excess moisture. Finely mince the kale and set it aside.

2. Heat the olive oil in a large skillet over medium heat. Add the onion, cover, and cook until softened, about 5 minutes. Add the garlic and cook, stirring, until softened, about 1 minute. Add the kale and cook until all of the liquid is absorbed, about 3 minutes.

3. Transfer to a food processor and add the tofu, lemon juice, dill, oregano, salt, pepper, and nutmeg. Process until smooth. Taste and adjust the seasonings, adding more salt if needed. Set aside.

4. Preheat the oven to 375°F. Lightly oil a shallow 10-inch square baking dish. Unwrap the phyllo pastry and remove 10 sheets. Cover with plastic wrap, then a damp towel. Tightly seal the remaining sheets and reserve for another use. Place 1 sheet in the prepared baking dish, pressing it gently into the bottom and sides of the dish. Using a pastry brush, lightly brush a small amount of olive oil on the pastry. Top with another sheet of pastry and brush with a little more oil. Repeat this layering procedure with 4 more sheets and oil. Spread the filling on the pastry and smooth the top.

5. Place a sheet of phyllo over the filling, gently pressing to smooth the top. Brush a small amount of oil on the pastry and repeat with the remaining 3 sheets, brushing each layer with oil. Trim the excess pastry to within 1 inch of the baking dish. Roll the trimmed edges inward and tuck into the rim of the dish to make a neat edge. Brush the rolled edge with oil.

6. Bake until golden brown, about 30 minutes. Let rest for 15 minutes, then cut into squares. Serve warm or at room temperature.

Serves 6

Vegetable Yuba Parcels

These versatile parcels lend themselves to a variety of sauces, from a fruity chutney or peanut sauce to a spicy salsa or mushroom sauce. You may alter the seasonings to complement the sauce you are using. For example, you might add some minced fresh ginger if using an Asian sauce or a little minced thyme if serving with a mushroom sauce. Use a leftover baked potato, if available. If not, peel, dice, and sauté or bake a medium-size potato until tender. (Cooking in water will add too much moisture to the patties.) If you can't find yuba, you can make these patties without it.

¼ cup toasted walnut or pecan pieces (page 203)

2 garlic cloves, crushed

3 scallions, chopped

1 cup diced cooked potato (see headnote)

1 cup cooked or canned Great Northern beans, drained, rinsed, and patted dry

½ cup rolled oats

½ cup broccoli florets, steamed until crisp-tender, then blotted dry

½ cup fresh or thawed frozen peas, blotted dry

2 tablespoons minced fresh parsley

1 teaspoon salt

⅛ teaspoon cayenne

2 tablespoons olive oil

2 large sheets yuba (page 379)

1. In a food processor, combine the walnuts, garlic, and scallions and process until finely ground. Add the potato, beans, oats, broccoli, peas, parsley, salt, and cayenne and pulse until finely chopped and well combined. Shape the mixture into 4 balls of equal size and flatten into patties about ½ inch thick. Place the patties on a plate and refrigerate for 30 minutes.

2. Heat 1 tablespoon of the olive oil in a large skillet over medium heat. Add the patties and cook until golden brown on both sides, about 4 minutes per side. Remove the patties from the skillet and set aside on paper towels to cool.

3. Cut the yuba sheets in half to make 4 pieces. Soften with a little water, if necessary, to make pliable. Place a vegetable patty on the lower third of each yuba piece. Fold the sides over onto the patty and roll up to enclose the patty and create a flat parcel.

4. Heat the remaining 1 tablespoon olive oil in another large skillet over medium heat. Add the parcels and cook until golden brown and crispy on both sides, about 3 minutes per side. Serve at once.

Serves 4

Red Quinoa Loaf

If red quinoa is unavailable, regular beige quinoa may be used. This is especially fun to serve in a heart-shaped pan on Valentine's Day, but if you don't have one, you can make the loaf in a square or round baking pan or in a loaf pan.

1 cup red quinoa, rinsed and drained

2 cups water

1½ cups cooked dark red kidney beans or 1 (15-ounce) can beans, rinsed and drained

¾ cup cooked or canned diced red beets plus 1 tablespoon beet cooking/canning liquid

¾ cup rolled oats

½ cup ground walnuts

½ cup vital wheat gluten

1 teaspoon onion powder

1 teaspoon garlic powder

1 teaspoon dried thyme

1 teaspoon dried savory

1 teaspoon dried basil

1 teaspoon salt

½ teaspoon freshly ground black pepper

1. Combine the quinoa and water in a medium saucepan and bring to a boil over high heat. Reduce the heat to low, cover, and simmer until the quinoa is tender and the water is absorbed, 12 to 15 minutes. Remove from the heat and set aside to cool. (You can cook the quinoa well ahead, if desired, and refrigerate in a covered container until needed).

2. Preheat the oven to 375°F. Lightly oil an 8- or 9-inch baking pan or a loaf pan or spray with nonstick spray and set aside.

3. In a food processor, combine all of the ingredients except the cooked quinoa and process to combine well. The mixture should be finely ground but with some texture remaining. Transfer the mixture to a bowl and add the reserved quinoa, stirring to mix well.

4. Taste and adjust the seasonings, then transfer the mixture to the prepared pan and smooth the top. Cover with aluminum foil and bake until firm, about 45 minutes. Remove the foil and let the loaf cool for 10 to 15 minutes, then carefully turn it out onto a plate by placing a plate over the loaf and inverting it. Slice and serve.

Serves 6

Simply Stuffed

W hen I look at a mushroom, bell pepper, or squash, I see more than a vegetable: I see an edible container.

Whether it is tiny cherry tomatoes filled with creamy hummus or large beefsteak tomatoes overflowing with rice and vegetables, fresh produce used as receptacles for other foods is a delicious and practical way to cook. In addition to tomatoes, consider stuffing mushrooms, peppers, squash, eggplants, and even cabbage. You can also stuff onions, artichokes, and, everyone's favorite, potatoes. When I'm in the mood to stuff, few vegetables are safe. One time I even stuffed carrots with a mushroom-shallot mixture and baked them in red wine. Fried stuffed zucchini flowers are an old family favorite. Stuffed vegetables can even be served as the main course of a meal, depending on the heartiness of the stuffing.

When you stuff vegetables, you can savor a delicious combination of ingredients that is made more flavorful by the permeating essence of the vegetable holding it. Adding to the enjoyment is the artful presentation and the fact that you get to eat the container. Once you start thinking of vegetables as containers, you may never look at produce the same way again.

But why stop with vegetables? As this chapter shows, not only is there more than one way to stuff a pepper, but you also can stuff tofu, seitan, and, of course, pasta. With all of these choices, you'll be simply stuffed in no time.

Thinking Outside the Stuffing Box

To me, my mother's chestnut stuffing was always the best part of Thanksgiving dinner. Even as a child, I bypassed the turkey in favor of the trimmings. These days, my mother's stuffing recipe finds its way into many a vegan seitan roast and stuffed winter squash. Just as stuffing doesn't have to be reserved for one day a year, neither does your stuffing recipe—or, for that matter, what you stuff it in. Cube cornbread or multigrain bread in place of white bread. Consider using leftover rice, millet, or other grains in place of bread. Experiment with different herbs, fruits, nuts, and chopped cooked vegetables. How about some pesto or sun-dried tomatoes?

Now that you have your stuffing, where should it go? It can, of course, stand on its own baked in a casserole or loaf pan. The seitan roast (page 380) is my personal favorite for holiday meals. And then there are vegetables: winter squash, summer squash, bell peppers, portobello mushrooms, eggplants, onions, and tomatoes—all of which make winning receptacles. So what are you waiting for? Get stuffing!

Paella-Stuffed Peppers

From artichokes, olives, and tomatoes to capers, saffron, and lemon zest, the stuffing in these delicious peppers features everything I love about paella—but in neat little packages.

4 large green bell peppers

1 tablespoon olive oil or ¼ cup water

3 garlic cloves, minced

1 (14.5-ounce) can diced fire-roasted tomatoes, drained

2 cups cooked brown rice

1 cup cooked or canned chickpeas, rinsed and drained

1 cup chopped marinated artichoke hearts

½ cup fresh or frozen peas

¼ cup sliced pimiento-stuffed green olives

2 teaspoons capers, drained

1 teaspoon finely minced lemon zest

1 teaspoon dried basil

½ teaspoon dried thyme

Large pinch of saffron threads

Salt and freshly ground black pepper

1. Preheat the oven to 350°F. Bring a large pot of water to a boil over high heat. Slice off the tops of the peppers and remove the seeds and ribs. Plunge the peppers into the boiling water and cook until slightly softened, 3 to 4 minutes. Remove from the water with tongs and set aside, cut sides down, to drain.

2. Heat the oil or water in a large saucepan over medium heat. Add the garlic and cook until fragrant, about 30 seconds. Stir in the tomatoes, rice, chickpeas, artichoke hearts, peas, olives, capers, lemon zest, basil, thyme, saffron, and salt and pepper to taste. Cook, stirring, for 5 minutes to blend the flavors. Taste and adjust the seasonings, if needed.

3. Fill the peppers with the paella mixture and place upright in a baking dish. Add a few tablespoons of water to the baking dish. Cover tightly and bake until the peppers are tender and the stuffing is hot, about 30 minutes. Serve hot.

Serves 4

Polenta-Stuffed Red Bell Peppers

These red bell peppers stuffed with yellow polenta studded with sun-dried tomatoes are as pretty as a picture—and they taste great, too. For easy cleanup, prepare them ahead of time so you can wash up all the pots and pans. Then, just pop in the oven at dinnertime and bake and serve in the same pan.

4 cups water

1½ teaspoons salt, plus more for seasoning

2 tablespoons olive oil

1½ cups medium-ground yellow cornmeal

4 large red bell peppers

1 small onion, minced

3 garlic cloves, minced

⅓ cup chopped oil-packed
or rehydrated sun-dried tomatoes

1 tablespoon minced fresh parsley

1 tablespoon minced fresh basil

Freshly ground black pepper

1. In a large saucepan, combine the water, salt, and 1 tablespoon of the oil and bring to a boil over high heat. Reduce the heat to medium and gradually whisk in the polenta, stirring constantly to avoid lumps. Cook, stirring, until the polenta begins to pull away from the sides of the pan, about 15 minutes. Remove from the heat and set aside.

2. Preheat the oven to 350°F. Bring a large pot of water to a boil over high heat. Slice off the tops of the peppers and remove the seeds and ribs. Plunge the peppers into the boiling water and cook until slightly softened, about 3 minutes. Remove from the water with tongs and set aside, cut sides down, to drain.

3. Heat the remaining 1 tablespoon oil in a large skillet over medium heat. Add the onion, cover, and cook until softened, about 5 minutes. Add the garlic and cook, stirring, until fragrant, about 30 seconds.

4. In a large bowl, combine the polenta, onion mixture, tomatoes, parsley, basil, and salt and pepper to taste. Mix well. Fill the peppers with the polenta mixture and place upright in a baking dish. Add a few tablespoons of water to the baking dish, cover, and bake until the peppers are tender and the stuffing is hot, about 30 minutes. Serve hot.

Serves 4

Poblanos Stuffed
with Cumin and Orange-Scented Rice

The symphony of flavors is sure to make this dish the center of attention at the dinner table. Poblanos are the flavorful, dark green chiles used to make *chiles rellenos*. They are available in well-stocked supermarkets and Hispanic grocery stores.

2 oranges, well scrubbed

2 tablespoons olive oil

1 small onion, minced

1 small carrot, grated

1 tablespoon ground cumin

2 cups cooked brown rice

Salt and freshly ground black pepper

8 poblano chiles, lightly roasted (page 129)

¼ cup chopped almonds

1. Preheat the oven to 350°F. Grate 2 tablespoons of zest from the oranges and set aside in a small bowl. Remove the remaining peel and pith from the oranges and discard. Coarsely chop the oranges, removing any seeds, if necessary, and add to the zest along with any juice. Set aside.

2. Heat 1 tablespoon of the olive oil in a large skillet over medium heat. Add the onion and carrot, cover, and cook until softened, about 5 minutes. Add the cumin, rice, orange mixture, and salt and pepper to taste. Mix well.

3. Lightly oil a baking dish. Cut a lengthwise slit in each roasted chile and remove the seeds. Spoon the stuffing mixture into the chiles and sprinkle with the almonds. Arrange the stuffed chiles in a single layer in the prepared dish. Drizzle with the remaining 1 tablespoon olive oil and bake until hot, about 30 minutes. Serve hot.

Serves 4

Sweet-and-Sour Chili-Stuffed Bell Peppers

The zesty filling makes a nice change from traditional stuffed peppers. Virtually any chili works well in this recipe.

4 medium-size green bell peppers

2 cups of your favorite vegan chili (pages 290–301)

1 cup cooked rice

⅔ cup Cheesy Sauce (page 128) or shredded vegan cheddar cheese

1 cup tomato juice

1 tablespoon cider vinegar

2 teaspoons natural sugar

1 teaspoon chili powder

1. Bring a large pot of water to a boil over high heat. Slice off the tops of the peppers and remove the seeds and ribs. Plunge the peppers into the boiling water and cook until slightly softened, 3 to 4 minutes. Remove from the water with tongs and set aside, cut sides down, to drain.

2. Preheat the oven to 350°F. In a large bowl, combine the chili, rice, and cheesy sauce until well mixed. Fill the peppers with the chili mixture and place them upright in a baking dish.

3. In a small bowl, combine the tomato juice, vinegar, sugar, and chili powder until well blended. Pour around the peppers and bake until hot, about 30 minutes. Serve hot.

Serves 4

Salsa-Spiced Chili-Stuffed Chiles

Any variety of large chile may be used in this recipe—or even bell peppers, if you prefer. I especially like the great taste of poblanos that can range from mild to hot. Serve them over rice.

8 poblano or other long green chiles, lightly roasted (page 129)

2 cups of your favorite vegan chili (pages 290–301)

1 cup Fresh Tomato Salsa (page 157) or purchased salsa

1 cup vegan sour cream, homemade (page 126) or purchased

Shredded vegan cheddar cheese (optional)

1. Preheat the oven to 350°F. Lightly oil a baking dish. Cut a lengthwise slit in each roasted chile and remove the seeds. Stuff with ¼ cup of the chili. Arrange the stuffed chiles in a single layer in the prepared dish and set aside.

2. In a small bowl, combine the salsa and vegan sour cream until well blended. Spread on top of the stuffed chiles and sprinkle evenly with the vegan cheese, if using. Bake until heated through and bubbly, about 30 minutes. Serve hot.

Serves 4

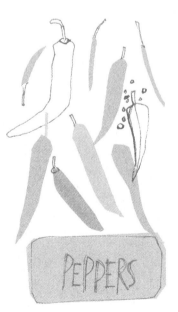

Stir-Fried Watercress in Japanese Eggplants

Be sure not to overcook the watercress—it should retain a slight crunch without tasting raw. For a dish with more substance, stir-fry some diced extra-firm tofu with a splash of tamari and add it to the stuffing. Add the red pepper flakes if you like a spicier dish.

4 Japanese eggplants, halved lengthwise

1 tablespoon neutral vegetable oil

4 scallions, chopped

3 garlic cloves, minced

2 bunches watercress, tough stems removed

2 tablespoons low-sodium tamari

½ teaspoon red pepper flakes (optional)

Salt and freshly ground black pepper

4 cups freshly cooked rice

1 tablespoon toasted sesame oil

1 tablespoon sesame seeds, toasted (page 171)

1. Preheat the oven to 400°F. Lightly oil a baking dish. Arrange the eggplant halves, cut sides down, in the dish and bake until just tender, about 15 minutes. Reduce the temperature to 250°F. Let the eggplants cool slightly, then scoop out the insides, leaving ⅓-inch-thick shells intact. Coarsely chop the flesh and set aside. Return the eggplant shells to the oven to keep warm.

2. Heat the oil in a large skillet over low heat. Add the scallions, garlic, and chopped eggplant and cook until fragrant, about 1 minute. Add the watercress, tamari, and red pepper flakes (if using). Stir-fry until the watercress is slightly limp, about 1 minute. Drizzle with the sesame oil and season to taste with salt and pepper.

3. To serve, spoon a bed of rice on a large platter or 4 individual plates. Arrange the eggplant shells on the rice and divide the watercress mixture between them. Sprinkle with the sesame seeds.

Serves 4

Barley-Stuffed Cabbage Rolls

These flavorful cabbage bundles are typically served in Eastern European countries, where they are called *halupki*. I especially like the barley in the stuffing, but the packets can be made with another grain, such as rice, bulgur, or quinoa. The tempeh combines especially well with the flavors of the cabbage and the sweet-and-sour tomato broth. You may prepare this dish on top of the stove, if you wish. Simply layer the cabbage packets in a large saucepan or Dutch oven and simmer over low heat. I prefer the oven method because I can arrange the *halupki* in one layer, pop them in the oven, and serve them from the same dish.

1 large head green cabbage, cored

1 tablespoon olive oil or ¼ cup water

1 cup grated onion

1 medium-size carrot, grated

3 cups water

1¼ cups pearl barley

8 ounces tempeh, steamed
(page 10) and finely chopped

2 tablespoons minced fresh parsley

¼ teaspoon ground allspice

Salt and freshly ground black pepper

1 (28-ounce) can crushed tomatoes

¼ cup cider vinegar

1 tablespoon natural sugar

1. Place the cabbage on a steamer rack set in a large pot. Add 2 to 3 inches of water, cover, and bring to a boil over high heat. Reduce the heat to medium and cook until the outer leaves are softened, about 10 minutes. Remove from the pot and let cool. Carefully remove the tender leaves and set aside.

2. Return the cabbage head to the steamer and cook, covered, to soften the remaining leaves, about 5 minutes. Remove from the steamer and let cool. Peel off the leaves and set aside with the others. You will need 14 to 16 leaves.

3. Heat the olive oil or water in a large skillet over medium heat. Add the onion and carrot, cover, and cook until tender, about 10 minutes.

4. Meanwhile, bring the 3 cups water to a boil in a medium-size saucepan over high heat. Salt the water, then add the barley. Reduce the heat to medium and simmer until just tender, about 10 minutes. Drain well and place in a large bowl. Add the tempeh, onion mixture, parsley, allspice, and salt and pepper to taste. Mix well.

5. Preheat the oven to 350°F. Lightly oil a shallow baking dish. Place 1 cabbage leaf, rib side down, on a flat work surface. Place approximately ⅓ cup of the stuffing mixture in the center of the leaf. Roll up the leaf around the stuffing, tucking in the sides as you roll. Repeat the process with the softened leaves until all of the filling is used. Arrange the cabbage rolls, seam sides down, in the prepared dish.

6. Combine the tomatoes, vinegar, and sugar in a medium bowl. Season to taste with salt and pepper and stir to mix. Pour the sauce over the cabbage rolls. Cover and bake until tender, about 45 minutes. Serve hot.

Versatile Cabbage

A member of the mustard family (*Cruciferae*), which also includes broccoli, cauliflower, and Brussels sprouts, cabbage is rich in potassium, folic acid, and vitamins B₆ and C. It can be enjoyed raw, fermented, or cooked in a variety of ways, from stuffed to soups to stir-fries. It is also good braised and goes well with potatoes, root vegetables, and sliced apples.

Turkish-Style Stuffed Eggplant with Walnut Sauce

To get the most juice from a fresh pomegranate, bring it to room temperature and roll it back and forth between a flat work surface and the palm of your hand. You can also buy bottled pomegranate juice, now available in most supermarkets.

2 medium-size eggplants, halved lengthwise

2 tablespoons olive oil or ¼ cup water

1 large onion, chopped

½ teaspoon turmeric

1 cup ground walnuts

1 cup vegetable broth

Salt and freshly ground black pepper

¼ cup fresh or bottled pomegranate juice

3 tablespoons natural sugar

2 tablespoons tomato paste

2 tablespoons fresh lemon juice

1 small green bell pepper, seeded and chopped

1 cup cooked basmati rice

2 tablespoons minced fresh mint

2 tablespoons minced fresh parsley

1. Preheat the oven to 400°F. Lightly oil a baking sheet. Place the eggplant halves, cut sides down, on the baking sheet and bake until partially softened, about 15 minutes. Remove from the oven and set aside to cool. Leave the oven on.

2. When cool enough to handle, scoop out the insides of the eggplants, leaving ¼-inch-thick shells intact. Coarsely chop the eggplant flesh and set aside, along with the shells.

3. Heat 1 tablespoon of the olive oil or 2 tablespoons of the water in a medium-size saucepan over medium heat. Add half of the onion, cover, and cook until softened, about 5 minutes. Add the turmeric, ½ cup of the walnuts, the broth, and salt and pepper to taste. Bring to a boil, then reduce the heat to medium-low and simmer, stirring occasionally, until the sauce begins to thicken, about 15 minutes.

4. In a small bowl, combine the pomegranate juice, sugar, tomato paste, and lemon juice and blend well. Add the mixture to the sauce, reduce the heat to low, and continue to simmer while you prepare the rest of the dish.

5. Heat the remaining 1 tablespoon olive oil or 2 tablespoons of the water in a large skillet over medium heat. Add the remaining onion and the bell pepper, cover, and cook until softened, about 5 minutes. Stir in the chopped eggplant and salt and pepper to taste. Continue cooking to blend the flavors, about 5 minutes, then transfer the eggplant mixture to a large bowl and stir in the rice, remaining ½ cup walnuts, the mint, and the parsley. Season to taste with salt and pepper.

6. Lightly oil a baking dish. Divide the stuffing among the eggplant shells and arrange them in the dish. Bake until the shells are tender and the filling is hot, 15 to 20 minutes. Serve topped with the walnut sauce.

================ *Serves 4* ================

NOTE: This dish may be prepared ahead of time, with the final baking done just before you're ready to serve it.

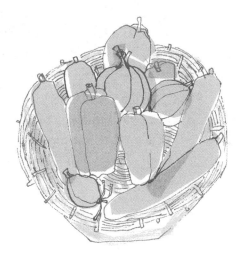

Portobello Mushrooms Stuffed with Chipotle Mashed Potatoes and Fried Leeks

There are a lot of flavors and textures going on in this deceptively simple dish. The earthy flavor of the mushrooms is enhanced by the spicy creaminess of the potatoes, and the crispy fried leeks add a surprising crunch. It's a great way to use up leftover mashed potatoes but delicious enough that you may want to prepare the potatoes especially for this recipe.

3 tablespoons olive oil

4 large portobello mushroom caps, gills scraped out

1 tablespoon low-sodium tamari

Salt and freshly ground black pepper

2 cups Chipotle Mashed Potatoes (page 182)

2 leeks (white parts only), washed well and slivered lengthwise

1. Heat 1 tablespoon of the olive oil in a large skillet over medium-high heat. Add the mushrooms, gill sides up, and sear until browned, about 30 seconds. Sprinkle the tamari over the mushrooms, turn them over, season to taste with salt and pepper, and cook for 30 seconds. Remove the mushrooms from the skillet and set aside.

2. Preheat the oven to 375°F. Lightly oil a baking dish. Spoon ½ cup of the mashed potatoes into each mushroom cap and smooth the top. Drizzle the stuffed mushrooms with 1 tablespoon of the olive oil and place in the prepared dish. Bake until hot, about 10 minutes.

3. While the mushrooms are baking, heat the remaining 1 tablespoon olive oil in a large skillet over medium-high heat. Add the leeks and cook, stirring, until crisp, about 5 minutes. Transfer to paper towels to drain. To serve, place the mushrooms on a plate and top with the fried leeks.

Serves 4

Shiitake-Stuffed Sesame Potatoes

Asian flavors abound in these rich and satisfying stuffed potatoes. Although they make a terrific side dish with a teriyaki- or hoisin-sauced entrée, they also are substantial enough to be enjoyed as the main event of a meal.

4 large baking potatoes, well scrubbed

1 tablespoon neutral vegetable oil or ¼ cup water

8 ounces fresh shiitake mushrooms, stems removed and caps chopped

1 tablespoon low-sodium tamari

½ cup cooked or canned white beans, mashed

1 tablespoon toasted sesame oil

Salt and freshly ground black pepper

1. Preheat the oven to 400°F. Prick the potatoes with a fork and bake until soft, about 1 hour. Remove from the oven but leave the oven on.

2. Heat the oil or water in a large skillet over medium heat. Add the mushrooms and cook, stirring, until the mushrooms are tender and the liquid evaporates, about 5 minutes. Stir in the tamari and set aside.

3. Lightly oil a baking dish. When the potatoes are cool enough to handle, cut in half lengthwise and, leaving the shells intact, carefully scoop out the flesh into a large bowl. Add the mashed beans, sesame oil, and salt and pepper to taste and mash until well combined. Add the mushroom mixture and mix well. Spoon the stuffing into the potato shells and arrange in the prepared dish. Bake until hot, 15 to 20 minutes. Serve hot.

Serves 4

One Potato, Two Potato

Potatoes are among the most popular vegetables, and there are seemingly infinite ways to prepare them. Rich in potassium, niacin, vitamins C and B₆, and iron, potatoes can be paired with root vegetables, squash, and dark leafy greens in soups, stews, and braised or roasted dishes. For a healthy alternative to French fries, cut potatoes into strips, arrange on a lightly oiled baking sheet, and bake at 425°F until soft and browned, turning once, 20 to 30 minutes. Then season with salt and pepper to suit your taste.

Sweet potatoes also taste great prepared this way, as well as baked, mashed, fried, or sautéed. They are delicious in soups and stews, and because they are naturally sweet, they can be used in pies, cookies, and other desserts. An excellent source of vitamin A, sweet potatoes also contain potassium, vitamins C and B₆, and riboflavin.

The best way to store potatoes and sweet potatoes is in a cool, dark, dry place.

Stuffed Pesto Potatoes with Fennel Compote

I love potatoes stuffed with everything from spinach to chili, but the aromatic combination of vegan pesto and fennel makes this version extra-special. In addition to adding creaminess to the stuffing, the silken tofu provides protein and helps make these potatoes hearty enough to serve as an entrée, allowing two halves per person.

4 large baking potatoes, well scrubbed

8 ounces soft silken tofu, drained and mashed

½ cup Basil Pesto (page 142) or purchased vegan pesto

1 tablespoon low-sodium tamari

Salt and freshly ground black pepper

Olive oil for drizzling

1 cup Fennel Compote with Black Olives and Pine Nuts (page 161)

1. Preheat the oven to 400°F. Pierce the potatoes with a fork and bake until soft, about 1 hour. Remove from the oven but leave the oven on.

2. Lightly oil a baking dish. When the potatoes are cool enough to handle, cut in half lengthwise and, leaving the shells intact, scoop out the flesh into a large bowl. Add the tofu, pesto, tamari, and salt and pepper to taste, blending until well combined. Spoon the stuffing back into the potato skins and arrange in the prepared dish. Drizzle with a small amount of olive oil and bake until hot, 15 to 20 minutes.

3. To serve, arrange the potato halves on a platter or 4 individual plates and top each with a spoonful of the fennel compote and another drizzle of olive oil, if desired.

Serves 4

Jalapeño Rice and Chili-Stuffed Squash

The complementary flavors of spicy chili and mellow squash join forces in this hearty and wholesome dish. It serves two as a main dish or four as a side dish. If you can find the sweet, orange-fleshed kabocha squash, also called Hokkaido pumpkin, you're in for a special treat.

1 medium-size butternut or other winter squash, halved and seeded

1 tablespoon olive oil or ¼ cup water

1 medium-size onion, minced

1 jalapeño, seeded and minced

2 cups of your favorite vegan chili (pages 290–301)

1 cup cooked rice

½ teaspoon salt

1. Preheat the oven to 375°F. Lightly oil a baking pan. Place the squash halves, cut sides down, in the pan and bake until just tender, about 30 minutes. Remove from the oven but keep the oven on.

2. Heat the olive oil or water in a large skillet over medium heat. Add the onion and jalapeño, cover, and cook until softened, about 5 minutes. Transfer to a large bowl and add the chili, rice, and salt. Mix well to combine.

3. Fill the squash cavities with the stuffing. Add ¼ inch of water to the baking pan, cover, and bake until the squash are tender and the filling is hot, about 20 minutes. Serve hot.

Serves 2 to 4

A Squash by Any Other Name: Winter Squash

Among the varieties of winter squash are acorn, butternut, buttercup, hubbard, kabocha, and turban, as well as the pumpkin. Most varieties are interchangeable in recipes. Winter squash is an excellent source of potassium and vitamins A and C. It can be steamed, braised, or baked and is especially good stuffed with a savory filling.

Winter Squash Stuffed with Moroccan Couscous

If kabocha squash is unavailable, substitute any sweet winter squash, such as butternut or acorn. The sweetness of the squash is enhanced by the aromatic spices.

1 large or 2 medium-size kabocha squash, halved and seeded

2 cups water, plus more as needed

1 cup instant couscous

½ teaspoon ground coriander

½ teaspoon ground cumin

¼ teaspoon ground cinnamon

1 tablespoon olive oil or ¼ cup water

1 large onion, chopped

1 carrot, grated

3 garlic cloves, minced

2 teaspoons grated fresh ginger

1 cup fresh or thawed frozen peas

Salt and freshly ground black pepper

½ cup raisins

½ cup chopped unsalted dry-roasted peanuts

1. Preheat the oven to 375°F. Place the squash halves, cut sides down, in a shallow baking dish. Add ¼ inch of water, cover tightly, and bake until just tender, about 30 minutes. Carefully turn the halves over and set aside.

2. While the squash is baking, bring the 2 cups water to a boil in a medium-size saucepan over high heat. Salt the water, then add the couscous, coriander, cumin, and cinnamon. Cover and turn off the heat.

3. Heat the olive oil or water in a large skillet over medium heat. Add the onion, carrot, and garlic, cover, and cook until softened, about 5 minutes. Add the ginger and peas, and salt and pepper to taste. Cook 1 to 2 minutes longer. Remove from the heat.

4. Fluff the couscous with a fork and transfer to a large bowl. Add the onion mixture, raisins, and peanuts. If the mixture seems too dry, add a little water to moisten. Divide the stuffing equally among the squash halves, cover the dish, and bake until hot, about 20 minutes. Serve hot.

Serves 4

Zucchini Stuffed with Corn, Tomatoes, and Dill

After a trip to the farmers' market, these stuffed zucchini will help solve your dilemma of which vegetables to cook up first, since they use a little bit of everything. When fresh corn and ripe tomatoes are out of season, frozen corn and canned tomatoes work well. Despite its appellation as a "summer" squash, fresh zucchini seems to be available year round.

4 medium-size zucchini, halved lengthwise

1 tablespoon olive oil or ¼ cup water

3 shallots, minced

3 tablespoons seeded and minced red bell pepper

3 garlic cloves, minced

Salt and freshly ground black pepper

3 large ripe tomatoes, finely chopped, or 1 (14.5-ounce) can petite diced tomatoes, drained

1 cup fresh or frozen corn kernels

2 teaspoons fresh lemon juice

3 tablespoons minced fresh dill

1. Use a sharp knife or melon baller to remove the zucchini flesh, leaving a ⅓-inch-thick shell. Chop the flesh well and set aside.

2. Place the zucchini shells on a steamer rack set in a large pot. Add 2 to 3 inches of water, cover, and bring to a boil over high heat. Steam the zucchini shells until tender, about 5 minutes. Set aside to cool.

3. Heat the olive oil or water in a medium-size skillet over medium heat. Add the shallots, bell pepper, garlic, chopped zucchini, and salt and pepper to taste. Cover and cook until tender, about 10 minutes. Add the tomatoes, corn, lemon juice, and 2 tablespoons of the dill. Simmer, stirring occasionally, until the liquid is absorbed, about 10 minutes. Remove from the heat and set aside.

4. Preheat the oven to 350°F. Lightly oil a baking dish. Spoon the stuffing mixture into the zucchini shells and arrange in the dish. Cover and bake until hot, about 30 minutes.

5. To serve, sprinkle with the remaining 1 tablespoon dill and finish with a few grindings of pepper.

===== *Serves 4* =====

Orzo-Stuffed Tomatoes with Yellow Pepper Coulis

This is a great way to use orzo, a small rice-shaped pasta usually reserved for soup. But keep this recipe in mind whenever you have a small amount of any leftover cooked grain and an abundance of firm, ripe tomatoes.

½ cup orzo

4 large ripe tomatoes

⅓ cup pine nuts, toasted (page 203)

2 garlic cloves, minced

2 tablespoons minced fresh parsley

2 tablespoons minced fresh basil

Salt and freshly ground black pepper

1 tablespoon olive oil

1 cup Yellow Pepper Coulis (page 141)

1. Bring a small pot of salted water to a boil over high heat. Cook the orzo, stirring occasionally, until tender, 8 to 10 minutes. Drain and set aside.

2. Preheat the oven to 375°F. Lightly oil a baking dish. Cut a ½-inch-thick slice off the top of each tomato. Scoop out the pulp, leaving a ½-inch-thick shell. Set aside.

3. Chop the tomato pulp and place in a large bowl. Add the orzo, pine nuts, garlic, parsley, basil, and salt and pepper to taste and mix well. Stuff the tomato shells with the mixture. Place them in the prepared dish, drizzle with the olive oil, and bake until hot, about 20 minutes.

4. To serve, spoon a small amount of the coulis onto 4 individual plates or a serving platter and carefully place the tomatoes on top.

Serves 4

Pesto-Stuffed Tofu Steaks with Summertime Tomato Sauce

The tofu readily absorbs the flavors of the pesto and tomato sauce in this light and luscious dish. Because of its resemblance to the Italian flag, this dish could be called "Tofu Bandiera." It makes a great dinner entrée served with pasta and a salad.

1 (12- to 16-ounce) package extra-firm tofu, drained and cut horizontally into four ¾-inch-thick slices

½ cup Basil Pesto (page 142) or purchased vegan pesto

Salt and freshly ground black pepper

1½ cups Summertime Tomato Sauce (page 136)

1 tablespoon olive oil

2 small roasted red bell peppers (page 129), cut into strips, for garnish

Fresh basil leaves, for garnish

1. Cut a slit in the side of each tofu slice and stuff 1 tablespoon of the vegan pesto into each pocket. Season to taste with salt and pepper and set aside.

2. Heat the tomato sauce in a small saucepan over low heat and keep warm.

3. Heat the olive oil in a large skillet over medium heat. Add the tofu and cook until golden brown on both sides, about 5 minutes. Reduce the heat to low and keep warm.

4. In a small bowl, combine the remaining ¼ cup pesto with 1 to 2 tablespoons water, blending well.

5. To serve, spoon a small amount of the warm tomato sauce on 4 individual plates. Top with a tofu steak. Drizzle 1 tablespoon of the diluted pesto over one-third of each tofu slice. Spoon a small amount of the tomato sauce over another third and leave the remaining portion unsauced. Garnish with the roasted pepper strips and basil leaves.

Serves 4

Yuba-Wrapped Seitan and Vegetable Rolls

Yuba, or bean curd skin, is a versatile ingredient in Asian cooking that is often used as a dumpling wrapper. Here it is used as a crispy outer wrapper for a flavorful seitan roll stuffed with julienned vegetables. These rolls can be served with a wide range of sauces, including Choron Sauce (page 131), Spicy Peanut Dipping Sauce (page 145), or Double Mushroom Sauce (page 135).

1 (1-pound) piece uncooked
seitan (page 12)

¼ cup low-sodium tamari

3 tablespoons neutral vegetable oil

1 large red bell pepper, seeded
and cut into thin strips

4 ounces fresh shiitake mushrooms, stems
removed and caps cut into thin strips

1 large yellow squash, cut
lengthwise into thin strips

4 scallions, sliced lengthwise

2 teaspoons toasted sesame oil

Salt and freshly ground black pepper

2 large sheets yuba (page 379)

1. Cut the raw seitan into 4 slices. Place the seitan slices between two sheets of parchment paper or plastic wrap. Use a rolling pin to roll out the seitan to about ¼ inch thick. Remove the parchment or plastic wrap. Place in a shallow bowl, cover with the tamari, and set aside.

2. Heat 1 tablespoon of the vegetable oil in a large skillet over medium heat. Add the bell pepper and cook until slightly softened, about 5 minutes. Add the mushrooms, squash, and scallions and cook until tender, about 5 minutes. Drizzle with the sesame oil, season to taste with salt and pepper, and set aside to cool.

3. Remove the seitan pieces from the marinade and place on a flat work surface. Divide the vegetable mixture among the slices, arranging the vegetable strips at one end of each slice, and roll up. Secure each roll with a toothpick or kitchen twine and place, seam sides down, on a platter.

4. Heat 1 tablespoon of the vegetable oil in a large skillet over medium-high heat. Add the seitan rolls and sear all over. Remove from the pan and set aside to cool.

5. Cut the yuba sheets in half and, if using dried yuba, soak in a shallow bowl of water to soften for about 5 seconds, then drain. Place a seitan roll on the lower third of each yuba sheet. Fold the sides of the yuba onto the seitan and roll up. Repeat with the remaining seitan rolls and yuba sheets.

6. Heat the remaining 1 tablespoon vegetable oil in the same large skillet over medium-high heat. Add the rolls and cook until golden brown and crispy on both sides, about 7 minutes total. Serve hot.

======================================= *Serves 4* =======================================

Yuba Is Only Skin-Deep

Yuba, also known as bean curd skin, is an unusual yet versatile ingredient used widely in Asian cooking. Made from the skin that forms on the surface of hot soy milk as it cools, yuba is available in Asian markets and is sold in fresh, partially dried, and dried sheets. The partially dried and dried versions need to be moistened or soaked just long enough to become pliable. Yuba can be used as dumpling or spring roll wrappers or to encase other ingredients. It fries up crisp and golden brown. Fresh yuba is sometimes cut into strips and used like noodles.

Seitan Roast
with Chestnut and Cranberry Stuffing

For meat-free holiday dining, it doesn't get much better than this. Even the skeptics at your dinner table will be impressed with the chewy wheat-meat surrounding a savory stuffing studded with chestnuts and cranberries. Serve with mashed potatoes and all the trimmings.

1 tablespoon olive oil or ¼ cup water

1 large onion, minced

½ cup minced celery

2 teaspoons dried thyme

1 teaspoon ground dried sage

½ teaspoon dried marjoram

2 tablespoons brandy, dry white wine, or water

6 cups cubed bread

8 ounces cooked chestnuts (page 381), coarsely chopped

⅓ cup sweetened dried cranberries

⅓ cup minced fresh parsley

1 cup vegetable broth or water

1 teaspoon salt

½ teaspoon freshly ground black pepper

1 (2-pound) piece uncooked seitan (page 12)

1½ cups Basic Brown Sauce (page 134)

1. Heat the olive oil or water in a medium-size skillet over medium heat. Add the onion and celery and cook until softened, 5 to 7 minutes. Add the thyme, sage, marjoram, and brandy and cook for 1 minute. Remove from the heat and set aside.

2. Place the bread in a large bowl. Add the chestnuts, cranberries, parsley, broth, salt, and pepper. Stir in the onion mixture and mix well. Taste and adjust the seasonings, adding more salt if needed, and a little more broth or water if the mixture is too dry. Set aside.

3. Preheat the oven to 350°F. Lightly oil a shallow baking pan. Place the raw seitan between two sheets of parchment paper or plastic wrap. Use a rolling pin to roll out the seitan to about ¼ inch thick. Remove the parchment or plastic wrap. Spread the surface of the seitan with the stuffing to within 1 inch of the edge and roll it up. Place the roast, seam side down, in the prepared pan. Bake until the surface is firm and golden brown, about 40 minutes.

4. Let stand at room temperature for 10 minutes. Using a serrated knife, cut the roast into ½-inch-thick slices and serve with the brown sauce.

Serves 6 to 8

Chestnuts, Roasted and Otherwise

Chestnuts have been eaten since ancient times, primarily in Italy, Spain, China, and Japan. They are especially popular in France, Italy, and North Africa, where they are usually eaten roasted or boiled. In many cities, street vendors sell hot roasted chestnuts on cold winter days.

George Washington and Thomas Jefferson were interested in growing chestnut trees during the late 1700s. Despite our forefathers' efforts, our country's once flourishing chestnut trees were nearly wiped out by a blight in the early 20th century. For that reason, to this day we import most of our chestnuts from Europe.

Chestnuts have a crumbly texture and a sweet, mild flavor. Unlike other nuts, they are low in fat. They have a fair amount of protein, are high in carbohydrates, and are a good source of calcium, potassium, B vitamins, magnesium, and iron.

In addition to eating them out of hand, you can use chestnuts in a variety of sweet and savory recipes, from soups to stuffings to desserts. Canned and bottled peeled chestnuts are available year round. Though expensive, they eliminate the labor-intensive job of peeling them yourself. Sweetened chestnuts, called *marrons glacés*, are also available, as are pureed chestnuts, dried chestnuts, and chestnut flour. Many of these items can be found in gourmet or specialty food shops.

When shopping for chestnuts, look for firm, heavy nuts with dark brown, shiny shells. If you can hear them rattling around in their shells, they are old and dried out. Unpeeled chestnuts can be stored in a cool, dry place for up to 2 weeks. It is important to note that the crisp, white water chestnuts used in Chinese stir-fries are not a substitute for regular chestnuts.

Both the shell and thin brown skin of the chestnut need to be removed before eating. Boiling or roasting the chestnuts beforehand makes them easier to peel. To cook chestnuts, pierce the shells with a sharp knife, cutting an X in the shell. Then boil or roast them at 400°F for 20 to 30 minutes, depending on the chestnuts. Peel them while still fairly hot, using a sharp knife to remove the outer shell and the inner skin. They are then ready to eat or use in recipes. Boiling is recommended if the chestnuts are to be used in another recipe, but for peeling and eating out of hand, roast them for maximum flavor.

Crispy Triple Soy Roast
with Double Mushroom Sauce

This protein-rich seitan roast uses soy in three ways: the uncooked gluten is seasoned with a tamari-miso paste, stuffed with tofu, and encased in crispy yuba. This roast lends itself to a variety of seasonings. Add a little grated fresh ginger when you sauté the garlic, or add some thyme or another herb when you throw in the parsley.

1 tablespoon olive oil or ¼ cup water

12 ounces white mushrooms, chopped

3 garlic cloves, minced

8 ounces extra-firm tofu, drained and crumbled

1 teaspoon dried thyme

½ teaspoon dried marjoram

½ teaspoon ground dried sage

½ teaspoon salt

¼ teaspoon freshly ground black pepper

4 cups cubed bread

3 tablespoons minced fresh parsley

¼ cup low-sodium tamari

2 teaspoons mellow white miso paste

1 (1-pound) piece uncooked seitan (page 12)

1 large sheet yuba (page 379)

1 cup Double Mushroom Sauce (page 135)

1. Heat the olive oil or water in medium-size skillet over medium heat. Add the mushrooms and garlic and cook, stirring, until tender, about 5 minutes. Stir in the tofu, thyme, marjoram, sage, salt, and pepper. Cook until the liquid is evaporated, about 10 minutes. Transfer to a large bowl and mix in the bread cubes and parsley. Set aside.

2. In a small bowl, combine the tamari and miso, stirring to blend well. Set aside.

3. Using a rolling pin, roll out the raw seitan between sheets of parchment or plastic wrap to about ¼ inch thick. Brush the surface with the tamari-miso mixture and spread the stuffing over all, to within 1 inch of the edge. Roll up the seitan to encase the stuffing and place, seam side down, on a platter.

4. Preheat the oven to 350°F. Lightly oil a shallow baking pan. If using dried yuba, soak it in water to soften for 5 seconds, if necessary, then drain. Spread out the yuba on a flat work surface, place the seitan roll at one end, and roll up, tucking in the sides as you roll. Place the wrapped roll, seam side down, in the prepared pan.

5. Bake until hot inside and golden brown and crisp outside, about 40 minutes.

6. Let stand at room temperature for 10 minutes. Using a serrated knife, cut into ½-inch-thick slices and serve with the mushroom sauce.

Serves 6 to 8

Chicory and Cannellini-Stuffed Pasta Shells

Chicory, also known as curly endive, is a slightly bitter green widely used in Italian cooking. It can be very sandy, however, so be sure to wash it well before using.

1 large head chicory, washed well and coarsely chopped

8 ounces large pasta shells

1 tablespoon olive oil or ¼ cup water

3 large garlic cloves, minced

1½ cups cooked cannellini or other white beans or 1 (15-ounce) can beans, rinsed and drained

Salt and freshly ground black pepper

2 cups Vegan Béchamel Sauce (page 132)

1 (12- to 16-ounce) package soft silken tofu, drained and mashed

2 tablespoons minced fresh parsley

1. Bring two large pots of salted water to a boil over high heat. Cook the chicory in one pot until tender, about 10 minutes. Drain well and set aside.

2. Meanwhile, cook the pasta shells in the other pot, stirring occasionally, until al dente, about 10 minutes. Drain well and set aside.

3. Heat the olive oil or water in a large skillet over medium heat. Add the garlic and cook, stirring, until fragrant, about 30 seconds. Add the chicory, beans, and salt and pepper to taste. Simmer until the flavors are well combined, about 5 minutes. Set aside to cool.

4. Preheat the oven to 350°F. Lightly oil a shallow baking dish. Spoon a thin layer of the sauce over the bottom of the dish and set aside.

5. In a medium-size bowl, combine the chicory-bean mixture, tofu, and salt and pepper to taste. Mix until well blended, then spoon the mixture into the pasta shells. Arrange the stuffed shells on top of the sauce and spoon the remaining sauce on top. Cover and bake until hot and bubbly, about 30 minutes. Sprinkle with the parsley and serve.

Serves 4

Sausage and Fennel Cannelloni

Although cannelloni is virtually indistinguishable from manicotti, the difference usually lies in the filling. Whereas manicotti usually contains a cheese filling, cannelloni is usually made with a meat filling.

12 cannelloni tubes

2 medium-size fennel bulbs, trimmed and coarsely chopped

1 tablespoon olive oil or ¼ cup water

1 small onion, minced

1 (14.5-ounce) can diced fire-roasted tomatoes, drained

3 cups chopped or crumbled vegan sausage, homemade (page 15) or purchased

½ teaspoon red pepper flakes

½ teaspoon dried oregano

½ teaspoon dried basil

Salt and freshly ground black pepper

½ cup ground toasted walnuts (page 203)

½ cup grated vegan mozzarella cheese or Cheesy Sauce (page 128)

3 cups tomato sauce, homemade (pages 136–137) or purchased

1. Bring a large pot of salted water to a boil over high heat. Cook the cannelloni, stirring occasionally, until al dente, about 8 minutes. Drain and rinse under cold running water, then set aside.

2. Lightly steam the fennel in a steamer basket set over boiling water until tender, about 5 minutes. Set aside.

3. Heat the olive oil or water in a large skillet over medium heat. Add the onion, cover, and cook until softened, about 5 minutes. Add the tomatoes, vegan sausage, red pepper flakes, oregano, basil, and salt and pepper to taste. Cook for 10 minutes, stirring to blend the flavors. Stir in the fennel.

4. Transfer to a large bowl, add the walnuts and ¼ cup of the vegan cheese, and stir to blend well. Set aside.

5. Preheat the oven to 350°F. Lightly oil a 9 x 13-inch baking dish. Spread a layer of the tomato sauce over the bottom of the dish. Using a teaspoon, fill the cannelloni, arranging the stuffed tubes in a single layer in the baking dish. Spoon the remaining sauce over the cannelloni, top with the remaining ¼ cup cheese, and cover with aluminum foil. Bake until hot, about 20 minutes. Uncover and bake until the top is golden brown, about 10 minutes more. Serve hot.

Serves 4

Florentine-Style Manicotti

This lovely dish is a good choice to prepare in advance for dinner guests. You can just pop it in the oven when needed. Featuring spinach and tofu, this manicotti is as nutritious as it is delicious.

12 manicotti tubes

2 tablespoons olive oil

1 large onion, minced

3 garlic cloves, minced

2 (10-ounce) packages frozen chopped spinach, cooked and well drained

1 teaspoon dried basil

¼ teaspoon freshly grated nutmeg

Salt and freshly ground black pepper

1 (12- to 16-ounce) package firm tofu, drained and crumbled

1 tablespoon fresh lemon juice

3 cups Vegan Béchamel Sauce (page 132)

½ cup ground toasted walnuts (page 203)

½ cup dry bread crumbs

½ cup shredded vegan mozzarella cheese (optional)

1. Bring a large pot of salted water to a boil over high heat. Cook the manicotti, stirring occasionally, until al dente. Drain and rinse under cold running water, then set aside.

2. Heat 1 tablespoon of the olive oil in a large skillet over medium heat. Add the onion and cook until softened, about 5 minutes. Add the garlic and cook 1 minute longer.

3. Squeeze the spinach to remove as much liquid as possible and add to the skillet. Add the basil, nutmeg, and salt and pepper to taste and cook for 5 minutes, stirring to blend the flavors.

4. Transfer the spinach mixture to a large bowl. Add the tofu and lemon juice and stir to blend well. Add salt and pepper to taste and set aside.

5. Preheat the oven to 350°F. Lightly oil a 9 x 13-inch baking dish. Spread a layer of the sauce in the bottom of the dish. Using a teaspoon, fill the manicotti with the tofu mixture until well packed. Arrange the stuffed tubes in a single layer in the baking dish. Spoon the remaining sauce over the manicotti.

6. In a small bowl, combine the walnuts, bread crumbs, and remaining 1 tablespoon olive oil with a fork. Sprinkle over the manicotti. Top with the vegan cheese, if using, and cover with aluminum foil. Bake for 30 minutes, then uncover and bake until the top is golden brown, about 10 minutes more. Let rest for a few minutes, then serve.

Serves 4

New World Pizza

Americans consume pizza at a rate of 350 slices per second, so it's hard to believe that it has been only 100 years since the first American pizzeria opened in New York. This savory pie became popular in 18th-century Italy, where it was topped with tomatoes, olive oil, garlic, and oregano. Mozzarella cheese was added later, when a patriotic pizza depicting the colors of the Italian flag (red tomato sauce, green basil, and white cheese) was made to honor Queen Margherita. However, long before Naples became the birthplace of the pizza we know today, ancient civilizations, including the Greeks and Egyptians, were enjoying savory baked flatbreads, often seasoned with oil, garlic, and herbs.

Inspired by pizza's ancient global history, this chapter sets out to explore a variety of ways pizza can be enjoyed without cheese, since vegan cheese products are not known for their melting ability—a trait one naturally associates with the popular cheese pizza. Of course, you can always load your pizza with vegan cheese and even vegan pepperoni, if you like. But with savory toppings that include tomatoes, mushrooms, fresh herbs, beans, eggplant, and even cabbage, you may not miss those traditional pizza trappings. In this chapter, you'll see that when you "hold the cheese," it doesn't mean you have to hold back on flavor.

The First Pizza Delivery

When pizza first became popular in Naples, bakers prepared it to sell to sailors as they returned from a day at sea. This classic "marinara" pizza was made with fresh tomatoes, garlic, oil, and oregano. At that time, pizza was baked in ovens and then sold in the streets by boys who would bring the pizza directly to the fishermen in tin stoves called *stufas*, which they balanced on their heads, to keep the pizza warm.

Traditional Pizza Dough

This basic dough recipe can be enhanced by the addition of a small amount of fresh or dried herbs. You also can replace up to half of the flour with whole-wheat flour, if you like. I like to use a food processor to make the dough, but you can make it by hand, if you wish.

1½ teaspoons active dry yeast

¾ cup warm water

2¼ cups unbleached all-purpose flour

1 teaspoon salt

Pinch of natural sugar

1 tablespoon olive oil, plus more for the bowl

1. Place the yeast in a small bowl. Add ¼ cup of the water and stir to dissolve. Set aside for 5 to 10 minutes.

2. To make the dough in a food processor, combine the flour, salt, and sugar, pulsing to blend. With the machine running, add the yeast mixture through the feed tube, along with the olive oil and as much of the remaining ½ cup water as necessary to make the dough hold together.

3. To make the dough by hand, combine the flour, salt, and sugar in a large bowl. Stir in the yeast mixture, olive oil, and the remaining ½ cup water until combined.

4. Turn the dough out onto a lightly floured work surface and knead until smooth and elastic, about 3 minutes. Transfer to a large oiled bowl. Spread a small amount of oil on top of the dough, cover with plastic wrap, and set aside in a warm place to rise until doubled in bulk, about 1 hour.

5. Use immediately or store, tightly wrapped in plastic, for up to 8 hours in the refrigerator or for up to 4 weeks in the freezer.

Makes 1 pizza crust

Enriched Pizza Dough

The addition of soy flour and sesame seeds provides extra protein and calcium in this pizza dough, along with a slightly nutty flavor. The texture is slightly coarser than that of Traditional Pizza Dough (page 388) and is ideal for some of the more nontraditional toppings in this chapter.

1½ teaspoons active dry yeast

¾ cup warm water

2 cups unbleached all-purpose flour

¼ cup soy flour

1½ tablespoons ground sesame seeds

1 teaspoon salt

Pinch of natural sugar

1 tablespoon olive oil, plus more for the bowl

1. Place the yeast in a small bowl. Add ¼ cup of the water and stir to dissolve. Set aside for 5 to 10 minutes.

2. To make the dough in a food processor, combine the flours, sesame seeds, salt, and sugar, pulsing to blend. With the machine running, add the yeast mixture through the feed tube, along with the olive oil and as much of the remaining ½ cup water as necessary to make the dough hold together.

3. To make the dough by hand, combine the flours, sesame seeds, salt, and sugar in a large bowl. Stir in the yeast mixture, olive oil, and remaining ½ cup water until combined.

4. Turn the dough out onto a lightly floured work surface and knead until smooth and elastic, about 3 minutes. Transfer to a large oiled bowl. Spread a small amount of oil on top of the dough, cover with plastic wrap, and set aside in a warm place to rise until doubled in bulk, about 1 hour.

5. Use immediately or store, tightly wrapped in plastic, for up to 8 hours in the refrigerator or for up to 4 weeks in the freezer.

Makes 1 pizza crust

Fresh Tomato Pizza with Basil Pesto

Fragrant vegan pesto combines with diced plum tomatoes for a fresh-tasting variation of the basic "tomato pie." If fresh, ripe tomatoes are out of season, use canned tomatoes, or even a canned pizza sauce. If you're in the mood for a more traditional pie, sprinkle with some vegan cheese.

1 recipe Traditional Pizza Dough (page 388)

½ cup Basil Pesto (page 142) or purchased vegan pesto

1 tablespoon olive oil

4 ripe plum tomatoes, peeled, seeded, and diced

Salt and freshly ground black pepper

1. Preheat the oven to 450°F. Punch the dough down. On a lightly floured work surface, roll out or stretch the dough into a circle about ¼ inch thick. Lightly oil a pizza pan or baking sheet and place the dough on it, stretching it to fit. Bake on the bottom oven rack for 8 minutes.

2. In a medium-size bowl, combine the pesto and olive oil, stirring to blend. Add the tomatoes and salt and pepper to taste. Toss gently to combine.

3. Remove the crust from the oven and top with the tomato-pesto mixture, spreading it to within ½ inch of the edge. Bake until the crust is golden brown, 10 to 12 minutes. Serve hot.

Makes 1 pizza

Pizza Variations

Pizza as we know it—a yeasty flatbread topped with tomato sauce and other toppings—became popular a couple of hundred years after Christopher Columbus brought the tomato back to Italy from the New World. Long before that time, however, ancient civilizations such as the Greeks and Etruscans were turning out their own versions of the delectable flatbread seasoned with oil, herbs, and spices that we know as focaccia, or "fireplace floor bread." Other regional Italian flatbreads include ciabatta, named for its "slipper" shape, and *pane carasau*, also known as *carta da musica*, or "music paper," since this Sardinian bread is thin, dry, and crisp.

White Pizza with Red Onion and Arugula

I love the combination of creamy white beans and assertive arugula sautéed with onion—no surprise it makes a wonderful pizza topping as well.

1 recipe Traditional Pizza Dough (page 388)

1½ cups cooked cannellini beans
or 1 (15-ounce) can beans, rinsed and drained

2 garlic cloves, crushed

⅓ cup nutritional yeast

2 teaspoons fresh lemon juice

¾ teaspoon dried basil

½ teaspoon dried oregano

Salt and freshly ground black pepper

1 to 2 tablespoons water

1 tablespoon olive oil

1 red onion, sliced very thin

1 cup arugula leaves

1. Preheat the oven to 450°F. Punch the dough down. On a lightly floured work surface, roll out or stretch the dough into a circle about ¼ inch thick. Lightly oil a pizza pan or baking sheet and place the dough on it, stretching it to fit. Bake on the bottom oven rack for 8 minutes.

2. In a food processor, combine the beans, garlic, nutritional yeast, lemon juice, basil, oregano, and salt and pepper to taste. Process until smooth and well blended. Add a tablespoon or two of water if the mixture is too thick and process again to blend.

3. Remove the crust from the oven and top with the bean mixture, spreading it to within ½ inch of the edge. Bake until the crust is nicely browned, 10 to 12 minutes.

4. While the pizza is baking, heat the oil in a medium-size skillet over medium heat. Add the onion and sauté until softened, about 4 minutes. Add the arugula and salt and pepper to taste and sauté until wilted, 2 to 3 minutes longer. When the pizza is done baking, top it with the sautéed onion and arugula. Serve immediately.

Makes 1 pizza

Wild Mushroom Pizza
with Garlic and Thyme

This is a mushroom pizza with a touch of class, topped with loads of juicy wild mushrooms redolent of garlic and thyme. Serve with a crisp green salad for a satisfying meal.

1 tablespoon olive oil

8 ounces fresh wild mushrooms, such as oyster, shiitake, and chanterelle, trimmed and sliced

3 garlic cloves, minced

1 teaspoon minced fresh thyme

Salt and freshly ground black pepper

1 recipe Traditional Pizza Dough (page 388)

1. Preheat the oven to 450°F.

2. Heat the olive oil in a large skillet over medium heat. Add the mushrooms and garlic and cook, stirring, until softened, about 5 minutes. Add the thyme and salt and pepper to taste. Continue to cook, stirring occasionally, until the liquid evaporates, 7 to 10 minutes.

3. Punch the dough down. On a lightly floured work surface, roll out or stretch the dough into a circle about ¼ inch thick. Lightly oil a pizza pan or baking sheet and place the dough on it, stretching it to fit. Bake on the bottom oven rack for 8 minutes.

4. Remove from the oven and top with the mushroom mixture, spreading it to within ½ inch of the edge. Bake until the crust is golden brown, 10 to 12 minutes. Serve hot.

Makes 1 pizza

Pizza Bandiera

Like pizza Margherita, which uses tomatoes, basil, and cheese to depict the colors of the Italian flag, this pizza is topped with sautéed tomatoes, green bell peppers, and onion. As in many Italian preparations, these vegetables are cooked until very soft. The word *bandiera* is Italian for "flag."

1 tablespoon olive oil

1 medium-size onion, chopped

2 small green bell peppers, seeded and chopped

3 large ripe tomatoes, peeled, seeded, and diced

1 tablespoon dry white wine

Pinch of natural sugar

Salt and freshly ground black pepper

1 tablespoon finely chopped fresh basil

1 recipe Traditional Pizza Dough (page 388)

1. Preheat the oven to 450°F.

2. Heat the olive oil in a large skillet over medium heat. Add the onion, cover, and cook until softened, about 5 minutes. Add the bell peppers, cover, reduce the heat to medium-low, and cook until tender, 5 to 7 minutes. Add the tomatoes, wine, sugar, and salt and pepper to taste. Cook for 10 minutes, stirring occasionally, to blend the flavors. Add the basil, then taste and adjust the seasonings.

3. Punch the dough down. On a lightly floured work surface, roll out or stretch the dough into a circle about ¼ inch thick. Lightly oil a pizza pan or baking sheet and place the dough on it, stretching it to fit. Bake on the bottom oven rack for 8 minutes.

4. Remove from the oven and top with the vegetable mixture, spreading it to within ½ inch of the edge. Bake until the crust is golden brown, 10 to 12 minutes. Serve hot.

Makes 1 pizza

Pizza Puttanesca

The classic pasta sauce made with capers and two kinds of olives is so delicious it deserves to be spread around—on pizza. Assemble a quick version of the sauce, as provided here, or use the recipe on page 226.

1 recipe Traditional Pizza Dough (page 388)

1 cup seasoned tomato or pizza sauce

¼ cup pitted and sliced black olives

¼ cup pitted and sliced green olives

1 tablespoon capers, drained and chopped

1. Preheat the oven to 450°F. Punch the dough down. On a lightly floured work surface, roll out or stretch the dough into a circle about ¼ inch thick. Lightly oil a pizza pan or baking sheet and place the dough on it, stretching it to fit. Bake on the bottom oven rack for 8 minutes.

2. Combine the sauce, olives, and capers in a small bowl.

3. Remove the crust from the oven and top with the sauce mixture, spreading it to within ½ inch of the edge. Bake until the crust is golden brown, 10 to 12 minutes. Serve hot.

Makes 1 pizza

Roasted Eggplant and Sesame Pizza

The combination of sesame and eggplant lends a Middle Eastern flavor to this pizza. Slender Japanese eggplant or small regular eggplant are used. If only a larger eggplant is available, chop it instead of slicing it into rounds and proceed with the recipe.

2 small eggplants (see headnote)

2 shallots, thinly sliced

3 tablespoons toasted sesame oil

Salt and freshly ground black pepper

1 recipe Enriched Pizza Dough (page 389)

1 tablespoon sesame seeds

½ teaspoon dried oregano

1. Preheat the oven to 450°F. Lightly oil a baking sheet.

2. Slice the eggplants into ¼-inch-thick rounds and place in a medium-size bowl. Add the shallots, sesame oil, and salt and pepper to taste and mix to combine. Arrange the eggplant-shallot mixture on the prepared baking sheet and roast, turning once, until tender but not browned, about 10 minutes. Remove from the oven and set aside.

3. Punch the dough down. On a lightly floured work surface, roll out or stretch the dough into a circle about ¼ inch thick. Lightly oil a pizza pan or baking sheet and place the dough on it, stretching it to fit. Bake on the bottom oven rack for 8 minutes.

4. Remove from the oven and top with the eggplant-shallot mixture, spreading it to within ½ inch of the edge. Sprinkle with the sesame seeds and oregano. Bake until the crust is golden brown, 10 to 12 minutes. Serve hot.

Makes 1 pizza

Spicy Black Bean and Salsa Pizza

This nontraditional pizza has a taste of the Southwest. The topping would feel right at home on a tortilla, but I prefer the more substantial pizza crust.

1 recipe Traditional Pizza Dough (page 388)

1 cup Fresh Tomato Salsa (page 157) or purchased salsa

1 cup cooked or canned black beans, rinsed and drained

1 chipotle chile in adobo, finely minced

2 tablespoons minced fresh cilantro

Salt and freshly ground black pepper

1. Preheat the oven to 450°F. Punch the dough down. On a lightly floured work surface, roll out or stretch the dough into a circle about ¼ inch thick. Lightly oil a pizza pan or baking sheet and place the dough on it, stretching it to fit. Bake on the bottom oven rack for 8 minutes.

2. In a medium-size bowl, combine the salsa, beans, chipotle chile, cilantro, and salt and pepper to taste. Stir to blend.

3. Remove the crust from the oven and top with the salsa-bean mixture, spreading it to within ½ inch of the edge. Bake until the crust is golden brown, 10 to 12 minutes. Serve hot.

Makes 1 pizza

Broccoli Rabe and White Bean Pizza

The combination of sautéed beans, greens, and garlic makes a great topping. Sprinkle some red pepper flakes into the sauté for a spicy accent. Broccoli rabe, also known as rapini, is available in well-stocked supermarkets.

1 bunch broccoli rabe, stems trimmed, leaves coarsely chopped

1 tablespoon olive oil

3 garlic cloves, minced

1½ cups cooked cannellini or other white beans or 1 (15-ounce) can beans, rinsed, drained, and mashed

Salt and freshly ground black pepper

1 recipe Traditional Pizza Dough (page 388)

1. Preheat the oven to 450°F. Bring a medium-size pot of salted water to a boil over high heat. Cook the broccoli rabe until tender, about 10 minutes. Drain very well and set aside.

2. Heat the olive oil in a large skillet over medium heat. Add the garlic and cook until fragrant, about 30 seconds. Add the broccoli rabe, beans, and salt and pepper to taste. Cook for about 5 minutes to blend the flavors. Set aside.

3. Punch the dough down. On a lightly floured work surface, roll out or stretch the dough into a circle about ¼ inch thick. Lightly oil a pizza pan or baking sheet and place the dough on it, stretching it to fit. Bake on the bottom oven rack for 8 minutes.

4. Remove from the oven and top with the broccoli rabe mixture, spreading it to within ½ inch of the edge. Bake until the crust is golden brown, about 10 to 12 minutes. Serve hot.

Makes 1 pizza

Did You Know?

It's a good idea to eat beans in combination with foods high in vitamin C, such as cruciferous vegetables or bell peppers. Doing so will increase the body's absorption of the iron in the beans.

Pizza with Sautéed Cabbage and Onion

In many eastern European countries, a yeasted flatbread is served topped with sautéed cabbage, onions, and sometimes potatoes. Pizza is truly a universal food.

1 tablespoon olive oil

1 medium-size Vidalia or other sweet onion, chopped

3 cups cored and finely shredded Savoy cabbage

Salt and freshly ground black pepper

1 recipe Enriched Pizza Dough (page 389)

1. Preheat the oven to 450°F.

2. Heat the olive oil in a large skillet over medium heat. Add the onion, cover, and cook until softened, about 5 minutes. Add the cabbage, cover, and cook until tender, about 7 minutes. Season with salt and pepper to taste and continue to cook, uncovered, until the vegetables are slightly caramelized, about 7 minutes. Set aside.

3. Punch the dough down. On a lightly floured work surface, roll out or stretch the dough into a circle about ¼ inch thick. Lightly oil a pizza pan or baking sheet and place the dough on it, stretching it to fit. Bake on the bottom oven rack for 8 minutes.

4. Remove from the oven and top with the cabbage mixture, spreading it to within ½ inch of the edge. Bake until the crust is golden brown, 10 to 12 minutes. Serve hot.

Makes 1 pizza

Pizza Bombay

I sometimes use Indian flatbread as a delicious stand-in for pizza crust, so I decided to turn the tables and use regular pizza dough to host an Indian-spiced topping made with spinach and lentils.

1 tablespoon olive oil

1 medium-size onion, chopped

1 tablespoon curry powder

1 pound fresh spinach, tough stems removed, leaves coarsely chopped

Salt and freshly ground black pepper

1 cup cooked or canned brown lentils, well drained

1 recipe Traditional Pizza Dough (page 388)

1. Preheat the oven to 450°F.

2. Heat the olive oil in a large skillet over medium heat. Add the onion, cover, and cook until softened, about 5 minutes. Add the curry powder, stirring to coat the onion. Add the spinach and salt and pepper to taste. Cook until the spinach is wilted and just tender, 2 to 4 minutes. Stir in the lentils, then taste and adjust the seasonings. Set aside.

3. Punch the dough down. On a lightly floured work surface, roll out or stretch the dough into a circle about ¼ inch thick. Lightly oil a pizza pan or baking sheet and place the dough on it, stretching it to fit. Bake on the bottom oven rack for 8 minutes.

4. Remove from the oven and top with the spinach-lentil mixture, spreading it to within ½ inch of the edge. Bake until the crust is golden brown, 10 to 12 minutes. Serve hot.

Makes 1 pizza

Cheesy Chili Pizza

Two of America's favorite foods combine for a hearty pizza with loads of flavor. Additional toppings may include chopped jalapeños, salsa, sliced olives, or chopped onion.

1 recipe Traditional Pizza Dough (page 388)

2 cups of your favorite vegan chili (pages 290–301)

1 cup shredded vegan mozzarella or cheddar cheese or Cheesy Sauce (page 128)

Additional toppings (see headnote; optional)

1. Preheat the oven to 450°F. Punch the dough down. On a lightly floured work surface, roll out or stretch the dough into a circle about ¼ inch thick. Lightly oil a pizza pan or baking sheet and place the dough on it, stretching it to fit. Bake on the bottom oven rack for 8 minutes.

2. Remove from the oven and top with the chili, spreading it to within ½ inch of the edge. Sprinkle on the vegan cheese and additional toppings (if using). Bake until the crust is golden brown, 10 to 12 minutes. Serve hot.

Makes 1 pizza

Caramelized Onion Tart

This French pizza, known as a *pissaladière*, is a savory specialty from Nice. Traditionally, the topping is caramelized onions, niçoise olives, and anchovies. For this version, we "hold the anchovies." The number of people this serves will depend on whether it is served as an appetizer (8 people) or as a main dish with a salad (4 people).

2 tablespoons olive oil

2 large Vidalia or other sweet onions, thinly sliced

Salt and freshly ground black pepper

1 recipe Enriched Pizza Dough (page 389)

½ cup pitted and halved niçoise olives

1. Heat 1 tablespoon of the olive oil in a large skillet over medium-low heat. Add the onions, cover, and cook until softened, about 5 minutes. Season to taste with salt and pepper, reduce the heat to low, and continue to cook, stirring a few times, until the onions are very soft, golden brown, and caramelized, 30 to 40 minutes. Remove from the heat and allow to cool.

2. Preheat the oven to 400°F. Punch the dough down. On a lightly floured work surface, roll out or stretch the dough into a rectangle about ¼ inch thick. Lightly oil a baking sheet and place the dough on it, stretching it to fit.

3. Drizzle the dough with the remaining 1 tablespoon olive oil. Bake on the bottom oven rack for 8 minutes.

4. Remove from the oven. Spread the onions on top and dot with the olives. Bake on the bottom oven rack until the crust is golden brown, 25 to 30 minutes. Let cool slightly, cut into squares, and serve warm or at room temperature.

Makes 1 tart

Focaccia with Kalamata Olives and Rosemary

Focaccia, a chewy Italian flatbread, is similar to pizza. But whereas pizza is usually oozing with toppings and eaten as a meal, focaccia is eaten with a meal or as a snack. Focaccia toppings tend to be spare, often just a sprinkling of herbs or chopped onion. In this version, I like the way the vibrant and contrasting flavors of the sweet onion, piquant olives, and fragrant rosemary complement one another.

2 tablespoons olive oil

1 small Vidalia or other sweet onion, chopped

2 garlic cloves, minced

2 teaspoons chopped fresh rosemary

½ cup pitted black olives, chopped or sliced

Salt and freshly ground black pepper

1 recipe Traditional Pizza Dough (page 388)

1. Preheat the oven to 400°F.

2. Heat 1 tablespoon of the olive oil in a large skillet over medium heat. Add the onion and garlic, cover, and cook until softened, about 5 minutes. Stir in the rosemary. Remove from the heat, add the olives, and season to taste with salt and pepper. Set aside.

3. Punch the dough down. On a lightly floured work surface, roll out or stretch the dough into a circle or rectangle. Lightly oil a pizza pan or baking sheet and place the dough on it, stretching it to fit. Drizzle with the remaining 1 tablespoon olive oil and press the olive mixture into the top. Bake on the bottom oven rack until the crust is golden brown, about 30 minutes. Serve warm or at room temperature.

Makes 1 focaccia

Mushroom and Shallot Focaccia

Thin slices of cremini mushrooms and shallots are baked right into the top of this crusty flatbread.

6 cremini mushrooms, stems removed and caps thinly sliced

2 shallots, halved lengthwise and thinly sliced

2 tablespoons olive oil

½ teaspoon dried marjoram

Salt and freshly ground black pepper

1 recipe Traditional Pizza Dough (page 388)

1. Preheat the oven to 400°F.

2. Place the sliced mushrooms and shallots in a medium-size bowl. Add the olive oil, marjoram, and salt and pepper to taste. Toss to coat well and set aside.

3. Punch the dough down. On a lightly floured work surface, roll out or stretch the dough into a circle or rectangle. Lightly oil a pizza pan or baking sheet and place the dough on it, stretching it to fit. Press the mushroom mixture into the top, keeping the mushroom slices in a single layer. Bake on the bottom oven rack until the crust is golden brown, about 30 minutes. Serve warm or at room temperature.

=== *Makes 1 focaccia* ===

Thai Pesto Focaccia

Sometimes when I'm eating hot Thai food, I wish for some crusty bread to help put out the fire. With this focaccia, I can enjoy the best of both worlds. Thai basil has a distinctive aromatic taste and fragrance that adds a special flavor to Thai cuisine. If it is unavailable, you can use regular basil, mint, or cilantro. Although the focaccia won't taste the same, it will still be tasty.

2 cups loosely packed fresh Thai basil leaves

2 garlic cloves, crushed

⅓ cup unsalted dry-roasted peanuts

1 or 2 small, fresh hot red chiles, seeded

½ teaspoon salt

¼ cup neutral vegetable oil

1 recipe Enriched Pizza Dough (page 389)

1. Preheat the oven to 400°F.

2. In a food processor, combine the basil, garlic, peanuts, chile, and salt. Process until the mixture forms a paste. With the machine running, add the oil through the feed tube and process until well blended. Set aside.

3. Punch the dough down. On a lightly floured work surface, roll out or stretch the dough into a circle or rectangle. Lightly oil a pizza pan or baking sheet and place the dough on it, stretching it to fit. Bake on the bottom oven rack for 8 minutes.

4. Remove from the oven and top with the pesto, pressing it lightly into the dough. Bake on the bottom oven rack until the crust is golden brown, about 20 minutes longer. Serve warm or at room temperature.

Makes 1 focaccia

Spinach and Tofu Calzones

Calzones are made by folding pizza dough over a savory filling to create large turnovers, which are then sealed and baked. What you stuff inside a calzone is limited only by your imagination. Basically, whatever you would put on top of a pizza, you can put inside a calzone.

1 cup cooked or thawed frozen chopped spinach, squeezed dry

1 cup cooked or canned cannellini beans, drained and mashed

Salt and freshly ground black pepper

1 tablespoon olive oil, plus more for brushing

3 garlic cloves, minced

1 (12- to 16-ounce) package extra-firm tofu, drained and crumbled

1 tablespoon minced fresh basil or 1½ teaspoons dried basil

1 teaspoon minced fresh oregano or ½ teaspoon dried oregano

1 recipe Traditional Pizza Dough (page 388)

1. Preheat the oven to 375°F.

2. In a blender or food processor, combine the spinach, cannellini beans, and salt and pepper to taste. Blend until smooth and set aside.

3. Heat the olive oil in a medium-size skillet over medium heat. Add the garlic and cook until fragrant, about 30 seconds. Add the tofu, basil, oregano, and salt and pepper to taste. Cook, stirring, until any liquid evaporates, about 5 minutes. Remove from the heat and stir in the spinach mixture. Taste and adjust the seasonings, then set aside to cool.

4. Punch the dough down and divide it in half. On a lightly floured work surface, roll out each piece into a 12-inch circle. Divide the filling equally between the dough circles, placing it on only half of each circle and leaving a 1-inch border at the edge. Fold the empty half of the dough circle over the filling and press down along the edges with your fingers, then crimp with a fork to seal.

5. Lightly oil a pizza pan or baking sheet and place the calzones on it. Use a sharp knife to slash them two or three times on top to allow the steam to vent, and brush the tops with a little oil. Bake until the crust is golden brown, about 30 minutes. Let stand at room temperature for 10 minutes before serving.

Serves 4

Spicy Mushroom Stromboli

If a calzone is a pizza turnover, a stromboli is a pizza roll. It's hard to imagine anyone wanting to improve on pizza, but this is one alternative to the familiar flat wedges.

1 tablespoon olive oil, plus more for brushing

1 large onion, sliced

1 small red bell pepper, seeded and sliced

2 garlic cloves, minced

8 ounces white mushrooms, sliced

1 (12- to 16-ounce) package extra-firm tofu, drained and crumbled

1 (14.5-ounce) can diced tomatoes, drained

1 tablespoon minced fresh basil or 1½ teaspoons dried basil

1 teaspoon minced fresh oregano or ½ teaspoon dried oregano

½ teaspoon red pepper flakes

Salt and freshly ground black pepper

1 recipe Traditional Pizza Dough (page 388)

1. Place a baking sheet in the oven and preheat the oven to 400°F.

2. Heat the olive oil in a large skillet over medium heat. Add the onion, cover, and cook until softened, about 5 minutes. Add the bell pepper and garlic, cover, and cook until softened, about 5 minutes. Stir in the mushrooms and cook, stirring a few times, until they release their liquid, about 3 minutes. Stir in the tofu, tomatoes, basil, oregano, red pepper flakes, and salt and pepper to taste. Cook until the liquid is evaporated, about 10 minutes. Remove from the heat and set aside to cool.

3. Punch the dough down. On a lightly floured work surface, roll out into a 9 x 13-inch rectangle. Top with the filling, spreading it to within 1 inch of the edges. Beginning on a long side, roll the stromboli into a log. Seal the dough by pinching it together along the ends and seam. Brush the top with olive oil.

4. Carefully place the roll, seam side down, on the preheated baking sheet. Bake until the crust is golden brown, 30 to 40 minutes. Let stand at room temperature for 10 minutes before cutting crosswise into slices.

Serves 4

Sandwiches, Wraps, & Burgers

Sandwiches have long been the mainstay of the American lunch, and with good reason. They are easy to make, portable, and tasty. But when they are made with animal products, they can also be loaded with fat and high in calories. Fortunately, many of our favorite sandwiches can be made with healthful vegan ingredients, so there's no need to deprive ourselves of that grilled Reuben, spicy po'boy, or juicy burger. We can enjoy these favorites and more when we start with ingredients such as tofu, tempeh, beans, and portobello mushrooms. In addition, natural foods stores and many supermarkets now carry an assortment of meat-free burgers, hot dogs, and cold cuts. Just read the labels carefully to be sure they are vegan. In addition, some brands taste better than others, so experiment to find ones you like.

In my house, we have some favorites that are just as satisfying as the original. We especially like BLTs overflowing with tempeh bacon, crisp lettuce, and juicy tomatoes and slathered with vegan mayonnaise.

Sandwiches are about more than the filling. The bread itself can be just as important as what is inside, and choices abound, from rustic artisan loaves to slender baguettes. Look to a variety of cultures for creative sandwich breads, including boules, tortillas, and pita breads. Add your favorite filling and garnish with the appropriate condiments—and lunch is served.

You Say Hero, I Say Hoagie

What do you call a large sandwich made with an elongated loaf of bread sliced horizontally and stuffed with a variety of fillings? Depending on where you live, the answer will be different. Throughout much of the United States, this popular sandwich is known as a hero. In some places, it is called a grinder. In New York, you would ask for a submarine, but in Philadelphia you would order a hoagie. There are specialized versions such as the Philly cheese steak, the New Orleans po'boy, the New England clam roll, and the Cuban sandwich found in Miami. Whatever you call these substantial sandwiches, they can be made with vegan ingredients. Fillings can range from sliced fresh tomatoes and avocados, to marinated mushrooms and artichokes, to grilled eggplant and onions. Slices of sautéed seitan or tofu that has been seasoned and breaded are also good choices. With a few slices of vegan cold cuts, you can even make a classic cold cut sub complete with olive oil, oregano, and hot pepper spread.

Bánh Mì Sandwiches

This Vietnamese sandwich is my absolute favorite. I love the combination of textures and flavors, from the crisp baguette and creamy, spicy mayo to the flavorful tofu and refreshing vegetables. If you have baked marinated tofu on hand (either homemade or purchased), these sandwiches can be assembled in a flash. Seitan may be substituted for the tofu.

8 ounces baked marinated tofu, homemade (page 8) or purchased

2 tablespoons hoisin sauce

⅓ cup vegan mayonnaise, homemade (page 125) or purchased

1 to 2 teaspoons sriracha

1 to 2 teaspoons fresh lime juice

4 (7-inch) baguettes, split horizontally

1 large carrot, shredded

½ medium-size English cucumber, peeled and cut into thin slices

1 cup fresh cilantro leaves

2 tablespoons sliced pickled jalapeños

1. Cut the tofu horizontally to create thin slabs. Spread each tofu slab with a thin layer of hoisin sauce. Set aside.

2. In a small bowl, combine the mayonnaise, sriracha, and lime juice. Mix well to combine.

3. Spread the mayonnaise mixture on the cut sides of the baguettes.

4. Layer each of the baguettes with the reserved tofu slices, shredded carrot, cucumber slices, cilantro, and jalapeños. Close up the sandwiches and serve immediately.

Serves 4

Tempting Tempeh Sandwiches

If you prefer a finer texture to this spread you can combine all of the ingredients in a food processor and pulse to the desired consistency. In addition to using for sandwiches, the spread is also great spooned into lettuce leaves or celery, or spread on crackers.

¼ cup vegan mayonnaise, homemade (page 125) or purchased

2 teaspoons prepared mustard

2 tablespoons rice vinegar

1 tablespoon low-sodium tamari

½ teaspoon sriracha

8 ounces tempeh, steamed (page 10) and cooled

½ to ¾ cup finely chopped fresh or canned pineapple, blotted dry

2 celery ribs, minced

4 scallions, minced

½ cup unsalted dry-roasted cashews, chopped or crushed

¼ to ½ teaspoon salt

¼ teaspoon freshly ground black pepper

8 slices bread

Lettuce leaves

1. In a mixing bowl, combine the mayo, mustard, vinegar, tamari, and sriracha. Mix until well blended. Finely chop the steamed and cooled tempeh and add it to the bowl. Stir in the pineapple, celery, scallions, and cashews and season with salt and pepper. Mix well. The sandwich filling can be used immediately or covered and refrigerated for later use.

2. To make the sandwiches, spread the tempeh mixture onto your favorite bread, top with lettuce leaves, and serve.

Serves 4

Pulled Portobello BBQ Sandwiches

Shredded portobello mushrooms combine well with a zesty barbecue sauce in these hearty sandwiches. For a variation, instead of mushrooms, try shredded canned jackfruit (packed in water), reconstituted soy curls, seitan, steamed tempeh, or even crushed cooked chickpeas.

½ cup ketchup

½ cup cider vinegar

1 chipotle chile in adobo, minced

2 tablespoons natural sugar

1 tablespoon low-sodium tamari

1 tablespoon prepared yellow mustard

1 tablespoon molasses

¼ teaspoon cayenne

4 large portobello mushroom caps, gills scraped out

1 tablespoon olive oil

1 sweet onion, halved lengthwise, then sliced thinly

Salt and freshly ground black pepper

Sliced rolls, to serve

1. In a saucepan, combine the ketchup, vinegar, chile, sugar, tamari, mustard, molasses, and cayenne. Stir to blend well and heat over medium heat to allow the flavors to meld.

2. Shred the mushrooms using the large holes on a box grater or in a food processer using the shredding disk. Set aside.

3. Heat the oil in a large skillet over medium heat. Add the onion and cook until softened, about 5 minutes. Add the mushrooms and cook until they soften, about 4 minutes. Season to taste with salt and pepper. Stir in as much of the sauce as desired, stirring to mix well. Cook for 5 to 7 minutes to reduce the sauce and blend the flavors. Pile the mushroom mixture onto sandwich rolls. Serve hot.

Serves 4

Pan Bagna

Pan bagna, or "bathed bread," is a layered vegetable sandwich that is popular picnic fare, since it must be prepared in advance and weighted down in order for the bread to soak up the flavors of the other ingredients. Crusty Italian bread is a must, and large round loaves are typically used. Slices of grilled portobello mushrooms, zucchini, or other vegetables can be added, if you like. The cannellini beans are added for substance, although a few thin slices of firm tofu work just as well—layered with the vegetables, the tofu will soak up all of the surrounding flavors.

1 cup cooked or canned cannellini or other white beans, rinsed and drained

¼ cup Basil Pesto (page 142) or purchased vegan pesto

1 loaf crusty Italian bread (preferably round, about 9 inches in diameter)

2 large roasted red bell peppers (page 129), cut into strips

6 marinated artichoke hearts, sliced

1 large ripe tomato, sliced

⅓ cup pitted and chopped black or green olives

¼ cup balsamic vinaigrette, homemade (page 147) or purchased

Salt and freshly ground black pepper

1. In a food processor, process the beans and vegan pesto together until smooth.

2. Using a serrated knife, cut the bread in half horizontally. Remove some of the inside of the loaf to make room for the filling.

3. Spread the pesto-bean mixture inside the bottom half of the loaf and top with layers of the roasted peppers, artichoke hearts, tomato, and olives. Drizzle with the vinaigrette and season to taste with salt and pepper.

4. Replace the top half of the loaf and wrap tightly in plastic. Place on a platter and top with a plate weighted down with some large canned goods or another weight. Refrigerate for at least 4 hours or up to 12 hours.

5. When ready to serve, unwrap the sandwich and cut into 4 wedges.

Serves 4

Chickpea and Avocado Muffaletta

Like *Pan Bagna* (page 412), the classic New Orleans muffaletta is usually made with a loaf of crusty bread. Although it traditionally contains several layers of meat and cheese, I maintain that its popularity is due primarily to the luscious olive salad that is an integral component of the filling. You can, of course, simply replace the meat and cheese with vegan cold cuts or thinly sliced baked tofu or seitan, but this version uses slices of creamy avocado and a tasty chickpea spread to complement the piquant olive mixture. A round loaf is traditional, but a long loaf or even individual sub rolls may be used instead.

1½ cups cooked chickpeas or 1 (15-ounce) can chickpeas, rinsed and drained

½ cup chopped roasted red bell peppers (page 129)

1 cup chopped pimiento-stuffed green olives

1 cup pitted and chopped imported black olives

½ cup seeded and chopped banana peppers, peperoncini, or other mild pickled peppers

2 large garlic cloves, minced

2 tablespoons capers, drained

2 tablespoons chopped fresh parsley

1 teaspoon dried oregano

3 tablespoons olive oil

1½ tablespoons white wine vinegar

Salt and freshly ground black pepper

1 loaf crusty Italian bread (preferably round, about 9 inches in diameter)

2 ripe Hass avocados, peeled, pitted, and sliced

1 large ripe tomato, thinly sliced

1. In a food processor, process the chickpeas and roasted peppers until smooth. Set aside.

2. In a medium-size bowl, combine the olives, banana peppers, garlic, capers, parsley, oregano, olive oil, vinegar, and salt and pepper to taste. Set aside.

3. Using a serrated knife, cut the bread in half horizontally. Remove some of the inside of the loaf to make room for the filling. Spoon some of the liquid from the olive salad onto the cut sides of the bread. Spread the chickpea mixture over the bottom half. Layer the avocado and tomato on top, then spread the olive salad evenly over all. Replace the top half of the loaf. Using a serrated knife, cut the sandwich into 4 wedges and serve.

Serves 4

Fried Green Tomato Po'Boys

Two southern favorites—the po'boy and fried green tomatoes—team up for a tempting sandwich that may just start a new tradition in your home. Po'boys are usually made with fried oysters, but succulent slices of fried green tomatoes make an engaging alternative. The tempeh "bacon bits" add a flavor reminiscent of a BLT.

3 green tomatoes, halved lengthwise and cut into ½-inch-thick slices

Salt and freshly ground black pepper

¾ cup dry bread crumbs

½ teaspoon Old Bay seasoning

2 tablespoons olive oil

2 (6-inch) sub rolls, split horizontally

2 tablespoons vegan mayonnaise, homemade (page 125) or purchased

2 romaine lettuce leaves

½ cup Tempeh "Bacon Bits" (page 11), kept warm

Tabasco sauce

1. Season the tomatoes with salt and pepper to taste. Combine the bread crumbs and Old Bay seasoning in a shallow bowl. Add the tomato slices and toss gently to coat evenly. Set aside.

2. Heat the olive oil in a large skillet over medium-high heat. Add the tomato slices and cook until golden brown on both sides, about 4 minutes per side. Remove from the heat and transfer to paper towels to drain.

3. Spread the vegan mayonnaise on the cut sides of the sub rolls. Line the bottom half of each roll with a lettuce leaf. Sprinkle each with half of the tempeh "bacon bits." Arrange the tomatoes on top, sprinkle with Tabasco, and replace the top half of the roll. Serve with the bottle of Tabasco on the table.

Serves 2

No-Egg Salad Sandwiches

This protein-rich sandwich filling tastes great and is quite similar to egg salad in texture and appearance—with no cholesterol. Here it is served on toasted whole-grain bread, but it's also good stuffed in a roll, pita, or lettuce leaves.

1 (12- to 16-ounce) package firm tofu, drained and crumbled

1 celery rib, minced

2 shallots, minced

1 tablespoon Dijon mustard

1 large dill pickle, minced

Pinch of turmeric

½ cup vegan mayonnaise, homemade (page 125) or purchased

Salt and freshly ground black pepper

8 slices whole-grain or other bread

4 lettuce leaves

1 large ripe tomato, thinly sliced

1. Place the tofu in a large bowl. Add the celery, shallots, mustard, pickle, turmeric, 6 tablespoons of the vegan mayonnaise, and salt and pepper to taste. Mix well. Cover and refrigerate for at least 1 hour to blend the flavors.

2. To assemble the sandwiches, toast the bread and place on a work surface. Spread a small amount of the remaining 2 tablespoons vegan mayonnaise on one side of the toast slices. Top 4 of the toast slices with a lettuce leaf and one or two tomato slices. Spoon a portion of the salad mixture onto each sandwich. Top the sandwiches with the remaining toast slices, cut in half, and serve.

Serves 4

Curried Tempeh Salad Sandwiches

If you like the flavor of curry in a salad sandwich, look no further. This tasty blend of tempeh seasoned with a curry mayonnaise dressing features the sweetness of golden raisins and the crunch of slivered almonds. I usually serve this salad stuffed into pita pockets, but you can use the bread or roll of your choice.

8 ounces tempeh, steamed (page 10) and cooled

1 celery rib, minced

2 scallions, minced

2 tablespoons minced red bell pepper

¼ cup golden raisins

2 tablespoons slivered almonds

1 tablespoon minced fresh parsley

½ to ¾ cup vegan mayonnaise, homemade (page 125) or purchased

1 tablespoon sweet pickle relish

2 teaspoons curry powder

1 teaspoon fresh lemon juice

½ teaspoon natural sugar

Salt and freshly ground black pepper

Shredded romaine lettuce

2 large or 4 small pita breads, cut in half

1. Grate or finely chop the tempeh and place in a large bowl. Add the celery, scallions, bell pepper, raisins, almonds, and parsley. Stir in the vegan mayonnaise, relish, curry powder, lemon juice, sugar, and salt and pepper to taste. Mix until thoroughly combined. Cover and refrigerate for at least 30 minutes to allow the flavors to blend.

2. To assemble, stuff a small amount of shredded lettuce into each pita half. Spoon the tempeh mixture into each half, dividing it evenly among the halves. Tuck a little more lettuce into each sandwich, if desired, and serve.

Serves 4

Tuna-Free Sandwiches

I'm always tinkering with ways to make a delicious tuna-free sandwich. This is my current favorite, which features a hearty blend of chickpeas with just a bit of kelp powder for a taste of the sea. Serve on your choice of bread, including rolls or pita pockets. Kelp powder is available at natural foods stores.

1½ cups cooked chickpeas or 1 (15-ounce) can chickpeas, rinsed and drained

½ cup blanched almonds

1 tablespoon fresh lemon juice

1 teaspoon kelp powder

⅓ cup minced celery

1 scallion, minced

¼ cup vegan mayonnaise, homemade (page 125) or purchased, or more as needed

1½ teaspoons Dijon mustard

Salt and freshly ground black pepper

Sliced bread, rolls, or pita loaves, to serve

In a food processor, pulse the chickpeas and almonds until coarsely chopped. Add the lemon juice and kelp powder. Blend until well combined. Transfer to a large bowl and add the celery, scallion, vegan mayonnaise, mustard, and salt and pepper to taste. Mix well, adding a little more mayonnaise if the mixture seems dry. Cover and refrigerate for at least 30 minutes before serving. To serve, spread the mixture onto the bread of choice.

Serves 2

Seitan Reubens

Thinly sliced seitan replaces the corned beef in this vegan version of the Reuben sandwich. Serve with vegan coleslaw, potato chips, and a dill pickle for a great deli-style lunch.

2 tablespoons vegan mayonnaise, homemade (page 125) or purchased

1 tablespoon ketchup

1 tablespoon sweet pickle relish

Salt and freshly ground black pepper

2 tablespoons olive oil

4 slices rye bread

6 ounces seitan, thinly sliced

½ cup sauerkraut, well drained

2 slices vegan cheese or ¼ cup Cheesy Sauce (page 128)

1. In a small bowl, combine the vegan mayonnaise, ketchup, and relish. Season to taste with salt and pepper, blend well, and set aside.

2. Brush a small amount of the olive oil on one side of each slice of bread. Place the bread, oiled sides down, on a flat surface and spread the mayonnaise mixture on the other side of each slice.

3. Layer the seitan, sauerkraut, and vegan cheese on 2 of the bread slices and top with the remaining 2 bread slices, oiled sides up.

4. Heat the remaining olive oil in a large skillet over medium heat. Place the sandwiches in the skillet and cook, turning once, until golden brown on both sides, about 2 minutes per side. Remove from the skillet, cut in half, and serve hot.

Serves 2

Three-Bean Burritos

Using three kinds of beans gives these burritos a more complex flavor and texture than if you used only one type. The filling is also quite good for tacos or similar dishes. The recipe can be easily stretched by adding more beans. You can also add a cup of cooked corn kernels to give it a deliciously sweet accent.

1 (15-ounce) can vegetarian refried pinto beans

1 cup cooked or canned black beans, rinsed and drained

1 cup cooked or canned dark red kidney beans, rinsed and drained

½ cup Fresh Tomato Salsa (page 157) or purchased salsa

1 teaspoon chili powder

Salt and freshly ground black pepper

4 large flour tortillas, warmed

½ cup Cheesy Sauce (page 128) or shredded vegan cheese

Minced red onion (optional)

1. In a large saucepan over medium heat, combine the refried beans, black beans, and kidney beans. Stir in the salsa, chili powder, and salt and pepper to taste. Cook, stirring, until the beans are hot, 7 to 10 minutes. Reduce the heat to low and keep warm.

2. Place the warmed tortillas on a flat work surface and spread a large spoonful of the bean mixture across the lower third of each tortilla. Sprinkle with the cheesy sauce and onion (if using). Fold up the burrito by bringing the bottom end over the filling, folding in the sides, and then rolling it up. Serve at once, seam side down.

Serves 4

Easy Jackfruit Tacos

There are many ways to make great vegan tacos, and one of my favorite ways is with shredded canned jackfruit. For this recipe you will need to buy canned jackfruit packed in water or brine—*not* packed in syrup. Canned jackfruit is available in Asian markets or online. If it is unavailable, you can substitute chopped seitan, steamed tempeh, or portobello mushrooms in this recipe. Or you can use reconstituted soy curls or TVP. Serve in crisp taco shells or warmed soft tortillas, according to personal preference, and remember to read the labels carefully to be sure that the products do not contain lard.

FILLING

1 (20-ounce) can young green jackfruit packed in water or brine, rinsed and drained

1½ tablespoons chili powder

1 teaspoon ground cumin

1 teaspoon dried oregano

½ teaspoon smoked paprika

¼ teaspoon cayenne

1 tablespoon olive oil

1 medium-size onion, finely chopped

3 garlic cloves, minced

2 cups Fresh Tomato Salsa (page 157) or purchased salsa

Salt and freshly ground black pepper

8 taco shells or tortillas

TOPPINGS

Shredded romaine lettuce

Chopped ripe tomatoes

Fresh Tomato Salsa (page 157) or purchased salsa

Cheesy Sauce (page 128) or shredded vegan cheddar cheese

Vegan sour cream, homemade (page 126) or purchased

Chopped red onion or scallions

Seeded and chopped fresh or canned jalapeños

Pitted and sliced black olives

Chopped avocado

Lime wedges

1. Press the moisture from the rinsed and drained jackfruit, then shred or chop it and transfer to a bowl. Add the chili powder, cumin, oregano, paprika, and cayenne, tossing to coat the jackfruit with the spices, or use your hands to rub the spices into the jackfruit. Set aside.

2. Heat the olive oil in a large skillet over medium heat. Add the onion and garlic and cook until softened, about 5 minutes. Add the jackfruit and any remaining seasonings from the bowl. Cook, stirring, until the jackfruit browns slightly. Stir in the salsa and season to taste with salt and pepper. Simmer, stirring occasionally, until the flavors are well infused into the jackfruit, 20 to 30 minutes. Keep warm.

3. Preheat the oven to 375°F. Wrap the taco shells or tortillas in aluminum foil and place in the oven to warm, 2 to 4 minutes.

4. To assemble the tacos, spoon about ¼ cup of the filling into each taco shell or tortilla. Top as desired with any combination of toppings. Serve immediately.

Serves 4

"Wrap" Stars

The popularity of Mexican food has brought tacos, burritos, fajitas, and many other "wrap" stars into our home kitchens. Virtually every cuisine has its own wrap foods, some of which are served sauced and eaten with a knife and fork, such as the French crêpe, while others are eaten out of hand and served with a dipping sauce, like Asian spring rolls. There is also the popular Japanese sushi wrap, a rice and seaweed roll known as a *maki*. Wrap sandwiches can be made with tortillas, lavash, pita pockets, or other flatbreads and a wide variety of fillings, including grilled or marinated vegetables. Many different versions of a veggie wrap can be found on the menus of cafés and restaurants and even in bakeries and fast-food shops.

Portobello Fajitas

Flavorful and juicy strips of portobello mushrooms are used to make these delicious fajitas.

1 tablespoon olive oil or ¼ cup water

1 large red onion, thinly sliced

1 large red or yellow bell pepper, seeded and thinly sliced

4 large portobello mushroom caps, gills scraped out, cut into strips

2 teaspoons chili powder

½ teaspoon salt

¼ teaspoon cayenne (optional)

4 large flour tortillas, warmed

Fresh Tomato Salsa (page 157) or purchased salsa

1. Heat the olive oil or water in a large skillet over medium-high heat. Add the onion and bell pepper and cook until softened, about 5 minutes. Add the mushrooms and cook, stirring a few times, until tender, about 3 minutes. Add the chili powder, salt, and cayenne (if using) and cook for 3 to 5 minutes, stirring to coat the vegetables with the spices. Reduce the heat to low and keep warm.

2. Place the tortillas on a flat work surface and spread a large spoonful of the mushroom mixture across the lower third of each tortilla. Top each portion of filling with salsa. Roll up the fajitas to enclose the filling and serve at once.

Serves 4

Soy Meets Grill Tortilla Wraps with Green Apple Salsa

Fruity, spicy, and oh soy good! Spice-rubbed slabs of grilled tempeh and bell pepper are cut into strips and wrapped inside a soft flour tortilla along with a generous helping of sweet-hot salsa.

1 teaspoon sweet paprika

1 teaspoon dried thyme or oregano

¾ teaspoon salt

½ teaspoon natural sugar

¼ teaspoon ground allspice

¼ teaspoon cayenne

⅛ teaspoon freshly grated nutmeg

8 ounces tempeh, steamed (page 10) and cut into 4 slabs

Olive oil

1 large red bell pepper, halved and seeded

4 large flour tortillas, warmed

1 cup Green Apple Salsa (page 156)

1. Preheat the grill. In a small bowl, combine the spices. Coat the steamed tempeh with olive oil and rub with the spice mixture. Place on the hot grill. Lightly oil the bell pepper halves and place, cut sides up, on the grill. Grill until the tempeh is well browned on both sides and the bell peppers are blackened and tender, turning once, about 10 minutes total. When the peppers are cool enough to handle, scrape the black bits from the skin. Then cut the peppers and tempeh into thin strips.

2. Place the tortillas on a flat work surface and divide the tempeh and pepper strips among them, placing the strips across the lower third of each tortilla. Spoon some of the salsa alongside the strips, roll up, and serve at once.

Serves 4

Grilled Vegetable Wraps

Grilled vegetables are great just about any way they are served, and wrap sandwiches are no exception. Lavash, a thin Middle Eastern flatbread found in ethnic markets or bakeries, is best for these sandwiches, but large tortillas may be used as well. The flatbread should be at room temperature for easier rolling. Instead of the vegan mayonnaise, you can use hummus or another bean spread for added flavor and nutrition, if you like. A grill basket or perforated metal grill pan will help keep the zucchini and other smaller pieces of vegetables from falling through the rack. If unavailable, you can skewer the vegetables before grilling.

1 large red onion, cut into ¼-inch-thick slices

1 large red bell pepper, halved and seeded

1 large portobello mushroom cap, gills scraped out

1 medium-size zucchini, cut diagonally into ¼-inch-thick slices

2 tablespoons olive oil

Salt and freshly ground black pepper

2 large lavash or flour tortillas

2 tablespoons vegan mayonnaise, homemade (page 125) or purchased

1. Preheat the grill. Brush the onion, bell pepper, mushroom, and zucchini with the olive oil and season to taste with salt and pepper. Grill the vegetables until tender on the inside and slightly charred on the outside, turning once. Cut the grilled vegetables into ½-inch-wide strips.

2. Place the lavash on a flat surface. Spread a thin layer of vegan mayonnaise over the surface and place the vegetable strips along the lower third of each flatbread. Beginning at the end with the filling, roll up into a cylinder. Cut each sandwich in half and serve seam side down.

Serves 2 to 4

Indian-Spiced Lentil Patties with Three-Fruit Chutney

Inspired by the flavors of India, these sandwiches are best made with roti or other Indian flatbread as the wrapper. If unavailable, use pita bread. A leftover baked potato is ideal for this recipe. Otherwise, peel, chop, and sauté a medium-size potato until tender. (Cooking in water will add too much moisture to the recipe.)

3 tablespoons olive oil

½ cup minced onion

1 cup cooked or canned brown lentils, rinsed and drained

1 cup chopped cooked potato (see headnote)

½ cup finely chopped unsalted dry-roasted cashews

⅔ cup dry bread crumbs

1 tablespoon minced fresh parsley

1 teaspoon curry powder, or more to taste

½ teaspoon salt

⅛ teaspoon cayenne (optional)

4 roti or other Indian flatbread, warmed

Three-Fruit Chutney (page 151) or other chutney

1. Heat 1 tablespoon of the olive oil in a large skillet over medium heat. Add the onion, cover, and cook until softened, about 5 minutes. Transfer to a food processor and add the lentils, potato, cashews, bread crumbs, parsley, curry powder, salt, and cayenne (if using). Process until well blended.

2. Shape the mixture into 8 small patties. Heat the remaining 2 tablespoons olive oil in a large skillet over medium heat. Add the patties and cook until browned on both sides, about 5 minutes per side.

3. Place 2 patties end to end on the lower third of each flatbread, spread with chutney, roll up, and serve hot.

Serves 4

Thai Peanut-Burger Wraps

This is a great way to enjoy fusion food: combine fragrant Thai ingredients to make an all-American burger, then surround it with a Middle Eastern or Mexican flatbread. The addition of peanut dipping sauce may seem a bit over the top for these already peanutty burgers, but the result is delicious. If you're using large flatbreads, allow half a sandwich per person. Otherwise, allow one sandwich per person.

½ cup chopped red onion

½ cup chopped green bell pepper

2 garlic cloves, minced

2 teaspoons minced fresh ginger

½ cup ground unsalted dry-roasted peanuts

8 ounces extra-firm tofu, drained, pressed (page 7), and mashed

3 tablespoons peanut butter

2 tablespoons chopped fresh Thai basil or cilantro

2 tablespoons low-sodium tamari

½ teaspoon Asian chili paste

Salt

½ cup dry bread crumbs

2 large or 4 small lavash, soft flour tortillas, or pita breads

Shredded romaine lettuce

½ cup Spicy Peanut Dipping Sauce (page 145)

1. Preheat the oven to 350°F. Lightly oil a baking sheet and set aside.

2. In a food processor, combine the onion, bell pepper, garlic, ginger, and peanuts. Pulse to blend, leaving some texture. Add the tofu, peanut butter, Thai basil, tamari, chili paste, and salt to taste and pulse until the mixture is well combined.

3. Shape the mixture into 4 large or 8 small patties and coat evenly with the bread crumbs. Arrange the burgers on the prepared baking sheet and bake, turning once, until browned on both sides, 25 to 30 minutes total.

4. To assemble, cut the burgers into halves or thirds, if necessary, so that they roll up easily. Place them end to end on the lower third of the flatbreads. Top with the lettuce, drizzle with the peanut sauce, and roll up. Cut in half crosswise if using large breads and place, seam side down, on 4 individual plates. Serve immediately.

===== *Serves 4* =====

Great Grain and Vegetable Burgers

Two grains and five vegetables add up to healthful veggie burgers that are loaded with flavor. Be sure the vegetables and grains are dry when combining them so no extra liquid gets into the mixture. Wheat gluten flour, also called vital wheat gluten or powdered wheat gluten, helps hold the burgers together. It is available in natural foods stores. Serve these burgers on rolls, tucked into pitas, or on a plate topped with your favorite sauce.

1 cup cooked brown rice

½ cup cooked medium-grind bulgur (page 198)

1 cup grated zucchini, squeezed dry

¼ cup grated onion, squeezed dry

¼ cup finely grated carrot

1 garlic clove, minced

½ cup vital wheat gluten

¼ cup chopped roasted red bell pepper (page 129)

2 tablespoons minced fresh parsley

Salt and freshly ground black pepper

2 tablespoons olive oil

1. Place the rice, bulgur, zucchini, onion, carrot, and garlic in a food processor and pulse to combine. Add the vital wheat gluten, roasted pepper, parsley, and salt and pepper to taste and process until well combined. Shape the mixture into four patties.

2. Heat the olive oil in a large skillet over medium-high heat. Cook the patties until golden brown on both sides, 5 to 8 minutes total. (Alternatively, place the patties on a lightly oiled baking sheet and bake at 350°F until browned on both sides, turning once, 20 to 30 minutes total.) Serve hot.

Serves 4

Three-Nut Burgers

The rich flavors of lentils, walnuts, and cashews combine to make these hearty veggie burgers, which are bound with creamy almond butter. Instead of serving them on burger rolls, you can serve them as an entrée topped with Basic Brown Sauce (page 134).

3 tablespoons olive oil

½ cup minced onion

1 cup cooked or canned brown lentils, rinsed and drained

1 cup chopped walnuts

⅔ cup dry bread crumbs

½ cup chopped unsalted dry-roasted cashews

2 tablespoons almond butter

1 tablespoon minced fresh parsley

½ teaspoon salt

⅛ teaspoon freshly ground black pepper

1. Heat 1 tablespoon of the olive oil in a large skillet over medium heat. Add the onion and cook until softened, about 5 minutes. Transfer to a food processor and add the remaining ingredients except the remaining olive oil. Process until well blended. If the mixture is too wet, add some vital wheat gluten or old-fashioned rolled oats, a tablespoon or two at a time, to reach the desired consistency.

2. Shape the mixture into 6 patties. Heat the remaining 2 tablespoons olive oil in a large skillet over medium heat and cook the burgers until well browned on both sides, about 5 minutes per side. (Alternatively, place the patties on a lightly oiled baking sheet and bake at 350°F until browned on both sides, turning once, 20 to 30 minutes total.) Serve hot.

Serves 6

Go Nuts!

Nuts add protein and "good" fat to your diet. Here are some other great ways to "go nuts."

- Sprinkle chopped nuts on your cereal at breakfast.

- Spread nut butter on toast or use in sandwiches.

- Enjoy nuts and raisins as a snack at work, at school, or on the road.

- Add nuts to salads, stir-fries, and grain and vegetable dishes.

- Include nuts in muffins, tea breads, and desserts.

- Slather nut butter on celery sticks, apple slices, or bananas.

The Ultimate Veggie Burgers

Most homemade veggie burgers lack the firm texture found in some of the purchased varieties. Flaxseeds and wheat gluten are used here to remedy that situation, resulting in protein-packed burgers. Serve these burgers on toasted rolls with lettuce, sliced tomato, and your favorite condiments.

1 tablespoon ground flaxseeds

2 tablespoons low-sodium tamari

½ cup walnut pieces

¾ cup cooked or canned brown lentils, rinsed and drained

½ cup vital wheat gluten

¼ cup grated onion

1 tablespoon minced fresh parsley

½ teaspoon browning sauce (see Note; optional)

½ teaspoon smoked paprika

½ teaspoon salt

¼ teaspoon freshly ground black pepper

2 tablespoons olive oil

1. In a blender, combine the flaxseeds and tamari, blending until viscous. Set aside.

2. In a food processor, pulse the walnuts to coarsely chop. Add the lentils, vital wheat gluten, onion, parsley, browning sauce (if using), flax mixture, paprika, salt, and pepper. Process until well combined but with some texture remaining. Shape the mixture into 4 patties and place on a platter. Refrigerate for 30 minutes.

3. Heat the olive oil in a large skillet over medium heat, add the patties, and cook until browned on both sides, about 4 minutes per side. Serve hot.

Serves 4

NOTE: Carefully read the label before buying a browning sauce (located with the gravies and sauces in the supermarket) to be sure it does not contain meat extract. One popular brand, Gravy Master, states "contains no meat" on its label, and the ingredients are clearly identifiable.

Stuffed Mushroom Burgers

For anyone who ever enjoyed sautéed mushrooms on a burger, this is the ultimate combination—a sautéed portobello mushroom cap "stuffed" with a veggie burger. Serve on toasted rolls with ketchup and onions, if you like. Purchase flavorful veggie burgers, such as Original Vegan Boca Burgers, or use one of the burger recipes in this chapter. The mushrooms and burgers also may be cooked on a grill.

2 tablespoons olive oil

4 large portobello mushroom caps, gills scraped out

Salt and freshly ground black pepper

4 vegan burgers, homemade (pages 426–429) or purchased

4 burger rolls, lightly toasted

1. Heat 1 tablespoon of the olive oil in a large skillet over medium heat. Add the mushrooms and cook until they begin to soften, about 5 minutes. Flip the mushrooms over, season to taste with salt and pepper, and cook until browned and tender, about 5 minutes more. Keep warm over very low heat.

2. While the mushrooms are cooking, heat the remaining 1 tablespoon olive oil in another large skillet over medium heat. Add the burgers and cook, turning once, until browned on both sides and hot inside, 8 to 10 minutes total.

3. To serve, place a burger inside each mushroom cap and place on the rolls. Serve hot.

Serves 4

Vegan Road Food

The thought of a vacation may conjure up images of four-star hotels, family visits, or fun day trips, but for a vegan, it often also includes the question "What am I going to eat?"

Although many urban restaurants now offer more choices in vegan fare, roadside restaurants generally do not. To get through any road trip, whether it be for a few hours or several days, it's best to plan ahead and pack a cooler.

One of my favorite road foods is hummus, a protein- and calcium-rich spread made with chickpeas and tahini that can be enjoyed with raw veggies, crackers, or as a pita sandwich filling. Other options include pasta or grain salads, marinated baked tofu, or even vegetable sushi. Kids always enjoy peanut butter and jelly sandwiches. Bring along a good supply of cut vegetables, fresh and dried fruits, trail mix, nuts, raisins, or energy bars. Eat the most perishable foods first, saving the nonperishables for later in the journey. On the return trip, look for a natural foods store or a well-stocked supermarket to replenish your supplies. For a quick lunch, there's usually a supermarket salad bar or a Taco Bell, where you can get a bean burrito (no cheese).

When seeking out a restaurant in an unfamiliar town, ethnic restaurants generally offer the best choices. Chinese, Thai, Indian, Italian, and Mexican menus usually include vegan alternatives. Many restaurants are willing to accommodate a vegan and will prepare a special meal upon request. If you don't see it, ask for it. If you're staying in a hotel, the concierge can help. You can also check online using resources such as HappyCow.net or travel sites such as TripAdvisor.com, where you can search vegetarian restaurant offerings in any location.

When traveling by air, I've been served everything from a lovely vegetable curry over rice pilaf to a wilted and gummy (canned) fruit plate. Since airline meal service varies greatly (most have no meal service in coach at all), it's best to call ahead. If there is meal service, ask for menu details and confirm your meal the day before and again just prior to boarding. If no meal service is provided, there are sometimes vegan choices available for purchase before boarding. As for a carry-on food stash, check with the airline to see what you can and cannot bring onboard. You wouldn't want your PBJ sandwich to be confiscated.

SEVENTEEN

Breads, Muffins, & Biscuits

Over the centuries to the present time, people throughout the world have relied on traditional breads for basic sustenance, baking them with their same time-tested methods, be it on an open fire or in a clay oven. These days in American supermarkets, you can find rustic, freshly baked artisan breads as a pricey luxury item.

Although a loaf of bakery bread can taste great, nothing beats the aroma, flavor, and satisfaction of home-baked bread. In addition, there are no additives in homemade bread—just natural ingredients and lots of love. Being in control of the ingredients is especially important to vegans, since commercial breads may contain eggs, dairy products, or honey.

Although hand-kneading can be relaxing, machines are often used to speed up the process, whether it be an electric mixer equipped with a dough hook or a bread machine that does all of the work from kneading to baking. As for me, I prefer to work the dough with my hands the old-fashioned way.

At its most basic, this "staff of life" is little more than a blending of flour and water that has been put to heat. But variety abounds within the two main divisions, yeast breads and quick breads. Loaves can be sweet or savory and include flatbreads, skillet breads, muffins, and biscuits. Among the most nutritious breads are hearty multigrain loaves, some of which include whole or cracked grains, nuts, and seeds. This chapter consists of a baker's dozen of samplings from the wide range of the world's breads.

Whole-Grain Herb Bread

This wholesome bread is delicious served with meals or used for sandwiches. The herbs may be varied according to personal preference. I like the look of freeform round or long loaves, but you can use traditional 5 x 9-inch loaf pans, if you prefer.

2¼ teaspoons (1 packet) active dry yeast

2¼ cups warm water

1 tablespoon pure maple syrup

2 tablespoons olive oil

1 tablespoon salt

4½ cups unbleached all-purpose flour or white whole-wheat flour

2 cups whole-wheat flour, plus more for kneading

2 tablespoons minced fresh parsley

1 teaspoon minced fresh chives

1 teaspoon dried marjoram

½ teaspoon dried thyme

1. In a large bowl, combine the yeast and ¼ cup of the water. Add the maple syrup and stir to dissolve. Let the mixture stand for 10 minutes, then stir in the remaining 2 cups water, the olive oil, and the salt.

2. In a separate large bowl, combine the flours and stir until well mixed. Add about half of the flour mixture to the liquid mixture, stirring to blend, then work in the remaining flour mixture to form a stiff dough. Sprinkle with the herbs, then transfer the dough to a lightly floured board.

3. With lightly floured hands, knead briefly to incorporate the herbs into the dough. Dust your work surface with whole-wheat flour as needed to prevent the dough from sticking and continue to knead well until smooth and elastic, 8 to 10 minutes.

4. Place in a lightly oiled large bowl and turn over once to coat with oil. Cover with a clean kitchen towel or a piece of lightly oiled plastic wrap. Let rise in a warm place until doubled in bulk, 1 to 2 hours.

5. Lightly oil two small baking sheets. Punch the dough down and turn out onto a lightly floured work surface. Divide the dough in half, shape into 2 round or long loaves, and place on the prepared baking sheets. Flatten the loaves slightly and cover with clean damp towels or lightly oiled plastic wrap. Set aside in a warm place and let rise again until doubled in bulk, about 1 hour.

6. Meanwhile, preheat the oven to 425°F. Use a sharp knife to cut one to three ¼-inch-deep diagonal slashes in each loaf. Bake on the center oven rack for 10 minutes, then reduce the oven temperature to 350°F and continue to bake until golden brown, about 30 minutes more. Tap the bottom of the loaves—if they sound hollow, the bread is done. Remove from the sheets and let cool on a wire rack before slicing.

Makes 2 loaves

Yeast Bread Types, Tips, and Techniques

Yeast breads can be made with unbleached all-purpose flour as well as whole-grain flours, such as whole wheat, to which other ingredients may be added, including other flours, vegetables, herbs, fruits, nuts, and seeds. Sourdough is a yeast bread that gets its name and distinctive flavor from a special yeast starter. Yeasted flatbreads include pita, focaccia, and pizza. Breakfast breads made with yeast include croissants, brioche, and cinnamon rolls, as well as skillet breads such as crumpets and English muffins.

- *Kneading and rising:* Yeast breads must be kneaded to activate the gluten-producing proteins in the flour. In addition, the dough needs time to rise. To knead dough, push the dough down and away from you with the palms of your hands, then turn it, fold it over, and push it down again. Kneading should be done for several minutes to activate the proteins. Well-kneaded dough should be smooth and elastic. After kneading, cover the dough and set it aside to rise in a warm place until doubled in bulk.

- *Baking:* For even baking, place the loaf in the center of the oven. The bread is done when the top is browned and the sides pull away from the pan and when a light tapping on the bottom produces a hollow sound.

- *Cooling and storing:* Bread should be removed from the pan as soon as it comes out of the oven and cooled on a wire rack. Cool the bread before slicing with a serrated knife, using a sawing motion. Cool the bread completely before storing to prevent condensation. Tightly wrapped bread will keep for several days at room temperature or for up to 3 months in the freezer (tightly wrap in plastic and aluminum foil).

Rustic Peasant Loaf
with Black Olives and Sun-Dried Tomatoes

Typical of the artisan breads popular in bakeries and gourmet markets, this rustic loaf is studded with bits of piquant olives and sun-dried tomatoes.

2¼ teaspoons (1 packet) active dry yeast

2 cups warm water

1 tablespoon natural sugar

3 tablespoons olive oil

1 tablespoon salt

5 cups unbleached all-purpose flour, plus more for kneading

1 cup whole-wheat flour

½ cup oil-packed or rehydrated sun-dried tomatoes, chopped

½ cup black olives, pitted and chopped

1. In a large bowl, combine the yeast and ¼ cup of the water. Add the sugar and stir to dissolve. Let the mixture stand for 10 minutes, then stir in the remaining 1¾ cups water, the olive oil, and the salt.

2. In a separate large bowl, combine the flours and stir until well mixed. Add about half of the flour to the liquid mixture, stirring to combine, then work in the remaining flour to form a stiff dough. Transfer to a lightly floured board.

3. Place the sun-dried tomatoes and olives on the dough and, using your hands, knead briefly to incorporate them. Continue to knead until smooth and elastic, 8 to 10 minutes. As you knead, keep your hands and work surface lightly floured so that the dough does not stick.

4. Place in a lightly oiled large bowl and turn over once to coat with oil. Cover with a clean kitchen towel or a piece of lightly oiled plastic wrap. Let rise in a warm place until doubled in bulk, 1 to 2 hours.

5. Lightly oil two small baking sheets. Punch the dough down and turn out onto a lightly floured work surface. Divide the dough in half, shape into 2 round or long loaves, and place on the prepared baking sheets. Flatten the loaves slightly and cover with clean damp towels or lightly oiled plastic wrap. Set aside in a warm place and let rise again until doubled in bulk, about 1 hour.

6. Meanwhile, preheat the oven to 375°F. Use a sharp knife to cut one to three ¼-inch-deep diagonal slashes in each loaf. Bake on the center oven rack until golden brown, 40 to 45 minutes. Tap the bottom of the loaves—if they sound hollow, the bread is done. Remove from the sheets and let cool on a wire rack before slicing.

Makes 2 loaves

Potato Bread with Chives

The addition of mashed potatoes gives this bread a moist, dense texture and delicate flavor that is accented by that of the chives. This bread is best eaten slightly warm from the oven on the day it is made. It is also good toasted.

2¼ teaspoons (1 packet) active dry yeast

1 cup warm water

1 teaspoon natural sugar or pure maple syrup

2 tablespoons neutral vegetable oil

2 teaspoons salt

1 cup cold mashed potatoes

1 cup plain unsweetened nondairy milk

5 cups unbleached all-purpose flour, plus more for kneading

¼ cup minced fresh chives

1. In a large bowl, combine the yeast and ¼ cup of the water. Add the sugar and stir to dissolve. Let the mixture stand for 10 minutes, then stir in the remaining ¾ cup water, the oil, and the salt. Mix in the potatoes, then stir in the nondairy milk. Add about half of the flour, stirring to combine, then work in the remaining flour to form a stiff dough. Transfer to a lightly floured board.

2. Lightly flour your hands and work surface. Knead the dough well until it is smooth and elastic, 8 to 10 minutes, using more flour as necessary so the dough does not stick. Place in a lightly oiled large bowl and turn over once to coat with oil. Cover with a clean kitchen towel or a piece of lightly oiled plastic wrap. Let rise in a warm place until doubled in bulk, 1 to 2 hours.

3. Lightly oil a large baking sheet or two 5 x 9-inch loaf pans. Punch the dough down and knead lightly. Turn out onto a lightly floured work surface, sprinkle with the chives, and knead until the dough is elastic and the chives are well distributed, 3 to 5 minutes. Shape the dough into 2 loaves and place on the prepared baking sheet or into the loaf pans. Cover the loaves with a clean damp towel or lightly oiled plastic wrap. Set aside in a warm place and let rise again until doubled in bulk, about 45 minutes.

4. Meanwhile, preheat the oven to 400°F. Use a sharp knife to cut an X into the top of the loaves. Bake on the center oven rack until golden brown, 35 to 40 minutes. Tap on the bottom of the loaves—if they sound hollow, the bread is done. Remove from the sheet and let cool briefly on a wire rack before slicing.

Makes 2 loaves

Banana-Split Tea Bread

This flavorful banana bread incorporates several banana-split ingredients for a surprising treat that sets it apart from ordinary tea breads. Vegan chocolate chips are available at natural foods stores.

2½ cups unbleached all-purpose flour

2 teaspoons baking powder

½ teaspoon salt

3 medium-size very ripe bananas, peeled and cut into chunks

¾ cup plain unsweetened nondairy milk

¾ cup natural sugar

1½ teaspoons pure vanilla extract

⅓ cup vegan semisweet chocolate chips

¼ cup chopped unsalted dry-roasted peanuts or other nuts

¼ cup drained crushed pineapple, blotted dry

¼ cup dried cherries

1. Preheat the oven to 375°F. Lightly oil a 5 x 9-inch loaf pan and set aside.

2. In a large bowl, combine the flour, baking powder, and salt and set aside.

3. In a food processor, combine the bananas, nondairy milk, sugar, and vanilla and process until smooth. Add to the flour mixture and mix well. Fold in the chocolate chips, nuts, pineapple, and cherries, then transfer to the prepared pan.

4. Bake on the center oven rack until a toothpick inserted in the center comes out clean, 50 to 60 minutes. Allow to cool in the pan on a wire rack before removing from the pan and slicing.

===================================== *Makes 1 loaf* =====================================

Three-Seed Lemon Tea Bread

A fresh lemon taste is the backdrop for this protein-packed tea bread loaded with three kinds of nutritious seeds. The light, not-too-sweet flavor makes it a terrific breakfast bread.

2 tablespoons flaxseeds	2 cups unbleached all-purpose flour
⅓ cup water	2 teaspoons baking powder
½ cup natural sugar	1 teaspoon salt
1 cup plain unsweetened nondairy milk	½ cup chopped hulled raw sunflower seeds
2 tablespoons neutral vegetable oil	¼ cup sesame seeds
Juice and grated zest of 1 lemon	

1. Preheat the oven to 350°F. Lightly oil a 5 x 9-inch loaf pan and set aside.

2. Grind the flaxseeds to a powder in a dry blender. Add the water and blend until thick, about 30 seconds.

3. In a large bowl, combine the sugar, nondairy milk, oil, and lemon juice and zest. Blend in the flaxseed mixture and set aside.

4. In a medium-size bowl, sift together the flour, baking powder, and salt. Using a few swift strokes, add the dry ingredients to the wet ingredients until just combined. Fold in the sunflower seeds and sesame seeds, then transfer to the prepared pan.

5. Bake on the center oven rack until golden brown and a toothpick inserted in the center comes out clean, about 1 hour. Let cool in the pan on a wire rack before removing from the pan and slicing.

Makes 1 loaf

Zucchini-Tahini Bread

Creamy sesame paste lends a delicious flavor to this zucchini bread, while also adding protein and calcium.

3 cups unbleached all-purpose flour or white whole-wheat flour

1 teaspoon baking powder

1 teaspoon baking soda

1 teaspoon ground cinnamon

1 teaspoon ground ginger

1 teaspoon salt

1 cup natural sugar

¼ cup tahini

1 cup plain unsweetened nondairy milk

2 cups grated zucchini, drained and squeezed dry

2 teaspoons pure vanilla extract

1 teaspoon lemon juice

2 tablespoons sesame seeds

1. Preheat the oven to 350°F. Lightly oil a 5 x 9-inch loaf pan and set aside.

2. In a large bowl, combine the flour, baking powder, baking soda, cinnamon, ginger, and salt.

3. In another large bowl, combine the sugar, tahini, and milk until well mixed. Stir in the zucchini, vanilla, and lemon juice.

4. Combine the wet ingredients with the dry ingredients, stirring until just blended. Transfer to the prepared pan and sprinkle evenly with the sesame seeds.

5. Bake on the center oven rack until golden brown and a toothpick inserted in the center comes out clean, about 1 hour and 5 minutes. Let cool in the pan on a wire rack before removing from the pan to slice.

Makes 1 loaf

Skillet Cornbread with Smoked Chiles

This recipe can be baked in a glass or metal baking pan, but if you have a cast-iron skillet, this is a great way to use it. If canned chipotles are unavailable, use dried ones that have been soaked in very hot water to cover for 30 minutes. Alternatively, canned hot green chiles may be used to add heat, but they won't impart the same smoky flavor as the chipotles do.

1¼ cups medium-ground yellow cornmeal

1 cup unbleached all-purpose flour

2½ teaspoons baking powder

1 teaspoon salt

1 (14-ounce) can creamed corn

3 tablespoons pure maple syrup

1 cup plain unsweetened nondairy milk

2 minced canned chipotle chiles in adobo

1. Preheat the oven to 400°F. Lightly oil a cast-iron skillet or 8-inch square baking pan and place in the oven to heat while you make the batter.

2. In a large bowl, combine the cornmeal, flour, baking powder, and salt and set aside.

3. In a medium-size bowl, combine the corn, maple syrup, ½ cup of the nondairy milk, and the minced chiles and set aside.

4. Add the wet ingredients to the dry ingredients and mix well with a few quick strokes. If the batter is too thick, stir in as much of the remaining ½ cup nondairy milk as needed.

5. Remove the skillet from the oven and scrape the batter evenly into it. Bake until golden brown and a toothpick inserted in the center comes out clean, about 30 minutes. Serve hot or warm.

===== *Serves 8* =====

Quick Breads

Since quick breads rise with the help of baking powder or baking soda instead of yeast, they require no rising or kneading time. Some varieties, called tea breads, are moist, slightly sweet loaves that are often made with pureed or grated fruits or vegetables and sometimes include nuts, seeds, and fragrant spices. Muffins resemble tea breads in flavor and texture—in fact, their recipes can be used interchangeably. The difference lies in the type of pan used and the baking time. Other quick breads include flaky and dropped biscuits, as well as many flatbreads, such as tortillas, *chapatis,* and *parathas.*

Molasses Bread with Walnuts and Raisins

This soft, luscious bread made with nutrient-rich walnuts, molasses, and raisins tastes great on its own or served with baked beans or a hearty stew. You can use either light or dark unsulphured molasses (the dark variety will have a deeper flavor and be less sweet than the light), but do not use blackstrap molasses, which has a strong, almost bitter flavor and is better suited to savory dishes.

1¼ cups plain unsweetened nondairy milk

1½ tablespoons white vinegar

2 cups unbleached all-purpose flour

1 cup medium-ground yellow cornmeal

1 teaspoon salt

1 teaspoon baking soda

¾ cup light or dark unsulphured molasses (not blackstrap)

½ cup coarsely chopped walnuts

½ cup raisins

1. Preheat the oven to 350°F. Lightly oil a 5 x 9-inch loaf pan and set aside.

2. In a small bowl, combine the milk and vinegar and set aside.

3. In a large bowl, combine the flour, cornmeal, salt, and baking soda, mixing well. Add the molasses and milk-vinegar mixture and stir until the batter is just mixed. Stir in the walnuts and raisins with a few quick strokes, then transfer to the prepared pan.

4. Bake on the center oven rack until firm and a toothpick inserted in the center comes out clean, about 1 hour. Let cool in the pan for 10 minutes before removing from the pan and slicing. Serve warm, soon after it is made.

Makes 1 loaf

Irish Soda Bread

I've been making soda bread on St. Patrick's Day for as long as I can remember. It's ideal served with a hearty stew or eaten on its own, still warm from the oven.

1½ cups plain unsweetened nondairy milk

1½ tablespoons white vinegar

4 cups unbleached all-purpose flour

1½ teaspoons salt

1 teaspoon baking soda

½ teaspoon baking powder

1. Preheat the oven to 375°F. Lightly oil a baking sheet and set aside.

2. Combine the milk and vinegar in a measuring cup and set aside.

3. In a large bowl, combine the flour, salt, baking soda, and baking powder and mix until blended. Add enough of the milk mixture to make a soft dough that is not too sticky. Knead just until the dough is smooth, about 3 minutes. Shape the dough into a round loaf and use a sharp knife to cut an X in the top. Place on the prepared baking sheet.

4. Bake on the center oven rack until golden brown, 40 to 45 minutes. The bread is done when it sounds hollow when tapped on the bottom. Remove from the sheet and let cool on a wire rack before slicing. This bread is best eaten the same day it is made.

Makes 1 loaf

Quick Tips for Quick Breads

- *Mixing and baking:* Because the leavening agents in quick breads react quickly with liquids, it is essential to mix the dry ingredients separately from the wet ingredients, combining them only at the last second. As you combine, avoid overmixing, which can toughen the bread. Quick breads should be baked in a preheated oven on the center oven rack. Test for doneness by inserting a toothpick in the center to see if it comes out clean.

- *Cooling and cutting:* Cool quick breads in the pan before cutting. Use a serrated knife and a sawing motion to slice.

- *Storing:* To store quick breads, cool in the pan for several minutes, then turn out onto a wire rack to cool completely before storing. (This prevents condensation.) Cooled bread that has been tightly wrapped in plastic will keep at room temperature for a day or two or in the refrigerator for several days. If stored tightly in the freezer in plastic wrap and aluminum foil, it will keep for up to 3 months.

Spiced Apple-Walnut Muffins

To save time, you may use a cup of applesauce instead of the grated fresh apple, if desired. For extra apple flavor, serve slices of this bread spread with apple butter.

1 large Granny Smith apple, peeled, cored, and grated, or 1 cup unsweetened applesauce

¾ cup plain unsweetened nondairy milk

½ cup natural sugar

2 tablespoons neutral vegetable oil

2 cups unbleached all-purpose flour

2½ teaspoons baking powder

1 teaspoon salt

1½ teaspoons ground cinnamon

¼ teaspoon ground allspice

½ cup chopped walnuts

1. Preheat the oven to 400°F. Lightly oil a standard muffin pan and set aside.

2. In a large bowl, combine the apple, nondairy milk, sugar, and oil and blend until smooth. Set aside.

3. In a medium-size bowl, combine the flour, baking powder, salt, cinnamon, and allspice. Using a few swift strokes, mix the dry ingredients into the wet ingredients until just blended. Fold in the walnuts, then transfer the batter to the prepared pan, filling the cups about two-thirds full.

4. Bake on the center oven rack until golden brown and a toothpick inserted in a muffin comes out clean, about 30 minutes. Let cool in the pan for 5 to 10 minutes. Serve warm.

Makes 12 muffins

Pumpkin Biscuits

Biscuits are convenient by nature because they come together easily and bake quickly. This variation on the classic sweet potato biscuit uses canned pumpkin, which I find even more convenient. These biscuits are ideal served with any autumn meal, from a bowl of chili to Thanksgiving dinner. For tender biscuits, be sure to mix lightly, since overmixing can result in tough biscuits.

2 cups unbleached all-purpose flour

2 teaspoons baking powder

¾ teaspoon salt

1 teaspoon ground cinnamon

¾ cup canned solid-pack or pure pumpkin puree

½ cup plain unsweetened nondairy milk

3 tablespoons neutral vegetable oil

1 tablespoon pure maple syrup

1. Preheat the oven to 450°F. Lightly oil a baking sheet and set aside.

2. In a large bowl, sift together the flour, baking powder, salt, and cinnamon, and set aside.

3. In a medium-size bowl, combine the pumpkin, nondairy milk, oil, and maple syrup and blend until smooth. Combine the pumpkin mixture with the flour mixture, stirring until the dough is just mixed and holds together.

4. Transfer to a lightly floured work surface and roll out to about ½ inch thick. Using a biscuit cutter or small drinking glass, cut the dough into 2-inch rounds and place on the prepared baking sheet. Reroll the dough scraps and cut out more biscuits.

5. Bake on the center oven rack until golden brown on top, 12 to 14 minutes. Serve hot.

Makes 20 biscuits

Getting a Rise

From baking powder to yeast, leavening agents are what make baked goods rise. Here are the most commonly used leaveners.

- *Active dry yeast:* This leavening agent is a living organism that makes bread rise by feeding off the sugars found in flour and giving off carbon dioxide bubbles, which makes the dough expand. Sold in granular form, it keeps well under refrigeration through the expiration date. Breads made with yeast require kneading and rising before they can be baked. Yeast should be dissolved in water that is around 110°F. If the water is too hot, it will kill the yeast; if it is too cool, the yeast will stay dormant.

- *Quick-rising yeast:* Made up of smaller particles than active dry yeast, this leavener works faster than the active variety but may be used in equal measure.

- *Fresh yeast:* Available in moist, crumbly cakes, it is highly perishable and less convenient than dry yeast. It can be stored in the refrigerator for about 2 weeks or until the expiration date.

- *Baking soda:* Breads made with this leavening agent require no kneading or rising time, but an acidic ingredient, such as vinegar, must be added for the bread to rise. Stored in an airtight container in a cool, dry place, baking soda will keep for up to 1 year.

- *Baking powder:* Like baking soda, this leavening agent requires no kneading or rising time to work. Baking powder is a combination of baking soda and cream of tartar or another acidic agent, so no additional acidic ingredient is needed. When stored in a cool, dry place, baking powder will keep for up to 6 months.

Ginger-Spiced Scones
with Cashews and Dates

Scones are similar in texture to biscuits, although slightly sweet. Unlike biscuits, which are usually served with a meal, scones are often served as a snack, much like muffins and tea breads. One of the great pleasures in life is a freshly baked scone served with a cup of hot coffee or tea.

2 cups unbleached all-purpose flour

½ cup natural sugar

2 teaspoons baking powder

1 teaspoon baking soda

½ teaspoon ground ginger

½ teaspoon salt

½ cup vegan butter, softened

⅓ cup dates, pitted and chopped

¼ cup chopped unsalted dry-roasted cashews

¼ cup plain unsweetened nondairy milk

1 teaspoon pure vanilla extract

1. Preheat the oven to 400°F. Lightly oil a baking sheet and set aside.

2. In a large bowl, combine the flour, sugar, baking powder, baking soda, ginger, and salt. Cut the vegan butter into the flour mixture until crumbly. Mix in the dates, cashews, nondairy milk, and vanilla, stirring until just blended. Do not overwork the dough.

3. Transfer the dough to a lightly floured work surface. Using a lightly floured rolling pin, roll out into a circle about ¾ inch thick. Cut into 12 wedges and place on the prepared baking sheet.

4. Bake on the center oven rack until golden brown, 15 to 20 minutes. Serve warm.

Makes 12 scones

Flour Storage

Keep whole-grain flours tightly covered and stored in the refrigerator or freezer to prevent them from turning rancid.

Cumin-Scented Sesame Flatbread

Simple flatbreads are made throughout the world—some with yeast, others without. This version uses no yeast and can, therefore, be prepared quickly. The cumin in this bread makes it especially complementary to Mexican or Indian foods.

2 cups unbleached all-purpose flour

½ teaspoon salt

¾ cup water, or as needed

Olive oil, for brushing

2 tablespoons sesame seeds

¾ teaspoon ground cumin

1. In a medium-size bowl, combine the flour and salt. Add enough water for the dough to hold together. Knead until smooth, about 5 minutes. Wrap the dough in plastic and set aside at room temperature for 15 minutes.

2. Divide the dough into 6 pieces. Lightly flour your hands and work surface, then shape the dough into balls and flatten them. Roll out into circles about 6 inches in diameter. Brush lightly with olive oil, then sprinkle with the sesame seeds and cumin, pressing lightly so the seeds adhere to the dough.

3. Lightly oil a large skillet and heat over medium-high heat. Place a dough circle in the skillet and cook, turning once, until brown spots begin to appear, about 3 minutes per side. Transfer to a platter and cover with aluminum foil or a clean towel to keep warm while you cook the rest. Serve at once.

Makes 6 flatbreads

Dessert Heaven

Although meat eaters and vegetarians may disagree on their entrées, most can find common ground at the dessert table. This is often not the case for vegans, since many popular desserts contain eggs or some form of dairy. Anyone who bakes knows that cakes, cookies, and other baked goods often rely on eggs and dairy products for their flavor and texture.

Fortunately, many traditional desserts can be made with vegan ingredients that produce similar results. For example, nondairy milk can be used instead of dairy milk, vegetable oil or vegan butter may replace dairy butter, and ground flaxseeds can be blended with water to use instead of eggs in many recipes.

Even such normally dairy-rich desserts as cheesecake, pudding, and ice cream can be made egg- and dairy-free. This comes as good news not only to vegans but also to people with dairy allergies or those looking for ways to reduce their cholesterol intake. In addition, many vegan desserts offer delicious opportunities to eat more soy foods.

Although I wouldn't recommend trying to replicate a particularly egg-centered dessert such as a vanilla soufflé, most recipes with only one or two eggs can be reproduced quite successfully. Some people may find that certain cakes made with vegan ingredients are denser than those prepared with eggs and butter, but the fact remains that vegan desserts are better for your health and can be delicious. Most vegans I know have quite a sweet tooth, and they readily devour every vegan dessert set before them with gusto. Still, I would be remiss if I did not point out that it may take some trial and error to get used to baking with egg and dairy alternatives—especially when trying to convert your favorite recipes. I have included a variety of dessert recipes that everyone can enjoy and that are easy to make, even for the beginner.

Regarding sweeteners, many health-conscious people choose to avoid sugar because of its lack of nutritional value, while vegans avoid honey because it is an animal byproduct. Still, a number of natural sweeteners are available to use in place of sugar or honey. As discussed on page 23 regarding the different sweeteners and their relative sweetness compared to sugar, you may need to make some adjustments when using natural alternatives in baking to regulate not only the degree of sweetness but also the ratio of dry to wet ingredients.

Once you become familiar with using egg and dairy alternatives in your dessert recipes, you will soon be able to whip up many of your favorite desserts without blinking an eye—and feel better for it.

Substituting Sweet for Sweet

When substituting a natural liquid sweetener for granulated sugar in recipes, you will need to reduce the amount of the other liquids in the recipe so that the finished product retains the intended texture. For each cup of liquid sweetener added, figure on reducing the total liquid by ¼ cup.

Tiramisu Cheesecake

Mascarpone cheese is traditional in tiramisu, but I use tofu and tofu cream cheese to transform the classic dessert into an amazing dairy-free cheesecake with bold flavors reminiscent of the classic "pick me up" dessert.

1½ cups vegan vanilla wafer crumbs

3 to 4 tablespoons vegan butter, melted

16 ounces vegan cream cheese, homemade (page 126) or purchased

1 (12- to 16-ounce) package firm silken tofu, drained

¾ cup natural sugar

2 tablespoons cornstarch

2 tablespoons strong brewed coffee

1 tablespoon brandy, rum, or Kahlúa or 1 teaspoon brandy extract or rum extract

Shaved vegan chocolate

1. Bring all of the ingredients to room temperature. Preheat the oven to 350°F. Lightly oil the inside of an 8- or 9-inch springform pan.

2. In a small bowl, combine the crumbs and as much of the melted butter as needed to moisten the crumbs when stirred with a fork. Press the crumb mixture evenly into the bottom and up the sides of the prepared pan. Bake for 5 minutes, then set aside to cool.

3. In a food processor, combine the cream cheese and tofu until smooth. Add the sugar, cornstarch, coffee, and brandy. Process until smooth.

4. Scrape the mixture evenly into the prepared crust. Bake on the center oven rack until firm, about 45 minutes. Turn off the oven and leave the cheesecake inside for 10 minutes. Remove from the oven and set aside to cool to room temperature. When the cheesecake is completely cool, cover and refrigerate for at least several hours or up to overnight.

5. To serve, remove the sides of the pan, using a knife to loosen it if necessary. Scatter the shaved chocolate over the top of the cheesecake, and cut into wedges.

Serves 8

Coconut-Macadamia Cheesecake

This taste of the tropics cheesecake is decadent and delicious. For an added taste treat and lovely color contrast, serve it with sliced fresh mango or mango puree.

½ cup plus 2 tablespoons ground macadamia nuts

1½ cups vegan graham cracker or vanilla wafer crumbs

2 tablespoons pure maple syrup

3 to 4 tablespoons vegan butter, melted

1 (12- to 16-ounce) package firm silken tofu, drained

16 ounces vegan cream cheese, homemade (page 126) or purchased

1 cup natural sugar

¼ cup unsweetened coconut milk

1 teaspoon pure coconut extract

⅓ cup unsweetened shredded coconut, toasted (page 453)

1. Bring all of the ingredients to room temperature. Preheat the oven to 350°F. Lightly oil an 8- or 9-inch springform pan.

2. In a large bowl, combine 2 tablespoons of the macadamia nuts, the cracker crumbs, maple syrup, and vegan butter until well blended. Transfer to the prepared pan and press the mixture evenly into the bottom and up the sides of the prepared pan. Bake for 5 minutes, then set aside to cool.

3. Place the tofu and vegan cream cheese in a food processor and process until smooth. Add the sugar, coconut milk, and coconut extract and process again until smooth. Pour into the prepared crust and bake on the center oven rack until firm, about 40 minutes. Turn off the oven and leave the cheesecake inside for 30 minutes.

4. Remove from the oven and let cool to room temperature, then refrigerate for several hours before serving.

5. To serve, remove the pan sides, using a knife to loosen it if necessary. Sprinkle the top evenly with the remaining ½ cup macadamia nuts and the shredded coconut, and cut into wedges.

Serves 8

Fresh Lime Cheesecake

The light and refreshing taste of this cheesecake makes it ideal to serve after a hot, spicy meal. This recipe uses regular limes, since Key limes are not widely available and are quite expensive. I use vegan gingersnaps for the crust because I like the combination of ginger and lime, but you may use vegan graham crackers instead.

1½ cups vegan gingersnap crumbs

3 to 4 tablespoons vegan butter, melted

1 (12- to 16-ounce) package
firm silken tofu, drained

16 ounces vegan cream cheese,
homemade (page 126) or purchased

1 cup natural sugar

2 tablespoons cornstarch

⅓ cup fresh lime juice (from 2 to 3 limes)

1 tablespoon grated lime zest

1. Bring all of the ingredients to room temperature. Preheat the oven to 350°F. Lightly oil an 8- or 9-inch springform pan.

2. In a medium-size bowl, combine the crumbs and the vegan butter and mix well. Transfer to the prepared pan and press the mixture evenly into the bottom and up the sides of the pan. Bake for 5 minutes, then set aside to cool.

3. In a food processor, process the tofu and vegan cream cheese together until smooth. Add the sugar, cornstarch, lime juice, and lime zest and process again until smooth. Pour into the prepared crust and bake on the center oven rack until firm, about 45 minutes. Turn off the oven and leave the cheesecake inside for 20 minutes.

4. Remove from the oven and let cool to room temperature, then refrigerate for several hours before serving. Remove the sides of the pan, using a knife to loosen it if necessary, and cut into wedges.

Serves 8

Toasting Coconut

Spread unsweetened shredded coconut in a dry skillet over low heat and cook, stirring frequently, until it begins to turn light brown. Or spread it on a baking sheet and toast in a preheated 325°F oven, stirring occasionally, for about 10 minutes. Coconut browns quickly and should be removed from the skillet or baking sheet right away to prevent overbrowning. Cool the coconut completely and store in an airtight container until ready to use. Properly stored, it will keep in the refrigerator for up to 2 weeks or in the freezer for up to 3 months.

Banana Swirl Cheesecake

Chocolate, bananas, and peanut butter are one of my favorite combinations, and for pure decadent indulgence, I can think of no better way to enjoy them than in this blissfully rich cheesecake. The three flavors are swirled together to create a marbleized cake that tastes as good as it looks.

1½ cups vegan chocolate cookie crumbs

3 to 4 tablespoons vegan butter, melted

16 ounces vegan cream cheese, homemade (page 126) or purchased

½ cup nondairy milk

¼ cup peanut butter

¾ cup natural sugar

3 large ripe bananas, peeled and mashed

½ cup vegan semisweet chocolate chips, melted

1. Bring all of the ingredients to room temperature. Preheat the oven to 350°F. Lightly oil an 8- or 9-inch springform pan.

2. In a medium-size bowl, combine the cookie crumbs and the vegan butter and mix well. Transfer to the prepared pan and press the mixture evenly into the bottom and up the sides of the pan. Bake for 5 minutes, then set aside to cool.

3. In a food processor, combine half of the cream cheese, half of the nondairy milk, and the peanut butter, and process until smooth. Pour into the prepared crust and set aside.

4. In the same food processor, process the bananas, the remaining cream cheese and nondairy milk, and the sugar until smooth. Pour over the peanut butter mixture and set aside.

5. Melt the vegan chocolate chips in a small saucepan over low heat or in the microwave. Stir until smooth. Using a circular motion, pour the melted chocolate over the banana mixture and use a thin spatula or knife to swirl all of the fillings around to create a marbleized pattern. Bake on the center oven rack until firm, about 45 minutes. Turn off the oven and leave the cheesecake inside for 20 minutes.

6. Remove from the oven and let cool to room temperature, then refrigerate for several hours before serving. Remove the sides of the pan, using a knife to loosen it if necessary, and cut into wedges.

Serves 8

Strawberry-Topped Cheesecake

You can serve this vegan version of the classic cheesecake plain or with a different fruit topping, if you prefer. Arrange the strawberries on top of the cheesecake whole or sliced, depending on their size.

1¼ cups vegan graham cracker crumbs

3 to 4 tablespoons vegan butter, melted

16-ounces vegan cream cheese, homemade (page 126) or purchased

1 (12- to 16-ounce) package firm silken tofu, drained

1 cup natural sugar

1½ teaspoons pure vanilla extract

½ cup fruit-sweetened strawberry spread

1 tablespoon water, fruit juice, or liqueur

2 to 3 cups fresh strawberries, hulled

1. Bring all of the ingredients to room temperature. Preheat the oven to 350°F. Lightly oil an 8- or 9-inch springform pan.

2. In a medium-size bowl, combine the crumbs and vegan butter until well blended. Transfer to the prepared pan and press the mixture evenly into the bottom and up the sides of the pan. Bake for 5 minutes, then set aside to cool.

3. In a food processor, process the vegan cream cheese and tofu until smooth. Add the sugar and vanilla and process again until smooth. Pour into the prepared crust and bake on the center oven rack until firm, about 40 minutes. Turn off the oven and leave the cheesecake inside for 30 minutes.

4. Remove from the oven and let cool to room temperature, then refrigerate for several hours.

5. While the cake is chilling, combine the strawberry spread and water in a small saucepan over medium heat, stirring until smooth. Set aside to cool.

6. Once the cake is chilled, slice the strawberries if they are large or vary greatly in size, or leave whole if they are small and uniform in size. Remove the sides of the pan, using a knife to loosen it if necessary. Arrange the strawberries on top of the cheesecake and brush with the strawberry glaze, then cut into wedges.

Serves 8

Chocolate Layer Cake

This richly flavored chocolate cake is enhanced by a decadent-tasting maple-chocolate frosting. For an interesting variation, make ginger-chocolate cake by adding 3 tablespoons minced crystallized ginger, 2 teaspoons ground ginger, and 2 teaspoons grated fresh ginger to the dry ingredients.

CAKE

2 tablespoons ground flaxseeds

½ cup water

2½ cups unbleached all-purpose flour

1½ cups natural sugar

⅔ cup unsweetened cocoa powder

2 teaspoons baking soda

½ teaspoon salt

1½ cups nondairy milk

½ cup pure maple syrup

¼ cup neutral vegetable oil

2 teaspoons apple cider vinegar

FROSTING

1¼ cups vegan semisweet chocolate chips

⅔ cup raw cashews, soaked for at least 3 hours or up to overnight, then drained

¼ cup pure maple syrup

1½ teaspoons pure vanilla extract

6 ounces extra-firm silken tofu

1. Preheat the oven to 350°F. Lightly oil two 9-inch round cake pans or coat them with nonstick cooking spray. Set aside.

2. In a medium bowl, combine the ground flaxseeds with the water and set aside to hydrate while you measure out the other ingredients.

3. In a large bowl, combine the flour, sugar, cocoa powder, baking soda, and salt. Mix well, using a whisk to thoroughly combine the dry ingredients. Set aside.

4. Once the flaxseed meal is hydrated (it will be thickened), stir in the nondairy milk, maple syrup, oil, and vinegar.

5. Add the wet ingredients to the dry ingredients and use the whisk to mix them together so that a smooth batter forms (do not overmix). Quickly pour the batter into the prepared pans and bake until a toothpick inserted in the middle comes out clean, 30 to 35 minutes. Do not overbake.

6. Let the cakes cool in the pans for 10 minutes. Run a knife around the edge of the cakes, between cake and pan, then turn them out onto cooling racks. Cool completely before frosting.

7. Meanwhile, make the frosting. Melt the chocolate chips in a microwave or in a double boiler over simmering water. Keep warm. In a high-speed blender, grind the drained cashews until smooth. Add the maple syrup and vanilla and blend until completely smooth. Add the tofu and blend until smooth. Add the melted chocolate and blend until smooth and creamy. Transfer to a bowl, cover, and refrigerate until well chilled, 2 to 4 hours.

8. When the frosting is chilled and the cake is completely cool, frost the cake by placing one layer on a plate. Spread it with about ¾ cup of the frosting. Top with the second layer and spread the top and sides of the cake with the remaining frosting. Cut into wedges and serve.

Serves 8 to 10

10 Ways to Replace Eggs in Baking

Use any of the following alternatives to replace 1 egg in baking recipes:

- *Applesauce:* Blend ¼ cup applesauce and ½ teaspoon baking powder.
- *Arrowroot:* Blend 2 tablespoons arrowroot in a blender with 3 tablespoons water.
- *Baking Powder:* Blend 2 tablespoons baking powder with 2 tablespoons water and 1 tablespoon oil.
- *Banana:* Puree ½ banana with ½ teaspoon baking powder.
- *Chia Seeds:* Combine 1 tablespoon chia seeds with ¼ to ⅓ cup water in a bowl and set aside for 15 minutes.
- *Chickpea Flour:* Blend 3 tablespoons chickpea flour with 3 tablespoons water.
- *Ener-G Egg Replacer:* Blend 1¼ teaspoons of the powder with 2 tablespoons water.
- *Flaxseeds:* Process 1 tablespoon ground flaxseeds plus 3 tablespoons water in a blender for 1 to 2 minutes, or until the mixture becomes viscous.
- *Nut Butter:* Use 3 tablespoons creamy nut butter (at room temperature).
- *Tofu:* Combine ¼ cup drained soft or silken tofu and ½ teaspoon baking powder.

Pumpkin-Rum Couscous Cake

This unusual no-bake cake has a moist texture similar to that of bread pudding, but it is made in a springform pan and is cut into wedges like a cheesecake.

¾ cup canned solid-pack
or pure pumpkin puree

½ cup natural sugar

2 tablespoons rum

1 teaspoon pure vanilla extract

¾ teaspoon ground cinnamon

¼ teaspoon ground allspice

¼ teaspoon ground nutmeg

1½ cups apple juice

Pinch of salt

1 cup instant couscous

1. In a food processor, combine the pumpkin, ¼ cup of the sugar, the rum, and vanilla until smooth. Add the spices and blend thoroughly until well combined. Set aside.

2. In a medium-size saucepan, combine the apple juice, remaining ¼ cup sugar, and salt and bring to a boil. Reduce the heat to low and stir in the couscous. Cover and simmer for 2 minutes, turn off the heat, and stir in the pumpkin mixture until well blended. Cover and set aside for 5 minutes.

3. Lightly oil an 8- or 9-inch springform pan. Spread the mixture into the pan, pressing the mixture firmly and evenly in the pan. Chill for several hours or overnight for easier slicing. Remove the sides of the pan, using a knife to loosen it if necessary. Cut into wedges.

Serves 8

Brandy-Apple Pie

A touch of brandy adds a bit of sophistication to "Mom's apple pie." You can, of course, omit it, if you prefer. Serve warm with a scoop of dairy-free vanilla ice cream for nostalgic decadence at its best. Be sure to place a baking sheet under your pie while it is baking to catch the drips.

2 cups unbleached all-purpose flour

1 teaspoon salt

⅔ cup chilled vegan butter, cut into small pieces

¼ cup ice water, or as needed

5 large Granny Smith or other tart baking apples

½ cup natural sugar

1 teaspoon ground cinnamon

¼ teaspoon ground allspice

1 tablespoon fresh lemon juice

1 tablespoon cornstarch

2 tablespoons brandy

1. Combine the flour and salt in a food processor. Blend in the vegan butter with short pulses until the mixture becomes crumbly. With the machine running, add just enough of the water through the feed tube until the dough just starts to hold together. Transfer to a work surface, divide in half, and flatten to form 2 disks. Wrap in plastic and refrigerate for 30 minutes.

2. Preheat the oven to 425°F. On a lightly floured work surface, roll out 1 piece of dough to fit a 9-inch pie plate. Fit the dough into the pie plate and trim and flute the edges. Roll out the remaining dough for the top crust and set aside or refrigerate if you will not be using it right away. Refrigerate the pie plate.

3. Peel, core, and slice the apples and place in a large bowl. Add the sugar, cinnamon, allspice, lemon juice, cornstarch, and brandy and stir to mix well. Spoon the apple mixture into the prepared bottom crust.

4. Place the top crust on the fruit, seal with the bottom crust, and flute the edges. Use a fork or knife to create several steam holes in the top crust. Bake for 10 minutes, then reduce the oven temperature to 350°F and bake until golden brown, about 45 minutes longer. Let cool to room temperature before slicing.

Serves 8

Asian Pear Tart with Toasted Almond Crust and Orange-Ginger Glaze

Asian pears taste and look like a cross between a pear and an apple. Primarily enjoyed raw and unadorned for their sweet flavor and crisp, juicy texture, Asian pears retain their shape and texture when cooked. Look for firm-fleshed, unbruised fruits that are heavy for their size. Color will range from pale yellow to golden brown. For a more traditional tart, use ripe regular pears, such as Anjou or Bartlett, or other fruits.

1½ cups toasted almonds (page 203)

½ cup pitted dates, soaked in hot water to cover until soft, then drained

3 to 4 Asian pears, peeled, cored, and thinly sliced

1 tablespoon plus 2 teaspoons fresh lemon juice

¼ cup natural sugar

¼ teaspoon ground ginger

⅓ cup orange marmalade

½ teaspoon grated fresh ginger

1. Preheat the oven to 375°F. Oil a 9-inch tart pan, pie plate, or springform pan or line it with parchment paper. In a food processor, coarsely grind the almonds. Add the dates and process until thoroughly combined. Press the mixture evenly into the bottom and up the sides of the prepared pan.

2. Toss the pears with 2 teaspoons of the lemon juice and arrange in the crust in a circular pattern. Sprinkle with the sugar and ground ginger and bake on the center oven rack until the pears soften, about 30 minutes. Let cool to room temperature.

3. In a small saucepan over low heat, combine the marmalade, remaining 1 tablespoon lemon juice, and the fresh ginger, stirring until blended. Brush on the pear slices and serve.

Serves 6 to 8

Sweet Choices

Following are explanations of the different sweeteners, from sugar to stevia. See page 23 for substitution guidelines. And note, honey is not vegan (see "The Buzz About Honey" on page 23).

- *White granulated table sugar, or sucrose:* A highly refined sweetener that contains empty calories and provides no nutritional benefit.

- *Brown sugar:* White sugar that contains a small amount of molasses.

- *Turbinado sugar:* A refined, light brown sugar that has not been bleached. It has no nutritional benefit.

- *Natural or raw sugar:* Made from sugar cane juice that is dehydrated and then milled into granulated powder. Retains its natural, though minimal, vitamins and minerals (brand names include Rapadura, Sucanat, and Florida Crystals).

- *Date or palm sugar:* Made from the fruit of the date palm tree, it has a rich, distinctive flavor but doesn't dissolve well in recipes. It is usually sold in Asian markets.

- *Stevia:* A heat-stable, highly concentrated natural sugar alternative with zero calories available at natural foods stores in liquid or powder form. Just a minuscule amount is needed for sweetening, but too much can produce a strong aftertaste.

- *Barley malt syrup:* A dark, thick sweetener made from roasted sprouted barley. It can replace honey or molasses in most baked goods.

- *Brown rice syrup:* A mild-tasting natural liquid sweetener made by adding sprouted barley or rice enzymes to cooked rice. It is about half as sweet as sugar.

- *Maple syrup:* Made by boiling the sap from maple trees, it has minimal nutrition. Buy only "pure maple syrup." Avoid pancake syrup, which can be little more than colored corn syrup.

- *Molasses:* This is the dark, thick liquid that remains after the sugar-making process. Blackstrap molasses is rich in iron and calcium. Generally, the darker the molasses, the greater its nutritional value.

Fresh Peach Crisp
with Almond Butter Cream

Besides eating them out of hand, this is my favorite way to enjoy fresh, ripe peaches. The crunchy topping, rather than a crust, allows the juicy fruit to take center stage. This dessert is best served warm out of the oven.

6 large ripe peaches, peeled, pitted, and sliced (or 4 cups frozen sliced peaches)

½ cup slivered almonds

½ cup plus 1 tablespoon unbleached all-purpose flour

½ cup natural sugar

2 tablespoons fresh lemon juice

¾ teaspoon ground cinnamon or allspice

½ cup old-fashioned rolled oats

3 tablespoons neutral vegetable oil

1 recipe Almond Butter Cream (recipe follows)

1. Preheat the oven to 375°F. Lightly oil a shallow 1½-quart baking dish and set aside.

2. In a large bowl, combine the peaches, almonds, 1 tablespoon of the flour, ¼ cup of the sugar, the lemon juice, and ¼ teaspoon of the cinnamon. Mix gently and transfer to the prepared dish.

3. In small bowl, combine the remaining ½ cup flour and ¼ cup sugar, the oats, oil, and remaining ½ teaspoon cinnamon. Use your hands or a pastry blender to mix well until crumbly. Sprinkle evenly over the peach mixture and bake on the center oven rack until the fruit bubbles in the middle and the topping is browned, about 30 minutes.

4. To serve, spoon into 8 individual dishes while still warm and top with a dollop of the almond cream.

Serves 8

ALMOND BUTTER CREAM

Seductively rich and deceptively healthful, this versatile topping can be served on pies, bread pudding, fruit, and even pancakes—just use your imagination.

¼ cup almond butter

¼ cup vegan butter

½ teaspoon pure vanilla or almond extract

½ cup confectioners' sugar

Almond milk, as needed

Combine the almond butter, vegan butter, and vanilla in a food processor and blend until smooth. Add the confectioners' sugar and process until smooth and creamy. If a thinner consistency is desired, add a little almond milk (up to ⅓ cup) and process until it is incorporated. Use right away or store in the refrigerator, tightly covered, for up to 1 week.

=== *Makes about 1½ cups* ===

Red, White, and Blueberry Cobbler

This is an ideal Fourth of July dessert, since fresh strawberries and blueberries are usually available at that time. The patriotic colors can be provided by the red and blue berries and the white crust, or you can go a step further and add a scoop of dairy-free vanilla ice cream topped with Strawberry–Grand Marnier Sauce (recipe follows) and a few fresh blueberries for garnish. Either way, you have a delicious all-American dessert. The amount of sugar needed will depend on the sweetness of your berries and also your personal taste. This recipe begins with ¼ cup, but you can add twice that amount, if you prefer.

3 cups fresh blueberries, picked over

3 cups fresh strawberries, hulled

¼ cup plus 2 tablespoons natural sugar, or more if needed

1½ cups plus 1 tablespoon unbleached all-purpose flour

½ teaspoon ground cinnamon

2 teaspoons baking powder

½ teaspoon salt

6 tablespoons chilled vegan butter, cut into small pieces

About ½ cup nondairy milk

1. Preheat the oven to 375°F.

2. In a medium-size saucepan over medium heat, combine the blueberries, strawberries, ¼ cup of the sugar, 1 tablespoon of the flour, and the cinnamon. Stir to blend and bring to a boil, then reduce the heat to low and stir gently until slightly thickened. Taste for sweetness, adding more sugar if desired. Remove from the heat and spoon into the bottom of a 9-inch round or square baking dish.

3. In a food processor, combine the remaining 1½ cups flour and 2 tablespoons sugar, the baking powder, and the salt. Blend in the vegan butter with short pulses, until the mixture becomes crumbly. With the machine running, add the milk through the feed tube and blend until the dough just starts to hold together.

4. Drop the dough by large spoonfuls on top of the fruit. Bake until the fruit is bubbly and the crust is golden brown, 30 to 40 minutes. Serve warm.

Serves 8

STRAWBERRY-GRAND MARNIER SAUCE

This multipurpose sauce can be used to top Red, White, and Blueberry Cobbler or to adorn a plain vegan cheesecake or a scoop of dairy-free ice cream.

2 cups ripe strawberries, hulled

2 tablespoons Grand Marnier
or other orange-flavored liqueur

1 teaspoon fresh orange juice or lemon juice

Superfine sugar, to taste

Place the strawberries in a food processor and process until smooth, or run them through a food mill. Pour the puree into a bowl and stir in the liqueur and juice. Stir in sugar to taste, 1 teaspoon at a time, until it reaches the desired sweetness. Use at once, or cover and refrigerate for up to 2 days.

===== *Makes about 2 cups* =====

In Search of Antioxidants

Antioxidants are special compounds present in certain vitamins and minerals that protect against oxidation, or cellular damage, caused by free radicals. This damage can lead to chronic diseases, including many cancers and diseases associated with aging. Among the best-known antioxidant vitamins are beta-carotene and vitamins C and E.

Beta-carotene can be found in orange, red, yellow, and dark green vegetables and fruits. Among the best sources are apricots, broccoli, cantaloupe, prunes, raisins, carrots, kale, mustard greens, spinach, beets, sweet potatoes, onions, and winter squash.

Vitamin C is found in abundance in citrus fruits (especially grapefruit), as well as broccoli, cantaloupe, cherries, bell peppers, kiwifruit, potatoes, strawberries, blueberries, blackberries, raspberries, red grapes, tomatoes, alfalfa sprouts, cauliflower, Brussels sprouts, and cabbage.

Vitamin E is found in almonds, oats, olive oil, peanuts, sunflower seeds, and wheat germ, as well as blackberries, cantaloupe, corn, black currants, and grapefruit.

Mango-Coconut Bread Pudding

Old-fashioned bread pudding takes a decidedly tropical turn with creamy coconut milk and luscious mangoes.

1 large ripe mango, peeled, pitted, and roughly chopped

½ cup Cashew Cream (page 127) or drained soft silken tofu

2½ cups unsweetened coconut milk

½ cup natural sugar

1 teaspoon pure vanilla extract

8 to 10 slices white bread, crusts removed

¼ cup unsweetened shredded coconut

1 large ripe mango (optional), peeled, pitted, and diced, for garnish

1. Preheat the oven to 350°F. Lightly oil a shallow 10-inch round cake pan or pie plate.

2. In a blender or food processor, puree the mango. Add the cashew cream, 1 cup of the coconut milk, the sugar, and vanilla and process until smooth. Set aside.

3. Cut the bread into small pieces and arrange in the bottom of the prepared dish. Pour the remaining 1½ cups coconut milk over the bread, tossing to coat and soak up the liquid. Add the mango mixture and bake on the center oven rack for 35 minutes. Remove from the oven and sprinkle with the coconut. Return to the oven and bake until firm, about 10 minutes more.

4. Serve warm or chilled, garnished with the diced mango, if desired.

Serves 8

Coconut-Cardamom Rice Pudding

Since I usually have cooked rice in the house, I often make rice pudding for a quick and wholesome dessert. Rose water adds a heavenly accent and is available at gourmet markets and Indian grocery stores. If unavailable, vanilla extract may be used instead.

2½ cups cooked basmati rice

2½ cups unsweetened coconut milk

½ cup natural sugar

¼ to ½ teaspoon ground cardamom

Pinch of salt

½ cup coarsely chopped raw pistachios

1½ teaspoons rose water or vanilla extract

1. Place the rice, coconut milk, and sugar in a medium-size saucepan over low heat and simmer for 20 minutes, stirring occasionally. Stir in the cardamom and salt and simmer until thick and creamy, 5 to 10 minutes.

2. Remove from the heat and stir in the pistachios and rose water. Let cool to room temperature before serving, or cover and refrigerate to serve chilled.

Serves 4

Chocolate Pudding Parfaits

A creamy chocolate pudding can be delicious on its own, but I enjoy serving it in parfait glasses (wineglasses also will work), layered with creamy whipped topping and chopped nuts. Crown each parfait with a fresh berry, and you have an easy and elegant dessert that's good for you, too.

1 cup vegan semisweet chocolate chips

½ cup pure maple syrup

1½ cups Cashew Cream (page 127) or 1 (12- to 16-ounce) package soft silken tofu, drained

1 teaspoon pure vanilla extract

1 cup Creamy Whipped Topping (recipe follows)

½ cup chopped almonds or other nuts, toasted (page 203)

4 fresh strawberries, hulled, or fresh raspberries (optional)

1. Place the vegan chocolate chips and maple syrup in the top half of a double boiler and heat over simmering water until the chocolate is melted, stirring to blend. Set aside to cool.

2. Place the cashew cream and vanilla in a blender or food processor and process until smooth. Add the chocolate mixture and process until smooth and well combined.

3. Spoon a small amount of the pudding into 4 individual parfait glasses. Top with a small amount of the whipped topping, and sprinkle lightly with nuts. Repeat the process until the glasses are full, ending with the chopped nuts. Cover tightly with plastic wrap and refrigerate for at least 2 hours before serving.

4. When ready to serve, top each serving with a fresh berry, if desired.

Serves 4

CREAMY WHIPPED TOPPING

This rich cashew-based whipped topping can be used in the same way as whipped cream: as a topping for cakes, pies, puddings, or other desserts.

1 cup raw cashews, soaked for at least 3 hours or up to overnight, then drained

⅓ cup almond milk

¼ cup confectioners' sugar

½ teaspoon pure vanilla extract

Place the soaked and drained cashews in a high-speed blender and process to a paste. Add the almond milk, sugar, and vanilla and process until completely smooth and creamy. Use immediately or transfer to a bowl, cover, and refrigerate until needed. Properly stored, it will keep for up to 3 days in the refrigerator.

===== *Makes 1¼ cups* =====

Chocolaty Peanut Butter Brownies

Chocolate and peanut butter join forces in these rich and chewy brownies. For extra flavor and texture, stir in some chopped peanuts or sprinkle them on top before baking. If you're not a fan of peanut butter, substitute another variety of nut or seed butter.

4 ounces vegan semisweet chocolate chips

⅓ cup peanut butter

¼ cup unsweetened applesauce
or mashed ripe banana

1 teaspoon pure vanilla extract

1¼ cups unbleached all-purpose flour

¾ cup natural sugar

1 teaspoon baking powder

1. Preheat the oven to 350°F. Lightly oil an 8-inch square baking pan and set aside.

2. Place the chocolate chips in the top half of a double boiler and melt over simmering water, stirring occasionally. Keep warm over very low heat.

3. In a blender or food processor, combine the peanut butter, applesauce, and vanilla and process until smooth. Set aside.

4. In a medium-size bowl, combine the flour, sugar, and baking powder. Stir in the melted chocolate and mix well. Scrape the batter into the prepared pan and swirl in the peanut butter mixture.

5. Bake until the top springs back when touched, about 30 minutes. Cool completely in the pan before cutting into squares.

Makes 9

Orange-Scented Almond Biscotti

These crisp, delicious biscotti with a hint of orange are ideal companions for a cup of tea or coffee, whether served alone or alongside a scoop of your favorite frozen dessert.

⅔ cup natural sugar

⅓ cup vegan butter, softened

¼ cup almond butter

¼ cup almond milk

1 teaspoon pure vanilla extract

2 cups unbleached all-purpose flour

2 teaspoons baking powder

⅓ cup slivered almonds

1½ teaspoons grated orange zest

1. In a mixing bowl, cream the sugar into the butter and almond butter until well blended. Blend in the almond milk and vanilla. Mix in the flour and baking powder, then stir in the almonds and orange zest. Chill the dough for 10 minutes. Preheat the oven to 350°F. Lightly oil a baking sheet.

2. Shape the dough into a slab about 1 inch high and place it on the prepared baking sheet. Flatten slightly.

3. Bake until golden brown, 25 to 30 minutes, or until a toothpick inserted in the center comes out clean. Remove from the oven and reduce the temperature to 300°F. Cool for 10 minutes, then cut into ½-inch-thick slices.

4. Place the sliced biscotti on their sides on the same baking sheet and bake until crisp and dry, 8 to 10 minutes. Cool completely before storing in an airtight container, where they will keep for up to 2 weeks.

Makes 12 to 16

Better Than Mom's Chocolate Chip Cookies

I gave my revision of my mother's time-tested recipe yet another makeover—this time, I've eliminated the oil! Now they're *really* better than Mom's—and better for you, too. Family and friends devour them with as much fervor as the originals.

2 cups unbleached all-purpose flour

½ teaspoon baking soda

½ teaspoon baking powder

½ teaspoon salt

1 cup natural sugar

½ cup unsweetened applesauce

¼ cup pure maple syrup

1½ teaspoons pure vanilla extract

1½ cups vegan semisweet chocolate chips

½ cup chopped nuts of your choice (optional)

1. Preheat the oven to 350°F. Lightly oil two baking sheets, spray them with cooking spray, or line them with parchment paper.

2. In a medium-size bowl, combine the flour, baking soda, baking powder, and salt. Set aside.

3. In a large bowl, combine the sugar, applesauce, maple syrup, and vanilla, mixing until blended. Add half of the dry ingredients and mix until just combined. Add the remaining dry ingredients and mix until just combined.

4. Fold in the vegan chocolate chips and nuts (if using). Drop the dough by the spoonful onto the prepared baking sheets, about 2 inches apart.

5. Bake until golden brown, 15 to 18 minutes. Let cool completely on the baking sheets before storing in an airtight container.

Makes about 36

Peanut Butter Chocolate Chip Oatmeal Cookies

These cookies are the solution when I can't decide whether to make peanut butter, chocolate chip, or oatmeal cookies.

1 cup white whole-wheat flour

1 teaspoon baking soda

¼ teaspoon salt

½ cup vegan butter, at room temperature

¾ cup natural sugar

½ cup peanut butter

¼ cup nondairy milk, or more if needed

1 teaspoon pure vanilla extract

½ cup vegan semi-sweet chocolate chips

½ cup old-fashioned rolled oats

¼ cup raisins or dried cranberries (optional)

1. Preheat the oven to 350°F. Lightly oil two baking sheets, spray them with cooking spray, or line them with parchment paper. Set aside.

2. In a small bowl, combine the flour, baking soda, and salt.

3. In a large bowl, cream together the butter and sugar, then blend in the peanut butter. Add the nondairy milk and vanilla and mix well.

4. Add the dry ingredients to the wet ingredients, then add the chocolate, oats, and raisins (if using), stirring until just mixed. If the dough is too dry, add a little more nondairy milk, one tablespoon at a time.

5. Drop the dough by the heaping tablespoon onto the prepared baking sheets, about 2 inches apart. Press down gently on the top of each cookie to flatten. Bake until golden brown, about 15 minutes. Remove from the oven and set aside to cool on the baking sheets before storing in an airtight container.

Makes 2 dozen

Cranberry-Walnut Oatmeal Cookies

Studded with bits of cranberries and walnuts, these tempting oil-free oatmeal cookies will disappear before you know it. You may substitute other dried fruits and nuts, if you prefer.

1¼ cups unbleached all-purpose flour

1½ teaspoons baking powder

¾ teaspoon ground cinnamon

Pinch of salt

½ cup unsweetened applesauce

¾ cup natural sugar

½ cup nondairy milk

2 teaspoons pure vanilla extract

1¾ cups old-fashioned rolled oats

½ cup chopped sweetened dried cranberries

½ cup chopped walnuts

1. Preheat the oven to 350°F. Lightly oil two baking sheets, spray them with cooking spray, or line them with parchment paper. Set aside.

2. In a medium-size bowl, combine the flour, baking powder, cinnamon, and salt.

3. In a large bowl, combine the applesauce, sugar, nondairy milk, and vanilla, mixing until blended. Add the reserved dry ingredients along with the oats, cranberries, and walnuts, stirring to mix well. Drop by the spoonful onto the prepared baking sheets, about 2 inches apart.

4. Bake for about 14 minutes or until done. Let cool completely on the baking sheets before storing in an airtight container.

Makes 24 to 30

Chocolate Macadamia Clusters

These tasty treats are sweetened only with dates, so they're better for you than a sugary candy bar while still being immensely satisfying. You may substitute a less pricey nut for the macadamias, if you prefer.

1½ cups macadamia nuts

1½ cups pitted dates, soaked in hot water to cover until soft, then drained

¼ cup unsweetened cocoa powder

1 teaspoon pure vanilla extract

1 cup unsweetened finely shredded coconut

1. Chop 1 cup of the macadamia nuts and set aside.

2. Place the remaining ½ cup macadamia nuts in a food processor and grind to a powder. Slowly add the dates through the feed tube until thoroughly mixed. Add the cocoa powder and vanilla and process until well blended. Stir in the chopped macadamia nuts.

3. Roll the mixture between your palms into 1-inch balls. Roll the balls in the coconut and flatten them somewhat. Arrange them on a platter and serve at once, or cover and refrigerate until ready to use. Tightly covered and refrigerated, they will keep for up to 2 weeks.

Makes about 36

Date and Cashew Truffles

Easy to make and infinitely versatile, these delicious morsels can be made with a different nut or the addition of grated orange zest. Instead of rolling them in ground nuts, you can coat them with unsweetened cocoa powder or finely shredded coconut.

2 cups raw cashews

1½ cups pitted dates, soaked in hot water to cover until soft, then drained

¼ cup nondairy milk, or as needed

1. Process the cashews in a blender or food processor until finely ground. Reserve ½ cup and set aside. Add the dates to the remaining cashews and process until well blended. Add just enough milk for the mixture to hold together.

2. Roll the mixture between your palms into 1-inch balls. Roll in the reserved ground cashews and place on a platter or baking sheet. Cover and refrigerate until ready to serve. Tightly covered and refrigerated, they will keep for up to 2 weeks.

Makes about 36

"Plain Vanilla" Ice Cream

With so many fruits and other flavorings available, I never make this as "plain vanilla" but rather use it as the base for flavored "ice creams." To do so, substitute ½ cup pureed fruit for ½ cup of the nondairy milk. You may add other ingredients, such as chopped nuts or extracts, if you wish, but keep the volume about the same.

2 tablespoons arrowroot	½ cup natural sugar
4 cups cold nondairy milk	1 teaspoon pure vanilla extract

1. In a small bowl, combine the arrowroot and ¼ cup of the nondairy milk. Blend until smooth and set aside.

2. In a medium-size saucepan over medium heat, heat the remaining 3¾ cups milk to a simmer, stirring constantly, then add the arrowroot mixture, stirring to thicken. Do not let it boil.

3. Once the mixture thickens slightly, remove from the heat and add the sugar, stirring until it dissolves. Stir in the vanilla and let cool to room temperature.

4. Refrigerate until chilled, then freeze in an ice-cream maker according to the manufacturer's directions.

Makes about 1 quart

Double-Chocolate Ice Cream

Real chocoholics may want to add more vegan chocolate chips near the end of the freezing process. Chopped nuts make a good addition as well.

4 cups cold nondairy milk

2 tablespoons arrowroot

¾ cup natural sugar

¼ cup unsweetened cocoa powder

½ cup vegan semisweet chocolate chips

1 tablespoon pure vanilla extract

1. In a small bowl, combine ¼ cup of the milk and the arrowroot. Blend well and set aside.

2. Place the remaining 3¾ cups milk in a medium-size saucepan over medium heat. Add the sugar and cocoa powder and bring to a simmer, stirring to dissolve the sugar. Stir in the arrowroot mixture, stirring constantly until the mixture thickens and starts to bubble, about 5 minutes. Do not let it boil. Remove from the heat and add the vegan chocolate chips. Let the chips sit in the hot liquid for a few minutes before whisking to combine thoroughly. Stir in the vanilla and let cool to room temperature.

3. Refrigerate until chilled, then freeze in an ice-cream maker according to the manufacturer's directions.

Makes about 1 quart

Frozen Coconut "Thaiphoon" with Mango, Lime, and Peanuts

When I first received my ice-cream maker as a gift, I was eager to create a vegan ice cream that would complement a spicy Thai meal. The result was this creamy and delicious "Thaiphoon," redolent of the flavors of Thailand.

2 tablespoons arrowroot

¼ cup cold nondairy milk

3 cups unsweetened coconut milk

½ cup natural sugar

1 large ripe mango, peeled, pitted, and halved

1 tablespoon fresh lime juice

1 teaspoon grated lime zest

1 teaspoon pure vanilla extract

¼ cup unsweetened shredded coconut, toasted (page 453), for garnish

¼ cup chopped unsalted dry-roasted peanuts, for garnish

1. In a small bowl, combine the arrowroot and nondairy milk. Blend until smooth and set aside.

2. In a medium-size saucepan over medium heat, heat the coconut milk to a simmer, stirring constantly. Add the arrowroot mixture and heat, stirring, to thicken slightly, about 5 minutes. Do not let it boil. Remove from the heat and add the sugar, stirring until it dissolves. Puree one mango half in a blender or food processor and stir it into the mixture along with the lime juice, lime zest, and vanilla. Let cool to room temperature.

3. Refrigerate until chilled, then freeze in an ice-cream maker according to the manufacturer's directions.

4. Cut the remaining mango half into dice. Garnish each serving with the mango, coconut, and peanuts and serve.

===== *Makes about 1 quart* =====

Double Espresso Affogato

This variation on the classic Italian dessert usually made with vanilla gelato is a coffee and chocolate lover's dream. For a dramatic presentation, bring the brewed espresso to the table and pour it over the ice cream at the last minute.

4 cups nondairy milk

2 tablespoons arrowroot

¾ cup natural sugar

¼ cup unsweetened cocoa powder

1 tablespoon instant espresso powder

½ cup vegan semisweet chocolate chips

1 tablespoon pure vanilla extract

1 cup warm or cold brewed espresso

1. In a small bowl, combine ¼ cup of the milk and the arrowroot. Blend well and set aside.

2. Place the remaining 3¾ cups milk in a large saucepan over medium heat. Add the sugar, cocoa powder, and instant espresso and bring to a simmer, stirring to dissolve. Stir in the arrowroot mixture, stirring constantly until the mixture thickens and starts to bubble, about 5 minutes. Do not let it boil. Turn off the heat and add the vegan chocolate chips. Let the chips sit in the hot liquid for a few minutes before whisking to combine thoroughly. Stir in the vanilla and let cool to room temperature.

3. Refrigerate until chilled, then freeze in an ice-cream maker according to the manufacturer's directions.

4. To serve, spoon the frozen dessert into stemmed glasses (martini glasses are best) and top with a few tablespoons of the brewed espresso.

Serves 6

NOTE: If using warm espresso rather than cold, be sure it isn't too hot, or it may crack the serving glasses.

Fresh Peach Sorbet

Use this recipe as a guide for making sorbet from your favorite fresh fruit. Peel, pit, or seed the fruit as necessary. Keep the amount of pureed fruit between 3 and 4 cups, using additional sugar if needed, depending on the sweetness of the fruit. Lemon juice is added here to help retain the color and to brighten the flavor of the peaches. Depending on the fruit you use, a splash of citrus juice or other flavoring is optional.

4 or 5 large ripe peaches, peeled, pitted, and cut into chunks

¾ cup natural sugar

1 teaspoon fresh lemon juice

1. Process the peaches in a food processor until smooth. You should have a little over 3 cups of puree. Transfer to a medium-size bowl.

2. Place the sugar in a small saucepan over low heat. Add enough of the puree to moisten the sugar and heat, stirring, to dissolve. Stir into the remaining puree along with the lemon juice.

3. Refrigerate until chilled, then freeze in an ice-cream maker according to the manufacturer's directions.

Makes about 1 quart

Cranberry-Walnut Sorbet
with a Hint of Orange

The walnuts offer a surprising crunch in this light and refreshing sorbet, although you can make it without them if you prefer a smooth texture. Especially festive when served in champagne flutes, this sorbet can be presented as an elegant dessert or an intermezzo. Or it can be used as an intriguing stand-in for cranberry sauce at holiday meals.

2¼ cups cranberry juice cocktail

2 cups fresh cranberries, picked over

1 cup natural sugar

Juice and grated zest of 1 large orange

½ cup chopped walnuts (optional)

Candied orange peel, for garnish (optional)

1. In a medium-size saucepan over medium heat, combine the cranberry juice, cranberries, and sugar and bring to a boil. Reduce the heat to low and simmer until the cranberries pop, about 5 minutes. Remove from the heat, then strain or run through a food mill to remove the skins. Set aside to cool.

2. Stir in the orange juice and zest and refrigerate until chilled. Freeze in an ice-cream maker according to the manufacturer's directions, adding the chopped walnuts, if using, about halfway through the freezing process. Serve garnished with candied orange peel, if desired.

Makes about 1 quart

NINETEEN

Smoothies, Shakes, & Other Quenchers

Smoothies are luscious, velvety blender beverages usually made with fresh or frozen fruits and naturally sweet fruit juices. They have been served at health food restaurants and juice bars for years and are now made in homes nationwide. Their growing popularity is proof positive that you don't need dairy products to enjoy a creamy, delicious drink. In addition to using fruits and juices, you can boost the nutritional content by adding a scoop of soy protein powder, nondairy milk, or tofu. Ground flaxseeds, rich in essential omega-3 fatty acids, also can be added to increase the nutritional value. People who normally skip breakfast may welcome a refreshing smoothie to provide the energy they need to get them through the morning. But don't let the virtuous health benefits fool you. Some of these concoctions can be as rich as the most decadent dessert.

Whether you're already a card-carrying smoothie addict or closet milk shake quaffer or you're simply looking for a healthful yet flavorful treat, you're sure to enjoy the drinks in this chapter, from cooling tropical smoothies to nutritious breakfast shakes.

Almond Milk

Versatile almonds can be used to make a nutritious milk alternative with a delicate nutty flavor. Although you can purchase almond milk in natural foods stores, you can make it easily from scratch at home. Soaking the almonds overnight softens them and activates their enzymes, making them more digestible.

1 cup raw almonds   4 cups water

1. Soak the almonds in the water overnight.

2. Drain the almonds, reserving the soaking liquid. Place the almonds in a blender with about half of the soaking liquid and blend until smooth. Add the remaining liquid and continue blending until very smooth.

3. Place a fine-mesh strainer over a bowl and strain the almond milk, stirring to push the liquid through. Refrigerate in a covered jar or airtight container and shake before using. Properly stored, almond milk will keep for up to 5 days.

Makes about 1 quart

Mango Tango Smoothie

It takes two to tango—in this case, a luscious ripe mango and a creamy banana. A splash of orange juice brings the two together. Frozen bananas make the smoothie thicker and creamier than unfrozen and do not dilute the smoothie the way ice can. Keep frozen chunks of peeled ripe bananas on hand for spontaneous smoothie making.

1 large ripe mango, peeled, pitted, and cut into chunks

1 cup cold fresh orange juice

1 large ripe banana, peeled, cut into chunks, and frozen

In a blender, combine the mango chunks and orange juice and process until smooth. Add the frozen banana chunks and blend until thick and frothy. Pour into two glasses and serve at once.

Serves 2

Ambrosia Breakfast Smoothie

Inspired by the classic dessert, this refreshing drink combines the flavors of banana, orange, and coconut and is loaded with potassium, vitamin C, and essential omega-3 fatty acids.

2 tablespoons finely ground flaxseeds

1 cup cold unsweetened coconut milk

1 cup cold fresh orange juice

2 large ripe bananas, peeled, cut into chunks, and frozen

In a blender, combine the flaxseeds and coconut milk and process until well blended. Add the orange juice and frozen banana chunks and blend until thick and smooth. Pour into two glasses and serve at once.

Serves 2

Berry Delicious Smoothie

This is a great way to enjoy fresh berries in season or frozen berries the rest of the year. The banana adds creaminess and sweetness, but if your berries are less than sweet, you might want to add a little maple syrup or agave nectar as well.

1 cup fresh strawberries, hulled, or frozen strawberries

⅔ cup fresh blueberries, picked over, or frozen blueberries

1 cup cranberry juice cocktail

1 medium-size ripe banana, peeled, cut into chunks, and frozen

In a blender, combine the strawberries, blueberries, and cranberry juice and process until smooth. Add the frozen banana chunks and blend until thick and smooth and creamy. Pour into two glasses and serve at once.

Serves 2

Peaches and Cream Smoothie

Make this smoothie when fresh peaches are in season; canned peaches just don't do the trick. The "cream" is nutritious and delicious almond milk. As with any smoothie, you can add some pure maple syrup, softened dates, or other natural sweetener, if desired.

3 to 4 medium-size ripe peaches, peeled, pitted, and quartered

1 cup cold almond milk

1 ripe banana, peeled, cut into chunks, and frozen

Combine all of the ingredients in a blender and process until smooth. Pour into two glasses and serve at once.

Serves 2

Tutti-Frutti Smoothie

Anything goes in this "fruit-full" smoothie. Use whatever fruit is on hand to create a creamy, fruity concoction whenever the mood strikes.

2 pitted dates, soaked in hot water
to cover until soft, then drained

¾ cup fresh or canned pineapple chunks

¾ cup fresh strawberries, hulled,
or frozen strawberries

1 large ripe banana, peeled, cut
into chunks, and frozen

1 cup apple juice or other fruit juice

In a blender, combine the dates, pineapple, and strawberries and process until smooth. Add the frozen banana chunks and apple juice and blend until thick and smooth. Pour into two glasses and serve at once.

Serves 2

Cantaloupe Tonight Melon Smoothie

Although this is best made with sweet, ripe melons, I've found that it can be a great way to use up a cantaloupe that is less than perfectly sweet—the banana and citrus juice work wonders at transforming the flavor into a luscious smoothie.

½ medium-size ripe cantaloupe,
seeded and cut from the rind

½ cup fresh orange juice

Juice of 2 large limes

1 medium-size ripe banana, peeled,
cut into chunks, and frozen

Fresh mint leaves, for garnish (optional)

Cut the cantaloupe into chunks and place in a blender. Add the orange juice, lime juice, and banana and process until thick and creamy. Pour into two glasses, garnish with mint leaves, if desired, and serve at once.

Serves 2

Spiced Pumpkin Smoothie

This is a favorite autumn drink at my house and a festive addition to holiday gatherings from Halloween right through the Christmas season, when it makes a colorful and delicious alternative to eggnog.

½ cup canned solid-pack
or pure pumpkin puree

3 tablespoons pure maple syrup

1 teaspoon pure vanilla extract

½ teaspoon ground cinnamon

¼ teaspoon freshly grated nutmeg

¼ teaspoon ground allspice

2 cups nondairy milk

Combine the pumpkin, maple syrup, vanilla, cinnamon, nutmeg, and allspice in a blender and process until smooth. Add the milk and blend again until smooth. Pour into two glasses and serve at once.

Serves 2

Make Mine Mocha

The popular combination of coffee and chocolate turns up in this delicious blender drink. It tastes like coffee and dessert all rolled into one.

2 cups nondairy milk

2 tablespoons unsweetened cocoa powder

2 tablespoons natural sugar

½ cup strong brewed coffee,
chilled or frozen into ice cubes

1 teaspoon pure vanilla extract

Combine all of the ingredients in a blender and process until thick and smooth. Pour into two glasses and serve at once.

Serves 2

Got (Nondairy) Milk?

There are lots of ways to have your milk without the moo. Choose among the following:

- *Almond milk:* Almond milk is now widely available in supermarkets. It has a delicious rich flavor, and the plain unsweetened variety is ideal for cooking. Homemade nut milks are also easy to make at home, with all the nutrients of the nut it is made from (see page 18). Use wherever a nutty flavor is desired.

- *Soy milk:* Soy milk can replace milk in recipes or be used on cereal or to make smoothies. Be aware that the flavors and textures vary by manufacturer, and you should experiment to find one you like.

- *Rice milk:* This milk alternative is thinner than soy milk but can be used in the same ways if you don't like soy.

- *Oat milk:* Oat milk has a mild flavor and thick, creamy texture. A good choice for "cream" soups and sauces.

- *Coconut milk:* Use this milk alternative to make Indian, Thai, or Indonesian dishes or in desserts or other dishes where a coconut flavor is desired. Make sure you buy unsweetened coconut milk, not coconut cream.

Sorbet Frappe

Blend your favorite fruit sorbet with almond milk and a splash of vanilla extract for a cool and creamy blender drink. For a lighter version, substitute seltzer water for the nondairy milk and omit the vanilla.

¾ cup fruit sorbet of your choice

1 cup almond milk

1 teaspoon pure vanilla extract

Combine all of the ingredients in a blender and process until smooth and creamy. Pour into two glasses and serve at once.

Serves 2

Banana Tips

- Unless you need to use them the same day, buy bananas with green tips. Then they can ripen at room temperature.

- Bananas will ripen faster if placed in a paper bag.

- Bananas are ripe when they turn yellow and brown speckles begin to appear.

- Once ripe, bananas may be stored in the refrigerator if you won't be using them right away. Refrigeration will turn the skin brown, but the inside will be fine.

- Ripe, peeled bananas may be cut or mashed and frozen for later use in baking or making smoothies.

Chocolate-Banana Shake

Bananas and chocolate are one of my favorite combinations, and they live up to my expectations in this decadent shake.

2 large ripe bananas, peeled, cut into chunks, and frozen

¾ cup vegan chocolate ice cream

1 cup nondairy milk

1 tablespoon chocolate syrup (optional)

2 fresh strawberries, for garnish (optional)

In a blender, combine the frozen banana chunks, ice cream, milk, and chocolate syrup (if using) and process until thick and smooth. Pour into two glasses, garnish each with a strawberry, if desired, and serve at once.

===== *Serves 2* =====

Creamy Cashew-Cardamom Shake

Naturally sweet and creamy, cashews are easily incorporated into a thick and delicious blender drink that is further enhanced by fragrant cardamom. Cardamom has a strong and distinctive flavor, so you may want to start with less of it and then add more if desired.

½ cup raw cashews, soaked for at least 3 hours or up to overnight, then drained

1 cup almond or unsweetened coconut milk

2 tablespoons pure maple syrup or agave nectar

1 teaspoon pure vanilla extract

½ teaspoon ground cardamom

1 large ripe banana, peeled, cut into chunks, and frozen

In a high-speed blender, grind the cashews to a paste. Add the nondairy milk, maple syrup, vanilla, and cardamom and blend until smooth. Add the frozen banana chunks and blend until thick and creamy. Pour into two glasses and serve at once.

===== *Serves 2* =====

Smoothie Savvy

The main rule about smoothies is that there are no rules. Use these recipes as guidelines to create your own concoctions. Here are some tips.

- *Frozen fruit:* Buy extra bananas to peel, cut into chunks, and keep on hand in the freezer to add creaminess, sweetness, and nutrients to almost any smoothie. It's also a good way to use up bananas that are very ripe. Frozen berries work well this way, too, because they thicken and chill the drink without diluting it the way ice cubes can. You can freeze fruit juice in an ice cube tray for this purpose. If no frozen fruit or juice is on hand, a few ice cubes can be blended into your smoothie.

- *Protein:* Smoothies are a great way to add it to your diet. Whether you add nut butter, tofu, or a scoop of vegan protein powder, you can get an extra serving of protein whenever you enjoy a smoothie.

- *Flax:* Flaxseeds are rich in essential omega-3 fatty acids, so when you add a tablespoon of ground flaxseeds to your smoothie, you increase its nutritional value.

- *Snack appeal:* A nutritious smoothie can help fill you up and not out, and it's a great way to curb your appetite between meals. Reach for the blender next time you crave something sweet and satisfying.

- *Sweet stuff:* Add softened dates, pure maple syrup, or another sweetener, if needed. All tastes are different, and some fruit is sweeter than others, so feel free to add a little sweetener.

- *Extra flavor:* Add vanilla or another extract to boost and brighten the flavor of a smoothie.

- *Extra liquid:* Despite the juiciness of many fruits, a certain amount of liquid is needed to make a smoothie drinkable. The liquid can be in the form of fruit juice, plain unsweetened nondairy milk (including coconut milk), or water.

- *Chill out:* Start with chilled ingredients for best results.

Creamsicle Redux

This smoothie is like a Creamsicle-in-a-glass for grown-up tastes, especially if you add the optional Grand Marnier.

½ cup vegan vanilla ice cream

1½ cups fresh orange juice

½ teaspoon pure vanilla extract

2 tablespoons Grand Marnier or other orange-flavored liqueur (optional)

In a blender, combine all of the ingredients and process until smooth. Pour into two glasses and serve at once.

===== *Serves 2* =====

Rum Nog

This vegan eggnog is always a hit at holiday parties. People are amazed at how rich and delicious it is, even though it contains no eggs or dairy products. I usually make it with rum, but you can substitute a teaspoon of rum extract, if you like, or omit it altogether.

1½ cups vegan vanilla ice cream

1½ cups nondairy milk

¼ teaspoon freshly grated nutmeg, plus more for dusting, if desired

3 tablespoons dark rum (optional)

In a blender, combine all of the ingredients and process until smooth. Pour into 6 eggnog cups, dust with an extra bit of nutmeg, if desired, and serve at once.

===== *Serves 6* =====

Luscious Lemon-Cranberry Cooler

This refreshing drink hits the spot on a hot, steamy day or warm, balmy evening. Use limeade concentrate instead of lemonade, if you like.

¼ cup frozen lemonade concentrate

2 cups cold cranberry juice cocktail

4 ice cubes

Combine all of the ingredients in a blender and process until smooth. Pour into two glasses and serve at once.

Serves 2

Tropical Paradise Quencher

A variety of sweet, ripe tropical fruits go into this refreshing smoothie. Feel free to vary the combination according to personal preference and availability.

1 medium-size ripe banana, peeled, cut into chunks, and frozen

1 small ripe papaya, peeled, seeded, and diced

1 small ripe mango, peeled, pitted, and diced

1 cup cold pineapple juice

2 fresh strawberries or fresh or canned pineapple chunks, for garnish

In a blender, combine the banana, papaya, mango, and pineapple juice and process until smooth. Pour into two glasses, garnish each with a strawberry, and serve at once.

Serves 2

TWENTY

Don't Skip Breakfast

Just because eggs and bacon are not on your menu doesn't mean you can't enjoy a hearty breakfast. Healthy vegan choices that are both satisfying and delicious abound. And they don't have to take extra time either.

If you enjoy cereal in the morning, simply substitute a nondairy milk for cow's milk, and you're on your way. Instead of butter, consider spreading your whole-grain toast with nut butter for a nutritious option, or try the yummy bagel spreads on page 515. If you don't care for a sit-down breakfast but realize you need a boost to get yourself through to lunch, whip up a smoothie such as the ones in Chapter 19. For extra protein to start the day, add a scoop of vegan protein powder and some ground flaxseeds to any smoothie recipe.

Tofu makes an ideal alternative to many high-cholesterol egg dishes: consider *Tomato-Zucchini Frittata* or *Salsa-Topped Spanish Tofu Omelet*. There are also several recipes for breakfast casseroles, wraps, and hash, as well as the more traditional pancakes and even French toast that can help make breakfast not just the most important meal of the day but perhaps the best-tasting one, too. And there's no need to stop at breakfast. Many of these recipes make great choices for lunch or dinner as well.

Scramble, Italian-Style

1 (12- to 16-ounce) package firm tofu, drained and crumbled

⅓ cup nutritional yeast

1 teaspoon dried basil

1 teaspoon dried oregano

¼ to ½ teaspoon red pepper flakes

½ teaspoon salt

¼ teaspoon freshly ground black pepper

1 tablespoon olive oil

1 medium-size onion, chopped

1 (6-ounce) jar marinated artichoke hearts, drained and chopped

⅓ cup chopped oil-packed or rehydrated sun-dried tomatoes

¼ cup kalamata olives, pitted and chopped

1. Combine the tofu, nutritional yeast, basil, oregano, red pepper flakes, salt, and pepper in a medium-size bowl. Mix to combine well.

2. Heat the oil in a large nonstick skillet over medium heat. Add the onion and cook until tender, about 5 minutes. Add the tofu mixture and cook, stirring, to heat through, about 4 minutes. Stir in the artichoke hearts, tomatoes, and olives and cook about 3 minutes longer. Taste and adjust the seasonings, if needed. Serve hot.

Serves 4

Farmers' Market Scramble

Scrambles are a great way to enjoy a variety of vegetables, especially when you have odds and ends to use up before you go to the farmers' market (or get your next CSA box). You can vary what goes into it depending on whatever vegetables are on hand.

1 tablespoon olive oil

¼ cup chopped red onion

3 scallions, minced

½ red bell pepper, seeded and chopped

1 cup sliced white mushrooms

1 cup chopped fresh spinach

6 cherry or grape tomatoes, halved

1 (12- to 16-ounce) package firm tofu, drained and crumbled

¼ cup nutritional yeast

¼ to ½ teaspoon red pepper flakes (optional)

Salt and freshly ground black pepper

1. Heat the olive oil in a large skillet over medium heat. Add the onion, scallions, and bell pepper, cover, and cook until softened, about 5 minutes. Add the mushrooms, spinach, and tomatoes and cook until softened, about 4 minutes.

2. Add the crumbled tofu, nutritional yeast, red pepper flakes (if using), and salt and pepper to taste. Cook, stirring, until any remaining liquid is evaporated and the ingredients are hot, 8 to 10 minutes. Serve hot.

Serves 4

Tomato-Zucchini Frittata

You can vary the filling ingredients in this luscious frittata according to your personal preference. Use cooked asparagus or mushrooms instead of zucchini, or try dill or tarragon instead of basil and oregano.

1 tablespoon olive oil

1 large sweet onion, minced

2 medium-size zucchini, shredded and squeezed dry

3 garlic cloves, minced

1 teaspoon dried basil

½ teaspoon dried oregano or marjoram

¼ cup chopped oil-packed or rehydrated sun-dried tomatoes

Salt and freshly ground black pepper

1 (12- to 16-ounce) package firm tofu, drained

¼ cup plain unsweetened nondairy milk

¼ cup nutritional yeast

3 tablespoons chickpea flour or unbleached all-purpose flour

1 tablespoon arrowroot or cornstarch

2 teaspoons fresh lemon juice or dry white wine

½ teaspoon onion powder

½ teaspoon baking powder

⅛ teaspoon turmeric

2 tablespoons chopped fresh basil

1½ cups grape tomatoes, halved

1. Preheat the oven to 375°F. Lightly oil a shallow round baking dish and set aside. Heat the olive oil in a large skillet over medium heat. Add the onion and cook until softened, about 5 minutes. Add the zucchini and garlic and cook, stirring occasionally, until softened, about 3 minutes. Stir in the dried basil, oregano, sun-dried tomatoes, and salt and pepper to taste. Transfer to the prepared baking dish and set aside.

2. In a food processor, combine the tofu, nondairy milk, nutritional yeast, flour, arrowroot, lemon juice, onion powder, baking powder, ½ teaspoon salt, ¼ teaspoon pepper, turmeric, and fresh basil. Process until smooth. Pour the tofu mixture evenly over the vegetables in the baking dish. Arrange the grape tomatoes on top of the tofu mixture, cut sides up. Bake until the tofu is set and the top is golden brown, about 30 minutes. Cut into wedges and serve hot.

Serves 4

Spinach Frittata

Tofu replaces eggs in this flavorful vegan frittata inspired by the classic Italian flat omelet.

1 tablespoon olive oil

1 small sweet onion, chopped

3 large garlic cloves, crushed

1 teaspoon dried basil

1 teaspoon dried oregano

1 (12- to 16-ounce) package firm tofu, drained and pressed (page 7)

2 tablespoons nutritional yeast

1 tablespoon cornstarch

1 tablespoon fresh lemon juice

Salt and freshly ground black pepper

4 cups fresh baby spinach

1 roasted red bell pepper (page 129), chopped

3 to 4 tablespoons chopped pitted kalamata olives

1 plum tomato, sliced very thin

1. Preheat the oven to 350°F. Lightly oil a deep-dish pie pan or shallow baking dish and set aside.

2. Heat the olive oil in a medium-size skillet over medium-high heat. Add the onion and sauté until softened, about 5 minutes. Add the garlic, basil, and oregano and cook until fragrant, 1 minute longer.

3. Transfer the mixture to a food processor or high-speed blender. Add the tofu, nutritional yeast, cornstarch, lemon juice, and salt and pepper to taste. Process until smooth. Scrape the mixture into the prepared pie pan.

4. In the same skillet, sauté the spinach until wilted, then transfer to a cutting board and coarsely chop. Blot the spinach dry and mix it into the tofu mixture along with the roasted bell pepper and olives. Spread the mixture evenly, smoothing the top. Bake until firm and golden brown, about 45 minutes. Arrange the tomato slices on top and bake 10 minutes longer, or run under the broiler for a minute or two. Serve hot.

Serves 4

Salsa-Topped Spanish Omelet

This vegan version of a Spanish omelet is a great way to use leftover cooked potatoes. I like to top this tasty dish with a fresh tomato salsa for extra flavor.

1 tablespoon olive oil

Coarse salt

3 cooked Yukon Gold potatoes, cut into ¼-inch thick slices

4 scallions, chopped

Salt and freshly ground pepper

1 (12- to 16-ounce) package firm tofu, drained and crumbled

¼ cup plain unsweetened nondairy milk

3 tablespoons chickpea flour or unbleached all-purpose flour

3 tablespoons nutritional yeast

1 tablespoon fresh lemon juice or dry white wine

½ teaspoon onion powder

¼ teaspoon ground cumin

½ teaspoon baking powder

1 cup Fresh Tomato Salsa (page 157) or purchased salsa

1. Preheat the oven to 375°F. Spread the olive oil in a 9- or 10-inch round baking dish. Sprinkle the surface of the olive oil with coarse salt. Arrange the potato slices evenly in the bottom of the baking dish. Sprinkle the scallions on top of the potatoes and season lightly with salt and pepper.

2. In a food processor, combine the tofu, nondairy milk, flour, nutritional yeast, lemon juice, onion powder, cumin, baking powder, ½ teaspoon salt, and ¼ teaspoon pepper. Process until completely blended and smooth.

3. Spread the tofu mixture evenly over the potatoes and scallions. Bake until the mixture is firm and set, 25 to 30 minutes. Remove from the oven and set aside to cool for 10 minutes. Cut into wedges, top each serving with a spoonful of the salsa, and serve hot.

Serves 4

Sausage Breakfast Casserole

This satisfying casserole can be enjoyed for breakfast, brunch, or supper. It can be assembled ahead of time and baked shortly before serving.

1 tablespoon olive oil

1 medium-size onion, chopped

3 garlic cloves, minced

2 cups chopped or crumbled vegan sausage, homemade (page 15) or purchased

1 (12- to 16-ounce) package soft tofu, drained and crumbled

2 cups plain unsweetened nondairy milk

1 teaspoon salt

1 teaspoon dried marjoram

½ teaspoon ground fennel seeds

½ teaspoon smoked paprika

¼ teaspoon freshly ground black pepper

8 slices bread

1. Heat the olive oil in a large skillet over medium heat. Add the onion, cover, and cook until softened, about 5 minutes. Add the garlic and vegan sausage and cook, stirring occasionally, until the sausage is browned, about 5 minutes. Remove from the heat and set aside.

2. In a large bowl, combine the tofu, nondairy milk, salt, marjoram, fennel seeds, paprika, and pepper. Mix well, then blend in the sausage mixture and set aside.

3. Lightly oil a shallow 9 x 13-inch baking dish. Tear the bread into bite-size pieces and place in the baking dish. Pour the sausage mixture evenly over the bread and set aside until the liquid is absorbed, about 20 minutes at room temperature, or cover and refrigerate overnight. (If refrigerating overnight, bring back to room temperature before baking.)

4. Preheat the oven to 350°F. Bake until puffy and lightly browned, about 45 minutes. Let stand for 10 minutes before cutting into squares. Serve warm.

Serves 6

Florentine Breakfast Casserole

Chock full of spinach with bits of onion and sun-dried tomato, this savory casserole makes an ideal brunch dish because it can be assembled the night before and baked shortly before serving. For a heartier version, add some crumbled vegan sausage to the mixture.

1 tablespoon olive oil

1 large Vidalia or other sweet onion, chopped

3 garlic cloves, minced

1 (10-ounce) package frozen chopped spinach, cooked according to package directions and well drained

1 (12- to 16-ounce) package soft tofu, drained and crumbled

⅓ cup minced oil-packed or rehydrated sun-dried tomatoes

3 cups plain unsweetened nondairy milk

1 tablespoon Dijon mustard

2 teaspoons fresh lemon juice

2 tablespoons chopped fresh dill or basil

1 teaspoon salt

¼ teaspoon freshly ground black pepper

1 loaf bread, sliced

1. Heat the olive oil in a large skillet over medium heat. Add the onion, cover, and cook until softened, about 5 minutes. Add the garlic and cook 2 minutes longer to soften. Set aside.

2. In a large bowl, combine the spinach, tofu, tomatoes, 1 cup of the nondairy milk, the mustard, lemon juice, dill, salt, and pepper. Mix well, then blend in the onion mixture and the remaining 2 cups nondairy milk. Set aside.

3. Lightly oil a shallow 9 x 13-inch baking dish. Tear the bread into bite-size pieces and place in the baking dish. Pour the spinach mixture over the bread, spreading it out evenly. Set aside until the liquid is absorbed, about 20 minutes at room temperature, or cover and refrigerate overnight. (If refrigerating overnight, bring back to room temperature before baking.)

4. Preheat the oven to 350°F. Bake until lightly browned and puffed, about 45 minutes. Let stand for 10 minutes before cutting into squares. Serve warm.

Serves 6

Spicy Sweet Potato Hash

This colorful hash is a yummy addition to a hearty breakfast, but it also makes a great lunch or dinner entrée. It's especially good served with a sweet, mild chutney. Adjust the amount of cayenne according to your heat tolerance, although the hash is delicious without it, too. This is a great way to use leftover baked sweet potatoes. Otherwise, the potatoes should be peeled and diced, placed on a lightly oiled baking sheet, and baked at 375°F until tender, 15 to 20 minutes.

1 tablespoon olive oil

1 large onion, chopped

1 red bell pepper, seeded and chopped

1½ pounds sweet potatoes, peeled, diced, and cooked (see headnote)

1 cup finely chopped mushrooms

½ teaspoon dried oregano

¼ teaspoon cayenne, or to taste

Salt and freshly ground black pepper

Heat the olive oil in a large skillet over medium heat. Add the onion and bell pepper, cover, and cook until soft, about 7 minutes. Add the sweet potatoes, mushrooms, oregano, cayenne, and salt and pepper to taste. Cook, stirring frequently, until lightly browned, about 10 minutes. Serve hot.

Serves 4

Skillet Vegetable Hash

Feel free to substitute different ingredients, including any leftover cooked vegetables you may have on hand. This is especially good made with leftover roasted or grilled vegetables, because they add an extra dimension of flavor. Serve with ketchup.

2 tablespoons olive oil

1 large red onion, chopped

1 small red or yellow bell pepper, seeded and chopped

1 carrot, shredded

1 medium-size zucchini, grated and well drained

1 pound Yukon Gold potatoes, scrubbed, diced, and steamed until tender

½ cup fresh or thawed frozen green peas

1 tablespoon low-sodium tamari

Salt and freshly ground black pepper

Heat the olive oil in a large skillet over medium heat. Add the onion, cover, and cook until softened, about 5 minutes. Add the bell pepper, carrot, and zucchini, cover, and cook until softened, about 5 minutes. Add the potatoes and cook, stirring frequently, until lightly browned, about 5 minutes. Add the peas, tamari, and salt and pepper to taste and cook until heated through, about 5 minutes. Serve hot.

Serves 4 to 6

Pan-Seared Breakfast Mushrooms

These mushrooms are terrific served whole and stuffed with Skillet Vegetable Hash (page 504) or your favorite vegan scramble. Alternatively, the mushrooms may be cut into ¼-inch-thick slices and fanned out on the plate.

1 tablespoon neutral vegetable oil

4 large portobello mushroom caps, gills scraped out

2 tablespoons low-sodium tamari

2 tablespoons pure maple syrup

Heat the oil in a large skillet over medium-high heat. Add the mushrooms and sear until well browned on the outside and slightly softened on the inside, about 5 minutes, turning once. Add the tamari and maple syrup and cook, turning to coat, until the mushrooms are glazed, about 5 minutes. Serve the mushrooms whole or sliced, as described in the headnote.

Serves 4

The Downside of "Sunny-Side Up"

Many vegetarians look to eggs as a source of protein, since no animal has to die to supply the product. But perhaps there is a fate worse than death, such as the short, miserable existence of "battery" hens. These naturally active birds are crammed into small cages for life, cruelly debeaked, and starved for periods of time to manipulate egg production. They become completely stressed out and often develop diseases such as cancer. In addition, after being imprisoned for a year or two in this way, they are slaughtered as soon as their egg production stops. Contrary to popular belief, free-range hens don't have it much better.

To vegans, therefore, the most compelling reason to give up eggs is often an ethical one, but there are a number of health reasons as well. Bacteria such as salmonella, poisonous ammonia fumes, and high doses of antibiotics can be passed into the eggs. In addition, an average egg contains more than 200 milligrams of cholesterol and is about 70 percent fat. In fact, the yolk of a chicken egg is one of the densest concentrations of animal fat there is. When eaten, it can raise cholesterol and help clog arteries. At the same time, albumin, which is concentrated animal protein, can leach the calcium out of your bones. A healthier alternative is to use tofu and other vegan ingredients to replace eggs in your diet.

Salsa Scramble Breakfast Wraps

Wrap sandwiches are a popular lunchtime meal, and now they can be a breakfast favorite as well.

1 tablespoon olive oil

1 medium-size red or yellow bell pepper, seeded and chopped

3 scallions, chopped

1 (12- to 16-ounce) package firm tofu, drained and chopped

2 teaspoons chili powder

Salt and freshly ground black pepper

3 tablespoons minced fresh cilantro

4 large flour tortillas, warmed

1 cup Fresh Tomato Salsa (page 157) or purchased salsa

1. Heat the olive oil in a large skillet over medium heat. Add the bell pepper and cook until softened, about 5 minutes. Add the scallions and cook for 2 minutes. Stir in the tofu, chili powder, and salt and pepper to taste, stirring to combine. Cook until the tofu is hot and any liquid is evaporated, about 5 minutes. Remove from the heat, stir in the cilantro, and set aside.

2. Place the tortillas on a work surface. Divide the tofu mixture among the tortillas, topping each with ¼ cup of the salsa. Roll up each tortilla to enclose the filling. Use a serrated knife to cut each wrap in half. Transfer to plates, seam side down, and serve at once.

Serves 4

Flax-Berry Pancakes

Many people include flaxseeds as part of their daily diets because they are an important source of omega-3 fatty acids. Ground flaxseeds blended with water are used to replace eggs in this pancake recipe—a nutritious way to start your day. Blueberries are the classic fruit choice, but feel free to substitute another fruit, if you like. Serve with pure maple syrup.

1½ cups unbleached all-purpose flour

3 tablespoons natural sugar

2 teaspoons baking powder

½ teaspoon salt

2 tablespoons ground flaxseeds

¼ cup water

1¼ cups nondairy milk

1 teaspoon pure vanilla extract

¾ cup fresh blueberries, picked over, or thawed frozen blueberries

1. In a large bowl, combine the flour, sugar, baking powder, and salt and set aside.

2. In a blender, combine the flaxseeds and water and blend until viscous. Add the nondairy milk and vanilla and blend until smooth.

3. Pour the wet ingredients into the dry ingredients, mixing with a few swift strokes until just moist. Fold in the berries.

4. Preheat the oven to 200°F. Heat a lightly oiled griddle or large nonstick skillet over medium heat. Ladle about 3 tablespoons of the batter onto the hot griddle. Cook on one side until small bubbles appear on top, about 2 minutes. Flip the pancake with a metal spatula and cook until the other side is lightly browned, about 1 minute more. Keep the cooked pancakes warm in the oven while you prepare the remaining pancakes.

Serves 4

Spiced Banana Pancakes

Banana pancakes are a special treat, and this recipe takes full advantage of that great banana flavor by using both sliced and pureed bananas in the batter. Top with pure maple syrup or blueberry syrup, as desired.

1½ cups unbleached all-purpose flour

3 tablespoons natural sugar

2 teaspoons baking powder

¼ teaspoon salt, or to taste

¼ teaspoon ground cinnamon

Pinch ground allspice

Pinch ground nutmeg

1¼ cups nondairy milk

3 medium-size ripe bananas, peeled and sliced

1. In a large bowl, combine the flour, sugar, baking powder, salt, cinnamon, allspice, and nutmeg and set aside.

2. In a food processor or blender, combine the milk and half of the bananas and process until smooth. Pour the wet ingredients into the dry ingredients, mixing with a few swift strokes until just combined. Fold in the remaining bananas.

3. Preheat the oven to 200°F. Heat a lightly oiled griddle or large nonstick skillet over medium heat. Ladle about ⅓ cup of the batter onto the hot griddle. Cook on one side until small bubbles appear on top, about 2 minutes. Flip the pancake with a metal spatula and cook until the other side is lightly browned, about 1 minute more. Keep the cooked pancakes warm in the oven while you prepare the remaining pancakes.

Serves 4

Pumpkin Pie Pancakes

The great taste of pumpkin pie in these moist, flavorful pancakes can make any morning special. Top with pure maple syrup or, for a delicious treat, Almond Butter Cream (page 463).

1½ cups unbleached all-purpose flour

3 tablespoons natural sugar

1 tablespoon baking powder

1 teaspoon pumpkin pie spice

½ teaspoon salt

1¼ cups nondairy milk

⅓ cup canned solid-pack or pure pumpkin puree

1 tablespoon neutral vegetable oil

1. In a large bowl, combine the flour, sugar, baking powder, pumpkin pie spice, and salt and set aside.

2. In a food processor or blender, combine the nondairy milk, pumpkin puree, and oil and process until well blended. Pour the wet ingredients into the dry ingredients, mixing with a few swift strokes until just combined.

3. Preheat the oven to 200°F. Heat a lightly oiled griddle or large nonstick skillet over medium heat. Ladle about 3 tablespoons of the batter onto the hot griddle. Cook on one side until small bubbles appear on top, about 2 minutes. Flip the pancakes with a metal spatula and cook until the other side is lightly browned, about 1 minute more. Keep the cooked pancakes warm in the oven while you prepare the remaining pancakes.

Serves 4

Maple-Pecan French Toast

The scent of pecans and maple from the kitchen can help warm up even the coldest winter morning. I like to use a heartier whole-grain or sprouted bread in this recipe, although it can be made with just about any bread you like.

¾ cup chopped pecans, toasted (page 203)

1¼ cups nondairy milk

4 ounces soft silken tofu, drained

1 teaspoon pure vanilla extract

¾ cup pure maple syrup

8 slices whole-grain or sprouted bread

1. Place ¼ cup of the pecans in a blender and grind into a powder. Add the nondairy milk, tofu, vanilla, and ¼ cup of the maple syrup and process until smooth.

2. Pour into a large, shallow bowl and dip in the bread, coating both sides evenly with the batter.

3. Preheat the oven to 200°F. Heat a lightly oiled griddle or large skillet over medium-high heat. Add the prepared bread in batches and cook until browned on both sides, 4 to 5 minutes total. Keep the cooked French toast warm in the oven while you prepare the remaining slices.

4. In a small saucepan, combine the remaining ½ cup maple syrup and the remaining ½ cup pecans and heat until warm. Spoon over the French toast and serve at once.

Serves 4

Apple-Cinnamon French Toast

Applesauce and cinnamon are blended into the batter in this egg- and dairy-free version of French toast. Instead of the usual maple syrup, the topping is warm sautéed apple slices. For an easy autumn supper, serve with vegan sausage patties or links.

1 cup nondairy milk

½ cup unsweetened applesauce

4 ounces soft silken tofu, drained

2 tablespoons natural sugar

1 teaspoon ground cinnamon

8 slices bread

1 tablespoon neutral vegetable oil

1 large apple, peeled, cored, and thinly sliced

1 teaspoon fresh lemon juice

1. Combine the nondairy milk, applesauce, tofu, 1 tablespoon of the sugar, and the cinnamon in a food processor or blender and process until smooth.

2. Pour into a large, shallow bowl and dip in the bread, coating both sides evenly with the batter.

3. Preheat the oven to 200°F. Heat a lightly oiled griddle or large skillet over medium-high heat. Add the prepared bread in batches and cook until just browned on both sides, 4 to 5 minutes total. Keep the cooked French toast warm in the oven while you prepare the remaining slices.

4. Heat the oil in a small skillet over medium heat. Add the apple slices, lemon juice, and remaining 1 tablespoon sugar and cook, stirring, until the apples are tender, about 5 minutes. Spoon the topping over the French toast and serve hot.

Serves 4

Couscous Breakfast Cake
with Pear and Dried Plum Compote

This unusual cake is an ideal addition to a brunch or breakfast for guests, as it can be prepared the day before. Made with couscous and fruit juice, the cake is dense and moist without being too sweet—a great way to start the day.

2½ cups apple or pear juice

Pinch of salt

2 cups instant couscous

Pear and Dried Plum Compote (page 513)

1. Place the juice and salt in a medium-size saucepan and bring to a boil over high heat. Reduce the heat to low and stir in the couscous. Cover and simmer for 2 minutes, then turn off the heat and set aside, covered, for 10 minutes.

2. Lightly oil an 8-inch springform pan and spoon the couscous into it, spreading it evenly. Use the back of a spoon or a spatula to press the couscous firmly into the pan. Cover and refrigerate for several hours or overnight to make it easier to slice.

3. To serve, remove the sides of the pan, cut into wedges, and top with the compote.

Serves 6

Pear and Dried Plum Compote

This compote is ideal with Couscous Breakfast Cake (page 512), but it is also wonderful on its own or served with Potato Pierogi and Cabbage (page 238).

3 medium-size ripe pears, peeled, cored, and sliced

2 cups dried pitted plums (prunes)

½ cup mixed dried fruit, chopped

⅓ cup natural sugar

Grated zest and juice of 1 large lemon

Grated zest and juice of 1 large orange

1 cinnamon stick

¼ teaspoon ground allspice

⅛ teaspoon freshly grated nutmeg

2 cups water

In a medium-size saucepan, combine all of the ingredients and bring to a boil over medium heat. Reduce the heat to low and simmer until the pears soften and the dried fruit plumps up, about 15 minutes. Set aside to cool, then transfer to a medium-size bowl, cover, and refrigerate for at least several hours. When ready to serve, return to room temperature for the best flavor. This will keep for up to 1 week in the refrigerator.

Serves 6 to 8

Maple-Cinnamon Oatmeal
with Slivered Almonds and Dried Cranberries

Few breakfasts are more satisfying on a cold winter morning than this fragrant oatmeal, studded with sweet-tart cranberries and crunchy toasted almonds. Serve with a little nondairy milk or an additional drizzle of maple syrup and a light dusting of cinnamon.

4 cups water

2 cups old-fashioned rolled oats

1 teaspoon ground cinnamon

¼ teaspoon salt

¼ cup sweetened dried cranberries

2 tablespoons pure maple syrup

¼ cup slivered almonds, toasted (page 203), for garnish

1. Bring the water to a boil in a medium-size saucepan over high heat. Reduce the heat to low and stir in the oats, cinnamon, and salt. Cover and simmer for 5 minutes, stirring occasionally.

2. Remove from the heat and stir in the cranberries and maple syrup. Cover and let stand for 2 to 3 minutes. To serve, spoon the oatmeal into bowls and garnish with the almonds.

Serves 4

Bagels-for-Breakfast Spread (Sweet)

This nutritious spread, loaded with protein, calcium, and potassium, is a great way to start your day. You can make it the night before so that you can quickly spread it on toast or a bagel the next morning.

4 ounces vegan cream cheese, homemade (page 126) or purchased

1 medium-size ripe banana, peeled and sliced

2 tablespoons almond butter

2 tablespoons pure maple syrup

1 teaspoon pure vanilla extract

½ teaspoon ground cinnamon

⅛ teaspoon ground allspice or nutmeg

In a food processor or blender, combine all of the ingredients and process until smooth. Transfer to a small bowl, cover, and refrigerate for several hours to allow the flavors to develop. This will keep for about 3 days in the refrigerator.

Makes about 1¼ cups

Bagels-for-Breakfast Spread (Savory)

This high-protein, calcium-rich spread is a wholesome, cholesterol-free way to enjoy your bagel or toast.

4 ounces vegan cream cheese, homemade (page 126) or purchased

¼ cup tahini

2 tablespoons mellow white miso paste

1 tablespoon fresh lemon juice

In a food processor or blender, combine all of the ingredients until well blended. Transfer to a small bowl, cover, and refrigerate until ready to use, up to 5 days.

Makes about 1¼ cups

Best-Ever Breakfast Bars

These wholesome bars have a delicious, not-too-sweet flavor and a great texture.

1 cup nondairy milk or apple juice

2 tablespoons almond butter

6 pitted dates, soaked in hot water to cover until soft, then drained

1½ teaspoons pure vanilla extract

½ teaspoon ground cinnamon

¼ teaspoon salt

¾ cup old-fashioned rolled oats

½ cup white whole-wheat flour

1 cup coarsely chopped cashews (or your favorite nut)

½ cup sunflower seeds

½ cup dried cranberries

1. Preheat the oven to 350°F. Lightly oil an 8-inch square baking pan or spray it with cooking spray.

2. In a food processor, combine the nondairy milk, almond butter, dates, vanilla, cinnamon, and salt. Process until blended. Add the oats, flour, cashews, sunflower seeds, and cranberries. Pulse until well combined.

3. Transfer the dough to the prepared pan and press it evenly into the pan. Bake for 20 minutes or until lightly browned. Remove from the oven and set aside to cool before cutting into bars.

Makes 8 bars

Resources

The following list of organizations, mail-order sources, and other resources is provided as a starting point for those interested in a vegan lifestyle. The list contains a representative sampling of what is available and is by no means exhaustive. Some of the sites listed may not be entirely vegan.

Mail-Order Products

These sources can be especially useful for hard-to-find ingredients or if you live in an area that does not have a natural foods store. Visit their websites to find vegan food items, shoes, clothing, accessories, books, and personal care products.

Alternative Outfitters
408 S. Pasadena Avenue #1
Pasadena, CA 91105
866.758.5837
www.alternativeoutfitters.com

Food Fight Grocery
1217 SE Stark Street
Portland, OR 97214
503.233.3910
www.foodfightgrocery.com

Herbivore Clothing Company
1211 SE Stark Street
Portland, OR 97214
503.281.TOFU (8638)
www.herbivoreclothing.com

**The Mail-Order Catalog
for Healthy Eating**
413 Farm Road
P.O. Box 180
Summertown, TN 38483
800.695.2241
www.healthy-eating.com

MooShoes
78 Orchard Street
New York, NY 10002
866.59.VEGAN (83426)
www.mooshoes.com

Pangea
2381 Lewis Avenue
Rockville, MD 20851
800.340.1200
www.veganstore.com

Vegan Cuts
RPO Glebe #14007
Ottawa, ON K1S 3T2
Canada
www.vegancuts.com

Vegan Essentials
1701 Pearl Street #8
Waukesha, WI 53186
866.88.VEGAN (83426)
www.veganessentials.com

(Resources continued on page 518)

Organizations

For more information on various aspects of veganism, contact or visit the websites of these nonprofit organizations.

American Vegan Society (AVS)
56 Dinshah Lane
P.O. Box 369
Malaga, NJ 08328
856.694.2887
www.americanvegan.org

EarthSave International
20555 Devonshire Street #105
Chatsworth, CA 91311
415.234.0829
www.earthsave.org

Farm Animal Rights Movement (FARM)
10101 Ashburton Lane
Bethesda, MD 20817
888.ASK.FARM (275.3276)
www.farmusa.org

Farm Sanctuary National Headquarters
3100 Aikens Road
P.O. Box 150
Watkins Glen, NY 14891
607.583.2225
www.farmsanctuary.org

In Defense of Animals (IDA)
3010 Kerner Boulevard
San Rafael, CA 94901
415.448.0048
www.idausa.org

Mercy for Animals
8033 Sunset Boulevard #864
Los Angeles, CA 90046
866.632.6446
www.mercyforanimals.org

North American Vegetarian Society (NAVS)
P.O. Box 72
Dolgeville, NY 13329
518.568.7970
www.navs-online.org

People for the Ethical Treatment of Animals (PETA)
501 Front Street
Norfolk, VA 23510
757.622.PETA (7382)
www.peta.org

Physicians Committee for Responsible Medicine (PCRM)
5100 Wisconsin Avenue #400
Washington, DC 20016
202.686.2210
www.pcrm.org

United Poultry Concerns (UPC)
P.O. Box 150
Machipongo, VA 23405
757.678.7875
www.upc-online.org

Vegetarian Resource Group (VRG)
P.O. Box 1463
Baltimore, MD 21203
410.366.8343
www.vrg.org

More Web Sites

In addition to the sites listed above, check out these websites:

www.happycow.net
www.meatlessmonday.com
www.notmilk.com
www.onegreenplanet.org
www.ourhenhouse.org

www.robinrobertson.com
www.vegan.com
www.vegan.org
www.veganoutreach.com
www.vegansociety.com

www.vegdining.com
www.vegnews.com
www.vegsource.com

Measurement Equivalents

Please note that all conversions are approximate.

Liquid Conversions	
U.S.	**Metric**
1 tsp	5 ml
1 tbs	15 ml
2 tbs	30 ml
3 tbs	45 ml
¼ cup	60 ml
⅓ cup	75 ml
⅓ cup + 1 tbs	90 ml
⅓ cup + 2 tbs	100 ml
½ cup	120 ml
⅔ cup	150 ml
¾ cup	180 ml
¾ cup + 2 tbs	200 ml
1 cup	240 ml
1 cup + 2 tbs	275 ml
1¼ cups	300 ml
1⅓ cups	325 ml
1½ cups	350 ml
1⅔ cups	375 ml
1¾ cups	400 ml
1¾ cups + 2 tbs	450 ml
2 cups (1 pint)	475 ml
2½ cups	600 ml
3 cups	720 ml
4 cups (1 quart)	945 ml (1,000 ml is 1 liter)

Weight Conversions	
U.S./U.K.	**Metric**
½ oz	14 g
1 oz	28 g
1½ oz	43 g
2 oz	57 g
2½ oz	71 g
3 oz	85 g
3½ oz	100 g
4 oz	113 g
5 oz	142 g
6 oz	170 g
7 oz	200 g
8 oz	227 g
9 oz	255 g
10 oz	284 g
11 oz	312 g
12 oz	340 g
13 oz	368 g
14 oz	400 g
15 oz	425 g
1 lb	454 g

Oven Temperature Conversions		
°F	**Gas Mark**	**°C**
250	½	120
275	1	140
300	2	150
325	3	165
350	4	180
375	5	190
400	6	200
425	7	220
450	8	230
475	9	240
500	10	260
550	Broil	290

Index